I0830783

A King Must Understand:

Thoughts of a Divine King:

A Manual Concerning the Art of Kingship

BOOK 2

Chronicles of the KING

Antionelle Owens

Kingdom Builders Publications LLC

THE TRILOGY
Prince Micah the Magnificent
BOOK 1 – Chronicles of the KING

A King Must Understand: Thoughts of a Divine King:
A Manual Concerning the Art of Kingship
BOOK 2 – Chronicles of the KING

For He Comes Out of Prison to be King The Gospel of Troy
BOOK 3 – Chronicles of the KING

Hardback

ISBN
978-0-578-82448-2

Library of Congress Control Number:
2021909345

Printed in the USA

Authored by
Antionelle Owens

Editors
Sandra L. O'Hern
Lakisha S. Forrester
Kingdom Builders Publications

Cover Design
Eric F. Quzack
LoMar Designs

DEDICATION

THIS BOOK IS DEDICATED TO KING ERMIAS JOSEPH ASGHEDOM, THE GREAT AKA NIPSEY HUSSLE. MAY YOUR NAME LIVE FOREVER. (THE MARATHON CONTINUES).

THIS BOOK IS ALSO DEDICATED TO THE MASTER WHICH DWELLS WITHIN THE HEART OF ALL BEINGS.

OWENS

CONTENTS

FOREWORD

In the 21ˢᵗ century, there are many ideologies to hear, learn, and follow, some of which have been around for many centuries. I can only speak to truth when I say this collection of writings by the auspicious author, Antionelle Owens, is an illumination to be experienced! I've not many times experienced in my years in this world the luxury of such passion in monologue, knowledge, wisdom, and understanding.

Of course, no one person has all truth to annihilate another's reasoning, but it does stand to reason that God drops portions of His nature, character, knowledge, wisdom, and understanding in each one of His human creation. God is the absolute and is the subject and knowledge in all matters. Nothing is known, made, or appreciated without HIM.

This is the exact dispensation men have been hungry for, for thousands of generations. It has passed the time for the man to realize his full potential, his honor, the authority in his mantle, his crown, and his kingship!

I am Woman, and I encourage every man to get influenced by the pages of these illustriously written volumes. It is the passport for your soul. It should be read for its truth, solidarity, for the newness and blossoming of himself, and to appreciate the life of the woman – from the youngest to the oldest ancestor. I believe this book is prophetic and could very well be the next classic knowledge for MANKIND as to the Vedas, Quran, the Holy Bible, and other such life-changing manuals.

No matter the culture in the eastern or western hemisphere, all men have a responsibility to learn his rightful place as priest and king of his own life, his home, his community, and the KINGDOM. This trilogy speaks more than information; it is impartation through revelation, which brings inspiration to better one's concepts and precepts.

Every child-bearing woman should read this purposeful manual to know how to love, nurture, and bring up a king to understand his king's nature and influence.

Soak in the pages of this manual. Your life will increase many degrees.

Louise Smith
Author and Life Coach

ACKNOWLEDGMENTS

To all who believed (You know who you are), I thank you for your belief. For it gave me the STRENGTH to carry on during my darkest hours. To all who didn't believe (You know who you are), for the exact same reason, I thank you for your disbelief.

Dear Master,

Son, **You were born to be a great KING.** This letter that **I AM** writing to you now is but a solemn testimonial to your magnificence. It is my humble offering to your supreme preeminence. For Master, you are so remarkable that even though you have not yet been born, and in truth, I do not even know if I have yet met your mother, **I AM** already prepared to die for you, my son. My entire life and every event which has taken place within it has served as crucial preparation for your arrival. However, my son, as one can never be completely sure what the future holds in the land of karma, there is no guarantee that I shall ever have the **HONOR** of meeting you in person. If destiny has penned in her scrolls that I shall, then, son, the words that **I AM** writing to you in this letter shall serve you merely as an embellishment to the aristocratic **KNOWLEDGE** that I shall impart to you personally during our time together. A study guide if you will. However, Master, if this is not the case and the fates have not decreed that this shall be so, then I pray that you allow my words to be the regal North Star that guides you along your journey to freedom. Master, there is so much that I have learned over the course of my travels around the sun, and so much that I have to tell you. Where shall I begin? Let's see. I suppose the most proper commencement of this testament to you would consist of a formal introduction of myself.

I AM POWER

THE WORD POWER IS DEFINED IN THE DICTIONARY AS "THE ABILITY OR CAPACITY TO ACT OR DO SOMETHING EFFECTIVELY," AND "THE ENERGY OR MOTIVE FORCE BY WHICH A SYSTEM OPERATES."[1] POWER IS MOTION OR THE ABILITY TO MOVE. IT IS THE FEMININE PRINCIPLE OF THE UNIVERSE. IT IS SHAKTI.

I AM THE TRUTH

THE TRUTH IS DEFINED IN THE DICTIONARY AS "REALITY OR ACTUALITY."[2] THE TRUTH IS WHAT IS. THE TRUTH IS STILLNESS, OR THAT WHICH ALLOWS MOVEMENT TO OCCUR. IT IS THE MASCULINE PRINCIPLE OF THE UNIVERSE. IT IS SHIVA.

THINK, SON, IF YOU WOULD FOR A MOMENT, OF THE OCEAN. IMAGINE IF SOMEONE TOOK ALL OF THE WATER OUT OF THE OCEAN. THINK OF ALL THE SPACE THAT WOULD BE PRESENT. ALL THAT SPACE IS THE CONTAINER OF ALL THAT FILLS IT. WITHOUT THIS SPACE, THERE OBVIOUSLY COULD BE NO OCEAN, FOR THERE WOULD BE NO SPACE TO PUT ANYTHING. THINK OF A CUP. WITHOUT THE EMPTY SPACE OF THE CUP, WHAT DO YOU HAVE? CERTAINLY, NO CUP. THE CUP'S REALITY IS TOTALLY DEPENDENT UPON SPACE, JUST AS THE OCEAN'S REALITY IS TOTALLY DEPENDENT UPON SPACE. IN FACT, REALITY ITSELF IS TOTALLY DEPENDENT UPON SPACE. FOR WHAT COULD YOU HAVE WITHOUT THE SPACE TO HAVE IT IN? SPACE DEFINES REALITY; THEREFORE, SPACE IS REALITY. SPACE IS THE TRUTH.

---

[1] https://www.ahdictionary.com/power
[2] https://www.ahdictionary.com/truth

OKAY, MASTER. THINK BACK TO THE OCEAN. THINK OF ALL THE WATER THAT FILLS THE SPACE. WITHOUT THIS WATER, THERE OBVIOUSLY COULD BE NO OCEAN EITHER, COULD IT? JUST A GIGANTIC CRATER OF EPIC PROPORTIONS. NO, SON. IN ORDER TO HAVE AN OCEAN, YOU MUST HAVE BOTH THE WATER AND THE SPACE. THE TWO MUST BECOME ONE IN ORDER TO HAVE MANIFESTATION. THINK OF FIRE AND LIGHT. THEY ARE TWO SEPARATE THINGS, AND YET THEY ARE ONE. IT IS IMPOSSIBLE TO SEPARATE THEM. THINK OF SILENCE AND SOUND. THE SILENCE IS WHAT GIVES THE SOUND ITS REALITY. FOR IF NOT FOR SILENCE, ONE COULD NOT HEAR ANYTHING. THE SILENCE IS WHAT ALLOWS THE SOUND TO EXIST.

NOW, MASTER. IMAGINE GOING TO THE BEACH AND LOOKING OUT OVER THE VAST EXPANSE OF WATERS. WHAT DO YOU SEE? DO YOU SEE THE OCEAN, OR DO YOU SEE THE WAVES? CAN YOU SEPARATE THE TWO? NO, YOU CANNOT BECAUSE THE TWO MAKE THE ONE. THEY ARE SEPARATE THINGS, AND YET THEY FORM THE ONE REALITY OF OCEAN. THE WAVES ARE THE OCEAN, AND THE OCEAN IS THE WAVES. IT IS THE WAVES THAT SHOW THE MOTION OF THE OCEAN. IT IS THIS MOTION THAT SHOWS THE FORCE OF THE OCEAN. NOW THINK OF THE SALT IN THE WATER OF THE OCEAN. SO WITHOUT THE SALT, YOU COULD HAVE NO OCEAN EITHER. THINK ABOUT THE MUD AT THE BOTTOM OF THE OCEAN THAT FORMS AUTOMATICALLY WHEN WATER AND EARTH COMBINE. THINK ABOUT THE CURRENTS OF THE OCEAN, ANOTHER MANIFESTATION OF THE FORCE OF THIS GREAT BODY OF WATER. THINK ABOUT THE ORGANISMS THAT LIVE IN THE OCEAN. WHERE DID THESE ORGANISMS COME FROM?

MOST SCIENTISTS AGREE THAT ALL LIFE ON THIS PLANET BEGAN IN THE WATERS OF THE OCEAN AND THEN SPREAD TO DRY LAND. SO

THE ORGANISMS THAT LIVE IN THE OCEAN MUST HAVE COME FROM THE WATERS THEMSELVES. ALL OF THESE THINGS ARE MANIFESTATIONS THAT ARISE WHEN THE COMBINATION OF WATER AND SPACE COME TOGETHER IN ORDER TO FORM THE REALITY OF THE OCEAN. IN THAT METAPHOR, THE OCEAN REPRESENTS THE UNIVERSE. THE WATER AND EVERYTHING THAT THE WATER CONTAINS REPRESENT **POWER**, AND THE SPACE IN WHICH THE WATER IS CONTAINED REPRESENTS **THE TRUTH**. SPACE, OR **THE TRUTH**, IS THE CONTAINER OF THE **POWER** OF THE UNIVERSE IN ALL OF ITS MANIFESTATIONS. **POWER** AND **THE TRUTH**. **THE TRUTH** AND **POWER**. TO HAVE **THE TRUTH** IS TO HAVE **POWER**, AND TO HAVE **POWER** IS TO HAVE **THE TRUTH**. TOGETHER, THEY FORM EXISTENCE ITSELF. THE TWO MAKE THE ONE. **POWER** IS **THE TRUTH**, AND **THE TRUTH** IS **POWER**.

AND JUST AS ALL OF THE MANY DIFFERENT PHENOMENA OF THE OCEAN ARE COMPOSED OF THE SAME SPACE AND WATER THAT MAKE UP THE OCEAN, ALL OF THE PHENOMENA OF THE UNIVERSE ARE MADE UP OF THE SAME SPACE AND ENERGY THAT COMPOSE THE UNIVERSE. SIMPLY **POWER** AND **THE TRUTH** IN DIFFERENT FORMS. NOTHING EXISTS BESIDES **POWER** AND **THE TRUTH**. EVERYTHING ELSE IS JUST AN ILLUSION. A FORM THAT **POWER** AND **THE TRUTH** HAVE TAKEN IN ORDER TO AMUSE THEMSELVES. ONLY **POWER** AND **THE TRUTH** ARE REAL BECAUSE ONLY **POWER** AND **THE TRUTH** ARE ETERNAL. ALL OF THEIR FORMS ARE BUT TEMPORARY APPARITIONS SUBJECT TO THE CYCLES OF BIRTH (BEGINNINGS) AND DEATH (ENDINGS). **POWER** AND **THE TRUTH** SUBJECT. THEY CANNOT BE SUBJECTED. BECAUSE I REALIZE THAT **I AM POWER,** AND I REALIZE THAT **I AM**

THE TRUTH, I have the POWER to shape myself into any form that I choose. For I AM POWER itself. And as POWER, there is only one form worthy of my essence.

I AM A DIVINE KING

THE dictionary defines DIVINE as belonging to or "having the nature of God."[3] It also defines DIVINE as "supremely good or beautiful; magnificent."[4] God is POWER and THE TRUTH, for POWER and THE TRUTH are all that exist. The dictionary defines KING as "one that is supreme or preeminent in a particular group, category, or sphere."[5] He that realizes that he is composed of POWER and THE TRUTH, the fundamental essences of the universe, is automatically supreme. And he that lives in accordance with this truth automatically takes the form of DIVINE KING. Therefore, a DIVINE KING is what I AM.

I AM WISDOM

Master, WISDOM is POWER, and to be wise is to be powerful. WISDOM is defined as the UNDERSTANDING of "what is true, right, or lasting."[6] Therefore, I AM WISDOM because I understand THE TRUTH. It is only with the companionship of WISDOM that you may reign and

---

[3] https://www.ahdictionary.com/divine
[4] https://www.ahdictionary.com/divine
[5] https://www.ahdictionary.com/king
[6] https://www.ahdictionary.com/wisdom

DECREE TRUE JUSTICE. FOR IT IS ONLY **WISDOM** THAT SHALL SUPPLY YOU WITH THE PRECIOUS JEWELS OF **KNOWLEDGE** WITH WHICH YOU MAY FORGE YOURSELF A MAJESTIC CROWN OF DISCERNING DISCRETION. UNFORTUNATELY, MASTER, IN THE PROCESS OF GAINING MUCH **WISDOM**, THERE SHALL BE MUCH GRIEF. I PERSONALLY CAN ATTEST TO THIS, FOR MY LIFE HAS INDEED BEEN A PAINFUL ONE. PAIN IS LIFE'S TEACHER, SON, AND THE MORE PAIN THAT YOU ARE ABLE TO PUSH YOURSELF THROUGH AND ENDURE, THE MORE **WISDOM** YOU SHALL ATTAIN. FOR THE MORE PAIN YOU ENDURE, THE MORE YOU SHALL COME TO KNOW AND UNDERSTAND YOURSELF.

I AM STRENGTH

STRENGTH IS **POWER**, AND **POWER** IS **STRENGTH**. FOR TO BE POWERFUL IS TO BE STRONG, MY SON, AND TO BE STRONG IS TO BE POWERFUL. **STRENGTH** IS DEFINED AS THE ABILITY TO ENDURE, AND THE CAPACITY OR POTENTIAL FOR ACTION.[7] NO MATTER HOW TALENTED YOU MAY BE, YOU STILL MUST MAKE A PARTNERSHIP WITH ENDURANCE AND PERSEVERANCE IF YOU WISH TO EMERGE VICTORIOUS IN ANY ENDEAVOR. IN FACT, THE GREATEST THING THAT A **KING** CAN BE KNOWN FOR IS FOR HAVING AN UNCONQUERABLE SPIRIT. BECAUSE THE GLORIOUS VIRTUE OF **STRENGTH** CAN ONLY BE DEVELOPED THROUGH EFFORT AND PRACTICE, WHEN DIFFICULT TIMES AND CIRCUMSTANCES COME UPON YOU, MASTER, YOU MUST NEVER GIVE UP. FOR YOUR **STRENGTH** CAN ONLY GROW FROM YOUR WEAKNESS, JUST AS AN OAK TREE CAN ONLY GROW FROM AN ACORN.

---

[7] https://www.merriam-webster.com/dictionary/strength

I AM FAITH

FAITH IS POWER, AND ALL OF ONE'S POWER LIES IN THEIR FAITH. FOR FAITH IS BELIEF. THE DICTIONARY DEFINES FAITH AS THE BELIEF OR TRUST IN A "PERSON, IDEA, OR THING."[8] FAITH IS LOYALTY. FAITH IS A PEN, AND WITH IT, YOU WRITE THE NARRATIVE OF YOUR LIFE. THERE IS NOTHING WHICH YOU MUST RELY MORE UPON THAN YOUR FAITH. FOR THERE IS NOTHING WHICH YOU MUST RELY MORE UPON THAN YOURSELF.

I AM KNOWLEDGE

KNOWLEDGE IS POWER. THUS, THOSE WHO POSSESS THE MOST KNOWLEDGE SHALL ALWAYS BE THE MOST POWERFUL. KNOWLEDGE IS DEFINED AS "FAMILIARITY, AWARENESS, OR UNDERSTANDING GAINED THROUGH EXPERIENCE OR STUDY."[9] IT IS ALSO DEFINED AS "THE SUM OR RANGE OF WHAT HAS BEEN PERCEIVED, DISCOVERED, OR LEARNED."[10] KNOWLEDGE, LIKE WISDOM, IS SO VALUABLE THAT ITS PRICE, MORE OFTEN THAN NOT, CAN ONLY BE PAID WITH THE CURRENCY OF PAIN. THUS IT IS, MY SON, THAT IN THE PROCESS OF GAINING MUCH KNOWLEDGE, THERE SHALL BE MUCH SORROW. NEVERTHELESS, KNOW THIS, MASTER. THERE IS NOTHING THAT SHOULD BE MORE DESIRED, NOR SHALL THERE EVER BE ANYTHING MORE PROPER AND BEFITTING TO YOU THAN KNOWLEDGE, AND IT IS THE EPITOME OF

---

[8] https://www.ahdictionary.com/knowledge
[9] https://www.ahdictionary.com/knowledge
[10] https://www.ahdictionary.com/knowledge

FOOLISHNESS FOR ANYONE TO EITHER SUGGEST OR BELIEVE THAT IT IS NOT ALWAYS A GOOD THING TO POSSESS OR PURSUE.

I AM UNDERSTANDING

UNDERSTANDING IS POWER, AND THE MOST POWERFUL POSSESSES THE GREATEST UNDERSTANDING. UNDERSTANDING IS DEFINED AS "THE QUALITY OF DISCERNMENT OR COMPREHENSION."[11] IT "IS THE FACULTY BY WHICH ONE UNDERSTANDS."[12] IT IS INTELLIGENCE. AT ALL TIMES, IN ORDER TO BE KING, YOU MUST SHOW THAT YOU POSSESS THAT QUIET FORCE AND INTELLIGENCE WHICH ALLOW YOU TO ACT BY INSTINCT IN SUCH A WAY THAT MEN HAVE NO RECOURSE BUT TO RESPECT YOU. IT IS ONLY BY WALKING THE PATH OF UNDERSTANDING THAT YOU SHALL ACQUIRE THE KNOWLEDGE WHICH YOU MAY RELY UPON FAITHFULLY IN ALL OF YOUR ENTERPRISES. KNOWLEDGE, WHEN COMBINED WITH UNDERSTANDING, IS ABLE TO BRING FORTH MANY WONDERS THAT SHALL BEAUTIFY YOUR KINGDOM. HOWEVER, SON, KNOWLEDGE WITHOUT UNDERSTANDING SHALL BRING FORTH A MULTITUDE OF AFFLICTIONS THAT SHALL EVENTUALLY LEAD TO THE DESTRUCTION OF YOUR REALM.

I AM DIGNITY

DIGNITY IS POWER, AND DIGNIFIED IS INVARIABLY THE POSE OF THE POWERFUL. DIGNITY IS DEFINED AS "THE

---

[11] https://www.aham.com

[12] https://www.thefreedictionary.com/reasoned

QUALITY OR STATE OF BEING WORTHY OF ESTEEM OR RESPECT."[13] It is also defined as "nobility of character, manner, or language."[14] There is nothing more worthy of respect than **THE TRUTH** and **POWER**, and no character so noble as that of a **DIVINE KING**. In fact, my son, to be a **DIVINE KING** is to be such a beacon of nobility that all others shall strive to behave in such a way as to be judged worthy of your noble company. No matter what trial or tribulation may threaten to overtake you, always adorn yourself in the armor of **DIGNITY** in order to combat it. By always assuming a pose that serenely radiates conviction in your belief that you have the ability to accomplish whatsoever your purposes and objectives are, you shall testify to the entire world that it has no dominion over you. Never, under any circumstances, must you allow yourself to lose a hold of your **DIGNITY**. For **DIGNITY** is the crown, and to lose your **DIGNITY** is to lose the **POWER** that the crown bestows upon you.

I AM HONOR

HONOR is **POWER**, and only the powerful are honored. **HONOR** is defined as "high respect,"[15] renown, or glory. To **HONOR** something is to respect it highly. A **KING** was made to be honorable, my son. Thus, as a **KING**, you should value nothing at all in

---

[13] https://ahdictionary.com/dignity
[14] https://ahdictionary.com/dignity
[15] https://www.ahdictionary.com/honor

THIS WORLD MORE THAN TO BE SO. **HONOR** IS SO BEFITTING TO THE CHARACTER OF A **KING** THAT ONCE YOU ARE IN POSSESSION OF IT, YOU SHALL SEEK NOTHING ELSE BESIDES IT. A TRUE **KING** IS INVARIABLY A MAN OF **HONOR** AND INTEGRITY. FOR IT IS IN THESE ATTRIBUTES THAT ONE FINDS PRUDENCE, GOODNESS, FORTITUDE, AND TEMPERANCE OF SPIRIT. THE VERY FOUNDATIONS OF GREATNESS LIE IN **HONOR**, MASTER. FOR GREATNESS ITSELF ARISES FROM ONE'S WILLINGNESS TO **HONOR** ALL OF THE SMALL THINGS WHICH COMPOSE THE PRESENT MOMENT.

I AM THE GREATEST KING THAT HAS EVER LIVED

POWER AND **THE TRUTH** ARE LIFE ITSELF, AND EVERYONE THAT YOU SHALL EVER MEET, WHETHER THEY REALIZE IT OR NOT, SHALL BE LOCKED IN A PERPETUAL SEARCH FOR THEM UNTIL THEY REALIZE **THE TRUTH** THAT THE SEARCH FOR **POWER** AND **THE TRUTH** IS LIKE A DOG CHASING ITS OWN TAIL, TURNING ENDLESSLY IN A CIRCLE OF TRIVIALITY. IT IS LIKE TRYING TO SEE YOUR OWN EYES WITHOUT THE AID OF A MIRROR. YOU ARE **POWER** ITSELF, AND WHEN YOU REALIZE THIS, YOU SHALL BECOME **THE GREATEST KING THAT HAS EVER LIVED**. FOR **POWER** IS ALL THAT HAS, DOES, AND EVER SHALL EXIST. **THE TRUTH** AND **POWER** ARE THE SOURCE OF ALL THINGS. THUS, THERE CAN BE NOTHING GREATER THAN **POWER** AND **THE TRUTH**. **POWER** IS THE **KING** OF THE UNIVERSE, FOR **POWER** IS THE UNIVERSE ITSELF.

I AM THE MASTER OF POWER

I AM THE MASTER OF POWER BECAUSE **I AM** THE MASTER OF MYSELF. **I AM** MY OWN AUTHORITY. **I AM** THE DEFINER OF MYSELF AS A TRUE **KING** ALWAYS IS. FOR HE WHO DEFINES, RULES. A TRUE **KING** MUST ALWAYS PAINT HIS OWN PICTURE OF REALITY. **THE TRUTH** IS THE CANVAS, AND **POWER** IS THE PAINT. WITH THESE, YOU MUST LEARN TO ILLUSTRATE THE MASTERPIECE OF YOUR OWN LIFE. FOR IF YOU DO NOT, AND YOU ALLOW OTHERS TO PAINT YOUR PICTURES FOR YOU, YOU CANNOT BE **KING**. FOR YOU SHALL BE LEADING A LIFE NOT OF YOUR OWN CHOOSING. YOU SHALL HAVE GIVEN YOUR **POWER** TO ANOTHER AND YOU SHALL NOT BE FREE. ONLY A **KING** IS TRULY FREE. NEVER FORGET, **POWER** IS THE MASTER, AND THE MASTER IS **POWER**.

A KING MUST UNDERSTAND

ABOVE ALL ELSE, MY SON, **A KING MUST UNDERSTAND**, FOR WHAT GOOD IS ANYTHING IF YOU DO NOT UNDERSTAND IT. IF YOU COULD NOT UNDERSTAND THE WORDS ON THIS PAPER, WISE AS THEY MAY BE, THEY COULD SERVE YOU NOT. IF YOU HAD THE GREATEST TOOL EVER CREATED, CAPABLE OF FIXING ANYTHING, OR SOLVING ANY PROBLEM, AND DID NOT UNDERSTAND HOW TO USE IT, HOW COULD IT HELP YOU? IMAGINE GIVING DIAMONDS TO A TWO-YEAR-OLD CHILD. INSTEAD OF BEING OF BENEFIT, LACK OF **UNDERSTANDING** MAKES THOSE DIAMONDS WORTHLESS TO THAT CHILD. IN FACT, THEY MAY EVEN BE A DETRIMENT TO THAT CHILD IF IT SWALLOWS ONE.

ALL RELATIONSHIPS EXIST IN **UNDERSTANDING**. YOUR MOTHER IS YOUR MOTHER NOT BECAUSE YOU CAME FROM HER WOMB, BUT BECAUSE YOU UNDERSTAND HER TO BE YOUR MOTHER. THIS IS WHY ADOPTED CHILDREN, EVEN THOUGH THEY DID NOT COME FROM THEIR ADOPTED MOTHER'S WOMB, STILL LIVE, AND TREAT HER AS IF SHE WERE THEIR MOTHER. AND IN FACT, SHE IS, BECAUSE THEY UNDERSTAND HER TO BE. THEIR **UNDERSTANDING** HAS SHAPED THEIR REALITY. THEIR **UNDERSTANDING** HAS BECOME **THE TRUTH** TO THEM. **UNDERSTANDING** SHALL KEEP YOU FROM DANGER AND DELIVER YOU FROM THE WAY OF MALEVOLENCE. HAPPY SHALL BE THEY WHO GAIN **UNDERSTANDING** AND LOST SHALL BE THEY WHO LACK IT. THE PROCEEDS FROM **UNDERSTANDING** ARE BETTER THAN THE PROFITS OF GOLD AND SHE IS MORE PRECIOUS THAN THE RAREST GEMS. NOTHING THAT YOU COULD EVER DESIRE CAN COMPARE TO HER, FOR WITHIN HER RESIDES LONG LIFE AND WEALTH. THE WAYS OF **UNDERSTANDING** ARE WAYS OF PLEASANTNESS, AND ALL OF HER PATHS SHALL DIRECT YOU TO PEACE. SHE IS LIFE TO ALL WHO GRASP HER, AND ALL WHO RETAIN HER ARE BLESSED.

IT IS BY **UNDERSTANDING** THAT YOUR KINGDOM SHALL BE ESTABLISHED, AND IT IS BY A LACK OF **UNDERSTANDING** THAT IT SHALL BE DESTROYED. NEVER TURN AWAY FROM **UNDERSTANDING**, FOR IF YOU DO NOT FORSAKE HER, SHE SHALL ALWAYS PROTECT YOU. IF YOU **LOVE** HER, SHE SHALL PRESERVE YOU. IF YOU EXALT HER, SHE SHALL RAISE YOU TO THE HEIGHTS OF SPLENDOR. IF YOU EMBRACE HER, SHE SHALL BRING YOU **HONOR**. SHE SHALL CROWN YOU WITH GRACE AND ROBE YOU IN GLORY. SHE SHALL MAKE ALL OF YOUR STEPS SECURE, AND IF SHE IS WITH YOU, EVEN

IF YOU WALK IN DARKNESS, YOU SHALL NOT STUMBLE. BE OF AN UNDERSTANDING HEART, MASTER, SO THAT YOU MAY FIND FAVOR AND TRAVEL IN THE WAY OF GOODNESS. ONLY SUFFERING IS RESERVED FOR THOSE WHOSE HEARTS VALUE NOT UNDERSTANDING.

A KING MUST UNDERSTAND, FOR ONLY A MAN OF UNDERSTANDING IS ABLE TO BRING PEACE TO HIS REALM. IT IS ONLY AN **UNDERSTANDING** HEART THAT SHALL ALLOW YOU TO JUDGE YOUR PEOPLE IN PROBITY AND EQUITABLENESS. **A KING MUST UNDERSTAND**, MY SON, FOR ALL IN THE KINGDOM RELY UPON THE **UNDERSTANDING** OF THE **KING**.

THOUGHTS OF A DIVINE KING

THINK FOR A MOMENT, MASTER, OF A WOODEN BOX. FILL THAT BOX WITH EXCREMENT, AND THAT BOX NOT ONLY BECOMES WORTHLESS, BUT IT IS NOW SUDDENLY REPUGNANT AS WELL. NOT MANY SHALL DESIRE THAT BOX. HOWEVER, IF YOU TAKE THAT SAME EMPTY BOX AND FILL IT WITH PRECIOUS JEWELS, EVERYTHING ABOUT THAT BOX CHANGES. NOT ONLY IS THAT BOX NOW EXTREMELY VALUABLE, BUT IT IS NOW RESPLENDENT AND DESIRED BY ALL. SO YOU SEE, ALL THE **POWER** OF THAT BOX IS LOCATED IN THE EMPTY SPACE AND WHAT FILLS IT. IT IS THE SAME WAY WITH THE MIND. THE SPACE OF THE MIND IS **THE TRUTH** AND THE THOUGHTS THAT ARE IN IT ARE THE **POWER** OF THE MIND. WHATEVER YOU FILL SPACE WITH IS WHAT THAT SPACE BECOMES. A BOX FILLED WITH EXCREMENT IS A DISGUSTING BIOHAZARD. THAT SAME BOX FILLED WITH PRECIOUS JEWELS IS A DREAM COME TRUE. A MIND FILLED WITH FOOLISH

THOUGHTS IS A FOOL. A MIND FILLED WITH THOUGHTS OF **WISDOM, STRENGTH, FAITH, KNOWLEDGE, UNDERSTANDING, DIGNITY,** AND **HONOR** IS A **DIVINE KING.** THUS, I OFFER YOU MY THOUGHTS, MASTER, THE THOUGHTS OF A **DIVINE KING** SO THAT YOUR TREASURE BOX MAY BE FILLED WITH SOME OF YOUR FATHER'S MOST PRECIOUS GEMS.

I OFFER YOU THESE JEWELS, MY SON, SO THAT YOU MAY BE THE NEXT STAGE IN MY EVOLUTION. FOR THE MASTER IS ALWAYS TEACHING ITSELF. WORDS ARE THOUGHTS AND THOUGHTS ARE WORDS. THESE WORDS THAT YOU HAVE BEEN READING AND SHALL CONTINUE TO READ ARE MY DISSERTATION ON THE SUBJECT OF **DIVINE** KINGSHIP. THIS LETTER IS A GUARANTEE THAT NO MATTER WHAT MAY HAPPEN, I SHALL ALWAYS BE HERE TO GIVE YOU ADVICE. SOME HELP ALONG YOUR WAY. THE HELP THAT I OFFER TO YOU IS **KNOWLEDGE** OF REGALITY. IF YOU WISH TO BE A **DIVINE KING,** YOU MUST FOREVER KEEP IN YOUR MIND THE THOUGHTS OF A **DIVINE KING.** I HAVE PAID MIGHTILY FOR THE JEWELS WITHIN THESE PAGES. THEREFORE, THEY ARE EXTREMELY VALUABLE.

A MANUAL CONCERNING THE ART OF KINGSHIP

EVEN NOW, MY SON, AS I WRITE THESE WORDS, MY EYES BURN WITH THE WEARINESS BORN OF YEARS SPENT READING, RESEARCHING, AND WRITING IN THE DARKNESS OF PRISON. PRISON IS A PLACE THAT IS FULL OF PAIN AND SORROW. I SERIOUSLY ADVISE THAT YOU DO NOT FIND OUT ABOUT IT PERSONALLY. THIS IS YET ANOTHER REASON WHY **I AM** WRITING

THIS LETTER TO YOU, MY SON. ANOTHER REASON WHY **I AM** GIVING YOU THESE JEWELS IS SO YOUR ROAD TO **POWER** MAY BE SMOOTHER THAN MINE WAS. YOU SEE, I HAD NO ONE TO TELL ME THESE THINGS THAT **I AM** WRITING TO YOU IN THIS LETTER AND JEWELS LIKE THESE DO NOT COME CHEAP. SO **I AM** GIVING THEM TO YOU SO THAT YOU MAY BE ABLE TO START FROM WHERE **I AM** AT THIS MOMENT, ADD YOUR OWN SPLASH OF GREATNESS TO THE MIX, AND INCREASE YOUR **POWER** EXPONENTIALLY. A GREAT MAN IN HISTORY ONCE SAID, "IF A MAN TREATS PRISON LIKE A UNIVERSITY, HE SHALL WALK OUT A **KING**."[16] A UNIVERSITY IS EXACTLY WHAT PRISON HAS BEEN TO ME, MY SON, AND THE SUBJECT THAT I HAVE STUDIED IS **THE TRUTH**. I HAVE A MASTER'S DEGREE, IF YOU WILL, IN **POWER**. I HAVE BECOME A **DIVINE KING**. I HAVE BECOME **THE GREATEST KING THAT HAS EVER LIVED**. NOW I REALIZE MY SON, THAT I HAVE BECOME THESE THINGS, MERELY SO THAT I MAY SERVE AS A FOOTSTOOL WHICH YOU MAY STEP UPON IN ORDER TO ASCEND TO THE GREATNESS THAT IS YOUR BIRTHRIGHT. THIS LETTER IS A COMPILATION OF ALL THE KINGLY **KNOWLEDGE** THAT I HAVE ATTAINED UP UNTIL THIS POINT IN MY LIFE.

THIS LETTER IS A MANUAL. A MANUAL WRITTEN FROM FATHER TO SON. A MANUAL WRITTEN FROM THE MASTER TO MY SON, MASTER. A MANUAL CONCERNING THE ART OF KINGSHIP.

---

[16] Author Unknown.

BOOK ONE

1

MASTER, AWARENESS CHANGES EVERYTHING. IMAGINE FOR A SECOND THAT IT IS THE FIRST DAY OF SCHOOL. CAT IS SEVEN YEARS OLD AND HAS EXCITEDLY BEEN ANTICIPATING THIS DAY FOR WEEKS. NOT ONLY IS SHE EXCITED TO SEE HER TEACHERS AND FRIENDS, BUT A FEW WEEKS AGO, HER FATHER BOUGHT HER A BEAUTIFUL NEW WHITE DRESS FOR HER BIRTHDAY AND WANTED HER TO WEAR IT AT HER BIRTHDAY PARTY, BUT SHE REFUSED. CAT COULD BE VERY DETERMINED WHEN SHE WANTED TO BE. SHE KNEW BIRTHDAY PARTIES WERE MESSY AFFAIRS WITH ALL THE CAKE, ICE CREAM, PUNCH, AND BOYS. SHE DID NOT WANT ANY OF THOSE MESSY THINGS TO RUIN HER BEAUTIFUL NEW SPARKLING WHITE DRESS. IT WAS THE MOST BEAUTIFUL DRESS SHE HAD EVER SEEN, MUCH LESS OWNED. SHE WAS DETERMINED TO WEAR IT ON THE FIRST DAY OF SCHOOL. SHE COULDN'T WAIT TO SHOW IT OFF TO HER FRIENDS, ESPECIALLY HER BEST FRIEND JULIE.

NOW THAT THE FIRST DAY OF SCHOOL HAD FINALLY ARRIVED, CAT'S PATIENCE WAS ABOUT TO FINALLY PAY OFF. SHE HAD BARELY SLEPT LAST NIGHT. NOT ONLY WAS SHE EXCITED, BUT SHE WORRIED AS WELL. FOR IT HAD RAINED LAST NIGHT AND SHE CERTAINLY COULD NOT WEAR HER NEW DRESS IN THE RAIN. HOWEVER, BY THE TIME SHE WOKE UP, THE RAIN HAD STOPPED, AND THE SUN WAS RISING, ALREADY SHINING BRIGHT ON THE HORIZON. WHEN CAT LOOKED OUT THE WINDOW OF HER ROOM, SHE COULD SEE THAT ALTHOUGH THERE WERE STILL A FEW MUD PUDDLES LEFT, THE GROUND WAS PRETTY MUCH DRY. SHE SMILED, GIDDY WITH ANTICIPATION FOR THE DAY SHE HAD BEEN WAITING ON FOR WHAT SEEMED LIKE, IN HER SEVEN-YEAR-OLD MIND, FOREVER.

HER FATHER AND MOTHER CHUCKLED TO THEMSELVES AS SHE SAT DOWN AT THE BREAKFAST TABLE COVERED IN TOWELS. SHE WAS DETERMINED NOT TO SPILL ANY FOOD ON HERSELF FOR WHAT WAS A SPECIAL MORNING. SHE DID NOT WANT TO GET A SMUDGE OF ANYTHING ON HER PRETTY NEW DRESS BEFORE JULIE SAW IT.

AS SHE WAS WALKING TO SCHOOL, SHE WAS VERY HAPPY. ALL OF HER FRIENDS WERE THERE, AND EVERYONE SEEMED REALLY EXCITED TO BE BACK AT SCHOOL. SUDDENLY, SOMEONE BEGAN TO POP SOME FIRECRACKERS. CAT LOVED FIRECRACKERS. SHE LOVED THE LOUD, POPPING SOUND THEY GAVE OFF WHEN THEY EXPLODED. SHE WONDERED IF ONE OF HER FRIENDS WERE POPPING THE FIRECRACKERS. IF SO, SHE WOULD ASK THEM TO LET HER LIGHT ONE SO THAT SHE COULD JOIN IN ON THE FUN TOO.

As soon as she was about to turn around to see who was setting off the firecrackers, out of nowhere, a man Cat had never seen before dove and pushed her right into a mud puddle, ruining her beautiful white dress. Then, to add insult to injury, the man got up and ran off without even bothering to apologize. Cat was mortified. When she stood up, she looked down at her dress and burst immediately into tears. It was no longer a pretty white dress. It was now a disgusting brown one. "Why would that man do this to me?" Cat wondered sorrowfully. "How could he be so cruel? He didn't even say sorry."

Heartbroken, little Cat ran all the way home, crying the entire way.

How do you feel about what happened to Cat? How do you feel about the man who pushed her down into the mud?

That very same morning, while Cat was eating breakfast at home, Derrick, the police officer that was assigned to the school zone where she went to school, was arriving at his post. He took his job very seriously. His job was to make sure that the children walking to school got across the street safely. He was these kids' guardian angel, so to speak, and he was determined not to let anything happen to any one of them.

As the kids began to trickle in, he could see all of their little faces beaming with innocent joy. All of a sudden, out of the corner of his eye, something caught his attention. Something was wrong and he could feel it. Years on the police force had trained him to be sensitive to his surroundings and to be aware of everything happening around him. Before he had a chance to

COMPLETELY FIGURE OUT WHAT WAS HAPPENING, TWO MEN PULLED PISTOLS OUT OF THEIR WAISTBANDS AND BEGAN SHOOTING AT EACH OTHER WITH THE CHILDREN WALKING RIGHT IN THEIR LINE OF FIRE.

WITHOUT EVEN THINKING, DERRICK TOOK OFF IN THE DIRECTION OF THE CHILDREN BETWEEN THE TWO GUNMEN. EVERYTHING WAS HAPPENING SO FAST. HE WATCHED AS ONE LITTLE BOY GOT SHOT, THE BULLET DESTROYING ALL OF HIS FUTURE ASPIRATIONS AS IT FLUNG HIM TO THE CONCRETE. DERRICK COULD SEE THERE WAS A LITTLE GIRL IN A WHITE DRESS ABOUT TEN FEET AWAY THAT WAS DIRECTLY IN THE LINE OF FIRE BETWEEN THE TWO GUNMEN. WITH EVERYTHING THAT HE HAD, DERRICK DOVE AND PUSHED THE LITTLE GIRL OUT OF THE WAY, A SPLIT SECOND BEFORE ANOTHER SHOT RANG OUT. THE BULLET WOULD HAVE HIT THE LITTLE GIRL HAD DERRICK NOT GOTTEN TO HER WHEN HE HAD. INSTEAD, IT HIT THE OTHER GUNMAN, KILLING HIM INSTANTLY. SEEING THAT ONE OF THE SHOOTERS WAS HIT AND DOWN, DERRICK GOT UP AND, WHILE CALLING FOR BACKUP, BEGAN PURSUING THE OTHER SHOOTER WHO WAS GETTING AWAY.

NOW, HOW DO YOU FEEL ABOUT WHAT HAPPENED TO CAT? NOW, HOW DO YOU FEEL ABOUT THE MAN WHO PUSHED HER INTO THE MUD? AWARENESS CHANGES EVERYTHING.

2

MASTER, EXCEPT YOUR OWN MIND, THERE IS NOTHING THAT IS ABSOLUTELY IN YOUR POWER. YOUR OWN THOUGHTS AND YOUR OWN OPINIONS ARE THE ONLY THINGS IN THIS UNIVERSE OVER WHICH YOU HAVE COMPLETE AND UNQUESTIONABLE CONTROL. BUT REST ASSURED, MY SON, THERE IS NOTHING ELSE

IN THE ENTIRE UNIVERSE THAT YOU NEED CONTROL. TO MASTER YOUR OWN THOUGHTS IS TO BECOME A BEING OF **POWER**. TO BECOME A BEING OF **POWER** IS TO BECOME THE SOLUTION TO ALL OF YOUR OWN PROBLEMS, AS WELL AS THE POSSESSOR OF THE ABILITY TO TRANSMUTE YOUR LIFE INTO WHATSOEVER YOU DESIRE IT TO BE. THERE SHOULD BE NO MORE INSPIRING FACT TO YOU THAN THAT OF YOUR ABILITY TO SHAPE AND ELEVATE YOUR LIFE BY THE USE OF YOUR OWN THOUGHTS. WHAT THE FUTURE HOLDS FOR YOU IS TOTALLY DEPENDENT UPON YOUR STATE OF CONSCIOUSNESS AND THE PERCEPTIONS THAT YOU ARE FORMING NOW. YOUR STATE OF MIND DETERMINES YOUR RELATIONSHIP WITH THE UNIVERSE. IF YOU HAVE THE STATE OF MIND OF A FOOL, THE UNIVERSE SHALL TREAT YOU LIKE A FOOL. IF YOU HAVE THE STATE OF MIND OF A **KING**, THE UNIVERSE SHALL TREAT YOU LIKE A **KING**. TO KNOW YOUR STATE OF MIND, YOU NEED ONLY TO LISTEN TO YOUR OWN THOUGHTS. IF YOU HEAR COMPLAINTS, BEWAILING, AND LAMENTATIONS, YOU HAVE A WEAK STATE OF MIND, AND THUS YOU SHALL BE DOMINATED AND ENSLAVED BY CIRCUMSTANCES. IF YOU HEAR FELICITATION, EXULTATION, AND GRATITUDE, YOU HAVE A POWERFUL STATE OF MIND, AND THUS YOU SHALL DOMINATE YOUR CIRCUMSTANCES AND BE FREE FROM THEIR DOMINION OVER YOU. KNOW THIS AND NEVER DOUBT IT, YOUR STATE OF MIND IS OF PRIMARY IMPORTANCE. EVERYTHING ELSE IS SECONDARY. FOR EVERYTHING THAT YOU PERCEIVE IS SIMPLY A REFLECTION OF YOUR STATE OF MIND. IF YOU DO NOT TAKE RESPONSIBILITY FOR YOUR OWN STATE OF MIND, YOU SHALL NEVER BE ABLE TO TAKE RESPONSIBILITY FOR YOUR OWN LIFE. YOUR LIFE SHALL BE PROGRAMMED, AND YOU SHALL BE SHAPED INTO A TOOL TO BE USED AT SOMEONE ELSE'S DISCRETION. YOU SHALL HAND OVER YOUR **POWER** TO ANOTHER. A **KING** COULD NEVER DO

THIS, FOR IF HE DID, HE WOULD NOT BE **KING**. THERE CAN ONLY BE ONE MASTER, MY SON. EITHER YOU ARE THAT OR YOU ARE NOT. IT IS TOTALLY UP TO YOU. WHATSOEVER YOU IMAGINE AND BELIEVE YOURSELF TO BE, THAT SHALL YOU BECOME. TO FORM YOUR OWN PERCEPTIONS AND DETERMINE YOUR OWN STATE OF MIND IS TO BE FREE. IT IS TO BE YOUR OWN AUTHORITY AND THE FASHIONER OF YOUR OWN DESTINY.

3

MASTER, BECAUSE DOING FOLLOWS THINKING, FREEDOM BEGINS IN YOUR THOUGHT, NOT IN YOUR ACTIONS. YOU SHALL NEVER BE FREE TO DO WHAT YOU DESIRE TO DO UNLESS YOU ARE FIRST FREE TO THINK WHAT YOU DESIRE TO THINK. ONLY A **KING** CAN DO AND THINK THAT WHICH HE WISHES, FOR ONLY A **KING** IS FREE. WHEN YOU ARE FREE, EVERY PLACE IN THE WORLD IS THE PERFECT PLACE TO BE. IT IS ONLY BY BEING FREE IN YOUR THOUGHTS THAT YOU SHALL BE ABLE TO TRANSMUTE OPPRESSING AND DEPRESSING CIRCUMSTANCES INTO THE LIBERATING AND ELEVATING CONDITIONS OF YOUR ENLIGHTENMENT. WHEN YOU FREE YOUR MIND AND GAIN THE ABILITY TO DEFINE YOUR OWN REALITY, YOU FREE YOURSELF FROM THE JUDGMENTS, EXPECTATIONS, AND CONCEPTIONS THAT OTHER PEOPLE AND SOCIETY ATTEMPT TO SHACKLE YOU WITH. TO FREE YOUR THOUGHTS IS TO FREE YOUR INTELLIGENCE TO WORK FOR ITS TRUE MASTER. ONCE YOUR INTELLIGENCE STARTS TO WORK, YOU SHALL NEED NOTHING ELSE. IT IS INTELLIGENCE AND ONLY INTELLIGENCE THAT INCREASES YOUR **POWER**. FOR IT IS ONLY INTELLIGENCE THAT ALLOWS YOU TO LEARN.

4

MASTER, LEARNING IS THE ONE THING THAT SHALL NEVER FAIL YOU. YOUR MIND CAN NEVER BE HARMED BY LEARNING; THUS, YOU SHOULD NEVER MISTRUST OR REGRET DOING SO. HOWEVER, ALL THE LEARNING IN THE WORLD IS USELESS VANITY IF IT DOES NOT TEACH YOU TO BE FREE. FOR FREEDOM IS THE PURPOSE OF LIFE. ONE WHO IS NOT A **KING** CAN NEVER TEACH YOU TO BE **KING**, FOR FREEDOM CAN NEVER BE TAUGHT BY SOMEONE WHO ISN'T FREE. THIS IS NOT TO SAY THAT YOU CANNOT LEARN FROM THOSE WHO ARE NOT **KINGS**, IT SIMPLY MEANS THEY CANNOT TEACH YOU TO BE **KING**. FOR THEY DO NOT UNDERSTAND WHAT IT IS TO BE ONE. IF THEY DID KNOW, THEY WOULD BE **KING**.

5

MASTER, THERE ARE THREE LEVELS OF INTELLECT. THERE IS ONE THAT COMPREHENDS **THE TRUTH** BY ITSELF. THIS IS THE MIND OF A MASTER. THERE IS ONE WHICH SEES **THE TRUTH** IN WHAT OTHERS HAVE COMPREHENDED. THIS IS THE MIND OF ONE ON THE WAY TO BECOMING A MASTER. AND THERE IS THE INTELLECT WHICH NEITHER COMPREHENDS **THE TRUTH** BY ITSELF, NOR BY THE SHOWING OF OTHERS. THIS IS THE MIND OF THE MAJORITY OF PEOPLE THAT YOU SHALL ENCOUNTER IN YOUR LIFE. FOR MOST PEOPLE ARE UNAWARE OF WHAT IS TAKING PLACE RIGHT IN FRONT OF THEIR VERY EYES. THEY ARE FOREVER SEEING BUT NEVER PERCEIVING. FOREVER HEARING BUT NEVER **UNDERSTANDING**. THEY ARE THE BLIND AND THE BLIND SEE THAT WHICH THEY DESIRE TO SEE. AND BECAUSE VERY FEW DESIRE TO SEE **THE TRUTH**, THEY REMAIN UNAWARE THAT THEY ARE BLIND.

6

ONCE UPON A TIME, THERE WAS AN OLD MASTER THAT LIVED AT THE TOP OF A STEEP HILL IN THE CENTER OF HIS TOWN. THERE WERE MANY THAT DESIRED TO LEARN FROM THE OLD MASTER, FOR HE WAS THE WISEST MAN IN ALL OF THE LAND. SCHOLARS FROM FAR AND WIDE CAME TO THE TOWN SO THAT THEY MAY HAVE THE OPPORTUNITY TO STUDY AT THE FEET OF THE OLD MASTER, BUT HE WOULD ACCEPT NONE OF THEM. IT WASN'T THAT THE OLD MASTER DID NOT WISH TO PASS DOWN HIS **WISDOM** TO A NEOPHYTE. IN FACT, HE DESIRED NOTHING MORE. IT WAS JUST THAT HE COULD FIND NONE THAT POSSESSED THE **UNDERSTANDING** NECESSARY TO PASS HIS FIRST TEST. IT WAS THIS TEST THAT DETERMINED WHETHER OR NOT THE PROSPECTIVE STUDENT POSSESSED THE **WISDOM** REQUIRED OF HE WHO COULD BE INITIATED. THUS, YEARS AND YEARS PASSED. MANY KNOCKED ON THE OLD MASTER'S DOOR, BUT NONE PASSED THE TEST.

One day, a penniless youth that lived in a tiny shack in the poor section of the town decided that he would climb the hill of the old master and see if he could pass the test. His family was very poor, and oftentimes the little boy would watch as his mother would go hungry just so that he could get a meager bite to eat. This made the little boy very sad, for he loved his mother very much and did not like to see her suffer, especially on account of him. He had heard that if you went to the old master's door at the top of the hill and passed his test, he would take you in and teach you to be master. The young boy heard that the old master would feed you as well. This sounded very good to the youth and he decided that he would go and see if he could take the old master's test. After all, what did he have to lose? If he failed the test, he would have at least tried to make things better for him and his mother. If he passed the test, then he would take half of the food that the master gave him and give it to his poor mother. To learn to be a master would be fine too he supposed, although he knew not exactly what that meant.
As the boy approached the steep hill that led to the old master's house, he passed by a group of men standing at the bottom of the hill looking very disgruntled.

"Where are you going, boy?" asked one of the sullen men.

"I'm going up there to the old master's house to see if he would accept me," answered the boy.

At the poor boy's words, all of the men burst into laughter.

"You!" laughed one of the men. "You think that you can pass the old master's test?"

THE MEN ALL ROARED HARDER WITH LAUGHTER.

"YOU ARE JUST AN ILLITERATE, DIRTY BOY FROM THE POOR SIDE OF TOWN. YOUR MOTHER CANNOT EVEN AFFORD TO FEED YOU. ALL OF US ARE VERY RICH AND WE HAVE READ MANY BOOKS. WE ALL HAVE MANY DEGREES FROM ALL KINDS OF UNIVERSITIES. EVEN WE COULD NOT PASS THE OLD MASTER'S TEST, AND NOW YOU ARE GOING TO TRY? GO HOME, STUPID, FILTHY BOY! YOU ARE WASTING BOTH THE MASTER'S AND YOUR OWN TIME."

THE LITTLE POOR BOY DROPPED HIS HEAD AND BECAME VERY SAD. "MAYBE THOSE MEN ARE RIGHT. MAYBE I SHOULD GO HOME," HE THOUGHT TO HIMSELF.

HE WAS ABOUT TO TURN AROUND WHEN HE REMEMBERED THAT HE HAD NOTHING TO LOSE BY TRYING. AFTER ALL, HE HAD NOTHING, AND THUS NOTHING COULD BE TAKEN AWAY FROM HIM IF HE FAILED. FOR SOME REASON, THIS THOUGHT GAVE THE LITTLE POOR BOY COURAGE AND HE WALKED UP THE HILL MORE DETERMINED THAN EVER. JUST AS HE WAS ABOUT TO KNOCK ON THE OLD MASTER'S DOOR, IT OPENED BY ITSELF. THERE ON THE OTHER SIDE STOOD THE OLD MASTER.

"MAY I HELP YOU?" ASKED THE OLD MASTER.

"I....I....I CAME TO PASS YOUR TEST SO THAT YOU MAY TAKE ME IN AND FEED...I MEAN, TEACH ME," STAMMERED THE LITTLE POOR BOY NERVOUSLY.

"IS THAT RIGHT?" RESPONDED THE OLD MASTER. "WELL, COME ON IN. HAVE A SEAT."

THE LITTLE POOR BOY WALKED INTO THE HOUSE AND SAT DOWN. THE OLD MASTER HAD INCREDIBLY BEAUTIFUL CARPETS THAT LOOKED VERY EXPENSIVE ALL ACROSS HIS FLOORS. THE LITTLE

POOR BOY HAD NEVER WALKED UPON CARPET, MUCH LESS WALKED UPON CARPET AS EXQUISITE AS THAT WHICH WAS IN THE OLD MASTER'S HOUSE. HE SUDDENLY LOOKED DOWN AT HIS DIRTY FEET AND GREW VERY EMBARRASSED. THE OLD MASTER THEN BROUGHT ANOTHER CHAIR AND A TABLE AND SAT THEM DOWN IN FRONT OF THE LITTLE POOR BOY. HE THEN GRABBED A TRAY THAT HAD UPON IT TWO CUPS AND A POT OF TEA AND SAT DOWN OPPOSITE HIM.

"SO YOU WANT ME TO TEACH YOU TO BE A MASTER, HUH? WELL, YOU MUST HAVE TEA WITH ME FIRST. YOUR CUP IS ALREADY FULL. HOWEVER, THE TEA IN YOUR CUP IS NO GOOD. IT IS QUITE UNDRINKABLE. SO IF YOU WANT ME TO TEACH YOU, YOU MUST POUR THE FRESH TEA OUT OF THE TEAPOT IN FRONT OF YOU INTO YOUR CUP WITHOUT CAUSING IT TO OVERFLOW ONTO THE TRAY. IF ANY TEA GETS ON THE TRAY, I SHALL NOT TEACH YOU. I SHALL NOT TEACH YOU IF YOU DRINK THE TEA EITHER. FOR THAT TEA IS NO GOOD. IT IS QUITE UNDRINKABLE. IF YOU DRINK IT, YOU SHALL BE NO GOOD EITHER."

AS THE POOR BOY LOOKED DOWN AT THE FULL CUP OF TEA IN FRONT OF HIM, HE WAS DUMBFOUNDED. IT DIDN'T LOOK LIKE ANOTHER DROP COULD FIT IN. HE LIFTED THE TEAPOT TO SEE HOW MUCH TEA WAS IN THERE. THERE WAS ENOUGH TEA IN THE POT FOR A WHOLE CUP PLUS MORE. THERE WAS ABSOLUTELY NO WAY HE COULD POUR ALL OF THAT TEA INTO THAT CUP WITHOUT IT OVERFLOWING. WHAT WAS HE TO DO? HE COULDN'T DRINK THE TEA OUT OF THE CUP. THE OLD MASTER HAD SAID THAT IT WAS NO GOOD AND UNDRINKABLE. HE HAD ALSO SAID THAT HE WOULD NOT TEACH HIM IF HE DRANK THE TEA BECAUSE IT WOULD MAKE HIM NO GOOD. THE LITTLE BOY WANTED MORE THAN ANYTHING TO BE GOOD. THE OLD MASTER SAT BACK,

SIPPED ON HIS TEA, AND WATCHED THE LITTLE BOY INTENTLY. THE LITTLE BOY SAT FOR A MOMENT LONGER BEFORE HE PICKED UP THE CUP, POURED THE TEA OUT ONTO THE EXPENSIVELY CARPETED FLOOR, AND THEN POURED THE TEA FROM THE TEAPOT INTO THE CUP. THE OLD MASTER SMILED AND SAID, "CONGRATULATIONS, YOU HAVE PASSED THE TEST. I SHALL TAKE YOU IN."

MY SON, MOST PEOPLE'S MINDS ARE LIKE THAT FULL CUP OF TEA. SO FULL OF CONCEPTS AND PRECONCEIVED NOTIONS THAT THERE IS NO ROOM LEFT FOR ANYTHING ELSE. EVEN TEA FROM THE MASTER. YOU MUST NEVER MAKE THAT MISTAKE, MASTER. IF YOU DO, YOU SHALL NEVER BE ABLE TO LEARN, FOR IT IS AN IMPOSSIBLE TASK TO TEACH SOMEONE SOMETHING WHO HAS ALREADY ASSUMED THAT THEY KNOW EVERYTHING. A PERSON SUCH AS THIS HAS A MIND LIKE A FULL CUP. HOWEVER, INSTEAD OF OVERFLOWING, THEIR MINDS REJECT ANY NEW INFORMATION THAT MAY COME THEIR WAY. HE WHO IS KEEN TO LEARN REJECTS NOTHING. FOR HE WHO IS KEEN TO LEARN UNDERSTANDS THAT IT IS NEVER POSSIBLE FOR A MAN TO BE FINISHED LEARNING, ESPECIALLY IF HIS PURPOSE IS ABOVE AVERAGE.

7

MASTER, YOU MUST DELVE AS DEEPLY AS POSSIBLE INTO WHATEVER FIELD OF STUDY THAT YOU WISH TO MASTER, FOR GENIUS LIES NOT IN THE EXTENSITY OF ONE'S KNOWLEDGE, BUT IN THE INTENSITY. HOWEVER, YOU MUST NEVER ALLOW THE VULGAR TO KNOW THE FULL EXTENT OF YOUR MENTAL PROWESS. FOR IF THEY DO, THEY MAY COME TO FEAR YOU. AND IF THEY COME TO

FEAR YOU, REST ASSURED, THEY SHALL COME TO HATE YOU. EDUCATION IS TRAINING, AND TO BE EDUCATED IS TO BE TRAINED. THE EDUCATION THAT A MAN MUST OBTAIN IF HE WISHES TO BE **KING**, IS AN EDUCATION IN **POWER**. AN UNEDUCATED **KING** SHALL BE THE RUIN OF HIS PEOPLE. FOR AN UNEDUCATED **KING** HAS NO **KNOWLEDGE** OF **POWER**. TO THE IGNORANT, EDUCATION IS LIKE HANDCUFFS THAT THEY CANNOT WAIT TO DISCARD. BUT TO THE INTELLIGENT, EDUCATION IS LIKE GOLD BRACELETS THAT THEY CANNOT WAIT TO EXHIBIT. EDUCATION IS **POWER**, MASTER, AND JUST AS YOU CANNOT MASTER THE ARTS OF READING AND WRITING UNTIL YOU HAVE STUDIED THEM PROPERLY, SO TOO IS IT IMPOSSIBLE TO MASTER THE ART OF KINGSHIP WITHOUT GIVING **POWER** PROPER STUDY.

8

MASTER, THOUGHT IS THE MASTER OF ALL OTHER FORMS OF ENERGY IN THE PHYSICAL UNIVERSE. FOR THOUGHT IS ENERGY MIXED WITH INTELLIGENCE. JUST AS THE AMOUNT OF LIGHT THAT THE SUN CAN FLOOD INTO A HOUSE IS DEPENDENT UPON WHETHER OR NOT THE CURTAINS OF THE HOUSE ARE OPEN, THE AMOUNT OF INTELLIGENCE THAT IS ABLE TO ENTER A PERSON'S MIND IS DEPENDENT UPON WHETHER OR NOT THAT PERSON'S MIND IS OPEN OR NOT.

9

MASTER, ONLY THOSE MINDS THAT INQUIRE, INVESTIGATE, AND EXPLORE, SHALL GAIN **KNOWLEDGE** AND **WISDOM**, AND THOSE MINDS THAT HAVE NO INTEREST IN

UNDERSTANDING AND INSIGHT SHALL GAIN ONLY FRIVOLITY AND FOOLISHNESS. Thoughts are the landmarks and lighthouses by which we navigate the journey of our lives. Wherever your thoughts go, your **POWER** goes as well. Your thoughts can either be weapons of destruction or the tools with which you construct creation. Every thought that you have shall either strengthen or weaken you. Thoughts are the seeds from which the mightiest of actions sprout. The physical universe is controlled by the mental. If you grasp **THE TRUTH** of this and truly gain an **UNDERSTANDING** of the **POWER** of the mind, you shall be well advanced along your path to **KINGSHIP**. Whether you cultivate it with intelligence or allow it to run wild, the soil of your mind shall yield a harvest. You must be the master horticulturist of the garden of your mind. As a gardener cultivates a plot of land, so too must you cultivate your mind. Weed out weak and vulgar thoughts and cultivate the beautiful flowers and luscious fruits of pure royal thought. As you sow, so shall you reap. The type of thought determines the type of action. The type of action determines the type of habit. The type of habit determines the type of character. The type of character determines the type of destiny. If you think royal thoughts, you shall act magnanimously. If you act magnanimously, you shall form noble habits. If you form noble habits, you shall create a regal character. To have a regal character is to have the destiny of a **KING**. Common minds gossip about people and average minds discuss events. However, truly noble minds contemplate the mysteries of reality.

For he who contemplates the mysteries of reality shall eventually discover that which shapes the fate of the entire universe.

10

Master, the events that have and shall continue to characterize your life are the result of the combination of your imagination, your ability to create, and your personality. Whether you are conscious of it or not, you use your imagination to shape not only your behavior, but your destiny as well. As you believe, so shall you act. As you act, so shall your destiny go. What you imagine and believe yourself to be shall determine how you shall act. How you act determines how the universe shall respond to you. How the universe responds to you is the determiner of your destiny. In the dance of reality, a **KING** takes the lead and the universe follows while everyone else follows the lead of the universe. While others are shaped by their circumstances, a **KING** shapes circumstances. You can ride fate into glory, or it can ride you into perdition if you allow it. It is your own mental attitude that shall decide which position you find yourself in.

11

Once, long ago, there was a mighty warrior **KING** who ruled his kingdom with an iron fist. It was in his nature to be a conqueror; thus, his empire grew daily it seemed. All who came before his sword fell before it, and

OFTENTIMES THE MERE ANNOUNCEMENT OF HIS ARMY'S APPROACH WAS ENOUGH TO INDUCE SUBMISSION. HOWEVER, AS THE YEARS PASSED BY, THE MIGHTY WARRIOR **KING** BEGAN TO GROW OLD. AS MOST DO WHEN THEY BEGIN TO GET OLD, HE BEGAN TO CONTEMPLATE DEATH. HE WANTED TO KNOW WHERE ONE WENT WHEN ONE DIED SO THAT HE COULD BEGIN PLANNING TO CONQUER THERE AS WELL. HE HAD CONQUERED EVERYWHERE ELSE HE WENT, HE REASONED TO HIMSELF. WHY SHOULD HE ALLOW DEATH TO STOP HIM?

THE MIGHTY **KING** CALLED IN ALL OF THE CLERGY FROM ALL OVER THE LAND SO THAT HE COULD QUESTION THEM ABOUT THE PLACE ONE GOES AFTER THEY DIE. AFTER ALL, THE CLERGY WERE SUPPOSED TO BE EXPERTS IN THE FIELD. THEY CLAIMED TO BE THE ONES WHO PREPARED YOU FOR THE AFTERLIFE. SURELY, THEY MUST HAVE SOME USEFUL INFORMATION. ALL OF THE CLERGYMEN TOLD THE **KING** PRETTY MUCH THE SAME THING WITH SLIGHT VARIATIONS. THEY ALL TOLD HIM THAT WHEN ONE DIES, THEY LEAVE THEIR BODY AND THIS WORLD AND GO TO EITHER HEAVEN OR HELL DEPENDING ON HOW THEY LIVED DURING THEIR LIVES. THEY ALL TOLD HIM THAT HEAVEN WAS PARADISE AND HELL WAS A PLACE OF TORMENT. ONLY THE DETAILS DIFFERED.

SOME SAID HEAVEN WAS A PLACE WITH STREETS OF GOLD AND HEAVENLY VOICES FILLING THE AIR. SOME SAID HEAVEN WAS A LAND OF PERPETUALLY FLOWING WINE AND EVERLASTING FEASTS. OF HELL, SOME SAID IT WAS AN ETERNALLY BURNING LAKE OF FIRE. SOME SAID IT WAS A VAST DESERT WITH NOTHING BUT PAIN AND DESOLATION WITHIN IT. HOWEVER, DESPITE ALL OF THE MANY DIFFERENT DESCRIPTIONS OF THE TWO PLACES, NONE COULD TELL HIM ANYTHING THAT HE COULD USE. THEY COULDN'T TELL HIM OF ANY STRATEGIC POINTS TO SET UP

DEFENSES OR FROM WHICH TO ATTACK. THEY COULDN'T TELL HIM ANYTHING ABOUT THE TERRAIN, NOT EVEN WHAT IT LOOKED LIKE. FOR NONE OF THEM HAD EVER BEEN TO EITHER PLACE AND NONE OF THEM KNEW ANY WHO HAD.

THIS FRUSTRATED **THE KING** VERY MUCH AND HE SENT THE WORD OUT THAT HE DESIRED TO MEET ONE WHO HAD BEEN TO EITHER HEAVEN OR HELL PERSONALLY. THE WORD OF THE **KING** SPREAD FAR AND WIDE. MANY MONTHS PASSED AND THE MIGHTY WARRIOR **KING** GREW MORE ANXIOUS BY THE DAY. FOR EVERY DAY HE WAS GROWING OLDER AND DRAWING CLOSER TO DEATH. FINALLY, ONE DAY, THE WORD GOT TO THE **KING** THAT ONE SUCH AS HE SOUGHT HAD BEEN FOUND AND WAS ON THE WAY TO MEET HIM. THE **KING** GREW EVEN MORE EXCITED ONCE HE LEARNED THAT THE MAN CLAIMED TO BE ABLE TO TAKE HIM TO BOTH HEAVEN AND HELL IF HE WISHED. THE MESSENGER WHO WAS DELIVERING THE MESSAGE TO THE **KING** TOLD HIM THAT THE MAN WAS AN OLD MASTER THAT LIVED DEEP IN THE MOUNTAINS AND IT WOULD TAKE HIM A COUPLE OF WEEKS TO MAKE THE JOURNEY TO THE PALACE. THE **KING** WAS ECSTATIC. HE RAN TO PREPARE HIMSELF FOR HIS JOURNEY AT ONCE. HE PREPARED HIS SWORD AND SHIELD, OILED HIS ARMOR, AND PACKED AWAY A TELESCOPE SO THAT HE COULD PROPERLY SURVEY THE LAND.

"IN FACT, I SHALL FORCE THIS OLD MASTER TO TAKE ME AND MY ARMY TO BOTH PLACES SO THAT IF THE OPPORTUNITY PRESENTS ITSELF, I CAN CONQUER THEM NOW. WHY WAIT UNTIL I DIE WHEN I COULD CONQUER THEM NOW?" THE **KING** THOUGHT TO HIMSELF.

SO, IN THE DAYS LEADING UP TO WHEN THE OLD MASTER WAS TO ARRIVE, THE **KING** DRILLED HIS TROOPS IN COMBAT MANEUVERS IN ORDER TO PREPARE THEM FOR THE IMMENSE TASK THAT LAY AHEAD. FOR THIS WOULD BE HIS GREATEST CONQUEST EVER. FINALLY, THE DAY CAME WHEN THE OLD MASTER ARRIVED. HE WALKED INTO THE THRONE ROOM SLOWLY, SUPPORTING HIMSELF WITH A CANE. AS THE OLD MASTER APPROACHED, THE **KING** GAVE HIS ARMY THE SIGNAL TO PREPARE THEMSELVES. THE **KING** GREW EVER MORE ASSURED WITH EVERY STEP THAT THE OLD MASTER TOOK TOWARDS HIM. FOR IF SOMEONE AS FRAIL AND WEAK LOOKING LIKE THIS OLD MAN COULD MAKE IT TO BOTH HEAVEN AND HELL, SURELY HE WOULD HAVE NO TROUBLE CONQUERING EITHER. ALSO, BECAUSE THE OLD MASTER WAS SO OLD AND FRAIL, SURELY HE COULD FORCE HIM TO TAKE HIS ENTIRE ARMY ALONG WITH THEM. AS THE OLD MASTER DREW NEAR, HE BOWED HIS HEAD SLIGHTLY BEFORE SAYING, "I HEAR YOU WISH TO SEE HEAVEN AND HELL. I KNOW THE WAY. I CAN TAKE YOU TO BOTH IF YOU WISH."

THE **KING** TOOK A STEP TOWARDS THE OLD MASTER FOR THE PURPOSE OF INTIMIDATING HIM. HE RESPONDED TO THE OLD MASTER BY SAYING, "NOT ONLY SHALL YOU TAKE ME TO BOTH, BUT YOU SHALL TAKE MY ENTIRE ARMY AS WELL. OR I SHALL HAVE YOU KILLED RIGHT HERE AND NOW."

THE OLD MASTER LOOKED THE **KING** DIRECTLY IN HIS EYES AND SAID SERENELY, "**I AM** NOT AS YOUNG AS I ONCE WAS. I ONLY HAVE ENOUGH **STRENGTH** TO TAKE YOU. HOWEVER, WHEN WE RETURN, YOU SHALL BE ABLE TO TAKE YOUR ARMY THERE YOURSELF IF YOU WISH TO."

The KING contemplated the master's words for a moment before giving him an acquiescent nod of the head.

"Before I take you to heaven, I must first take you through hell. Are you ready to go, sire?" asked the old master.

"I AM," said the KING.

THE OLD MASTER SMILED, DROPPED HIS CANE, AND THEN SUDDENLY WITH ALL OF HIS MIGHT, HE SLAPPED THE **KING** ACROSS THE FACE. TIME ITSELF SEEMED TO STOP. EVERYONE IN THE THRONE ROOM FELL INTO SHOCKED SILENCE. NO ONE COULD BELIEVE WHAT THEY HAD JUST WITNESSED. EVEN THE **KING** HIMSELF JUST STOOD THERE FOR A MOMENT TRANSFIXED AND CONFUSED BY THE IMPOSSIBILITY OF WHAT HAD JUST OCCURRED. ALTHOUGH IT INDEED TOOK HIM A MOMENT TO RECOVER, THAT MOMENT WAS BUT A SPLIT SECOND. ALMOST FASTER THAN THE EYES COULD SEE, THE **KING** HAD HIS LEFT HAND WRAPPED AROUND THE OLD MASTER'S THROAT AND HIS RIGHT HAND CLUTCHING HIS SWORD.

"HOW DARE YOU!" THE **KING** ROARED IN RAGE. "I SHALL GUT YOU LIKE A PIG, YOU FOOL!"

THE OLD MASTER SAID NOTHING. HE JUST KEPT LOOKING THE **KING** STEADILY IN THE EYE.

"BEFORE I KILL YOU, YOU TREACHEROUS OLD DOG," BELLOWED THE **KING**, "TELL ME WHY YOU WOULD DARE DO SUCH A STUPID THING."

THE OLD MASTER GAZED DEEPER INTO THE EYES OF THE **KING** AND SAID CALMLY, "SIRE, YOU SAID THAT YOU WISHED TO GO TO HELL. HELL IS WHERE I HAVE TAKEN YOU. HELL IS WHERE YOU ARE RIGHT NOW."

UPON HEARING THE WORDS OF THE OLD MASTER, THE EYES OF THE **KING** WENT IN RAPID SUCCESSION FROM CONFUSED TO IRRITATED AND THEN FROM COMPREHENSION TO **UNDERSTANDING**.

READING THOSE LOOKS, THE OLD MASTER SAID, "AHH...I CAN SEE THAT YOU HAVE MADE IT TO HEAVEN. IT IS UP TO YOU TO TAKE YOUR ARMY TO BOTH PLACES NOW IF YOU WISH."

THE **KING**, STUNNED SILENT ONCE AGAIN, RELEASED THE OLD MASTER'S NECK AND DROPPED HIS SWORD TO THE FLOOR. AND WITH THAT, THE OLD MASTER PICKED UP HIS CANE, TURNED AROUND, AND LEFT.

HEAVEN AND HELL ARE AROUND YOU AT ALL TIMES. FOR HEAVEN AND HELL ARE MERELY STATES OF MIND. A PEACEFUL, SERENE, AND JOYFUL STATE OF MIND IS HEAVENLY AND ANGELIC, WHILE A MIND SHACKLED WITH ANGER AND RAPACITY IS HELLISH AND DEMONIC.

12

ONCE, THERE WAS A PROSTITUTE THAT LIVED ACROSS THE STREET FROM A CHURCH. EVERY DAY, MEN WENT INTO THE PROSTITUTE'S HOUSE. ALL OF THIS MADE THE PRIEST OF THE CHURCH VERY ANGRY. HE DETESTED THE FACT THAT THE PROSTITUTE HAD HER HOUSE DIRECTLY IN FRONT OF HIS CHURCH. "WHO DOES THAT HARLOT THINK SHE IS?" HE THOUGHT. HE HATED IT WHEN MEN WOULD LEAVE THE CHURCH AND GO DIRECTLY OVER THERE. "THOSE INGRATES. DIDN'T THEY APPRECIATE THE WORDS THAT I HAD JUST SPOKEN? DID THEY HATE THEIR OWN SOULS THAT MUCH?" HE REALLY DESPISED IT WHEN MEN WOULD LEAVE THE PROSTITUTE'S HOME AND WALK STRAIGHT INTO THE CHURCH. HE HATED SEEING THOSE IMPOSTERS JUST SITTING UP IN THE PEWS OF HIS CHURCH ACTING LIKE THEY WERE GOOD, SINCERE BELIEVERS. "THOSE HYPOCRITES!" HE THOUGHT. MOST OF ALL, HE ABHORRED THE

PROSTITUTE HERSELF. SHE WAS THE CORRUPTOR OF THE MEN OF THAT TOWN AND THE REASON WHY THE FAMILIES WERE IN SUCH DISARRAY. EVEN AS HE PERFORMED THE SERVICES OF THE LORD, HE COULD THINK OF NOTHING ELSE BUT THE DESPICABLENESS OF THE PROSTITUTE AND HER HOUSE.

THE PROSTITUTE, ON THE OTHER HAND, WAS VERY GRATEFUL THAT FATE HAD PLACED HER HOUSE IN FRONT OF A CHURCH. IN FACT, SHE LOVED NOTHING MORE THAN THAT FACT. AFTER ALL, WHO WAS SHE? ACCORDING TO HERSELF, SHE WAS JUST A LOWLY PROSTITUTE, AND IT WAS A GREAT **HONOR** TO BE LIVING IN FRONT OF A HOUSE OF GOD. MAYBE SOME OF THE PIOUS ENERGY FROM THE CHURCH WOULD FIND ITS WAY INTO HER HOUSE OF ILL REPUTE. GOD KNOWS THE MEN WHO CAME TO VISIT HER NEEDED IT. THEY WERE ALL SO SAD WHEN THEY CAME TO SEE HER. SHE TOOK IT AS HER SOLEMN DUTY TO MAKE THEM HAPPY BEFORE THEY LEFT HER. SHE LOVED IT WHEN MEN WOULD COME TO HER HOUSE RIGHT AFTER CHURCH AND TELL HER ALL THEY HAD HEARD THAT DAY ABOUT GOD. BLESS THEM AND THEIR KEEN MINDS AND EARS. THEY MUST LOVE THEIR SOULS VERY MUCH TO RETAIN THOSE WORDS IN THEIR HEART LIKE THAT AND THEN GENEROUSLY SHARE THEM WITH HER, A HUMBLE SINNER.

SHE LOVED THINKING OF THOSE GOOD MEN SITTING IN THE SEATS OF THE LORD'S CHURCH. "THOSE SAINTS!" SHE SAID TO HERSELF. SHE LIKED TO THINK THAT SHE HAD A HAND IN SENDING THEM THERE. MAYBE GOD WOULD SPARE HER SOUL ON THE DAY OF JUDGMENT FOR HER SERVICE TO HIM. MOST OF ALL, SHE ADMIRED THE PRIEST AND BELIEVED HE WAS THE UPLIFTER OF THE MEN OF THAT TOWN AND THE REASON WHY THE FAMILIES OF THAT TOWN WERE IN SUCH HARMONY. EVEN AS SHE

PERFORMED THE SERVICES OF A PROSTITUTE, SHE COULD THINK OF NOTHING ELSE BUT THE HOLINESS OF THE LORD AND HIS HOUSE.

AS FATE WOULD HAVE IT, BOTH THE PROSTITUTE AND THE PRIEST DIED ON THE EXACT SAME DAY. WHEN THE PROSTITUTE DIED, THEY WRAPPED HER BODY IN A SHEET AND THREW IT IN A HOLE IN THE GROUND. THEY DIDN'T MARK THE GRAVE AT ALL. THEY JUST THREW DIRT ON HER BODY. OUTSIDE OF THE MEN WHO DUG HER HOLE, NO ONE SAW HER BEING BURIED. THE PRIEST, ON THE OTHER HAND, HAD A GRAND FUNERAL. EVERYONE IN THE TOWN CAME OUT TO SEE THE HOLY MAN GET BURIED. HIS CASKET WAS THE MOST DAZZLING, RESPLENDENT COFFIN THAT ANYONE HAD EVER SEEN. HIS GRAVE WAS MARKED BY AN ENORMOUS SCULPTURE BARING HIS LIKENESS. EVERYONE WHO ATTENDED THE FUNERAL REMARKED AFTERWARDS HOW SUCH A MAGNIFICENT FUNERAL BEFITTED SUCH A GREAT MAN.

AND SO IT WAS, THE PRIEST AND THE PROSTITUTE BOTH ARRIVED AT THEIR TABLES OF JUDGMENT AT EXACTLY THE SAME TIME. THE PRIEST LOOKED OVER AT THE PROSTITUTE AND GAVE HER A CURT NOD AND AN ARROGANT SMIRK. THE PROSTITUTE RESPONDED TO THE MAN'S RUDENESS WITH A PLEASANT WAVE AND A GRIN OF VENERATION. AS THE JUDGE ON THE RIGHT GAVE THE PROSTITUTE HER ENVELOPE, HE GAVE IT TO HER WITH A LOVING SMILE. WHEN THE JUDGE ON THE LEFT GAVE THE PRIEST HIS, HE GAVE IT WITH A LOOK THAT BORE THE TAINT OF REGRET. THE PRIEST, HOWEVER, DID NOT NOTICE. HE WAS TOO BUSY PREPARING HIS REBUKE FOR THE PROSTITUTE. HE HAD BEEN WAITING ON THIS OPPORTUNITY FOR YEARS. HE COULDN'T WAIT UNTIL SHE OPENED HER ONE-WAY TICKET TO HELL. HE COULDN'T WAIT TO TELL HER HOW GLAD HE WAS THAT SHE WAS

GOING TO BURN FOREVER FOR HER TERRIBLE SINS. HE COULDN'T WAIT TO TELL HER HOW HORRIBLE SHE WAS. HOW DIRTY SHE WAS. "I MIGHT EVEN SPIT ON HER," HE THOUGHT TO HIMSELF, "IF THE ANGEL JUDGES TURN THEIR HEADS. AFTER ALL, WHO WOULD CARE? SHE WAS JUST A FILTHY PROSTITUTE ON HER WAY TO HELL."

The prostitute opened her envelope and instead of the look of horrified chagrin that the priest expected, a look of elation lighted her face with effulgent luminosity. The priest was livid. He shot the judge on the right a dirty look and then shook his head in disgust.

"Incompetent fool," the priest muttered below his breath. "Surely, he had made a mistake. I will have to straighten this out when I get up to heaven. We can't just have anyone up in heaven with us."

As the priest looked at his envelope, a feeling of smug satisfaction came over him. Finally, all of his years of service and devotion to the church were about to pay off. After all, it had been such a chore saving all of those sinners' souls. Finally, he could reap his rewards. However, when the priest opened his envelope and looked at his destination, he was floored with desperate outrage. For his card said that he was going to hell.

"This most definitely is a mistake. I am not going to stand around for this. Obviously, the judge on the right and the judge on the left mixed up their cards. Heaven must have a lot of changes that need to be made," the priest thought to himself.

The priest stormed up to the judge that handed him his envelope and said, "You made a mistake, sir. I was a priest! You and that other judge over there must have mixed up your envelopes. The prostitute got my card and I have hers!"

THE JUDGE LOOKED AT THE PRIEST SADLY AND SAID, "I'M SORRY, PRIEST. THERE WAS NO MISTAKE."

"BUT SHE WAS A PROSTITUTE! I WAS A PRIEST! I WORKED FOR THE CHURCH, YOU FOOL!" THE PRIEST SCREAMED IN RESPONSE.

THE JUDGE, GROWING IMPATIENT WITH THE PRIEST'S ARROGANCE, SAID, "YES, PRIEST. YOU DID SPLENDID WORK FOR THE CHURCH. THUS, YOUR FUNERAL WAS THE GREATEST IN THE CHURCH'S HISTORY. EVERYBODY FROM THE TOWN CAME TO YOUR BURIAL AND TALKED ABOUT HOW SUCH A GREAT MAN DESERVED SUCH A GREAT FUNERAL. THE PROSTITUTE, ON THE OTHER HAND, HAD NO FUNERAL. NO ONE CAME TO HER BURIAL. NO ONE TALKED OF HER GREATNESS BECAUSE NO ONE CARED THAT SHE HAD DIED. HER BODY WAS USED FOR SINFUL MEANS, SO SHE GOT A BURIAL BEFITTING A SINNER. YOUR BODY WAS USED FOR SAINTLY MEANS, SO YOU GOT A BURIAL BEFITTING A SAINT."

"THAT'S WHAT I'VE BEEN TRYING TO TELL YOU, DUMMY!" BLURTED OUT THE PRIEST RUDELY.

"HOWEVER, PRIEST," BEGAN THE ANGEL JUDGE, UNPERTURBED BY THE PRIEST'S INSULT, "THE WHOLE TIME THAT YOU WORKED AT THE CHURCH YOU THOUGHT OF NOTHING BUT THE PROSTITUTE'S SIN AND HOW MUCH YOU HATED HER. YOU THOUGHT OF NOTHING BUT HOW SHE WAS CORRUPTING MEN AND DESTROYING THE SANCTITY OF THE TOWN. WHILE SHE WAS DOING HER WORK, SHE THOUGHT OF NOTHING BUT THE GLORY OF THE LORD AND HOW MUCH SHE LOVED HIM. SHE THOUGHT OF HOW MUCH YOU SANCTIFIED THE TOWN, AND HOW YOU PLAYED SUCH A HUGE PART IN MAKING MEN HOLY. SHE THOUGHT OF NOTHING BUT RIGHTEOUSNESS, YOU THOUGHT OF NOTHING BUT

SIN. THUS, HER SOUL SHALL GO IN THE DIRECTION THAT HER THOUGHTS PROPELLED HERS TO GO, AND YOUR SOUL SHALL GO IN THE DIRECTION THAT YOUR THOUGHTS PROPELLED YOURS TO GO. AFTER ALL, WE CAN'T JUST HAVE ANYONE UP IN HEAVEN WITH US."

AND WITH THAT, THE PRIEST WENT TO HELL AND THE PROSTITUTE WENT TO HEAVEN.

THOSE THAT TRY TO KEEP OTHERS OUT OF HEAVEN DO NOT REALIZE THAT THEY ARE HOLDING THE DOOR SHUT ON THEMSELVES.

13

MASTER, THERE ARE MANY DIFFERENT RELIGIONS IN THIS WORLD. MANY WAYS TO VIEW GOD. MANY DIFFERENT WAYS TO RELATE TO THE EXACT SAME THING.

ONCE, THERE WERE FOUR BLIND MEN. THEY HAD ALL BEEN BLIND SINCE BIRTH. OBVIOUSLY, BECAUSE THEY WERE BLIND, THEY HAD NEVER SEEN AN ELEPHANT BEFORE. HOWEVER, THEY HAD HEARD A GREAT DEAL ABOUT THESE WONDROUS CREATURES AND WANTED TO TRULY UNDERSTAND WHAT AN ELEPHANT REALLY WAS. THE FOUR BLIND MEN ALL STAYED TOGETHER IN ONE HOUSE AND EVERY DAY THEY TALKED ABOUT HOW THEY WISHED THEY COULD GET TO KNOW PERSONALLY WHAT AN ELEPHANT WAS BECAUSE EVERYTHING THAT THEY HAD HEARD ABOUT THEM WAS FANTASTIC.

One day, a young man that tended to the blind men took pity upon them. He had been tending to them for quite a while now and every day he heard them talk about how badly they wanted to know what an elephant was. So the young man arranged for the four blind men to have their wish. He was going to take them to the zoo to meet a real elephant. The four blind men were ecstatic. Finally, they would learn what an elephant truly was. When the young man arrived at the zoo with the four blind men, he led each one to a different part of the elephant so that they could all feel it at the same time. He led one to the foot. He led one to the ear. He led another to the tail. The last, he took to the elephant's side.

The blind man at the foot said, "An elephant is like a tree. Thick and round."

The blind man at the ear said, "What are you talking about, fool? An elephant is like a giant leaf or a huge fan. Flat, thin, and broad."

The blind man at the tail said, "What are you two dummies talking about? An elephant is like a rope. Long, slender, and limber."

The blind man at the side of the elephant said, "All of you idiots shut up! An elephant is like a wall!"

The four blind men argued for hours about what an elephant was, each refusing to move from his position to feel what the others were feeling. They just kept using different words to describe that which they were feeling

AND GREW MORE AND MORE INCENSED WHEN THE OTHERS DIDN'T AGREE WITH THEIR DESCRIPTIONS. ALL ARGUING FURIOUSLY, NOT REALIZING THAT THEY ALL FOUR WERE TELLING **THE TRUTH** YET LYING AT THE SAME TIME. FOR THEY WERE ALL SPEAKING FROM A PARTICULAR POINT OF VIEW AND NOT FROM THE POINT OF VIEW OF THE WHOLE.

IN REALITY, THERE IS NOTHING FALSE EXCEPT REALITY ITSELF. THE FOUR BLIND MEN OF THE METAPHOR ARE LIKE THE MAJORITY OF PEOPLE THAT PRACTICE RELIGION. THEY ARE ALL FEELING A PART OF GOD, BUT BECAUSE THEY ARE BLIND, THEY CANNOT SEE THE PART THAT THEY ARE FEELING IS NOT THE WHOLE STORY. ASSUMING THAT THEY KNOW THE WHOLE THING, THEY DENY THE VALIDITY OF ANYONE ELSE'S POSITION. A MAN'S RELIGIOUS POINT OF VIEW IS MERELY THE FORMULATION AND EXPRESSION OF HIS ESSENTIAL PSYCHOLOGICAL ATTITUDES AND SPECIFIC PREJUDICES. RELIGION HAS A TENDENCY TO MAKE GOD INTO MAN'S IMAGE, RATHER THAN SHAPING MAN INTO GOD'S. RELIGIONS DO THIS BY DEFINING AND DESCRIBING GOD, AND THEN PRESENTING THIS INFORMATION AS **THE TRUTH** RATHER THAN JUST TRUE.

MOST PEOPLE WHO PRACTICE RELIGION, BECAUSE THEY ARE BLIND, MISTAKE THE INFORMATION THEY HAVE BEEN GIVEN AS REALITY. INFORMATION CAN NEVER TRULY REVEAL **THE TRUTH** THAT LIES BEHIND REALITY. I COULD GIVE YOU ALL TYPES OF INFORMATION ABOUT HOW ORANGE JUICE TASTES. I COULD WRITE BOOKS ON TOP OF BOOKS DESCRIBING ITS TASTE. EVERYTHING THAT I WOULD BE TELLING YOU WOULD BE TRUE, AND YET YOU WOULD NEVER KNOW HOW ORANGE JUICE TASTES UNLESS YOU TASTED SOME YOURSELF. THIS IS WHY YOU MUST NEVER DELUDE YOURSELF INTO BELIEVING THAT KNOWING THE

DEFINITION AND DESCRIPTION OF A THING IS THE SAME AS KNOWING THE THING ITSELF. GOD IS FORMLESS AND INFINITE, AND THUS BEYOND ANY DESCRIPTION. TO DESCRIBE SOMETHING IS TO PUT A LABEL OVER REALITY. IT IS TO PUT SOMETHING FINITE, A WORD, OVER SOMETHING INFINITE, REALITY. GOD IS **POWER** AND **THE TRUTH**. IT IS ENERGY AND SPACE. IT IS AWARENESS. IT IS **LOVE**. ALL THE FORMS OF IT ARE MERELY WAVES UPON THE OCEAN OF IT. IT IS THE AWARENESS INSIDE YOU, THE **POWER** WITHIN YOU, YOUR DIVINE SOUL THAT IS ALERT TO ALL THINGS, ADAPTS TO ALL THINGS, TAKES WHATEVER FORM IT WISHES, AND CLOTHES THAT WHICH LIES OUTSIDE ITSELF IN ANY FASHION THAT IT CHOOSES.

EVERYTHING IS SIMPLY **LOVE** IN DIFFERENT FORMS. WE CALL OURSELVES DIFFERENT NAMES AND SEEM TO DIFFER FROM EACH OTHER BECAUSE WE WANT TO DEFINE OURSELVES. WE EACH WANT TO HAVE OUR OWN DEFINITION. **LOVE** IS CREATIVE AND SO WE ARE CREATORS. WE CREATE OURSELVES AND EVERYTHING ELSE. BUT, IN REALITY, WE CANNOT DIFFER. WE ARE ALL THE SAME THING. WE ARE MERELY BRANCHES ON THE TREE OF REALITY. EVERYTHING IS ROOTED IN BEING BECAUSE EVERYTHING IS. THE VARIATIONS AND DEFINITIONS ONLY BECOME REAL WHEN WE IDENTIFY WITH THE MIND AND BODY INSTEAD OF REALITY ITSELF. THOUGHTS ARE THE CLOTHING OF **THE TRUTH**, JUST AS LIGHT IS THE CLOTHING OF THE SUN. JUST AS A MAN WEARING A POLICE OFFICER'S UNIFORM IS SEEN AS A POLICE OFFICER, **THE TRUTH** WEARING THE THOUGHTS OF A **KING** SHALL BE VIEWED AS A **KING**. EVEN THE LOWLIEST AND MOST HUMBLE OF MEN HAVE THE **POWER** TO FASHION THEMSELVES AFTER **THE TRUTH**, AND BY SO DOING, DRESS

HIMSELF IN THE ROYAL ROBES OF THE **DIVINE** IF THEY WOULD BUT USE THEIR THOUGHTS IN THAT MANNER.

14

MASTER, JUST AS ICE IS SIMPLY WATER MADE SOLID, ALL PHYSICAL MATTER, INCLUDING YOUR BODY, IS YOUR MIND MADE SOLID. YOUR MIND AND BODY ARE ONE. IT IS IMPOSSIBLE TO SEPARATE THE TWO. ANYTHING THAT AFFECTS THE HEALTH, VIGOR, AND VITALITY OF YOUR MIND SHALL ALSO AFFECT YOUR BODY. THERE IS NOTHING THAT AFFECTS THE HEALTH OF THE MIND MORE THAN YOUR OWN THOUGHTS AND OPINIONS. A CORRUPT MIND IS FAR WORSE THAN A CONTAMINATED BODY. FOR THE BODY GROWS FROM THE MIND. CORRUPT THOUGHTS OF MALICE, ENVY, DISAPPOINTMENT, AND DEPRESSION ROB THE BODY OF ITS SOUNDNESS AND GRACE. HONORABLE THOUGHTS OF BENEVOLENCE, MAGNANIMITY, GENEROSITY, AND HAPPINESS BUILD THE BODY UP IN **STRENGTH, POWER**, AND HEALTH. IT IS OUT OF A CLEAN MIND THAT A CLEAN LIFE AND A CLEAN BODY MAY SPRING FORTH. IT IS OUT OF A DEPRAVED MIND THAT A DEFILED LIFE AND A TAINTED BODY MANIFEST. ONLY A CALM, SERENE MIND COUPLED WITH A HEALTHY AND RELAXED BODY SHALL ALLOW THE TRUE LIGHT OF YOUR **POWER** TO SHINE FORTH WITHOUT DISTORTION.

15

Master, your thoughts are just as important, perhaps more so than your actions. Thoughts are the directors of **POWER** and the seeds of all action. Your thoughts compose your character; thus, it is imperative that you keep your thoughts pure. Because action follows thought, someone with a mind full of noble, excellent, and beautiful thoughts does noble, excellent, and beautiful things. You are **POWER**. **POWER** is the impresser. If you impress impressive thoughts upon the fabric of your consciousness, you can do nothing but impress. You shall save much valuable time and effort by paying no attention to what others are saying, doing, or thinking. Instead, concentrating upon your own behavior, make it regal and majestic. There is nothing outside of yourself that can prevent you from having thoughts that are pure, composed, and just. If you would purify your mind of thoughts of anxiety, fear, and despair, the whole world shall become your friend.

16

Master, pain follows weak, ignorant, unfocused thoughts as the cart follows the horse, but joy follows strong, aware, focused thoughts like wetness follows the rain. Vile thoughts are the jailors of fate, while noble thoughts are the keys to freedom. If you wish to become wise and royal in character and rise into a position of blessed influence, all that is necessary of you is that you live constantly in the conception of lofty

THOUGHTS AND DWELL UPON ALL THAT IS MAJESTIC. IGNOBLE, WICKED, AND LOW THOUGHTS CRYSTALLIZE INTO FEEBLE AND AIMLESS HABITS, WHICH IN TURN SOLIDIFY INTO BEWILDERING AND DISASTROUS CIRCUMSTANCES. REGAL, NOBLE, AND HIGH THOUGHTS CRYSTALLIZE INTO HABITS OF TEMPERANCE, SELF-CONTROL, AND INTEGRITY, WHICH SOLIDIFY INTO CIRCUMSTANCES OF TRANQUILITY, ABUNDANCE, AND PEACE. TO CONTINUALLY DWELL IN THOUGHTS OF HATRED, ENVY, AND CYNICISM IS TO INCARCERATE YOURSELF INTO A SELF-MADE PRISON. HOWEVER, TO THINK WELL OF ALL, TO BE CHEERFUL WITH ALL, TO PATIENTLY LEARN TO FIND THE GOOD IN ALL, IS TO FIND THE KEYS TO THE GATES OF HEAVEN. THOUGHTS OF PEACE, DWELLED IN DAY AFTER DAY, SHALL BRING ABOUT ABOUNDING PEACE TO THE POSSESSOR OF THOSE THOUGHTS. CONVERSELY, THE FIRE OF HATEFUL THOUGHTS SHALL DRY YOU UP AND BLIND YOU TO THE GOODNESS THAT IS PRESENT IN ALL THINGS. ONCE HATRED OVERCOMES A PERSON, IT IS SO CORROSIVE AND RUINOUS THAT IT SHALL TARNISH EVERYTHING THEY TOUCH AND SULLY EVERYTHING THEY THINK ABOUT. TO FOLLOW THE PATH OF HATRED IS TO DESCEND INTO THE DEPTHS OF HELL; BUT, TO WALK THE PATH OF **LOVE** IS TO ASCEND TO THE HEIGHTS OF HEAVEN. INSIDE ALL, THERE IS SOME SEED OF VIRTUE OR SOME SEED OF FOLLY, WHICH IF STIRRED CAN GROW INDEFINITELY. IT IS THE VIRTUOUS SEED OF REGALITY THAT LIES WITHIN YOUR HEART THAT YOU MUST PURPOSELY STIR IF YOU WISH TO GROW INTO THE GREATNESS THAT YOU WERE BORN TO MANIFEST.

17

MASTER, THE LAWS OF CREATION THAT GOVERN THE UNIVERSE ARE BASED IN THE REALITY THAT ANYTHING THAT CAN BE THOUGHT OF CAN BE. IT IS FOR THIS REASON THAT YOU MUST NEVER BE AFRAID TO EXPRESS YOUR OWN THOUGHTS AND FOLLOW YOUR OWN INCLINATIONS. FOR YOU ARE THE CREATOR, AS WELL AS THE RULER OF YOUR OWN REALITY. NEVER FEEL THAT YOU SHALL LOSE ANY **DIGNITY** OR **HONOR** BY CHANGING YOUR MIND AND ACCEPTING THE CORRECTION OF SOMEONE WHO MAY POINT OUT AN ERROR THAT YOU HAVE OVERLOOKED. FOR INDEED, IT IS YOUR OWN INITIATIVE, YOUR OWN JUDGMENT, AND YOUR OWN INTELLIGENCE THAT MAKE THE CHANGE POSSIBLE.

18

MASTER, WHO OR WHAT YOU DETERMINE YOURSELF TO BE DETERMINES HOW YOU THINK, HOW YOU USE YOUR IMAGINATION, HOW YOU USE YOUR CREATIVITY, YOUR LEVEL OF SELF-DISCIPLINE, AND YOUR ACTIONS. WHAT SHALL RAISE YOU UP TO THE HEIGHTS OF GREATNESS IS YOUR ABILITY TO THINK IMMORTAL THOUGHTS EVEN WHILE YOU EXIST WITHIN THE LIMITATIONS OF YOUR OWN MORTALITY. OF ALL THE THINGS THAT INFLUENCE A PERSON'S SENSE OF WHO THEY ARE, THEIR CAPACITY TO IMAGINE IS THE GREATEST. PEOPLE'S BELIEFS ABOUT THE ISSUES OF LIFE, THEIR ABILITY TO KNOW, AND THEIR ABILITY TO ACHIEVE ALL FOLLOW AUTOMATICALLY FROM THEIR SELF-IMAGE, WHO THEY IMAGINE THEMSELVES TO BE. YOU ARE WHAT YOU BELIEVE THAT YOU ARE. THE ONLY QUESTION IS, WHAT DO YOU BELIEVE YOURSELF TO BE? TO BE **KING**, YOU MUST FIRST LEARN TO THINK AS A **KING** DOES. A ROYAL CHARACTER IS

NOT A THING OF FAVOR OR CHANCE BUT IS THE NATURAL RESULT OF A CONTINUED EFFORT IN ROYAL THINKING. IT IS THE EFFECT OF A LONG-CHERISHED ASSOCIATION WITH ROYAL THOUGHTS.

19

MASTER, IT IS ONLY NATURAL THAT A KING SHOULD HAVE A KINGDOM. THINK OF THE MORNING STAR, THE SUN. EVERYTHING THAT THE SUN'S POWER REACHES IS CALLED THE SOLAR SYSTEM. THE SOLAR SYSTEM IS THE KINGDOM OF THE SUN. ALL THAT LIES WITHIN THE SOLAR SYSTEM REVOLVES AROUND THE SUN. ALL MOVE IN RESPONSE TO THE SUN'S POWER. TO BECOME KING IS TO BECOME THE SUN THAT THE SOLAR SYSTEM OF YOUR REALITY REVOLVES AROUND. TO BE KING IS TO HAVE EVERYTHING AROUND YOU MOVE AND ROTATE IN RESPONSE TO YOUR POWER. THE GREATER YOUR POWER, THE STRONGER YOUR LIGHT; THUS, THE GREATER SHALL BE YOUR DOMINION. FOR THE STRONGER THE LIGHT, THE FARTHER IT REACHES OUT INTO SPACE. THE STRONGEST OF THOSE LIGHTS EVEN TRANSCEND TIME. LOOK UP AT THE SKY. SEE THE STARS? YOU THINK SO? ACTUALLY, WHAT YOU ARE SEEING IS THE LIGHT THAT THOSE STARS PRODUCED. LIGHT THAT HAS TAKEN MILLIONS, EVEN BILLIONS OF YEARS TO REACH THE EARTH. LIGHT THAT HAS TAKEN SO LONG TO REACH YOUR EYES THAT THE SOURCE THAT CREATED THAT LIGHT HAS ALREADY EXPIRED. THE LIGHT FROM THOSE STARS WAS SO GREAT THAT IT TRANSCENDED TIME.

THINK OF THE GREAT MEN OF THE PAST WHOSE LIGHT WAS SO STRONG THAT IT STILL MOVES MULTITUDES ALTHOUGH THOSE MEN DIED HUNDREDS, OR EVEN THOUSANDS OF YEARS AGO.

THINK OF JESUS, BUDDHA, OR THE PROPHET MUHAMMED. SOME PEOPLE'S ENTIRE LIVES ARE SPENT REVOLVING AROUND THE LIGHT OF ONE OF THOSE GIANTS OF YESTERDAY. THEY EACH POSSESSED THE LIGHT OF A **DIVINE KING**.

THE STARS IN THE SKY ARE THE KINGS OF THE UNIVERSE. LOOK HOW FEW THEY ARE COMPARED TO THE VAST AMOUNT OF DARKNESS THAT SURROUNDS THEM. AS THE SUN'S **POWER** GUIDES AND CONTROLS THE MATERIAL BODIES OF THE SOLAR SYSTEM, ITS KINGDOM, THE **POWER** OF THE SPIRIT OF A **KING** DIRECTS AND INFLUENCES THOSE ETHEREAL INTELLECTS THAT LIE WITHIN REACH OF ITS LIGHT. THE STRONGER THE SPIRIT, THE GREATER THE REACH. WHATEVER FILLS THE SPACE OF YOUR DOMAIN, YOUR SOLAR SYSTEM IS YOUR KINGDOM. ONE OF THE DEFINITIONS THAT THE DICTIONARY GIVES FOR KINGDOM IS AN AREA "IN WHICH ONE THING IS DOMINANT."[17] THAT AROUND WHICH EVERYTHING REVOLVES SHALL ALWAYS BE THE MOST DOMINANT THING IN THAT AREA. EVERYTHING REVOLVES AROUND **POWER**. FOR **POWER** DOMINATES. **POWER** ATTRACTS AND MOVES THINGS THROUGH SPACE. IN HUMAN BEINGS, THIS **POWER** MANIFESTS ITSELF AS, OR RATHER, CARRIES THE LABEL OF CHARISMA. YOUR CHARISMA IS THE **POWER** THAT SHALL ATTRACT AND MOVE THE MINDS IN YOUR KINGDOM.

HUMANS ARE SOCIAL BY NATURE. THUS, THE INSTINCT FOR HUMAN COMPANIONSHIP SHALL NEVER BE DENIED. FOR THE MIND IS POWERFULLY ATTRACTED TO AND COMBINES WITH THAT WHICH IS LIKE IT. THIS IS WHY FAMILIES, NATIONS, AND OTHER FORMS OF KINGDOMS FORM. THESE FORM WHEN THE MINDS OF

---

[17] https://www.ahdictionary.com/kingdom

A GROUP OF PEOPLE MERGE INTO ONE AND THAT GROUP MOVES AS ONE UNIT. THE STRONGEST SPIRIT SHALL BE THE SPIRIT THAT CONTROLS THE UNIT. IT SHALL BE THE SPIRIT THAT POSSESSES THE MOST CHARISMA. THE STRONGEST SPIRIT IS **KING**. THE GREATER THE AMOUNT OF PEOPLE YOU FASCINATE, THE GREATER THE AMOUNT OF PEOPLE YOU SHALL CAPTIVATE. THE MORE PEOPLE YOU CAPTIVATE, THE MORE PEOPLE YOU SHALL HAVE INFLUENCE OVER. THE MORE INFLUENCE YOU POSSESS, THE MORE **POWER** YOU HAVE. THE CHARISMA OF A **KING** BESTOWS UPON HIM A PRESENCE THAT EXCITES OTHERS. HE STANDS OUT BECAUSE OF THE COMBINATION OF HIS SELF-BELIEF, HIS BOLDNESS, AND HIS SERENITY. THE LIGHT OF HIS CONFIDENCE AND CONTENTMENT CAN BE FELT BY ALL, FOR IT RADIATES OUTWARD LIKE THE SUN'S RAYS RADIATE OUTWARD FROM THE SUN.

THE **POWER** OF THE CHARISMA OF A **KING** IS MYSTERIOUS AND INEXPLICABLE, NEVER OBVIOUS, YET IT SHALL CAUSE PEOPLE TO BELIEVE IN HIM, OFTEN WITHOUT ANY RATIONAL REASON FOR DOING SO. "THERE'S JUST SOMETHING ABOUT HIM," PEOPLE OFTEN SAY. NEVER FORGET, MY SON, THERE IS NOTHING MORE ATTRACTIVE, NOTHING MORE POWERFUL, MORE CHARISMATIC, THAN GIVING PEOPLE SOMETHING TO BELIEVE IN AND FOLLOW. IF YOU HAVE A PLAN, IF YOU KNOW WHERE YOU ARE GOING, PEOPLE SHALL FOLLOW YOU INSTINCTIVELY. YOU MUST GAIN A VISION, MASTER, AND SHOW THAT YOU SHALL NOT BE SWAYED FROM YOUR GOAL. THOSE AROUND YOU SHALL FEEL THE **POWER** OF YOUR CONFIDENCE. THEY SHALL BELIEVE IN YOU BECAUSE OF THE **STRENGTH** OF YOUR CHARACTER. BECAUSE THE MAJORITY OF THE TIMID MASSES HESITATE BEFORE TAKING BOLD ACTION, THE SINGLE-MINDED FOCUS AND SELF-ASSURANCE OF A **KING** MAKES HIM ALWAYS THE FOCUS OF ATTENTION.

Mystery provides a **KING** with immense **POWER**. This mystery manifests itself in the form of paradox, for a **KING** realizes that although he is in this world, he is not of this world. Think of an ancient battlefield. On the battlefield, it is chaos. The clang of steel swords striking other swords and shields is deafening. Men are yelling and the smell of blood fills the air. Men are dying all around you. You are virtually always under attack or in fear of being attacked. It is total madness. Now look up to the top of the hill overlooking the battle. The **KING** is up there. It is peace up there. He is viewing the battle from above it. He has a greater perspective of the whole battle than those enmeshed in it. It is from up here that he directs all. For he sees all. He has not killed a single man with his own hands, and yet he is responsible for hundreds of deaths. He is intimately involved in the battle, yet he is distant from it at the same time. This is how a **KING** views life. Looking down upon it from the mountain top allows him to be both in it and removed from it. This paradox makes him impossible to fathom. For his mind goes too deep. It adds richness to his character and makes people talk about him. He has an uncanny aura about him and appears to have prophetic gifts. A **KING** lives out his ideals and cares not about consequences. He knows **THE TRUTH** and lives it.

On the stage that is life, it is not the actor that screams the loudest or gesticulates the most vehemently that emits the most charisma. Flamboyancy, which mostly attracts spite and hatred should rarely, if ever, be

SHOWN BY A **KING**. IT IS NOT THE FLAMBOYANT ACTOR, BUT THE ACTOR WHO IS ALWAYS CALM AND RADIATING SELF-ASSURANCE THAT THE ENTIRE PLAY REVOLVES AROUND. FOR HE IS THE EYE OF THE STORM. EVEN IN THE MOST TURBULENT OF CIRCUMSTANCES, THE COMPOSURE OF A **KING** REMAINS OLYMPIAN DESPITE THE HYSTERIA WHICH SURROUNDS HIM. A **KING** HAS NO FEAR OF DEATH, FOR HE KNOWS THAT **POWER** AND **THE TRUTH** ARE ETERNAL, AND THUS CAN NEVER DIE. FOR THEY SHALL NEVER CHANGE. ONLY THOSE FORMS WHICH THEY MANIFEST SHALL. THIS **KNOWLEDGE** ALONE RAISES A **KING** TO SUPREMACY IN ANY GROUP. THE FEAR OF DEATH IS THE WORST EPIDEMIC IN THE HISTORY OF MANKIND. BECAUSE THEY ARE ALWAYS IN THE FLOW OF THE PRESENT MOMENT, A **KING** IS DELIGHTFULLY SPONTANEOUS AND HAS A FLUIDITY OF SPIRIT, AN EASE AND ADAPTABILITY THAT SHOWS THAT THEY ARE OPEN, AND THUS PREPARED TO USE ANY AND ALL MATERIAL THAT THE UNIVERSE MAY SEND TO THEM TO MOLD INTO WHATEVER FORM MAY SUIT THEIR NEEDS. A **KING** BELIEVES IN HIMSELF AND THIS BELIEF ANIMATES ALL OF HIS GESTURES AND MAKES HIS EYES CATCH FIRE WITH THE ETERNALLY BLAZING INCANDESCENT FLAME OF **FAITH**. THE FLAME WHICH BURNS AWAY ALL THAT DARE STAND IN ITS OPPOSITION. A **KING** SHARES NONE OF THE DOUBTS THAT PLAGUE THE MASSES.

20

MASTER, THERE IS NOTHING MORE COMPELLING TO PEOPLE AND PEOPLE **LOVE** NOTHING MORE THAN THE FEELING THAT THEY ARE DESIRED. A **KING** IS ALWAYS OPEN TO HIS PEOPLE, FOR HE FEEDS OFF OF THEIR ENERGY AND BELIEF IN HIM. THE PEOPLE ARE YOUR **POWER**, AND YOU ARE THE **POWER** OF THE

PEOPLE. A **KING** HAS AN AIR OF ADVENTURE THAT HYPNOTIZES THE BORED MASSES. BRAZEN AND COURAGEOUS ARE TWO ATTRIBUTES THAT SHALL ALWAYS BE ADORNED BY A **KING**. THE REASON WHY HE SHALL ALWAYS BE WILLING TO TAKE RISKS IS BECAUSE A **KING** THRIVES IN TROUBLED WATERS. FOR HE UNDERSTANDS THAT CRISIS SITUATIONS GIVE HIM THE OPPORTUNITY TO FLAUNT HIS BRAVERY AND ENHANCE HIS AURA AND TO ENHANCE HIS **POWER**.

HEROISM SHALL GIVE YOU **POWER** THAT SHALL LAST A LIFETIME, BUT COWARDICE SHALL STRIP YOU OF WHATEVER **POWER** YOU THOUGHT YOU HAD. THE DEMEANOR OF A **KING** MAY BE POISED AND CALM, BUT THEIR EYES EXUDE **POWER**. THEY HAVE A PIERCING GAZE THAT EXERTS FORCE WITHOUT THEIR EVEN HAVING TO USE WORDS OR ACTIONS. THE EYES OF A **KING** SHALL NEVER SHOW FEAR, FOR FEAR HAS NO **POWER** OVER A **KING**. IN TIMES OF DISTRACTION AND DISORDER, A **KING** REMAINS SUPREMELY FOCUSED. THEIR **STRENGTH** IS THEIR FOCUS. THEY HAVE NO SELF-DOUBT, FOR THERE IS NO DOUBTING **POWER**. THIS IS WHAT GIVES A **KING** THE **POWER** TO BE GENUINE. A **KING** UNDERSTANDS THAT THE QUALITY OF SINGLE-MINDEDNESS IS DEVASTATINGLY POWERFUL. THIS **POWER** IS ENHANCED IN YOU WHEN YOU EXHIBIT CALMNESS, RESOLUTION, AND CLEAR-MINDED PRACTICALITY DURING TIMES OF TROUBLE. ONCE PEOPLE IMAGINE THAT YOU CAN SAVE THEM FROM CHAOS, THEY SHALL FALL UNDER YOUR SPELL AUTOMATICALLY. BECAUSE HE IS FULFILLED, A **KING** GIVES OFF THE APPEARANCE THAT HE HAS NO MATERIAL NEEDS. HE EMITS PEACE LIKE A FURNACE EMITS HEAT. HIS PEACE IS SHOWN IN HIS GENTLE SMILE, HIS UNHURRIED MANNER, AND IN HIS EASE AND COMFORT. HE IS

CONTENT BECAUSE HE IS DETACHED. A **KING** SHOULD NEVER ALLOW HIS EMOTIONS TO BE UNCONTROLLABLE. FOR NOT ONLY DOES CALMNESS AND CONTROL HYPNOTIZE, BUT PEOPLE ALWAYS ADMIRE SELF-CONTROL AND ADAPTABILITY.

21

MASTER, YOUR KINGDOM IS YOUR POWER. WHAT YOU THINK OF YOUR KINGDOM IS WHAT YOU THINK OF YOURSELF. YOUR KINGDOM IS MERELY A REFLECTION OF YOU AND YOUR THOUGHTS. YOU SHALL ALWAYS BE ABLE TO CHANGE THE NATURE OF YOUR KINGDOM SIMPLY BY CHANGING YOUR THOUGHTS CONCERNING IT. FOR THE OUTER CONDITIONS OF YOUR KINGDOM SHALL ALWAYS BE FOUND TO BE HARMONIOUSLY RELATED TO THE THOUGHTS OF YOUR MIND. IF YOU THINK GENEROUS AND LOVING THOUGHTS, YOUR KINGDOM SHALL BE ONE OF ABUNDANCE AND GLORY. IF YOU THINK MISERLY, HATEFUL THOUGHTS, YOUR KINGDOM SHALL BE ONE OF INADEQUACY AND SHAME. WHAT YOU THINK AND DO AFFECT YOUR ENTIRE KINGDOM. FOR IT IS YOUR CURRENT THOUGHTS THAT ARE BUILDING YOUR FUTURE KINGDOM, THOUGHT BY THOUGHT. TRUE AND LASTING KINGDOMS ARE BUILT UPON FOUNDATIONS OF INTELLIGENCE AND WILL. IT IS THE WISE **KING** THAT DIRECTS HIS **POWER** WITH **UNDERSTANDING** AND FORETHOUGHT AND ORIENTATES HIS THOUGHTS TO FRUITFUL ISSUES. AS LONG AS YOU CONTROL YOUR OWN MIND, YOUR KINGDOM SHALL NEVER BE CONTROLLED BY THE MINDS OF OTHERS.

22

MASTER, ALL OF YOUR THOUGHTS ARE SEEDS AND THE HARVEST YOU REAP SHALL DEPEND ENTIRELY UPON THE SEEDS THAT YOU CHOOSE TO PLANT. AN acorn shall always grow into an oak tree. It shall never grow to be an apple tree. All seeds bear fruit of their own kind. This is the law. Thoughts of magnanimity shall always bear royal fruit, while thoughts of savagery shall always bear ignoble fruit. Nothing shall sprout from a mind but that which was planted into it. This is the purpose of education. To plant seeds of productive thought into fertile minds. The more seeds planted, the greater the harvest shall be.

23

MASTER, ANY IDEA CAN BE IMPLANTED WITHIN A PERSON'S MIND SIMPLY BY BEING REPEATED OFTEN ENOUGH. This is how beliefs are formed. For a belief is merely a thought that you habitually think. Whatever thoughts you meditate upon most often shall become your reality. Thus, you must never dwell upon any images that would be detrimental to your well-being. Rather, dwell upon those ideas that shall be beneficial to your kingdom. It is a law of the mind that it shall gradually adapt itself and become one with the subject upon which it has been trained to dwell. Your life shall reflect that which your mind dwells upon. Education, because it teaches you to think intensively and critically, gives you the ability to add intelligence and UNDERSTANDING to your character. How great

YOU BECOME SHALL BE DETERMINED BY THE AMOUNT OF FOCUS AND DETERMINATION YOU HAVE, HOW MUCH EFFORT YOU PUT FORTH, AND THE TYPES OF SEEDS YOU PLANT.

24

MASTER, IN ORDER TO BE **KING**, YOU MUST LOOK AT THE WORLD THROUGH THE EYES OF A **KING**. TO HAVE THE THOUGHTS OF A **KING** IS TO BE A **KING** IN REALITY. FOR IT IS IMPOSSIBLE TO TRAVEL WITHIN AND STAND STILL WITHOUT. YOU MUST ALWAYS SEEK TO ACQUIRE **KNOWLEDGE**. YOU MUST ALWAYS BE READY TO LEARN. TO LEARN MOST EFFECTIVELY, YOU MUST KEEP YOUR MIND IN A STATE OF CONSTANT READINESS WHERE YOU ARE NEVER ATTACHED TO WHAT YOU USED TO THINK.

25

ONCE, THERE WAS AN OLD PECAN TREE. IT HAD LIVED MANY YEARS AND IT WAS VERY PROUD, RIGID, AND UNYIELDING. IT HAD PRODUCED MANY PECANS THROUGHOUT THE YEARS, AND IT STOOD VERY TALL. NOT VERY FAR AWAY FROM THE PECAN TREE WAS PLANTED A HUMBLE BLACKBERRY VINE. IT WAS VERY PLIABLE AND YIELDING. IT GREW LOW TO THE GROUND, SO SOME PEOPLE HAD PLACED A FENCE AROUND IT SO THAT IT WOULD NOT BE STEPPED ON AND HAVE ITS SOFT FRUIT SMASHED. ALTHOUGH, OVER THE YEARS, THE BLACKBERRY VINE HAD CREPT UP THE SIDE OF THE FENCE, IT WAS NOT EVEN A QUARTER OF THE HEIGHT OF THE PECAN TREE.

ONE DAY, AS VINES AND TREES OFTEN DO WHEN THERE IS NO ONE AROUND TO HEAR, THE PECAN TREE AND THE BLACKBERRY

VINE BEGAN TO CHAT. THE PECAN TREE, LIKE USUAL WAS BRAGGING ABOUT HOW STURDY AND TALL HE STOOD. HE WAS VERY PROUD.

"HEY, VINE!" HE YELLED DOWN TO THE BLACKBERRY VINE. "DON'T YOU WISH YOU WERE AS STRONG AND AS TALL AS ME? YOU ARE SUCH A WIMP. SOMEONE EVEN HAD TO BUILD A FENCE AROUND YOU SO THAT YOU WOULD NOT GET STEPPED ON. HA! NO ONE CAN STEP ON ME! MANY PEOPLE CAN CLIMB ON ME AT ONE TIME AND I WOULDN'T FEEL A THING. IF MANY PEOPLE CLIMBED ON YOU, IT WOULD KILL YOU. EVEN YOUR FRUIT IS SOFT AND SQUISHY. MINE IS HARD AS A STONE. WHAT A WEAKLING."

THE BLACKBERRY VINE DID NOT GET ANGRY. HE DID NOT EVEN BOTHER TO RESPOND. IT WAS POINTLESS. HE HAD KNOWN THIS PECAN TREE FOR MANY YEARS AND HAD HEARD THESE THINGS OFTEN. BESIDES, EVERYTHING THAT THE PECAN TREE WAS SAYING WAS TRUE, ALTHOUGH HE SAW THESE TRUTHS FROM A DIFFERENT PERSPECTIVE. HE WAS NOWHERE NEAR AS IMPORTANT, STRONG, AND TALL AS THE PECAN TREE, YET SOMEONE HAD THOUGHT HIM REMARKABLE ENOUGH TO TAKE THE TIME TO BUILD A FENCE AROUND HIM. NOT ONLY DID THIS FENCE KEEP HIM FROM BEING STEPPED ON, BUT IT ALSO ALLOWED HIM TO ASCEND TO THE TOP OF THE FENCE SO THAT HE COULD LOOK AROUND THE ORCHARD A BIT. SOMETHING HE COULD NEVER HAVE DONE WITHOUT THE FENCE. HE WAS VERY GRATEFUL TO THE PEOPLE THAT HAD BUILT THE FENCE IN HIS **HONOR**. THUS, HE MADE SURE TO PRODUCE THE SWEETEST, SOFTEST, JUICIEST BERRIES THAT HE COULD SO THAT THE PEOPLE COULD ENJOY THEM EASILY. HE HAD SEEN THE TROUBLE THAT THE PEOPLE HAD TO GO THROUGH IN ORDER TO ENJOY THE PECANS AND HE DID NOT WANT TO PUT

ANYONE THROUGH THAT TYPE OF STRUGGLE. HE KNEW THAT HE WAS NOT PHYSICALLY STURDY, BUT HE ALSO KNEW THAT SOMETIMES A WEAKNESS CAN TURN OUT TO BE REALLY A **STRENGTH**, AND SOMETIMES A **STRENGTH** CAN TURN OUT TO BE REALLY A WEAKNESS DEPENDENT UPON THE SITUATION THAT ONE FINDS THEMSELVES IN.

ONE DAY, A HORRIBLE STORM CAME. IT WAS THE MOST FRIGHTFUL, MALEVOLENT STORM THAT PARTICULAR AREA HAD EVER SEEN. THERE WAS TERRIBLE LIGHTNING AND HORRENDOUSLY POWERFUL WINDS. IT STORMED NIGHT AND DAY FOR THREE DAYS STRAIGHT. WHEN THE STORM FINALLY HAD FINISHED RAVAGING THE LAND AND THE SUN SHYLY PEEKED OUT FROM BEHIND THE CLOUDS, THE SIGHT IN THE ORCHARD WAS ONE OF POOR DEVASTATION. THE PECAN TREE HAD REPEATEDLY BEEN STRUCK BY LIGHTNING AND THE STRONG WINDS HAD TORN AWAY ALL OF ITS MIGHTY LIMBS.

THE HARD STURDY WOOD OF THE TREE HAD BEEN CHARRED TO A BRITTLE CRISP. THE GREAT PECAN TREE WAS RUINED. THE BLACKBERRY VINE, ON THE OTHER HAND, HAD SURVIVED THE WHOLE ORDEAL JUST FINE. OH, THE FENCE THAT IT HAD CLIMBED UP OVER THE YEARS HAD BEEN TORN DOWN BY THE WINDS, BUT THAT WAS ALRIGHT. THE FENCE COULD BE REBUILT. HE HAD WEATHERED THE STORM. WHEN THE POWERFUL WINDS HAD BLOWN, HIS LIMBER NATURE ALLOWED HIM TO FLOW WITH THEM, WHEREAS THE RIGID NATURE OF THE PECAN TREE HAD PREVENTED HIM FROM DOING THE SAME. WHEN THE LIGHTNING STRUCK, BECAUSE HE WAS NOWHERE AS TALL AS THE PECAN TREE, HE HAD NOT BEEN SUBJECTED TO THE LIGHTNING'S FURY. THE SAME CHARACTERISTICS THAT THE PECAN TREE HAD BEEN SO PROUD OF HAD PROVED TO BE HIS DOWNFALL. THE SAME RIGIDNESS THAT HE HAD VIEWED AS HIS **STRENGTH** HAD BEEN THE VERY REASON THAT HE HAD BEEN TORN APART. THE SAME HEIGHTS THAT HE WAS SO PROUD OF REACHING HAD BEEN THE VERY SAME THING THAT HAD ATTRACTED THE LIGHTNING'S RUTHLESS VIOLENCE. HOWEVER, THE SAME CHARACTERISTICS THAT THE PECAN TREE HAD RIDICULED THE BLACKBERRY VINE FOR HAVING PROVED TO BE THE BLACKBERRY VINE'S SALVATION.

MY SON, IN THIS WORLD, YOU HAVE PEOPLE WHOSE MINDS ARE LIKE THE PECAN TREE AND YOU HAVE PEOPLE WHOSE MINDS ARE LIKE THE BLACKBERRY VINE. THOSE PEOPLE WHOSE MINDS ARE LIKE THE PECAN TREE ARE THOSE WHO ARE SO PROUD IN THEIR **KNOWLEDGE** THAT THEY BECOME RIGID AND INFLEXIBLE. THEY MISTAKE THEIR UNYIELDING NATURE FOR **STRENGTH** AND THE LOFTY POSITIONS THEY ATTAIN IN THE WORLD FOR SECURITY, NOT **UNDERSTANDING** THAT WHEN THE TEMPESTS AND ASSAULTS OF LIFE COME AS THEY INVARIABLY SHALL, THESE THINGS JUST MAY PROVE TO BE THEIR UNDOING. ON THE OTHER HAND, THOSE WITH MINDS LIKE THE BLACKBERRY VINE

MAY APPEAR TO BE WEAK TO THE MASSIVE PECAN TREES OF THE WORLD, BUT THEIR SWEET, HUMBLE NATURE ENCOURAGES THOSE THAT ENJOY THEIR FRUITS TO HELP THEM BY PROTECTING THEM AND ASSISTING THEM IN THEIR ASCENSION. JUST LIKE THE PEOPLE OF THE ORCHARD DID WHEN THEY BUILT THE FENCE AROUND THE BLACKBERRY VINE. INSTEAD OF BEING UNYIELDING, THOSE WITH MINDS LIKE THE BLACKBERRY BUSH REMAIN EVER GRACEFUL, FLEXIBLE, AND IN HARMONY WITH THE PRESENT MOMENT, FLOWING WITH THE WINDS OF TIME RATHER THAN STANDING IN STUBBORN DEFIANCE OF THEM. THEIR HUMILITY, WHICH SOME SEE AS WEAKNESS, IS THEIR **STRENGTH**, WHILE THE PRIDE OF THE PECAN TREES, WHICH SOME SEE AS **STRENGTH**, IS NOTHING BUT WEAKNESS WEARING A CLEVER DISGUISE.

26

MASTER, FLEXIBILITY OF MIND IS STRENGTH. FOR IT IS WHAT ALLOWS YOU TO GROW. STAYING LIMBER IN YOUR THINKING IS WHAT SHALL ALLOW YOU TO SCALE THE MOUNTAIN OF LIFE WITH THE MINIMUM AMOUNT OF SORENESS AND PAIN. WHILE FLEXIBILITY OF THE BODY IS ATTAINED BY STRETCHING THE BODY, FLEXIBILITY OF MIND IS GAINED BY ALWAYS BEING WILLING TO ADOPT NEW PERSPECTIVES. ALWAYS BE WILLING TO LEARN AND GROW, MY SON, FOR GROWTH IS **STRENGTH** MANIFESTED. GROWTH IS THE MEANS BY WHICH **STRENGTH** BECOMES KNOWN. YOU SHALL NEVER KNOW THE TRUE NATURE OF YOUR FORCES, OF YOUR **STRENGTH**, UNTIL YOU REACH THE MOUNTAIN TOP OF KINGSHIP AND ARE ABLE TO LOOK DOWN UPON ALL WITH **UNDERSTANDING**. GROWTH IS MERELY THE JOURNEY TO THE MOUNTAIN TOP. GROWTH IS MERELY THE

HIKE THAT ONE UNDERTAKES ON THEIR EXPEDITION TO THE THRONE. JUST AS A MAN WITH A WEAK BODY SHALL FIND IT NEARLY IMPOSSIBLE TO CLIMB A STEEP MOUNTAIN, A MAN WITH A WEAK MIND SHALL NEVER BE ABLE TO SCALE THE HEIGHTS OF **DIGNITY** NECESSARY TO BE DESERVING OF THE MAJESTIC APPELLATION OF **KING**. HOWEVER, JUST AS A PHYSICALLY WEAK MAN CAN MAKE HIS BODY STRONG BY CAREFUL AND PATIENT PHYSICAL TRAINING, SO TOO CAN A MAN OF WEAK THOUGHT MAKE HIS MIND STRONG BY EXERCISING IT IN REGAL THINKING.

27

MASTER, A MAN IS MERELY A COMPILATION OF HIS BELIEFS, IDEAS, AND ACTIONS. A MAN LITERALLY IS WHAT HE THINKS AND HIS CHARACTER. THE IDENTITY THAT HE HAS ASSUMED IN THIS WORLD IS BUT A COMPLETE SUM OF HIS THOUGHTS. YOUR THINKING, THE CONTENT OF YOUR MIND, IS DETERMINED SOLELY BY YOUR PAST EXPERIENCES AND WHAT YOU THOUGHT DURING THEM. ALL THAT YOU MANIFEST IN THIS WORLD IS A RESULT OF ALL THAT YOU HAVE THOUGHT. EVERY THOUGHT CREATES CHANGE, FOR THOUGHT AND CHANGE ARE ONE AND THE SAME. GROWTH, EVOLUTION, AND INCREASE ARE ALL MANIFESTATIONS OF CHANGE, AS ARE DEGRADATION, DEGENERATION, AND STAGNATION. GROWTH, EVOLUTION, AND INCREASE CARRY WITH THEM JOY AND FULFILLMENT. DEGRADATION, DEGENERATION, AND STAGNATION BRING WITH THEM PAIN AND SUFFERING. GROWTH, EVOLUTION, AND INCREASE ARE BROUGHT ABOUT BY THE STRONG LIBERATING THOUGHTS OF A **KING**. CHARACTER CHANGES. THOUGHTS ARE THE MEANS OF THE CHANGE. THIS CHANGE IS THE SOURCE OF MAN'S TRIUMPHS, AS WELL AS TRAGEDIES. TRIUMPH OCCURS WHEN YOUR EVOLUTION IS

KEEPING PACE WITH THE PRESENT MOMENT. THIS CAN ONLY HAPPEN IF YOU BECOME ONE WITH THE PRESENT MOMENT. ONE WITH **POWER**. FOR ALL **POWER** LIES IN THE PRESENT MOMENT. TRAGEDY OCCURS WHEN, SHACKLED TO OLD THOUGHTS AND VIEWPOINTS, YOU RESIST THE PRESENT MOMENT, MAKE A STAND AGAINST THE WINDS OF TIME, GET PUMMELED BY DEBRIS, AND ARE TORN APART. THIS IS THE CAUSE OF ALL OF THE PAIN THAT YOU FEEL. THE ATTACHMENT TO YOUR OLD FORM PREVENTS YOU FROM GROWING BECAUSE IT PREVENTS YOU FROM LEARNING. THUS, IT ENSLAVES YOU TO THE WRETCHEDNESS OF YOUR OWN IGNORANCE.

28

IN THE JUNGLES OF SOME LANDS, IT IS SURPRISINGLY EASY TO CATCH SOME MONKEYS. THESE TYPES OF MONKEYS LOVE SHINY OBJECTS. I MEAN THEY ARE ABSOLUTELY CRAZY ABOUT THEM. THEY GREEDILY TRY TO HOARD THEM. IN FACT, AT TIMES, IT SEEMS THAT THIS IS THEIR VERY PURPOSE IN LIFE. THOSE THAT HUNT THEM KNOW THAT ALL YOU NEED TO DO IS TO GET A BOTTLE, STUFF A SHINY OBJECT INSIDE THAT WON'T COME OUT IF YOU TURN THE BOTTLE UPSIDE DOWN AND TIE THE BOTTLE TO A TREE. THE MONKEY'S HANDS ARE SMALL ENOUGH TO PUT INSIDE THE BOTTLE IF IT DOESN'T MAKE A FIST. IF IT DOES MAKE A FIST, ITS HAND CANNOT FIT INSIDE OF THE BOTTLE'S OPENING. WHEN ONE OF THESE MONKEYS SEES ONE OF THESE BOTTLES, THEIR LITTLE MONKEY EYES LIGHT UP. FINALLY, THEY HAVE FOUND THEIR HEART'S DESIRE. THEY RUSH DOWN QUICKLY TO THE GROUND SO THAT THEY MAY CLAIM THEIR TREASURE. THE OBJECT IN THE BOTTLE IS SO SHINY! AS THE MONKEY FITS HIS HAND THROUGH THE OPENING, IT IS A TIGHT SQUEEZE, BUT NO

MATTER. ALL THE MONKEY IS THINKING ABOUT IS THE SHINY OBJECT.

EVERYTHING FOR THE MONKEY CHANGES WHEN IT TRIES TO PULL ITS HAND OUT OF THE BOTTLE, HOWEVER. THE DREAM COME TRUE BECOMES A NIGHTMARE. TRY AND TRY AS HE MIGHT, THE POOR MONKEY JUST CANNOT GET HIS HAND OUT SINCE THE OBJECT IS INSIDE OF IT. HE SCREAMS IN PROTEST. HE JUMPS UP AND DOWN. HE EVEN CUTS A COUPLE OF BACKFLIPS. NOTHING SEEMS TO WORK. EVERYTHING FOR THE MONKEY CHANGES WHEN IT TRIES TO PULL ITS HAND OUT OF THE BOTTLE, HOWEVER. THE DREAM COME TRUE BECOMES A NIGHTMARE. TRY AND TRY AS HE MIGHT, THE POOR MONKEY JUST CANNOT GET HIS HAND OUT SINCE THE OBJECT IS INSIDE OF IT. HE SCREAMS IN PROTEST. HE JUMPS UP AND DOWN. HE EVEN CUTS A COUPLE OF BACKFLIPS. NOTHING SEEMS TO WORK. THE MONKEY IS SO DISTRAUGHT THAT IT DOESN'T EVEN SEE THE CONUNDRUM THAT IT HAS PLACED ITSELF IN. IT DOES NOT SEE THAT THE ONLY THING THAT IT HAS TO DO TO BE FREE IS TO JUST LET THE SHINY OBJECT GO. BLINDED TO HIS IGNORANT ATTACHMENT TO SHINY OBJECTS, HE REFUSES TO LET GO EVEN WHEN THE TRAPPER IS UPON HIM. HE JUST SCREAMS IN PROTEST AT THE CRUELNESS OF FATE.

EVERYTHING FOR THE MONKEY CHANGES WHEN IT TRIES TO PULL ITS HAND OUT OF THE BOTTLE, HOWEVER. THE DREAM COME TRUE BECOMES A NIGHTMARE. TRY AND TRY AS HE MIGHT, THE POOR MONKEY JUST CANNOT GET HIS HAND OUT SINCE THE OBJECT IS INSIDE OF IT. HE SCREAMS IN PROTEST. HE JUMPS UP AND DOWN. HE EVEN CUTS A COUPLE OF BACKFLIPS. NOTHING SEEMS TO WORK. THE MONKEY IS SO DISTRAUGHT THAT IT DOESN'T EVEN SEE THE CONUNDRUM THAT IT HAS PLACED ITSELF

IN. IT DOES NOT SEE THAT THE ONLY THING THAT IT HAS TO DO TO BE FREE IS TO JUST LET THE SHINY OBJECT GO. BLINDED TO HIS IGNORANT ATTACHMENT TO SHINY OBJECTS, HE REFUSES TO LET GO EVEN WHEN THE TRAPPER IS UPON HIM. HE JUST SCREAMS IN PROTEST AT THE CRUELNESS OF FATE.

29

MASTER, THAT FROM WHICH YOU DETACH YOURSELF SHALL NEVER BE ABLE TO ENSLAVE YOU. FOR IT IS ONLY ATTACHMENTS THAT ENSLAVE YOU. ATTACHMENTS TO SHINY OBJECTS. ATTACHMENTS TO OTHERS. ATTACHMENTS TO BELIEFS AND IDEAS. ESPECIALLY THOSE THAT ARE NO LONGER IN HARMONY WITH THE PRESENT MOMENT. ATTACHMENTS ARE CHAINS THAT BIND YOU TO FORM, AND THUS PREVENT YOUR EXPANSION. **POWER** IS FORMLESS AND ETERNALLY EXPANDING. TO ATTACH YOURSELF TO ANYTHING THAT IS NOT FORMLESS AND ETERNALLY EXPANDING IS TO MAKE YOURSELF A SLAVE TO THAT WHICH YOU ARE ATTACHED. A SLAVE CAN NEVER BE **KING**.

30

MASTER, ALTHOUGH YOUR BELIEFS ARE WHAT HOLD TOGETHER THE FORM THAT YOU DESIRE TO PRESENT TO THE WORLD, IT IS MUCH MORE POWERFUL NOT TO BE ATTACHED TO ANY BELIEFS AND REMAIN FORMLESS. FOR TO BE FORMLESS IS TO BE **POWER**. BEING FORMLESS ALLOWS YOU TO BE FREE. ONLY A **KING** IS FREE. IT ALLOWS YOU TO BE OPEN TO LIFE AS IT COMES YOUR WAY SO THAT YOU MAY BE ABLE TO USE YOUR OWN INTELLIGENCE AND INNER **UNDERSTANDING**, RATHER

THAN STORED, STUCK, STALE JUDGMENTS, AND OUTDATED CONCEPTIONS THAT NO LONGER FIT REALITY. IT ALLOWS YOU TO BE WHO YOU TRULY ARE.

31

MASTER, THOUGHTS ARE THE SHAPERS OF CHARACTER. ALL OF YOUR THOUGHTS AND ACTIONS LEAVE AN IMPRESSION ON YOUR MIND. THESE IMPRESSIONS CREATE A FORM. BECAUSE A **KING** IS FREE TO THINK HIS OWN THOUGHTS, A **KING** IS FREE TO CREATE HIS OWN FORM. A **KING** SHAPES CIRCUMSTANCES SO THAT THEY MAY FIT HIS DESIRES. OTHERS ARE SHAPED BY CIRCUMSTANCES DESPITE THEIR DESIRES.

32

MASTER, EVERY THOUGHT THAT YOU HAVE SHALL EITHER HEAL OR HARM. THE IMMUTABLE LAW OF CAUSE AND EFFECT GUARANTEES THAT YOU SHALL EXPERIENCE THE RESULT OF WHATEVER IT IS THAT YOU CHOOSE TO THINK. FREE, ROYAL THOUGHTS LEAD TO FREEDOM. BARBARIC THOUGHTS LEAD TO BONDAGE. WHERE DO YOU WISH TO GO? EVERY MIND STATE, THOUGHT, OR EMOTION THAT YOU REPEATEDLY EXPERIENCE SHALL BECOME STRONGER AND MORE HABITUATED TO EITHER YOUR BENEFIT OR DETRIMENT. NEVER THINK THAT YOU SHALL NOT BRING TO A NATURAL AND LOGICAL CONCLUSION WHATEVER THOUGHTS THAT YOU PERMIT TO DOMINATE YOUR MIND. FOR IT IS YOUR THINKING, MASTER, NOT OTHER PEOPLE, OR CIRCUMSTANCES THAT MAKE YOU WHAT YOU ARE AND SHALL BE.

33

MASTER, DESIRES ARE THE LIGHTS THAT CAUSE US TO MOVE THROUGH THE MAZES OF OUR LIVES. OUR DESIRES GUIDE US IN THE DARKNESS AND KEEP US MOVING ALONG OUR PATH. NOT REALIZING THAT OUR DESIRES ARE MERELY THE REFLECTION OF OUR OWN LIGHT, WE CHASE THEM ENDLESSLY, JUST AS A DOG CHASES ITS OWN TAIL. DESIRE IS THE ROOT CAUSE OF EVERYTHING THAT OCCURS IN YOUR LIFE. FOR DESIRES CAUSE YOU TO ACT. WHEN AN ACTION IS PERFORMED, THE REACTION IS ALWAYS RIGHT THERE WITH IT, EVEN IF IT HAS NOT YET MANIFESTED. EVEN THE BODY THAT YOU NOW POSSESS IS THE OUTCOME OF YOUR PAST DESIRES. IF YOU DESIRED TO BE HEALTHY, THEN YOU EXERCISED AND ATE WELL. YOUR HEALTHY BODY IS THE REACTIONS TO THOSE ACTIONS. IT IS EVIDENCE OF YOUR DESIRE. THE STRONGER THE DESIRE, THE MORE OVERWHELMING SHALL BE THE EVIDENCE. DESIRES DESIRED WITH AWARENESS ARE THE CAUSE OF GROWTH, EVOLUTION, AND INCREASE. IGNORANT DESIRES ARE THE CAUSE OF DEGRADATION, DEGENERATION, AND STAGNATION. DESIRES ARE THE BEWITCHING, SEDUCTIVE LIGHT OF YOUR OWN **POWER** SHINING THROUGH SPACE AND BEING REFLECTED BACK TO YOU BY THE MIRROR OF THE PHYSICAL UNIVERSE.

YOU SEE YOUR OWN LIGHT IN OBJECTS "OUT THERE" AND ARE MESMERIZED. YOU ASSUME THOSE OBJECTS THAT YOU SEE "OUT THERE" ARE THE SOURCE OF THE LIGHT, AND THUS ARE TOTALLY SEDUCED BY THEM. THIS WOULD BE LIKE THE SUN LOOKING OUT INTO SPACE AND DESIRING THE LIGHT OF THE EARTH. BECAUSE YOUR LIGHT IS ETERNAL, YOU SHALL ALWAYS SEE ITS REFLECTION "OUT THERE" FOR AS LONG AS YOU LOOK. HOWEVER, REMEMBER

YOUR JOURNEY TO THOSE LIGHTS SHALL ALWAYS LEAD YOU BACK TO YOUR OWN. TO REALIZE THIS IS TO GAIN THE **POWER** TO CONSCIOUSLY CHOOSE AND CONTROL YOUR DESIRES. WHEN YOU ARE UNAWARE OF THIS, YOUR DESIRES CONTROL YOU AND THEY ARE OFTEN NOT EVEN YOUR OWN. WHEN YOU ARE UNAWARE, OTHER PEOPLE'S DESIRES CONTROL YOU. ALWAYS GUARD YOUR DESIRES WITH AWARENESS. FOR YOUR WORST ENEMY COULD NOT HARM YOU AS MUCH AS YOUR OWN DESIRE UNGUARDED. BUT ONCE MASTERED, THERE IS NOTHING THAT COULD HELP YOU AS MUCH. DESIRE IS THE REFLECTION OF YOUR **POWER**; THUS, IT SHALL NEVER END. EVEN TO DESIRE TO HAVE NO DESIRES IS STILL A DESIRE. THE IGNORANT MIND WANTS TO DESIRE MORE THAN IT WISHES TO HAVE. THUS, IN A MIND SUCH AS THIS, THE SHALLOW SATISFACTION OF HAVING SHALL ALWAYS SOON BE REPLACED BY MORE DESIRES. IT IS TRULY LIKE A DOG CHASING ITS OWN TAIL. FOR ONCE YOU OBTAIN THE OBJECT OF YOUR DESIRE, YOU SHALL FIND THAT IT WAS NOT WHAT YOU IMAGINED IT WOULD BE. THERE IS NO **POWER** IN IT. THE **POWER** THAT YOU THOUGHT IT HELD WAS MERELY A REFLECTION OF YOUR OWN. TO BE AWARE OF THIS IS TO GAIN THE **POWER** TO DIRECT YOUR DESIRES. TO DIRECT YOUR **POWER** IN WHATEVER DIRECTION THAT YOU CHOOSE.

34

MASTER, YOUR SENSE OF WHO YOU ARE SHALL DETERMINE WHAT YOU PERCEIVE TO BE YOUR NEEDS AND WHAT MATTERS TO YOU IN LIFE. YOUR SENSE OF WHO YOU ARE DETERMINES YOUR DESIRES. A **KING** THINKS OF FEEDING HIS PEOPLE AND DESIRES THE MEANS TO DO SO. THUS, HE IS GIVEN ABUNDANCE. FOR ABUNDANCE IS HOW ONE FEEDS A MULTITUDE. A **KING**

DESIRES TO ENLIGHTEN THE DARKNESS OF IGNORANCE; THUS, HE ATTRACTS INTELLIGENCE AND DISCERNMENT. A **KING** DESIRES **POWER** AND **THE TRUTH**; THUS, HE ATTRACTS EVERLASTING **WISDOM**, PERPETUAL **STRENGTH**, INFINITE **FAITH**, TIMELESS **KNOWLEDGE**, ENDLESS **UNDERSTANDING**, IMMORTAL **DIGNITY**, AND INCESSANT **HONOR**. NEVER FORGET, MY SON, THE TRUE "MEASURE OF A MAN IS THE WORTH OF THOSE THINGS" WHICH CONCERNS HIM.

35

MASTER, IT IS BECAUSE MOST PEOPLE DESIRE MATERIAL OBJECTS TO MAKE THEM HAPPY, THAT THE DESIRE FOR MATERIAL OBJECTS IS THE MAIN SOURCE OF THEIR UNHAPPINESS. THIS IS WHY IT IS OF THE UTMOST IMPORTANCE THAT YOU FREE YOURSELF FROM THE ATTACHMENT TO MATERIAL OBJECTS. IN ORDER TO CREATE A KINGDOM, YOU MUST CULTIVATE AN UNFETTERED MIND FREE FROM THE WEIGHT OF MATERIALITY. THIS IS THE ONLY WAY THAT YOU SHALL EVER BE ABLE TO SOAR WITH THE EAGLES. ATTACHMENT TO THINGS DROPS AWAY BY ITSELF[18] ONCE YOU CEASE SEEKING HAPPINESS IN THEM. YOU SHALL NEVER FIND HAPPINESS IN THINGS BECAUSE YOU ARE HAPPINESS. TO SEARCH FOR HAPPINESS IN THINGS IS LIKE THE EYES TRYING TO SEE THEMSELVES. OBSESSION IS THE KINSMAN OF DEATH, FOR IT BLOCKS THE FLOW OF LIFE. THOSE THINGS "OUT THERE" THAT YOU DESIRE ARE SHADOWS. CHASE THEM AND THEY SHALL RUN AWAY FROM YOU AT THE SAME SPEED THAT YOU ARE CHASING THEM. HOWEVER, IF YOU WALK TOWARD THE LIGHT OF YOUR

---

[18] Eckhart Tolle Quote

OWN **POWER** AND THEN LOOK OVER YOUR SHOULDER, YOU SHALL SEE THAT THOSE SAME SHADOWS ARE NOW CHASING YOU. TO TRANSCEND DESIRE IS TO TRANSCEND THE MIND AND TAKE YOUR POSITION AS THE **KING** UPON THE HILL, OVERLOOKING THE BATTLE, WHO DIRECTS HIS FORCES AS INTELLIGENCE AND **UNDERSTANDING** SEE FIT.

WHEN YOU THINK GREATLY, YOU BECOME GREAT. A NEGATIVE MIND CANNOT MANIFEST A POSITIVE REALITY. UNTIL YOU EXHAUST THE HABIT OF THINKING IN IGNORANCE, INTELLIGENCE AND **UNDERSTANDING** SHALL NOT APPEAR. LEARN TO LIMIT YOURSELF ONLY TO THOSE THOUGHTS WHICH, IF SOMEONE WERE TO ASK WHAT YOU ARE THINKING IN THIS MOMENT, WOULD ALLOW YOU TO ANSWER THEM WITHOUT HESITATION, EQUIVOCATION, OR HUMILIATION. REALITY IS WHATEVER IDEA OF IT YOU IDENTIFY WITH. THEREFORE, LIFE SHALL BE WHATEVER YOU DECIDE IT SHALL BE. ULTIMATELY, ONE BECOMES WHAT ONE IMAGINES. YOUR AURA IS STAINED BY THE DYE OF YOUR THOUGHTS. AS ARE YOUR HABITUAL THOUGHTS, SO TOO SHALL YOU BE.

36

MASTER, FROM THE UNIVERSAL PERSPECTIVE, THE PERSPECTIVE OF A **KING**, THE UNIVERSE, AND EVERYTHING WHICH OCCURS IN IT IS PERCEPTION, AND PERCEPTION IS CHANGE. A **KING** UNDERSTANDS THAT JUDGING THIS CHANGE OR ATTEMPTING TO STOP THIS CHANGE FROM OCCURRING IS AS FUTILE AS ENDEAVORING TO GRASP THE WIND. FOR WITHOUT CHANGE, NOTHING CAN COME INTO EXISTENCE.

37

MASTER, PERCEPTION IS POWER. POWER IS FOREVER IN MOTION. SHE IS FOREVER DANCING. SHE IS ETERNALLY LOCKED IN A PERPETUAL DANCE FOR THE ENTERTAINMENT OF HER OTHER HALF, **THE TRUTH**. FOR THIS IS HER NATURE. IT IS THE NATURE OF **THE TRUTH** TO BE FOREVER THE WATCHER, THE KNOWER, THE STILLNESS THAT CONTAINS ALL MOTION. **THE TRUTH** IS THE PERCEIVER OF ALL PERCEPTION; THUS, **POWER** SHALL FOREVER GIVE HIM SOMETHING TO PERCEIVE. **THE TRUTH** FEELS NO NEED TO JUDGE THESE PERCEPTIONS, FOR HE REALIZES THAT THEY ARE ALL FOR THE PURPOSE OF HIS ENTERTAINMENT AND UNDER COMPLETE CONTROL. FOR **THE TRUTH** AND **POWER** ARE ONE. PERCEPTION IS THE LIGHT AND HEAT OF THE FIRE THAT IS **THE TRUTH**. THEY ARE SEPARATE, AND YET THEY ARE ONE. **THE TRUTH** IS THE STILLNESS OF THE UNIVERSE. THE SPACE OF THE UNIVERSE. PERCEPTION, OR **POWER**, IS THE MOTION OF THE UNIVERSE. CHANGE IS HOW THE UNIVERSE SHOWS ITS **POWER**, JUST AS WAVES ARE HOW THE OCEAN'S **POWER** SHOWS. FROM THE PERSPECTIVE OF THE OCEAN, THE WAVES DO NOT EXIST. ONLY THE OCEAN IS THERE. THE WAVES ARE MERELY ILLUSIONS. TEMPORARY APPEARANCES, OR FORMS THAT THE OCEAN HAS TAKEN.

THINK OF A TREE. A TREE IS STILL. A TREE DOESN'T MOVE, AND YET AT THE SAME TIME A TREE IS IN CONSTANT MOTION. ITS LEAVES ARE ALWAYS COMING AND GOING. THEY ARE CONSTANTLY RUSTLING IN THE WIND. THE LIMBS OF A TREE ARE CONSTANTLY GROWING ABOVE GROUND AND ITS ROOTS ARE STEADILY GROWING BELOW GROUND. ALL THIS MOTION, ALL THIS

CHANGE, IS TAKING PLACE, YET THE TREE ITSELF NEVER MOVES FROM WHERE IT IS. THIS IS THE NATURE OF YOU AND YOUR PERCEPTIONS. **THE TRUTH** AND **POWER**. YOU, **THE TRUTH**, ARE OMNIPRESENT. YOU ARE EVERYWHERE. THERE IS NO PLACE FOR YOU TO MOVE, FOR THERE IS NOWHERE ELSE TO GO. YOU, **THE TRUTH**, ARE STILLNESS. **POWER**, YOUR PERCEPTIONS, IS THE MOVEMENT TAKING PLACE WITHIN YOUR STILLNESS. IT IS THE ILLUSION OF CHANGE.

38

MASTER, YOU ARE ETERNAL. YOU ARE THE ABILITY TO PERCEIVE. THE ABILITY TO PERCEIVE SHALL NEVER CHANGE. ONLY WHAT YOU PERCEIVE, YOUR PERCEPTIONS, SHALL CHANGE. FOR THIS IS THEIR NATURE. EVERYTHING THAT YOU CAN PERCEIVE IS A PERCEPTION. EVEN DEATH. FOR DEATH IS MERELY THE CHANGE FROM ONE FORM TO THE NEXT.

39

MASTER, THE UNIVERSE IS PERCEPTION. IT IS AN ILLUSION THAT YOU HAVE CREATED WITH YOUR **POWER**. THINK OF A STAINED GLASS WINDOW. THE LIGHT THAT SHINES THROUGH THE STAINED GLASS IS PURE. IT IS COLORLESS. IT IS PURE **POWER**. WHEN THAT LIGHT SHINES THROUGH THE STAINED GLASS, IT SHINES ON THE OTHER SIDE AS THE COLOR OF THE GLASS THROUGH WHICH IT SHINED. THE LIGHT ITSELF NEVER CHANGED. ONLY THE APPEARANCE DID. IF THE STAINED GLASS IS STAINED PURPLE, THEN THE LIGHT THAT SHINES THROUGH THAT GLASS SHALL APPEAR TO BE PURPLE. IF THE GLASS IS STAINED

GOLD, THEN THE LIGHT THAT SHINES THROUGH THAT GLASS SHALL APPEAR TO BE GOLD. THIS IS HOW PERCEPTION WORKS. POWER SHINES THROUGH THE STAINED GLASS OF THE MIND AND COLORS ALL THAT IT SHINES UPON THE SAME HUE AS THE MIND THROUGH WHICH IT SHINED. IF THE LIGHT OF POWER SHINES THROUGH A MIND TARNISHED WITH THE WEAKNESSES OF FEAR AND DOUBT, THEN A WEAK LIFE FULL OF FAILURE AND SUFFERING IS WHAT IT SHALL PERCEIVE. HOWEVER, IF THE LIGHT OF POWER SHINES THROUGH A MIND POLISHED CLEAN WITH THE CONSCIOUSNESS OF A KING, THEN A POWERFUL FREE LIFE, FULL OF STRENGTH AND HAPPINESS IS WHAT YOU SHALL PERCEIVE.

ABOVE ALL ELSE, REALITY IS SUBJECTIVE. PEOPLE SHALL ALWAYS FILTER EVENTS, THE CHANGES IN THE UNIVERSE, AND LIFE ITSELF, THROUGH THEIR EMOTIONS AND PRECONCEPTIONS. FOR THESE ARE THE COLORINGS OF THEIR MIND. ONLY THE CALM, CLEAR MIND OF A KING IS ABLE TO SEE THE CLEAR LIGHT OF THE TRUTH WHICH FLOWS THROUGH HIM. ONLY A KING IS ABLE TO PERCEIVE THE TRUE NATURE OF THE POWER THAT FLOWS THROUGH EVERYTHING. IN THIS WORLD OF CHANGE IN WHICH WE LIVE, PERCEPTION IS REALITY. FOR IT IS ONLY THAT WHICH ONE BELIEVES AND NOT THE TRUTH OF THEIR THOUGHTS THAT SHALL BE THE DETERMINING FACTOR IN THEIR DANCE WITH THE UNIVERSE. YOUR PERCEPTIONS SHALL DETERMINE HOW LIFE RESPONDS TO YOU. ALWAYS REMEMBER, MY SON, YOU ARE NOT THE MIND OR THE BODY. YOU ARE THAT WHICH IS PERCEIVING THEM. YOU ARE THAT POWER THAT IS SHINING THROUGH THEM.

40

MASTER, BECAUSE THE PHYSICAL WORLD MIRRORS THAT MIND WHICH IS PERCEIVING IT, EVERYTHING THAT YOU PERCEIVE IS A REFLECTION OF YOURSELF. THE UNIVERSE COMPLETELY IS A MIRROR AND LIKE ANY MIRROR, IT IS COMPLETELY NEUTRAL. IT REFLECTS THAT WHICH IS BEFORE IT WITHOUT JUDGMENT OR DISTORTION. THERE IS NOTHING OUTSIDE OF YOU IN THE UNIVERSE THAT JUDGES YOU OR YOUR PERCEPTIONS BECAUSE YOU AND YOUR PERCEPTIONS ARE THE UNIVERSE. THIS WORLD IS MERELY A REFLECTION OF THAT WHICH IS ALREADY INSIDE YOU, FOR EXTERNAL REALITY SHALL ALWAYS REFLECT BACK TO YOU YOUR OWN INNER STATE. IF YOUR INNER STATE IS ONE OF GOODNESS AND INTELLIGENCE, THEN LIFE SHALL REFLECT THIS TO YOU, AND YOU SHALL SEE ALL OF THE GOODNESS AND INTELLIGENCE THAT THE WORLD HAS TO OFFER. IF YOUR INNER STATE IS ONE OF IGNORANCE AND WICKEDNESS, THEN YOU SHALL SEE ALL OF THE IGNORANCE AND WICKEDNESS THAT THE WORLD HAS TO OFFER.

ALL PEOPLE SEE THE WORLD NOT AS IT IS, BUT AS THEY ARE. PERCEPTIONS ARE MERELY DIFFERENT WAYS OF SEEING **THE TRUTH**. THEY ARE DIFFERENT MANIFESTATIONS OF **POWER**. THEY ARE ILLUSIONS. TEMPORARY APPEARANCES OF THE MIND. YET, THEY ARE REAL. FOR ALL PERCEPTIONS ARE REAL TO THE PERCEIVER, AND THE PERCEIVER IS ALL THAT TRULY EXISTS. THE WORLD IS AS YOU SEE IT. EVERYTHING SHALL BE TO YOU WHAT YOUR OPINION ALLOWS YOU TO MAKE OF IT. YOU ARE THE MAGICIAN THAT CREATES THE ILLUSIONS, FOR YOU ARE THE **POWER** BEHIND THE ILLUSIONS. THE MAJORITY OF THE PEOPLE IN THIS WORLD LIMIT THEMSELVES BECAUSE THEY ARE UNABLE TO SEE SITUATIONS AS THEY TRULY ARE. THEY ARE ONLY

ABLE TO SEE THE WORLD THROUGH THE LENS OF THEIR PRE-PROGRAMMED PERCEPTIONS.

41

ONCE, THERE WAS AN EXPLORER THAT JOURNEYED TO THE HEART OF THE JUNGLE. IN THE HEART OF THE JUNGLE, HE DISCOVERED A VILLAGE OF PEOPLE THAT HAD NEVER LEFT THE JUNGLE. THEY WERE COMPLETELY UNAWARE OF ANYTHING OUTSIDE OF THE DENSE JUNGLE IN WHICH THEY LIVED, FOR EVERYTHING THAT THEY NEEDED, THE JUNGLE PROVIDED. THE EXPLORER, WITH THE HELP OF A TRANSLATOR, TOLD THE PEOPLE OF THE VILLAGE OF THE GREAT WONDERS THAT WERE BEYOND THE JUNGLE. AFTER MUCH INSISTENCE, HE CONVINCED ONE BRAVE SOUL TO COME WITH HIM OUTSIDE THE JUNGLE SO THAT THE PEOPLE MAY KNOW **THE TRUTH** OF HIS WORDS. WHEN THE EXPLORER AND THE BRAVE VILLAGER FINALLY REACHED THE EDGE OF THE JUNGLE, THE AREA WHERE THEY EXITED OVERLOOKED AN ENORMOUS PLAIN. AN IMMENSE AREA OF WIDE-OPEN SPACE.

In the distance, they could see a herd of buffalo grazing. When the explorer told the villager that what they were, in fact, looking at were animals many times larger than themselves, the incredulous villager refused to believe the explorer. In fact, he ridiculed the explorer for his idiocy. The villager had never seen a buffalo, as no buffalo ever came into the dense jungle. Nor had he ever been in such a wide-open space, so he didn't know that the farther that one was from something, the smaller it appeared.

The villager, shaking his head at what he perceived to be the explorer's ignorance, told the explorer, "That which we are looking at are only ants. They cannot possibly be what you are describing because those things that we are looking at are too small. Only ants are that small. They have to be ants."

Refusing to go any farther with the stupid explorer, the villager returned to the jungle, appalled at his own foolishness for even venturing out and wasting his time with the confused explorer. He could not wait to tell everyone in the village how the man, as intelligent as he had appeared, did not even know what ants were.

The villager's perceptions were based upon his personal experiences in the dense, closed space of the jungle. He had never been to a wide-open space before. Thus, his ignorant mind could not grasp the fact that the farther things were in the distance, the smaller they appeared. To his mind, the only things that could possibly be that small were ants and even to suggest anything else was ludicrous. He even ridiculed the

EXPLORER. HE HAD NOT THE ABILITY, NOR THE FLEXIBILITY OF MIND TO BE ABLE TO PERCEIVE THE HUGE WORLD THAT EXISTED BEYOND THE EDGES OF THE DENSE JUNGLE. THUS, HIS REALITY REMAINED LIMITED TO THE TINY REALITY OF THE JUNGLE.

42

MASTER, LIFE SHALL GIVE YOU EXACTLY THE WORLD THAT YOU HAVE THE CAPABILITY TO PERCEIVE. NO MATTER WHAT MAY HAPPEN, YOUR MIND SHALL MAKE ALL CIRCUMSTANCES APPEAR TO BE IN AGREEMENT WITH YOUR PERCEPTIONS. IF YOU HAVE THE PERSPECTIVE OF A SLAVE, THEN THE WORLD SHALL APPEAR TO BE SMALL. FOR A SLAVE WEARS THE SHACKLES OF IGNORANCE, AND THUS CAN ONLY GO TO THE BOUNDARY OF HIS PERSPECTIVE. IF YOU PERCEIVE **THE TRUTH** THAT YOU ARE **POWER**, THAT YOU ARE **KING**, THEN THE WORLD SHALL APPEAR IMMENSE. A **KING** IS FREE, AND THUS CAN TRAVEL TO ANY PERSPECTIVE. TO HAVE THE PERSPECTIVE OF A SLAVE IS TO BE LIMITED. TO HAVE THE PERSPECTIVE OF A **KING** IS TO BE LIMITLESS. LIFE SHALL ALWAYS REFLECT THE BELIEFS OF HE THAT LIVES IT.

IN THE INFINITE DIVERSITY OF REALITY, EVERY PERCEPTION OF LIFE THAT YOU HAVE SHALL GIVE RISE TO A WORLD THAT MIRRORS IT. YOUR REALITY CHANGES AS YOU DO. WHEN YOU CHANGE YOUR PERCEPTIONS, REALITY SHALL RESPOND BY SHIFTING TO FIT YOUR PERCEPTION. THE OBSERVER IS THE DECIDING FACTOR IN EVERY OBSERVATION, AND THE OBSERVER CHANGES REALITY BY THE VERY ACT OF OBSERVATION. FOR ONLY THE OBSERVER CAN INTERPRET THAT WHICH HAS BEEN OBSERVED. THIS IS WHY YOU MUST NEVER RELINQUISH CONTROL OF YOUR PERCEPTION TO ANOTHER. A **KING** IS THE RULER OF HIMSELF AND THE

PAINTER OF HIS OWN PICTURES. IF YOU CAN CONTROL A PERSON'S PERCEPTION OF REALITY, YOU CAN CONTROL THEM. A **KING** ALWAYS CONTROLS HIMSELF. THIS IS WHY HE IS FREE.

43

MASTER, BECAUSE THE DEPTH OF REALITY IS UNFATHOMABLE, ULTIMATELY EVERYTHING IS UNKNOWABLE. PERCEPTIONS COVER UP THE MYSTERY WITH A LABEL, WITH AN EXPLANATION. IT IS THESE CONCEPTS, OR MENTAL LABELS THAT TAKE YOU AWAY FROM THE FLEXIBILITY OF REALITY. THE QUICKER YOU ARE IN ATTACHING LABELS TO THAT WHICH YOU PERCEIVE, THE MORE YOU PERCEIVE REALITY THROUGH A MENTAL SCREEN OF CONCEPTUALIZATION, THE MORE LIFELESS, FLAT, AND SHALLOW YOUR REALITY SHALL BECOME. WHEN YOU ARE FREE FROM CONCEPTS, OR THE NEED TO CONCEPTUALIZE, REALITY COMES TO LIFE AND BECOMES WHATEVER YOU NEED IT TO BE. WHEN YOU ARE NOT FREE FROM CONCEPTS, OR THE NEED TO CONCEPTUALIZE, REALITY BECOMES DEAD AND YOU BECOME WHATEVER CIRCUMSTANCES DICTATE. IN THIS WORLD, THE MAJORITY OF PEOPLE DON'T INHABIT A LIVING REALITY, BUT ONE THAT IS CONCEPTUALIZED. IN THIS WORLD, MOST ARE SLAVES TO THEIR OWN ILLUSIONS. ALL THE GOODNESS IN LIFE LIES IN THE STILL GAP THAT LIES BETWEEN THE PERCEPTION OF A THING AND YOUR INTERPRETATION OF THAT PERCEPTION. FOR IN THAT GAP LIES THE FREEDOM OF CHOICE AND THE AWARENESS OF THAT FREEDOM.

44

MASTER, WHILE ALL HAVE THE POTENTIAL TO BE KING, FEW ARE AWARE OF THIS POTENTIAL. EVEN FEWER POSSESS THE FOCUS TO CROWN THEMSELVES WITH THE **UNDERSTANDING** NECESSARY TO SIT ON THE THRONE. BECAUSE OF THIS, MASTER, THERE ARE FEW THAT SHALL BE ABLE TO UNDERSTAND YOU. THEY SHALL BE BLINDED BY THEIR OWN REFLECTION. THEY SHALL NOT BE ABLE TO PERCEIVE YOUR GREATNESS; THUS, THEY SHALL ATTEMPT TO TELL YOU THAT YOU ARE NOT GREAT. THEY SHALL ATTEMPT TO CONVINCE YOU THAT YOU ARE NOT **KING**. AND BECAUSE IT SEEMS TO BE THE TENDENCY OF ORDINARY MEN TO MAKE IT THEIR SOLEMN DUTY NEVER TO OPEN THEIR MINDS, NOTHING THAT YOU SHALL BE ABLE TO SAY SHALL MAKE THEM SEE OTHERWISE. IF YOU TAKE HEED OF NOTHING ELSE WRITTEN IN THESE PAGES, TAKE HEED OF THIS. ALL THAT MATTERS IS WHAT YOU BELIEVE YOURSELF TO BE. NOTHING ELSE MATTERS. LEAST OF ALL, ANYONE ELSE'S OPINION. UNAWARE OF WHO THEY ARE THEMSELVES, THERE SHALL BE MANY THAT YOU ENCOUNTER IN YOUR LIFE THAT SHALL ATTEMPT TO TELL YOU WHO YOU ARE. NEVER ALLOW HOW YOU ARE SEEN BY OTHERS TO BECOME A MIRROR THAT TELLS YOU WHO YOU ARE. IN THE WAR THAT IS LIFE, IT IS THE REPORT OF YOUR OWN INTELLIGENCE THAT SHOULD BE MOST HOSPITABLY RECEIVED AND TREATED WITH RESPECT. STAY FAR FROM THE COMPANY OF THOSE WHO DO NOT KNOW WHO THEY ARE, AND YET HAVE THE AUDACITY TO TRY TO CONVINCE YOU THAT YOU ARE WHO THEY SAY. THERE IS NOTHING MORE DANGEROUS THAN A CONFUSED PERSON WHO IS SURE OF EVERYTHING.

45

MASTER, EVERYTHING THAT YOU REGARD AS GOOD OR BAD IS ONLY THAT WAY BECAUSE OF YOUR OPINION OF IT. NOT ONLY DO YOU HAVE THE OPTION OF HAVING NO OPINION, BUT YOU ALSO HAVE THE FREEDOM TO CHOOSE WHAT OPINION OF A THING THAT YOU WISH TO HAVE. IT IS EVEN WITHIN YOUR **POWER** TO REFUSE TO REGARD PAIN AS BAD. FROM THE PERSPECTIVE OF THE UNIVERSE, THAT WHICH WE CALL PAIN IS MERELY CHANGE. ONLY THE MIND LABELS THIS CHANGE AS BAD, AND BECAUSE OF THIS LABELING, THE CHANGE IS SEEN AS PAINFUL. HOWEVER, IF YOU RECLAIM YOUR **POWER** TO FORM YOUR OWN JUDGMENTS AND REFUSE TO LABEL THE CHANGE AS BAD, YOUR SOUL SHALL REMAIN UNCLOUDED, IN PERFECT EQUANIMITY, AND IN COMPLETE CONTROL OF ITS FORCES. YOU SHALL BE COMPLETELY FREE OF THE WEAKNESS THAT PAIN INDUCES. NOTHING BAD CAN ENTER YOUR SOUL WITHOUT THE CONSENT OF YOUR MIND. YOUR PAIN BECOMES YOUR **STRENGTH** WHEN YOU ARE FREE TO USE IT AS MOTIVATION. WHEN YOU ARE ABLE TO USE IT AS MOTIVATION, IT SHALL BECOME THE FUEL THAT PROPELS YOU TO GREATNESS.

A **KING** IS ABLE TO USE ANY AND ALL THINGS TO AID HIS PURPOSES. WHATEVER MEANING YOU WANT THE UNIVERSE TO REFLECT, IT SHALL PROVIDE. FOR ALL EVENTS COME FROM THE CREATIVE SOURCE WITHIN YOURSELF. RATHER THAN THINKING, "THIS EXPERIENCE IS HAPPENING TO ME," THINK, "**I AM** CREATING THIS EXPERIENCE." IT IS IMPOSSIBLE FOR WORLDLY CIRCUMSTANCES TO TOUCH, ALTER, OR MOVE YOUR MIND. THE MIND ALTERS AND MOVES ITSELF, WHILE MOLDING THE WORLD INTO THE SHAPE OF WHATEVER JUDGMENTS THAT IT PLEASES

ITSELF TO MAKE. NEVER, UNLESS YOU ARE SEEKING TO ACHIEVE SOME GREAT GOOD ON THE BEHALF OF ANOTHER, MUST YOU CONCERN YOURSELF WITH WHAT ANOTHER IS SAYING, DOING, OR THINKING.

UNDERSTAND, THERE IS NOTHING MORE PATHETICALLY PITIFUL THAN THE MAN WHO, FAILING TO REALIZE THAT THE ONLY MIND WHICH HE NEED CONCERN HIMSELF WITH AND SERVE WITH DEVOTION IS HIS OWN, RELENTLESSLY WALKS AROUND, SEEMINGLY WITH THE SOLE PURPOSE OF GUESSING WHAT OTHERS ARE THINKING. BECAUSE HE KNOWS THAT THE WORLD REFLECTS BACK TO A MAN THAT WHICH HE HAS ALREADY DECIDED IN HIS HEART, A **KING** CULTIVATES HIS HEART WITH MAGNIFICENCE. FOR HE KNOWS THAT THIS IS EXACTLY WHAT IS NECESSARY TO DO IN ORDER TO PERCEIVE A MAGNIFICENT REALITY. A **KING** SEEKS AT ALL TIMES TO BE EXCELLENCE PERSONIFIED. A **KING** UNDERSTANDS THAT EVERYTHING IS THE WAY THAT IT IS BECAUSE YOU PERCEIVE IT THAT WAY. AND BECAUSE YOU ARE YOUR PERCEPTION, EVERYTHING IS THE WAY THAT IT IS BECAUSE YOU ARE THAT WAY. BECAUSE A **KING** UNDERSTANDS THE DEEP INTERRELATEDNESS BETWEEN ONE'S STATE OF CONSCIOUSNESS AND THEIR EXTERNAL REALITY, A **KING** SEEKS TO GROW SPIRITUALLY AND MENTALLY BEFORE HE SEEKS TO GROW IN THE WORLD. FOR A **KING** UNDERSTANDS THAT IT IS IMPOSSIBLE FOR ONE'S CONSCIOUSNESS TO UNFOLD WITHOUT ALSO UNFOLDING OUTSIDE EVENTS THAT MIRROR IT. ALTHOUGH A **KING** IS BOMBARDED CONSTANTLY BY THE OBSERVATIONS AND OPINIONS OF OTHERS, HE RECOGNIZES THAT NONE OF THESE OBSERVATIONS OR OPINIONS SHALL BE ABLE TO AFFECT HIM UNLESS HIS MIND ACKNOWLEDGES AND ACCEPTS THEM.

46

MASTER, WHILE IT IS PEOPLE THAT CREATE ASSUMPTIONS, ASSUMPTIONS OFTEN CONTROL PEOPLE. ASSUMPTIONS ARE NAUGHT BUT STUCK FROZEN PERCEPTIONS THAT NO LONGER HARMONIZE WITH THE PRESENT MOMENT. THUS, YOU SHOULD NEVER MAKE ASSUMPTIONS. YOU MUST ALWAYS REMAIN PREPARED TO CHANGE YOUR PERCEPTION IF IT IS NO LONGER CONCORDANT WITH THE PRESENT MOMENT. ASSUMPTIONS INHIBIT YOUR GROWTH, FOR ASSUMPTIONS ARE THE ONLY ADVERSARY CAPABLE OF DEFEATING LEARNING. ASSUMPTIONS ARE PERCEPTIONS THAT YOU ARE UNAWARE THAT YOU HAVE EVEN MADE. THEY ARE PERCEPTIONS WITHOUT AWARENESS. THEY ARE IGNORANT PERCEPTIONS. THIS IS WHY IT IS SO IMPORTANT THAT YOU CULTIVATE AWARENESS, THE DESTROYER OF IGNORANCE.

AWARENESS IS LIKE THE RISING SUN OVER THE DARK HORIZON. JUST AS THE LIGHT FROM THE RISING SUN SIGNALS THE END OF DARKNESS, THE LIGHT FROM RISING AWARENESS SIGNALS THE END OF IGNORANCE. THE RECOGNITION OF YOUR OWN DARKNESS IS THE ARISING OF YOUR LIGHT. THE RECOGNITION OF YOUR INSANITY IS THE ARISING OF SANITY. THE RECOGNITION OF YOUR OWN IGNORANCE IS THE ARISING OF **WISDOM**.

47

MASTER, THERE IS NO UNIVERSE EXCEPT THE ONE THAT YOU PERCEIVE RIGHT NOW. NOTHING EXISTS OUTSIDE OF THE PRESENT MOMENT. THE PRESENT MOMENT IS **THE TRUTH**. THUS, IT IS IN THIS MOMENT THAT YOU MUST BE AWARE. IT IS IN THIS MOMENT THAT YOU MUST BE A **KING**. YOUR

WILLPOWER IS DIRECTLY TIED TO WHAT YOU BELIEVE IS POSSIBLE. WHEN YOU BECOME AWARE OF **THE TRUTH** OF YOUR OWN **POWER**, YOU SHALL BECOME AWARE THAT ANYTHING IS POSSIBLE. WHEN YOU ARE AWARE THAT ANYTHING IS POSSIBLE, YOUR WILLPOWER SHALL SHOW EVIDENCE OF YOUR BELIEF.

48

MASTER, FOR THE WELL-BEING OF YOUR KINGDOM, IT IS VITAL THAT YOU ALWAYS MAINTAIN A CONFIDENT, CONSTRUCTIVE, AND EVER FORWARD MOVING DISPOSITION OF THE MIND OVER ANY GIVEN SET OF CIRCUMSTANCES WHICH MAY AFFLICT YOU. ON YOUR PATH TO THE THRONE, NOT ALL OF THE ROADS THAT YOU SHALL TRAVEL SHALL BE SMOOTH. IN FACT, BECAUSE THE PATH TO KINGSHIP IS A PATH THAT FEW HAVE OR EVER SHALL VENTURE UPON, IF YOU DO DECIDE TO BE **KING**, YOUR ROAD SHALL BE LARGELY UNDEVELOPED AND FULL OF UNKNOWN PERILS. BE COURAGEOUS, MY SON, AND TAKE HEART. FOR THERE IS NO DILEMMA OR DIFFICULTY THAT HAS EVER EXISTED THAT WAS ABLE TO WITHSTAND THE ASSAULT OF PROTRACTED, ORGANIZED THOUGHT.

ORGANIZED THOUGHT IS FOCUSED THOUGHT. IT IS CONCENTRATED THOUGHT. WHILE UNFOCUSED, UNORGANIZED THOUGHT IS LARGELY INEFFICIENT AND IMPOTENT, ORGANIZED, FOCUSED THOUGHT IS AN IRRESISTIBLE FORCE THAT SHALL ERADICATE ALL IMPEDIMENTS FROM YOUR PATH. THE MIND HAS THE **POWER** TO TRANSMUTE ALL THAT OBSTRUCTS ITS ACTIVITY INTO THINGS THAT HELP IT, ALL THAT HINDERS ITS LABOR INTO AID, AND ALL THAT ATTEMPTS TO BARRICADE ITS PATH INTO AN ESCORT ON ITS JOURNEY. THINK OF A FIRE. EVERYTHING THAT

STANDS IN A FIRE'S PATH NOT ONLY FAILS TO HINDER IT BUT ADDS FUEL TO THE FIRE'S DETERMINATION.

49

MASTER, IT IS BY RESERVING ITS OPINIONS AND JUDGMENTS AND BEING EVER READY TO HARMONIZE WITH THE PRESENT MOMENT AND CHANGE THAT YOUR MIND SHALL BE ABLE TO BYPASS OR DISPEL ANY AND ALL OBSTACLES THAT DARE ATTEMPT TO IMPEDE ITS PROGRESS TO THE THRONE. IT IS BY MAINTAINING YOUR MIND IN THIS STATE THAT YOU SHALL BE ABLE TO USE WHATEVER OPPOSES YOU AS A MEANS TO ACHIEVE YOUR OWN INTENTIONS, AND IN THE PROCESS, TURN ROADBLOCKS INTO ROADS. IT IS BY FREEING YOUR MIND OF ALL SELF-IMPOSED LIMITATIONS THAT YOU SHALL BE ABLE TO FIND SOLUTIONS TO ALL OF YOUR PROBLEMS, REGARDLESS OF THEIR NATURE. AMIDST THE STORMS OF LIFE, THE MORE YOU ARE ABLE TO STAY FOCUSED, THE BETTER YOU SHALL BE ABLE TO ADAPT YOUR THOUGHTS TO CHANGING CIRCUMSTANCES, AND THE MORE POWERFUL YOUR RESPONSES SHALL BE. THE MORE DISTRACTED YOU BECOME BY THE ILLUSIONS OF DOUBT, THE WEAKER YOUR RESPONSES TO REALITY SHALL BE. JUST AS A HEALTHY STOMACH IS ABLE TO DIGEST ALL SORTS OF FOOD, SO TOO CAN A FOCUSED MIND HANDLE WHATSOEVER MAY BEFALL IT.

50

MASTER, CIRCUMSTANCES ARE MERELY THE MEANS BY WHICH THE MIND IS ABLE TO VIEW ITSELF. THE MIND CAN ONLY ATTRACT THAT WHICH IT PRIVATELY SHELTERS. YOUR INNER WORLD AND YOUR OUTER WORLD ARE ALWAYS LINKED. THUS, TO CLEAR YOUR

LIFE OF DIFFICULTIES, YOU MUST ADDRESS AND CLEAR UP THE
INNER CONFUSION WITHIN YOUR MIND BY FOCUSING YOUR
THOUGHTS. IF YOU MANAGE TO DO THIS, ALL CONFUSION AND
DISORDER SHALL DISAPPEAR FROM YOUR EXTERNAL WORLD AS
WELL. THE CHANGES IN YOUR CIRCUMSTANCES SHALL ALWAYS BE
IN EXACT RATIO WITH THE CHANGES IN YOUR THOUGHTS. THE
RESULTS SHALL INVARIABLY BE FAILURE WHEN YOU ATTEMPT TO
CHANGE YOUR EXTERNAL REALITY WITHOUT FIRST CHANGING
YOUR INNER REALITY.

51

MASTER, IT IS NOT YOU, BUT ONLY YOUR MIND THAT GETS
AGITATED, DISTURBED, OR VEXED WHEN IT ENCOUNTERS
HARDSHIPS. THE MIND FEELS THIS WAY WHEN IT IS NOT IN
HARMONY WITH THE PRESENT MOMENT. IT GETS OUT OF
HARMONY WITH THE PRESENT MOMENT WHEN IT GETS STUCK IN
THE BELIEF THAT WHAT IS NOW HAPPENING SHOULD NOT BE
HAPPENING. BECAUSE IT IS ATTACHED TO A PERCEPTION THAT IS
OUT OF SYNC WITH THE PRESENT MOMENT, IT RESISTS WHAT IS
AND CLASHES WITH **THE TRUTH**. THIS IS WHAT CAUSES
SUFFERING.

52

MASTER, THERE ARE NO SUCH THINGS AS STRESSFUL SITUATIONS.
THE STRESS FELT IN SITUATIONS IS THE PRODUCT OF A PERSON'S
FAILURE TO CULTIVATE HIS MIND TO REMAIN CALM IN THE FACE
OF THE STIMULUS. THERE IS NOTHING IN EXISTENCE THAT IS
CAPABLE OF MAKING YOU UPSET IF YOU DO NOT GIVE IT YOUR
CONSENT TO DO SO. THERE IS NOTHING OUTSIDE OF YOUR

MIND THAT CAN DISTURB IT. ALL OF YOUR PERTURBATIONS COME FROM YOUR MIND'S OPINION OF WHAT LIES OUTSIDE OF IT. BECAUSE THE THINGS THAT BOTHER YOU ARE THE PRODUCTS OF YOUR OWN OPINIONS, YOU ALWAYS HAVE THE **POWER** TO STRIKE THEM FROM YOUR MIND AND FREE YOURSELF OF THEM. IT IS ESSENTIAL THAT YOU LEARN TO DETACH YOURSELF FROM YOUR OPINIONS. FOR ONLY THAT WHICH YOU ARE ATTACHED TO HAS THE **POWER** TO DISTURB YOU. THERE IS NO EVIL OR HARM THAT CAN EVER IMPAIR YOUR ABILITY TO THINK UNLESS YOU ALLOW IT.

53

MASTER, CHANGE IS NEVER AS SERIOUS AS YOUR MIND MAKES IT OUT TO BE. THERE IS NOTHING LIKE CHANGE TO ELEVATE YOUR MIND AND HEIGHTEN YOUR PERCEPTIVITY. WHEN IT IS YOUR TURN TO EXPERIENCE CHANGE, INSTEAD OF RAILING AGAINST IT AND COMPLAINING, YOU SHOULD WELCOME IT AS YOU WOULD AN OLD FRIEND, EVEN IF YOUR MIND IS OF A DIFFERENT OPINION. FOR YOU MUST NEVER WAIT ON YOUR MIND TO GIVE YOU PERMISSION TO ENJOY LIFE.

54

MASTER, PEOPLE WALLOW IN HATRED ONLY WHEN THEY BELIEVE THEY ARE UNABLE TO ASCEND HIGHER. YOUR SELF-IMAGE IS A REFLECTION OF YOUR SELF-ESTEEM. NO MATTER WHAT VILENESS OTHERS MAY PROJECT UPON YOU, YOU MUST NEVER ALLOW THIS TO AFFECT YOUR GENIALITY. TO MAKE YOUR MIND STATE SUBJECT TO THE OPINION THAT OTHERS HAVE OF YOU IS TO FORFEIT RESPECT FOR YOURSELF. NEVER BLAME SOMEONE ELSE

FOR YOUR OWN PROBLEMS. FOR EVEN IF THIS BLAME SEEMS JUSTIFIED, AS LONG AS YOU BLAME OTHERS FOR YOUR CONDITION, THEY SHALL ALWAYS HAVE A CERTAIN MEASURE OF **POWER** OVER YOU. A **KING** IS DEPENDENT UPON NONE BUT HIMSELF. FOR A **KING** IS **THE TRUTH**. OTHERS' THOUGHTS AND OPINIONS ARE IRRELEVANT TO YOUR REALITY. IT IS ONLY THE **UNDERSTANDING** OF THE WORKINGS OF YOUR OWN MIND THAT SHALL LEAD YOU TO THE THRONE. ALTHOUGH YOUR ACTIONS MAY BE HINDERED BY ANOTHER, DUE TO THE ABILITY OF YOUR MIND TO ADAPT TO ANY CHANGE, NEVER CAN ANOTHER HINDER YOUR MOTIVATION. AS A **KING**, YOUR STATE OF MIND MUST BE FREE FROM THE CHAINS OF DOUBT AND FEAR. WHEN THERE IS DOUBT AND FEAR IN RELATION TO THE COURSE OF ACTION YOU HAVE DECIDED TO TAKE, YOU SHALL FIND GREAT DIFFICULTY IN SUITING YOUR THOUGHTS TO YOUR VISION.

55

MASTER, THE CAUSE OF VIOLENCE AND WAR LIE WITHIN THE MIND. MEN ONLY INJURE BECAUSE OF THOUGHTS OF FEAR OR HATRED. BOTH FEAR AND HATRED STEM FROM A LACK OF **UNDERSTANDING**. MEN FEAR WHAT THEY DO NOT UNDERSTAND AND HATE THAT WHICH THEY FEAR. THAT WHICH MEN DO NOT UNDERSTAND, THEY MAKE AN ENEMY OUT OF AND SEEK TO DESTROY. THE LACK OF **UNDERSTANDING** IS THE GERM FROM WHICH ALL ENEMIES GERMINATE. HE WHO POSSESSES **UNDERSTANDING** HAS NO ENEMIES. FOR HE UNDERSTANDS, THAT IN A WAR, THE ONLY MAN SURE TO PREVAIL IS THE MAN WHO HAS NOT AN ENEMY.

56

MASTER, THE CELESTIAL POWER OF INTELLIGENCE SHALL ALWAYS DEFEAT THE INIQUITOUS POWER OF IGNORANCE. THE MOST IMPORTANT ASPECT OF YOUR MIND IS YOUR ATTENTION. IT IS YOUR ATTENTION THAT MAKES IT POSSIBLE FOR YOU TO FOCUS UPON A SINGLE THOUGHT, OBJECT, OR AIM OUT OF AN INFINITE RANGE OF POSSIBILITIES. TO GIVE YOUR ATTENTION TO SOMETHING IS TO PROJECT AN EXTENSION OF YOUR MENTAL ENERGY THAT SHALL LINK YOUR MIND TO THAT WHICH YOU ARE FOCUSED UPON. THIS EXTENSION OF MENTAL ENERGY SERVES AS A BRIDGE FOR KNOWLEDGE AND ALLOWS IT TO TRAVEL FROM THAT WHICH YOUR ATTENTION IS PLACED TO YOUR MIND. ATTENTION IS WHAT LINKS ONE MIND TO ANOTHER AND IS THE CHANNEL THAT ONE MUST USE TO SEND AND RECEIVE MESSAGES FROM PERSON TO PERSON. IT IS THROUGH ATTENTION THAT KNOWLEDGE FROM OUTSIDE YOUR MIND IS COMMUNICATED TO THE INSIDE OF YOUR MIND, AND KNOWLEDGE FROM INSIDE YOUR MIND IS TRANSMITTED OUTSIDE. IT IS IMPOSSIBLE TO TEACH SOMEONE IF YOU DO NOT HAVE THEIR ATTENTION, NOR IS IT POSSIBLE TO LEARN SOMETHING IF YOU DO NOT GIVE THAT WHICH YOU WISH TO LEARN YOUR ATTENTION.

57

MASTER, IT IS YOUR WILL THAT DIRECTS YOUR ATTENTION. THE MORE POWERFUL YOUR WILL, THE LONGER YOU SHALL BE ABLE TO HOLD YOUR ATTENTION UPON AN OBJECT, AND THE MORE KNOWLEDGE YOU SHALL BE ABLE TO GAIN FROM THAT OBJECT. CONVERSELY, THE WEAKER YOUR WILL, THE SHORTER

YOUR ATTENTION SPAN SHALL BE AND THE LESS **KNOWLEDGE** YOU SHALL BE ABLE TO ATTAIN FROM AN OBJECT. A SHORT ATTENTION SPAN SHALL MAKE ALL OF YOUR PERCEPTIONS AND RELATIONSHIPS BOTH SHALLOW AND MEDIOCRE. FOR THE LESS **KNOWLEDGE** YOU HAVE OF SOMETHING, THE LESS YOU SHALL UNDERSTAND IT.

58

MASTER, YOUR ATTENTION AND THAT WHICH YOU FOCUS YOUR ATTENTION UPON SHALL DETERMINE YOUR REALITY. BY CHOOSING WHICH THOUGHTS YOU GIVE YOUR ATTENTION TO, YOU GAIN THE ABILITY TO CHANGE THEM FROM INHIBITORS TO EMPOWEREES. IT IS VITAL THAT YOU ARE AWARE OF WHAT YOU ARE FOCUSING YOUR MIND UPON. ATTENTION IS PAID RIGHT NOW IN THE PRESENT MOMENT, OR IT IS NOT PAID AT ALL. WHATEVER YOU PAY ATTENTION TO SHALL GROW. THIS IS WHY, AS MUCH AS POSSIBLE, YOU MUST FOCUS UPON **THE TRUTH** THAT RESIDES WITHIN YOU. FOR **THE TRUTH** IS THE FOUNDATION OF ALL THAT IS GOOD, AND IT SHALL ALWAYS WILLINGLY POUR FORTH GOODNESS IF YOU WOULD PERSISTENTLY TURN YOUR ATTENTION TO IT.

59

MASTER, ONCE YOU DEVELOP THE **POWER** OF SELF-DISCIPLINE, WHICH IS THE **POWER** OF FOCUS, NOTHING WITHIN THE REALM OF HUMAN POSSIBILITY SHALL BE IMPOSSIBLE FOR YOU TO ACHIEVE. FOR EQUIPPED WITH THIS **POWER**, YOU SHALL GAIN THE **DIVINE** ABILITY TO ORGANIZE THOUGHT INTO MATTER, AND MATTER INTO FORM. TO FOCUS YOUR MIND IS TO MAKE IT

EVER SHARPER AND MORE EXACT. IT IS THE ABILITY TO FOCUS EXCLUSIVELY ON YOUR OWN THOUGHTS THAT SHALL BESTOW UPON YOU THE **POWER** TO CHANGE THE ENTIRE WORLD.

60

MASTER, NO GREAT THING WAS EVER ACHIEVED WITH IMPATIENCE. ONE CANNOT HELP BUT BE IMPATIENT WHEN THEY POSSESS AN UNFOCUSED MIND. YOU MUST MAKE IT YOUR DAILY OBJECTIVE TO PURGE YOUR MIND OF ALL AIMLESS AND VAIN THOUGHTS. ESPECIALLY THOSE THAT INQUIRE INTO THE AFFAIRS OF OTHERS OR WISH THEM HARM. BECAUSE A FOCUSED MIND HAS NO ROOM IN IT FOR ANXIETY, OR THE EFFECTS OF AN OVERACTIVE, FEARFUL IMAGINATION, THERE IS NO SAFER PLACE TO TAKE ASYLUM THAN A FOCUSED MIND. THE VERY BEST QUALITY THAT ANY LEADER CAN HAVE IS A COOL, STRONG, AND FOCUSED MIND WHICH ABSORBS PRECISE IMPRESSIONS OF PHENOMENA, NEVER GETS HEATED, AND NEVER ALLOWS ITSELF TO BE BLINDED OR BEWILDERED BY EITHER GOOD OR BAD REPORTS.

61

MASTER, THE KEY TO VICTORY IN ANY ENTERPRISE LIES IN YOUR ABILITY TO CONCENTRATE AND FOCUS YOUR THOUGHTS ON ONE TASK AT A TIME. THE DIVISION OF YOUR ATTENTION SHALL LEAD YOU ONLY TO CONFUSION. CONCENTRATION IS THE SECRET OF **STRENGTH**. ANY **POWER**, WHETHER THOUGHT OR PHYSICAL, IS ACHIEVED BY THE CONCENTRATION OF ENERGY. TO TAKE THE TIME TO CONCENTRATE YOUR MENTAL ENERGY ON THE ACQUISITION OF SOME USEFUL AND BENEFICIAL **KNOWLEDGE**, IS TO TAKE THE TIME TO STOP IT FROM

FLITTING ABOUT FUTILELY. IT IS OF THE UTMOST IMPORTANCE THAT YOU TAKE THE TIME TO LEARN TO FOCUS YOUR MIND AND CONCENTRATE YOUR THOUGHTS. FOR FOCUSED, POSITIVE THOUGHTS ARE INFINITELY MORE POWERFUL IN THE ACCOMPLISHMENT OF DESIRES THAN NEGATIVE, CONFUSED THOUGHTS SHALL EVER BE.

62

MASTER, IN TIMES OF ADVERSITY ESPECIALLY, A STRONG MIND SHALL PAY IMMENSE DIVIDENDS. CREATIVITY FLOURISHES UNDER PRESSURE IN THOSE WHO HAVE A STRONG MIND. A **KING** MUST HAVE A STRONG MIND, FOR A WEAK, UNFOCUSED MIND IS ONE THAT IS EASILY LED ASTRAY. ANY NEW **KNOWLEDGE**, EVEN THAT WHICH IS ALTOGETHER COMPOSED OF FOLLY, IS CAPABLE OF ARRESTING A WEAK MIND AND IMPRISONING IT TO THE EXTENT THAT IT NO LONGER SEES, HEARS, OR LEARNS ANYTHING ELSE. IT IS ONLY THROUGH A COMBINATION OF THEORY (WHICH THIS LETTER IS TO YOU), CONTEMPLATION, AND PRACTICE THAT YOU SHALL DEVELOP THE MENTAL **STRENGTH** NECESSARY TO MOLD ANY SET OF CONDITIONS INTO CIRCUMSTANCES THAT SHALL MEET THE REQUIREMENTS OF YOUR DESIRES AND NEEDS. IT IS INTENSITY OF THOUGHT, MY SON, NOT EXTENSITY, THAT SHALL GIVE RISE TO BRILLIANCE IN THE MIND, IN WHICH IT IS CONTAINED, AND CAUSES THE ONE WHO POSSESSES THAT MIND TO RISE TO THE HEIGHTS OF SUBLIME REGALITY.

63

MASTER, IT IS A QUEER PECULIARITY OF HUMAN NATURE, THAT WHILE MOST MEN LOVE THEMSELVES MORE THAN THEY LOVE OTHERS, MOST MEN CARE MORE ABOUT WHAT OTHERS THINK OF THEM THAN WHAT THEY THINK OF THEMSELVES. THIS IS WHY THE MAJORITY OF PEOPLE IN THE WORLD ARE MORE OR LESS THE SLAVES OF HEREDITY, ENVIRONMENT, OR CIRCUMSTANCE, AND THUS MANIFEST VERY LITTLE FREEDOM. THEY ARE SWAYED FROM THEIR POSITION BY THE OPINIONS, CUSTOMS, AND THOUGHTS OF THE OUTSIDE WORLD. NO MAN SHALL EVER BE TRULY FREE UNTIL HE LEARNS TO DO HIS OWN THINKING AND GAINS THE COURAGE TO ACT ON HIS OWN INITIATIVE. THERE SHALL BE NO GREATER DAY IN ANY MAN'S LIFE THAN THE DAY WHEN HE FREES HIMSELF FROM HIS SOCIAL CONDITIONING AND BEGINS TO ACT UPON HIS OWN INCLINATIONS WITH GUMPTION. FOR THIS IS THE DAY WHEN HE SHALL BEGIN HIS JOURNEY TO THE THRONE. THE LESSON THAT ALL EXPERIENCES TEACH IS THE LESSON OF SELF-RELIANCE. IT IS YOUR EXPERIENCES, AS WELL AS YOUR ABILITY TO LEARN FROM THEM THAT SHALL GIVE YOU THE FREEDOM TO BE YOUR OWN AUTHORITY.

64

MASTER, YOU MUST VALUE THE FREEDOM TO THINK INDEPENDENTLY MORE THAN ANY OTHER FREEDOM THAT YOU COULD POSSIBLY IMAGINE. UNDER NO CIRCUMSTANCES ARE YOU EVER TO ALLOW ANYONE TO DO YOUR THINKING FOR YOU. WHILE IT MAY BE TRUE THAT YOU SHOULD OBTAIN FACTS, INTELLIGENCE, AND COUNSEL FROM OTHERS, YOU MUST ALWAYS RESERVE THE RIGHT TO HONOR OR DISCARD SUCH COUNSEL,

EITHER IN WHOLE OR IN PART, AS YOU SEE FIT. FOR TO DO OTHERWISE IS TO ALLOW ANOTHER TO RULE YOUR KINGDOM.

65

MASTER, CHANGE IS THE REAL NATURE OF EXISTENCE. WHEN YOU TRULY REALIZE THIS, YOUR MIND SHALL BECOME PREPARED AND ABLE AT ALL TIMES TO EMBRACE CHANGE. THIS, IN TURN, SHALL MAKE IT ADAPTABLE AND ALERT. AN ADAPTABLE AND ALERT MIND IS A REQUISITE FOR ALL WHO WISH TO WEAR THE CROWN. FOR THE MIND THAT CAN NO LONGER ADAPT IS DEAD, AND AN ALERT THINKING MIND IS THE ONLY TYPE OF MIND THAT SHALL CONTINUE TO GROW AND EVOLVE THROUGHOUT ITS ENTIRE LIFE. LIKE A MACHINE, YOUR MIND SHALL RUST IF YOU ALLOW IT TO REMAIN IDLE FOR TOO LONG. THE MINDS OF THE GREATEST KINGS IN HISTORY WERE FOREVER MOVING AND AT ALL TIMES, ENTHUSIASTIC AND CURIOUS. JUST AS YOURS MUST BE.

66

MASTER, YOUR WILL IS WHAT GIVES YOU THE **POWER** TO CHOOSE THAT WHICH YOU WISH TO DO OR FOCUS UPON. YOUR WILL IS **KING**, BECAUSE YOUR WILL IS FREE. WHILE IT IS NOT POSSIBLE FOR YOU TO BE ROBBED OF YOUR FREE WILL, IT IS POSSIBLE FOR YOU TO SURRENDER IT. TO SURRENDER YOUR WILL TO SOMETHING OUTSIDE OF YOURSELF IS TO CEDE YOUR AUTHORITY TO SOMETHING OUTSIDE OF YOURSELF. A **KING**, BY THE USE OF HIS WILL, IS ABLE TO ATTAIN A DEGREE OF POISE AND MENTAL FOCUS THAT IS ALMOST IMPOSSIBLE TO BELIEVE, BY THOSE WHO ALLOW THEMSELVES TO BE SWUNG BACKWARD AND FORWARD BY THE MENTAL PENDULUM OF THEIR DESIRES AND

IMPULSES. THE UNFOLDMENT OF YOUR AWARENESS IS DEPENDENT TOTALLY UPON YOUR WILL.

THE MORE YOU EXERCISE YOUR WILL AND USE IT TO FOCUS UPON, AND SEARCH FOR THE ULTIMATE MEANING OF YOUR LIFE, THE MORE YOU SHALL HEIGHTEN YOUR AWARENESS AND GAIN ACCESS TO THE INFINITE **POWER** OF **THE TRUTH**. WHEN YOU FOCUS ON **THE TRUTH**, YOU SHALL BECOME AWARE OF WHO YOU ARE NOT. WHEN YOU BECOME AWARE OF WHO YOU ARE NOT, THE REALITY OF WHO YOU ARE SHALL EMERGE ALL BY ITSELF.

67

MASTER, IN ORDER TO ESTABLISH THE THRONE OF YOUR WILL AND TRULY BECOME KING, YOU MUST FREE YOUR WILL FROM THE TYRANNY OF YOUR EMOTIONS. YOUR EMOTIONS ARE SERVANTS. YOUR WILL IS **KING**. IF YOU ALLOW SERVANTS TO RULE, THEY SHALL CRUELLY ENSLAVE YOUR MIND AND THEN DEVASTATION, DISCORD, AND EMBARRASSMENT SHALL ENSUE. YOUR EMOTIONS, STUCK IN THE MIRE OF THEIR UNAWARENESS, SHALL BRUTALIZE THOSE IN YOUR CIRCUMFERENCE WITH IGNORANCE AND BE THE CAUSE OF YOUR KINGDOM'S DEMISE. THIS WOULD BE THE SAME AS ALLOWING THE SOLDIERS ON THE BATTLEFIELD TO DIRECT THE BATTLE INSTEAD OF THE **KING** WHO SITS HIGH ABOVE ALL WITH THE **POWER** OF AWARENESS. UNABLE TO SEE THE ENTIRETY OF THE BATTLEFIELD, THEIR STRATEGIES SHALL BE INACCURATE. FOR THEY SHALL BE BASED UPON INADEQUATE **KNOWLEDGE** AND PETTY INDULGENCES. THEY SHALL BE TOO CAUGHT UP IN FEELINGS OF FEAR AND THE OVERALL CHAOS OF THE BATTLE TO STRATEGIZE EFFECTIVELY. YOUR EMOTIONS SHALL TURN UPON YOU AND BETRAY YOU TO

YOUR ENEMIES EVEN AS YOU SLEEP, ULTIMATELY PROVING TO BE THE SOURCE OF YOUR RUIN. ALL OF THE INFORMATION THAT YOUR INTELLIGENCE ATTEMPTS TO PROVIDE, YOU SHALL BE DISTORTED AND WARPED BY THESE DESPOTS. YOU SHALL BE UNABLE TO SEE THE EXTENT OF THEIR TREACHERY UNTIL IT IS TOO LATE, AND YOUR REALM LIES IN DEVASTATION AROUND YOU.

THE SERVANTS THAT ARE YOUR EMOTIONS SHOULD NEVER BE ALLOWED TO RULE YOUR WILL, WHICH IS THE **KING**. TO FREE YOUR WILL FROM YOUR EMOTIONS, IS TO FREE YOURSELF FROM THE TYRANNY OF THE WORLD. IT IS ESSENTIAL THAT YOU LIBERATE YOUR **KING**, SO THAT HE MAY BE FREE TO TAKE HIS PROPER PLACE AS THE ORCHESTRATOR OF YOUR FORCES. WHEN YOU FREE YOUR WILL, AWARENESS SHALL ADVISE HIM AND HE SHALL EMANCIPATE YOUR MIND, ALLOWING PROSPERITY, ACCOMPLISHMENT, AND SUCCESS TO BE ATTENDANTS TO YOUR MAJESTY. FREE FROM THE MIRE OF IGNORANCE AND COMPULSION, YOUR WILL SHALL AMELIORATE ALL THOSE IN YOUR EMPIRE AND BE THE PROGENITOR OF YOUR KINGDOM'S TRIUMPH. TO ALLOW YOUR WILL TO RULE WITH AWARENESS IS TO SIT HIGH ABOVE THE BATTLEFIELD ON THE MOUNTAIN TOP. ALL OF YOUR DESIGNS SHALL BE CARRIED OUT WITH INTELLIGENCE, FOR THEY SHALL BE BASED UPON ACCURATE **KNOWLEDGE** AND HEROIC MOTIVATIONS. FREE FROM FEELINGS OF PETTINESS, YOU SHALL BE FILLED WITH MAGNANIMITY. FREE FROM THE OVERALL CONFUSION OF THE BATTLE, YOU SHALL BECOME INDOMITABLE. YOUR WILL SHALL PROTECT YOU EVEN AS YOU SLEEP, AND ULTIMATELY PROVE TO BE THE CAUSATION OF YOUR TRIUMPHS. ALL **KNOWLEDGE** THAT LIFE ATTEMPTS TO PROVIDE YOU; YOU SHALL RECEIVE WITH CLARITY. YOU SHALL BE FREE TO BE

ABLE TO APPRECIATE THE BEAUTY OF NOBILITY AND YOUR REALM SHALL RISE TO THE HEIGHTS OF RENOWN.

68

MASTER, THERE IS A GRAVE DIFFERENCE BETWEEN FEELING AN EMOTION AND BECOMING ONE. TO FEEL ANGER IS TO BE THE MASTER. IT IS TO BE AWARE OF THE ANGER. IT IS THE ABILITY TO USE ITS FIRE TO MELT AWAY IGNORANCE. IT IS TO BE ABLE TO USE ITS ENERGY TO FORTIFY THE FORTRESS OF YOUR FORTITUDE SO THAT YOU MAY BECOME IMPERVIOUS TO ALL AFFLICTIONS. HOWEVER, TO BE ANGRY IS A COMPLETELY DIFFERENT STORY. TO BE ANGRY IS TO BE A SLAVE TO ANGER AND IN TOTAL SUBMISSION TO ITS CAPRICIOUS DEMANDS. IT IS TO BE UNAWARE OF THE EFFECTS OF YOUR ACTIONS. IT IS TO BE BLIND TO HOW THEY ARE RUINING THE MERITS OF YOUR SUPREMACY. AN EMOTIONAL MAN, ESPECIALLY AN ANGRY MAN IS ONE THAT RARELY THINKS STRAIGHT. A DISTURBED MIND IS ONE THAT CAN EASILY BE CONTROLLED. A MIND THAT IS EASILY OVERCOME BY EMOTION CANNOT SEE THE WORLD WITH CLARITY AND SHALL ALWAYS CREATE STRATEGIES THAT SHALL MISS THE MARK. IT IS ONLY WHEN YOU STILL THE WATERS OF YOUR HEART THAT YOU SHALL BE ABLE TO SEE YOUR REFLECTION CLEARLY IN ALL THINGS. WHEN UNDERSTANDING TRIUMPHS, THE PASSIONS WITHDRAW THEMSELVES. FOR EMOTIONS SUBMIT AUTOMATICALLY TO THE OMNIPOTENT SOVEREIGNTY OF AWARENESS.

69

MASTER, LEARNING TO CONTROL YOUR EMOTIONS DOES NOT MEAN REPRESSING THEM. IT MEANS MASTERING THEM AND

LEARNING TO USE THEM TO THEIR BEST EFFECTS. TO MASTER YOUR EMOTIONS IS TO GAIN THE ABILITY TO IGNORE THEM. PEOPLE FAIL TO SOLVE THEIR PROBLEMS, NOT BECAUSE THEY ARE INCAPABLE OF FINDING A SOLUTION, BUT BECAUSE THEIR EMOTIONAL RESPONSES CLOUD AND DERAIL THE PROCESS OF **UNDERSTANDING.**

70

MASTER, NOBLE JOY IS THE PURE ENERGY THAT FUELS THE MIND'S OPTIMISM AND POSITIVE THOUGHTS. JOY IS THE MAGNET THAT ATTRACTS JOYFUL ENERGIES, AND AS A RESULT, JOYFUL SITUATIONS, AND CIRCUMSTANCES. IT IS FOR THIS REASON THAT YOU MUST ALWAYS BE VERY SELECTIVE ABOUT WHO YOU ALLOW TO INFILTRATE YOUR REALM. FOR EVERYONE IS EXTREMELY SUSCEPTIBLE TO THE EMOTIONS OF THOSE AROUND THEM. MUTINY BEGINS WITH BUT A SINGLE TREACHEROUS THOUGHT. NEVER FORGET, MY SON, YOUR JOY IS MUCH TOO IMPORTANT TO BE DEPENDENT UPON THE ILLUSIONS OF THE UPS AND DOWNS OF LIFE.

71

MASTER, YOUR MIND IS THE TOOL YOUR TRUE SELF USES TO CREATE REALITY. YOU SHALL ONLY BECOME FREE ONCE YOUR WILL, AND YOUR WILL EXCLUSIVELY, BEGINS TO CONTROL YOUR THOUGHTS AND DESIRES. ONCE YOU LEARN TO CONTROL YOUR THOUGHTS, YOU SHALL BE ABLE TO CREATE ANY THOUGHT YOU WISH. IT IS THIS MASTERY THAT SHALL MAKE YOUR MIND YOUR TOOL INSTEAD OF SOMEONE ELSE'S. IT IS THE MIND THAT CREATES ALL. MIND IS THE GREATEST FORCE ON THIS EARTH.

HE WHO HAS MASTERED HIS OWN MIND IS ABLE TO BRING ALL OTHER MINDS UNDER HIS INFLUENCE. NEVER ALLOW YOUR MIND TO CONTROL YOU. INSTEAD, CONTROL IT BY IGNORING THOSE THOUGHTS THAT DISTURB IT. IT IS THE MAN WHOSE THOUGHTS ARE ALWAYS OF ANIMAL INDULGENCES THAT SHALL NEVER BE ABLE TO THINK CLEARLY OR PLAN METHODICALLY.

72

ONCE, THERE WAS A MAN WHO LOVED HIS CAMEL. THE MAN WHO LOVED HIS CAMEL LIVED IN THE DESERT KINGDOM OF SETANIA. HIS MOST PRIZED POSSESSION WAS HIS CAMEL. HE WAS EXTREMELY PROUD OF IT, FOR THE CAMEL WAS VERY HANDSOME AND SWIFT OF FOOT. THE MAN LOVED HIS CAMEL SO MUCH THAT HE ALLOWED THE CAMEL TO NOT ONLY COME INTO HIS HOME BUT SLEEP IN THERE AS WELL. HE EVEN COOKED FOOD FOR THE CAMEL AND ALLOWED IT TO EAT FROM THE TABLE. HE HARDLY EVER DISCIPLINED THE CAMEL, EVEN WHEN THE CAMEL DID MISCHIEVOUS THINGS THAT THE MAN DIDN'T LIKE. HE PRETTY MUCH ALLOWED THE CAMEL TO DO WHATEVER IT LIKED.

ONE DAY, WORD GOT BACK TO THE MAN THAT THE **KING** NEEDED THE SWIFTEST CAMEL IN THE KINGDOM TO PERFORM A SPECIAL SERVICE TO THE LAND. IT WAS WARTIME AND THE **KING** NEEDED TO DELIVER A MESSAGE TO THE NEIGHBORING KINGDOM OF NETERIA. THE **KING** ALSO SENT WORD THAT HE WOULD REWARD THE CAMEL'S OWNER HANDSOMELY FOR THEIR SERVICES. AT ONCE, THE MAN RUSHED TO THE **KING**. HE WAS SO PROUD OF HIS CAMEL. TO HIM, HIS CAMEL WAS THE VERY BEST IN THE LAND. WHEN HE CAME BEFORE THE **KING**, THE VEHEMENCE WITH WHICH HE SPOKE OF THE SPEED OF HIS

CAMEL WAS VERY CONVINCING, AND IT WASN'T LONG BEFORE THE MAN CONVINCED THE **KING** TO GIVE HIM THIS IMPORTANT MISSION. THE **KING** TOLD THE MAN THAT THE ROAD TO NETERIA WAS LONG, BUT IF HE TRAVELED AT A STEADY PACE HE WOULD MAKE IT TO HIS DESTINATION BEFORE DARK. IT WAS VERY IMPORTANT THAT HE DID, FOR NETERIA CLOSED HER GATES AT NIGHT AND DID NOT OPEN THEM AGAIN UNTIL MORNING. THEY DID THIS BECAUSE THE DESERT WAS VERY DANGEROUS. IN FACT, TO BE STUCK IN THE DESERT AT NIGHT WAS GUARANTEED DEATH. NOT ONLY DID BANDITS AND SOLDIERS FROM THE ENEMY'S TROOPS LURK UNSEEN EVERYWHERE, BUT ALL TYPES OF WILD ANIMALS THAT HID FROM THE DESERT SUN CAME OUT AT NIGHT TO FIND A MEAL.

THE MAN ASSURED THE **KING** THAT HIS CAMEL WAS SWIFT OF FOOT AND WOULD HAVE NO TROUBLE COMPLETING THE MISSION. AS HE LAY DOWN BESIDE HIS CAMEL THAT NIGHT, HE DREAMED OF THE RICHES AND GLORY THAT HE WOULD GAIN. AS THE MAN SET OUT THE NEXT MORNING, HE WAS VERY ENTHUSIASTIC. THERE HAD BEEN AN INTENSE BATTLE THE NIGHT BEFORE SO THERE WOULD BE NO ENEMIES ABOUT TODAY. IT WAS AN UNUSUALLY HOT DAY, EVEN FOR THE DESERT, AND ALL WOULD MOST ASSUREDLY BE HIDING FROM THE SUN'S HEAT AS THEY RECOUPED FROM LAST NIGHT AND PREPARED FOR THIS ONE.

BEFORE THE MAN SET OUT, THE **KING** THANKED HIM AGAIN FOR HIS SERVICE AND GAVE HIM SOME FINAL ADVICE FOR HIS JOURNEY. HE TOLD THE MAN THAT HE HAD TO BE CAREFUL NOT TO STOP AT ALL OF THE OASES ALONG THE WAY. HE ALSO TOLD HIM TO BE CAREFUL NOT TO STAY TOO LONG AT THE ONES HE DID STOP AT. FOR IF HE DID, HE WOULD NOT MAKE IT TO NETERIA BEFORE DARK. THE MAN ASSURED THE **KING** AGAIN

THAT HIS CAMEL WAS SWIFT OF FOOT AND WOULD SURELY MAKE IT TO NETERIA IN TIME.

AS HE STARTED ON HIS JOURNEY, HE WAS IN GREAT SPIRITS. HE WOULD FINALLY HAVE A CHANCE TO SHOW EVERYONE HOW GREAT HIS CAMEL WAS. AFTER HE RODE ON THE TRAIL FOR A COUPLE HOURS, HE CAME UPON AN OASIS. HE DID NOT REALLY WANT TO STOP SO EARLY IN THE JOURNEY, AS HE WANTED TO MAKE IT TO NETERIA AS QUICKLY AS POSSIBLE. HOWEVER, AS SOON AS THE CAMEL SMELLED THE WATER, IT RAN STRAIGHT FOR THE OASIS. "OH WELL," THOUGHT THE MAN, "A LITTLE REST WON'T HURT."

AS HE ACQUIESCED TO THE CAMEL'S WISHES, HE DIDN'T PULL THE REINS. AFTER SPENDING A BIT OF TIME AT THE OASIS, THE MAN TUGGED THE CAMEL UP ON ITS FEET AND ONCE AGAIN HE SET OUT. TO MAKE UP FOR THE TIME THAT HE HAD LOST, HE SET OUT AT A QUICKER PACE. AFTER CONTINUING ON FOR A COUPLE OF MORE HOURS, THEY BEGAN TO APPROACH ANOTHER OASIS. THEY WERE MAKING GOOD TIME AND THE MAN DID NOT WANT TO STOP. HOWEVER, THE SMELL OF RIPE DATES AND COOL WATER ENCHANTED THE CAMEL DEEPLY AND IT IMMEDIATELY TOOK OFF RUNNING TOWARDS THE OASIS. THE MAN TRIED TO PULL THE REINS GENTLY TO KEEP THE CAMEL ON COURSE, BUT THE CAMEL RESISTED AND KEPT RIGHT ON RUNNING TO THE OASIS. THE MAN ACQUIESCED TO THE CAMEL'S DESIRES YET AGAIN, AND HE AND HIS CAMEL ATE DATES AND DRANK WATER IN THE SHADE FOR A WHILE BEFORE HE DECIDED IT WAS TIME TO START OFF AGAIN. THE DATES WERE VERY SWEET AND THE WATER VERY REFRESHING. THE MAN WAS FULL OF VIGOR AS HE GOT UP TO GET STARTED BACK OUT ON THE JOURNEY. HIS CAMEL, HOWEVER, WAS VERY DROWSY AND LETHARGIC. THE CAMEL HAD GOTTEN COMFORTABLE IN THE SHADE AND DID NOT WANT TO MOVE.

With great effort, the man pulled his camel to its feet and started it out along the road. This time, the man set his camel out at a very hard fast pace. He pushed the camel to a gallop. As he looked up into the sky, he could see that the sun was no longer ascending. It wouldn't be long at all before the sun began to descend.

After a few more hours, the man and his camel approached yet another oasis. This time, the man was determined not to stop. He knew that daylight was waning quickly, and they couldn't afford to stop. As the camel had done both times before, it bolted towards the oasis. The man tugged mightily on the camel's reins. But no matter how hard he pulled; the camel refused to deviate from its course. "Oh well," the man thought, "my camel is swift. He won't stay as long as last time. We shall make it. A quick drink won't hurt."

The man figured that once the camel got a quick drink, it would be ready to go. However, the opposite occurred. After drinking some water, the man's camel laid down as if it were going to take a nap. The man tugged and tugged on the camel's reins, but the camel refused to budge.

EXASPERATED, THE MAN GRABBED THE CAMEL BY THE NECK AND TRIED TO PULL IT UP. STILL THE CAMEL WOULD NOT MOVE. IN FACT, THE CAMEL TRIED TO BITE THE MAN. FINALLY, EXHAUSTED BY THE STRUGGLE, THE MAN SAT DOWN IN THE SHADE BY THE NAPPING CAMEL. "OH WELL," THOUGHT THE MAN, "I MIGHT AS WELL GET SOME REST. MY CAMEL IS SWIFT. WE SHALL SURELY MAKE IT BEFORE DARK."

THE MAN THEN CLOSED HIS EYES FOR WHAT TO HIM SEEMED LIKE SECONDS. WHEN HE OPENED THEM, HOWEVER, HIS HEART DROPPED. WHAT SEEMED LIKE SECONDS HAD BEEN HOURS, AND IT WOULD SOON BE DARK. THE MAN LEAPT UP AND STRUCK THE CAMEL WITH A STICK. STARTLED FROM ITS DREAMS, THE CAMEL LEAPT UP AS WELL. THE MAN QUICKLY MOUNTED HIS CAMEL AND WHIPPED IT INTO A FURIOUS GALLOP. THE SUN WAS SETTING QUICKLY, AND THE MAN WAS GROWING QUITE FEARFUL. ALREADY HE COULD HEAR THE FORLORN HOWLS OF RAVENOUS WOLVES IN THE DISTANCE. THE MORE HOWLS HE HEARD, THE MORE FURIOUSLY HE WHIPPED HIS CAMEL TO RUN ON FASTER.

JUST AS THE SUN WAS BEGINNING TO SINK BELOW THE HORIZON, THE GATES TO THE KINGDOM BEGAN TO COME IN SIGHT FAR OFF IN THE DISTANCE. THE MAN WHIPPED HIS CAMEL WITH RENEWED VIGOR AND THE CAMEL, SENSING THE MAN'S URGENCY, PUSHED ON HARDER THAN IT EVER HAD BEFORE. HOWEVER, BY THE TIME THE MAN AND HIS CAMEL MADE IT TO NETERIA'S GATES, IT WAS TOO LATE. IT WAS DARK AND THE GATES HAD BEEN LOCKED FOR THE NIGHT. THE MAN WHO LOVED HIS CAMEL SUDDENLY THOUGHT TO HIMSELF THAT HE DID NOT LOVE HIS CAMEL SO MUCH ANYMORE. HE THOUGHT BACK, WITH GREAT REGRET, AT THE TIMES THAT HE HAD ALLOWED HIS CAMEL TO STOP AT THE

OASES. IF HE HAD MORE CONTROL OVER HIS CAMEL, THEY SURELY WOULD HAVE MADE IT IN TIME. BY THE TIME MORNING CAME AND THE GATES WERE OPENED, NEITHER THE MAN NOR HIS CAMEL WERE ANYWHERE TO BE FOUND. THE DESOLATION OF THE DESERT HAD SWALLOWED THEM WHOLE AND THEY WERE NEVER HEARD FROM AGAIN. BECAUSE OF THE MAN'S INABILITY TO CONTROL HIS CAMEL, THE KINGDOM OF SETANIA WAS LOST.

THOSE WHO HAVE NO CONTROL OVER THEIR MINDS ARE LIKE THE MAN WHO LOVED HIS CAMEL. INSTEAD OF THE CAMEL BEING THE MAN'S SERVANT, THE MAN WAS HIS CAMEL'S SERVANT. THE CAMEL HAD NO AWARENESS OF ANY WAR, ANY MESSAGES TO BE DELIVERED, OR ANYTHING OF THAT SORT. IT ONLY SOUGHT ITS OWN PLEASURE. IT ONLY DESIRED TO REST IN THE SHADE OF THE OASES, DRINK WATER, AND EAT DATES. MAKING IT TO NETERIA'S GATES BEFORE THE SUN SET WAS NONE OF ITS CONCERN, EVEN THOUGH ITS AND THE MAN'S VERY LIVES DEPENDED UPON IT. BECAUSE THE MAN HAD NEVER DISCIPLINED HIS CAMEL AND ALWAYS LET IT HAVE ITS WAY, WHEN HE NEEDED THE CAMEL TO DO WHAT HE WISHED IT TO DO, IT REFUSED TO COMPLY. IN THIS STORY, THE MAN CORRESPONDS TO THE WILL. IF YOU ALLOW YOUR MIND TO BE THE MASTER OF YOUR WILL, IT IS ONLY A MATTER OF TIME BEFORE YOUR KINGDOM SHALL PERISH.

73

MASTER, YOU SHALL BE ABLE TO CONTROL YOUR DESTINY ONLY TO THE EXTENT THAT YOU ARE ABLE TO CONTROL YOUR OWN THOUGHTS. NEVER SHOULD YOU SEEK TO CONTROL ANOTHER'S THOUGHTS. ONLY SEEK TO CONTROL YOUR OWN. TO SEEK TO CONTROL WHAT ANOTHER THINKS IS TO ALLOW THEM TO

CONTROL HOW YOU ARE THINKING. ONCE YOU GAIN THE **STRENGTH** TO CONTROL YOUR MIND AND ARE ABLE TO FOCUS IT UPON **THE TRUTH**, IT IS INEVITABLE THAT YOU SHALL GAIN CLARITY. CLARITY IS ONE ATTRIBUTE THAT ALL WHO DESIRE TO BE **KING** MUST ACQUIRE. IT IS ONLY WITH CLARITY THAT YOUR MIND SHALL BE ABLE TO LOOK INTO ANY PROBLEM AND SEE THE SOLUTION. YOUR THOUGHTS, FEELINGS, AND THE PHENOMENA OF THE UNIVERSE ARE SIMPLY DIFFERENT MANIFESTATIONS OF CHANGE. THOSE WHO POSSESS CLARITY OBSERVE CHANGE AS ONE WOULD OBSERVE CLOUDS IN THE SKY. FOR CLOUDS NEITHER DISTURB THE SKY OR THOSE WHO OBSERVE THEM.

74

MASTER, THERE IS NO GREATER REFUGE TO BE FOUND THAN THE CLEAR MIND THAT IS FREE FROM ALL DISTURBANCES. THE MIND THAT IS FREE FROM ALL DISTURBANCES IS A FOCUSED AND CONCENTRATED MIND. IT IS ONLY WHEN YOU ARE ABLE TO STILL AND SILENCE YOUR MIND, AND THEN ROOT YOURSELF IN THIS STILL SILENCE THAT YOU SHALL BE ABLE TO CONTROL AND CREATE THOUGHTS AT WILL. THIS STILL SILENCE IS NONE OTHER THAN OMNISCIENT, OMNIPOTENT, OMNIPRESENT AWARENESS. THIS STILL SILENCE IS WHERE **DIVINE** INTELLIGENCE RESIDES, AND TO ROOT YOURSELF IN IT IS TO GIVE YOUR MIND ACCESS TO THE VERY SAME INTELLIGENCE THAT CREATED THE UNIVERSE. AN INTELLIGENT MIND IS THE GREATEST ALLY THAT ANY **KING** COULD EVER HAVE. A MIND THAT THINKS THINGS THROUGH INTELLIGENTLY IS LIKE A FIRM WALL IN A SPLENDID MANSION. IT IS ONLY ONCE YOU HAVE TURNED YOUR ATTENTION AWAY FROM THE CONFUSION OF CHAOS AND PLACED IT UPON THE CERTITUDE

OF **THE TRUTH** THAT YOU SHALL COME TO UNDERSTAND THAT IT IS WITHIN YOUR **POWER** EVERYWHERE AND ALWAYS TO BE CONTENT WITH THE HAND THAT FATE HAS DEALT YOU, DEAL HONORABLY WITH THOSE WHOM YOU ENCOUNTER ON YOUR TRAVELS AROUND THE SUN, AND GUARD YOUR MIND AGAINST THE INGRESS OF BOTH MALIGNANT AND ACRIMONIOUS OPINIONS.

75

MASTER, YOUR TRUE SELF IS UNLIMITED IN ITS POTENTIAL TO BE, KNOW, AND DO. THE POSSIBILITIES THAT YOU CAN THINK INTO EXISTENCE ARE INFINITE. LITERALLY, WHATSOEVER YOUR MIND CAN VISUALIZE AND BELIEVE, YOU YOURSELF CAN READILY ACHIEVE. YOU ARE THE CREATOR OF ALL. THUS, THE ONLY LIMITATIONS THAT SHALL EVER INHIBIT YOU ARE THE ONES WHICH YOU CONJURE UP IN YOUR VERY OWN MIND. IF YOU BELIEVE IN YOUR SELF-IMPOSED LIMITATIONS, THEY SHALL BECOME YOUR REALITY. WHILE ALL MEN ARE BORN WITH THE POTENTIAL TO ACHIEVE ALL THAT IS HUMANLY POSSIBLE TO ALL HUMANS, BECAUSE MOST ARE ACCUSTOMED TO ACCEPTING AND ACQUIESCING TO WEAK PUSILLANIMOUS THOUGHTS, THEY ARE LIMITED TO A MINISCULE PERCENTAGE OF THEIR POTENTIAL. BECAUSE MOST MEN DO NOT VIEW THEMSELVES AS **KING** AND THEIR OWN AUTHORITY, MOST DERIVE THEIR BELIEFS ABOUT THEIR OWN POTENTIALITIES LARGELY FROM THE OPINIONS FORMED OF THEM BY OTHERS. IF NOTHING GREAT OR EXCELLENT IS THOUGHT OR EXPECTED OF THEM BY OTHERS, THEY ADOPT THESE OPINIONS AS THEIR OWN, AND AS A RESULT, THEY BECOME INCAPABLE OF THINKING OR EXPECTING ANYTHING GREAT OR EXCELLENT OF THEMSELVES.

Despite the nescience of those who may surround you, you must always treat with the utmost respect your own ability to form your own opinions concerning your own capabilities. If you say that you can't achieve and believe that this is so, then you shall be unable to achieve and prove yourself right only because you believe that this is so. However, if you say that you can achieve and believe that this is so, you shall be able to achieve because you believe it so. It is simple, Master. If you think that you can do a thing, you are correct. If you think that you cannot do a thing, you are also correct. You must only make the choice to believe.

76

Master, the POWER to live an exemplary life resides within you. The physical world is merely an illusion created by your mind. What you must come to understand is that the outside world is never the cause of anything, but is only the effect of thought. Wherever the mind goes, the body has no choice but to follow. Thus, if your mind dwells in the edifying pools of royal nobleness, circumstances of goodness shall envelop you in their benevolent glory. However, if you allow your mind to dwell in the decrepit cistern of malignant iniquity, conditions of wickedness shall smother you in their malefic shame.

77

MASTER, REALITY IS BUILT EXCLUSIVELY BY THE INVISIBLE HANDS OF IMAGINATION AND BELIEF. BEFORE YOU CAN ACCOMPLISH ANYTHING, THAT WHICH YOU ASPIRE TO ACCOMPLISH MUST FIRST BE CONCEIVED BY YOU IN YOUR IMAGINATION. NEVER THINK THAT A THOUGHT IS MERELY AN IDEA OR IMAGE FLOATING THROUGH YOUR MIND. EACH AND EVERY ONE OF YOUR THOUGHTS IS A VERITABLE FORCE OF NATURE AND CREATIVE ACT THAT PUSHES YOU FORTH IN YOUR JOURNEY UPON THE GREAT SEA OF EVOLUTION. ALL OF YOUR PAST EXPERIENCES AND ALL THAT YOU EVER SHALL EXPERIENCE ARE EFFECTS. ALL THAT YOU HAVE THOUGHT OR SHALL EVER THINK ARE THE CAUSES OF THESE EFFECTS. IF YOU MAKE WHAT YOU DESIRE THE DOMINANT THOUGHT IN YOUR MIND, YOUR MIND SHALL MANIFEST YOUR THOUGHTS INTO THE PHYSICAL WORLD. EVERYTHING THAT YOU ACHIEVE, AND EVERYTHING THAT YOU FAIL TO ACCOMPLISH IS THE DIRECT RESULT OF YOUR OWN THOUGHTS. THUS, IT IS VITAL THAT YOU ALWAYS MAINTAIN AN AWARENESS OF WHAT YOU ARE THINKING. IF YOU ARE AWARE OF YOUR THOUGHTS, YOU SHALL BE ABLE TO CONTROL HOW YOU THINK, AND CONSEQUENTLY, YOUR DESTINY. THE PROCLIVITIES, ASPIRATIONS, AND PREDILECTIONS THAT YOU ALLOW TO DOMINATE YOUR MIND SHALL DETERMINE YOUR DESTINATION. THE HIGHER YOU LIFT YOUR THOUGHTS, THE GREATER SHALL BE YOUR SUCCESS, AND THE MORE BLESSED AND ENDURING SHALL BE YOUR ACHIEVEMENTS. YOUR MIND SHALL ALWAYS CREATE EXCELLENT IDEAS AS LONG AS YOU DON'T KEEP IT TOO OCCUPIED WITH TERRIBLE THOUGHTS. THOSE THOUGHTS THAT YOU THINK TODAY SHALL BE THE REALITY THAT YOU LIVE TOMORROW. AS YOU THINK, YOU SHALL BECOME. THEREFORE, IT IS A MUST THAT

YOU MAKE IT YOUR MAIN OBJECTIVE IN YOUR DAILY THOUGHTS TO KEEP YOUR MIND ON THOSE THINGS THAT SHALL BRING YOU JOY AND OFF THOSE THINGS THAT SHALL BRING YOU PAIN.

78

MASTER, ALL OF YOUR FUTURE CIRCUMSTANCES ARE TOTALLY DEPENDENT UPON AND INSEPARABLE FROM THE CONSCIOUSNESS OUT OF WHICH YOUR ACTIONS EMANATE. THE ANCESTOR TO EVERY ACTION IS A THOUGHT. JUST AS ALL PLANTS COME FROM SEEDS, EVERY ACTION SPRING FROM A THOUGHT. YOUR AMBITIONS AND LONGINGS SHALL ONLY FIND FULFILLMENT WHEN THEY ATTAIN SYNCHRONIZATION WITH YOUR THOUGHTS AND ACTIONS. ACHIEVEMENT IS THE CROWN OF EFFORT AND THE CORONATION OF INTELLIGENT THOUGHT. IF YOU CAN THINK AND ACT CORRECTLY, IT SHALL ALWAYS BE WITHIN YOUR POWER TO MAKE LIFE FLOW FAVORABLY. LIFE SHALL NEVER GIVE YOU ANYTHING, NOR SHOULD YOU EXPECT LIFE TO GIVE YOU ANYTHING BESIDES OPPORTUNITY. HOWEVER, MY SON, REJOICE. FOR OPPORTUNITY IS ALL THAT YOU SHALL EVER NEED. IT IS ONLY OPPORTUNITY THAT SHALL BRING YOU THE MATERIAL FROM WHICH YOU MAY CARVE OUT AND FASHION YOUR SUCCESS. WHILE IT IS TRUE THAT WITHOUT OPPORTUNITY, A STRONG, FOCUSED MIND WOULD BE WASTED, IT IS EQUALLY TRUE THAT WITHOUT A STRONG, FOCUSED MIND, ALL OPPORTUNITY SHALL COME TO YOU IN VAIN. TO ACHIEVE SUCCESS, IT IS NOT NECESSARY FOR YOU TO HAVE THE BEST OF EVERYTHING. IT IS ONLY NECESSARY THAT YOU MAKE THE BEST OUT OF WHATEVER YOU HAVE. INSTEAD OF SEEING THE TROUBLE IN EVERY OPPORTUNITY, TRAIN YOUR MIND TO SEE THE OPPORTUNITIES IN ALL OF YOUR TROUBLES. IF YOU WOULD EXPEL ALL OF THE

CRAVEN, DASTARDLY THOUGHTS FROM YOUR MIND, AND THINK ONLY VALIANT, HEROIC THOUGHTS, THE WORLD SHALL SOFTEN TOWARDS YOU AND BE EVER READY TO HELP YOU. OPPORTUNITIES SHALL ARISE AT EVERY TURN TO ACCOMMODATE YOUR INDOMITABLE DETERMINATION, AND NO CIRCUMSTANCE SHALL EVER BE ABLE TO BIND YOU TO IGNOMINY OR DISGRACE. IF YOU WOULD ACHIEVE GREATNESS, IT IS A MUST THAT YOU FOCUS AND CONTINUALLY SHARPEN YOUR MIND. FOR WHILE AN INTELLIGENT, ALERT MIND SHALL BE ABLE TO BOTH PERCEIVE AND GRASP OPPORTUNITY WHENEVER AND WHEREVER IT MAY PRESENT ITSELF, A TORPID AND APATHETIC MIND SHALL WALK RIGHT BY OPPORTUNITY WITHOUT EVEN RECOGNIZING IT FOR WHAT IT IS.

79

MASTER, ANY MAN WHO SEEKS TO ACHIEVE GREATNESS SHALL BE CRITICIZED AND SLANDERED BY THE IGNORANT WHO CANNOT COMPREHEND THEIR OWN LIGHT, MUCH LESS APPRECIATE ANOTHER'S. IT IS FOR THIS REASON THAT YOU MUST NEVER CONCERN YOURSELF WITH CYNICS OR ALLOW THE CHATTER OF YOUR CRITICS TO HOLD YOUR ATTENTION. AS LONG AS YOU ARE BEHAVING JUSTLY, IT IS YOUR RIGHT TO SAY OR DO ANYTHING THAT ACCORDS WITH YOUR NATURE. IF YOU TRULY BELIEVE THAT YOU ARE DESTINED FOR GREAT THINGS, THIS ASSUREDNESS SHOWN BY YOU SHALL RADIATE OUTWARD AND INFECT THOSE AROUND YOU WITH A BELIEF IN YOU THAT SHALL SHATTER ALL LIMITS AND BOUNDARIES THAT SEEK TO BESIEGE YOU.

80

Master, great achievements can only come from minds that are relaxed and at peace with themselves. The reason why geniuses are so proficient in their arts is that every genius either consciously or unconsciously relaxes during their work. In whatever it is that you seek to attain achievement, you must allow peace to rule the kingdom of your mind so that you shall be able to relax and allow the goddess of victory to crown you with success. The best way to ease and relax your mind in any undertaking is to form a strategy and plan a course that is able to allow you to envision your enterprise coming to a glorious conclusion. Even if you may have to change plans during your journey to eminence, the mind shall always be comfortably content with the harmony of action shown in a well-organized plan, while it shall always suffer from doubt in a poorly organized one.

81

Master, whatever you wish to find outside of you is within you, and that which you seek, you already are. The reason why anyone wants to achieve or gain anything is the good feeling that they shall have once they achieve or gain it. That good feeling comes from within you; thus, it shall always be there with you. This feeling is what all people value most in the world. All feelings of fulfillment come from within. Thus, it is pointless to search for it outside of yourself.

A KING MUST UNDERSTAND: THOUGHTS OF A DIVINE KING

BOOK TWO

1

Master, the very particles that make up your body were once forged inside of the stars themselves. You were born to evince greatness. Your evolution is more momentous than the formation of a galaxy. You are an expression of the very same intelligence and energy that created the cosmos. This very same **POWER** resides within you awaiting your command. It is for this reason that you must dream whatever it is that you dare to dream so that you may go where it is that you wish to go and become whatsoever you desire to become. Dreams are the seedlings of awe-inspiring realities, and even the most magnificent of kingdoms was at first but a whisper of a fantasy.

2

Master, your imagination is merely the preview to your future. You shall only become as great as your dominant aspiration. You must never allow the vision that you have for your kingdom to become circumscribed by doubt. To transcend mediocrity is a necessity which you must always view as such. People limit their own visions by clouding their minds with thoughts of their own limitations. Perception is everything; thus, perceiving yourself as weak, unworthy, inferior, or inadequate in any fashion shall impede any progress that you seek to make in your life. People limit their visions also by

BELIEVING POSSIBLE ONLY THAT WHICH THEY ARE FAMILIAR WITH. BECAUSE WHAT IS POSSIBLE SHALL ALWAYS BE MORE ATTRACTIVE THAN WHAT IS CONSIDERED NOT POSSIBLE, THOSE WHO BELIEVE POSSIBLE ONLY THAT WHICH THEY ARE FAMILIAR WITH ARE NOT ATTRACTED TO THE UNKNOWN, AND THUS SHALL NEVER VENTURE PAST THE BOUNDARIES OF THEIR OWN INSIPIDITY. THEY SHALL NEVER BE ABLE TO ACHIEVE GREATNESS, FOR THEY DO NOT BELIEVE THEMSELVES CAPABLE OF IT. THINGS ALWAYS SEEM IMPOSSIBLE UNTIL THEY ARE DONE. THEREFORE, IN ORDER TO ACHIEVE GREATNESS, YOU MUST DEEM IT ONE OF YOUR MAIN RESOLUTIONS IN LIFE TO ACCOMPLISH THOSE THINGS WHICH OTHERS DEEM IMPOSSIBLE.

NEVER MAKE THE ASININE MISJUDGMENT THAT OTHERS DO WHO COME TO THE CONCLUSION THAT A THING IS HUMANLY IMPOSSIBLE JUST BECAUSE THEY FIND IT DIFFICULT TO DO. MY SON, IF AN ACT CAN AND SHOULD BE DONE BY A MAN, THEN YOU TOO ARE CAPABLE OF DOING IT. FOR IF SOMETHING IS HUMANLY POSSIBLE AND CORRESPONDS TO WHAT IT IS IN THE NATURE OF HUMANS TO DO, THEN AS A HUMAN, IT IS IN YOUR **POWER** TO ACHIEVE THIS THING AS WELL. AT ALL TIMES, WALK WITH THE ABSOLUTE CERTAINTY THAT YOU ARE DESTINED TO ATTAIN GREATNESS. IT IS THIS CERTAINTY THAT SHALL GIVE YOU THE **STRENGTH** AND FORTITUDE NECESSARY TO CARRY ON AND VANQUISH DESPAIR EVEN WHEN YOU FEEL LIKE STEPPING OFF OF THE PATH TO MAGNIFICENCE.

3

MASTER, IN THE SETTING OF YOUR AMBITIONS AND GOALS, YOU SHOULD FOLLOW THE EXAMPLES OF ARCHERS WHO DESIRING

TO HIT A TARGET WHICH IS A GREAT DISTANCE AWAY, AIM MUCH HIGHER THAN THEIR TARGET SO THAT THE ALTITUDE OF THEIR ASPIRATIONS MAY AID THEM IN REACHING THEIR MARK. MAKE YOUR GREATEST ANXIETY AND FEAR NOT THAT YOU SHALL AIM TOO HIGH AND MISS YOUR GOAL, BUT THAT YOU SHALL AIM TOO LOW AND HIT IT. ALWAYS AIM HIGH, MY SON, AND ALWAYS EXPECT THE BEST IN ANY ENDEAVOR THAT YOU DESIRE TO UNDERTAKE. THE EXPECTATION OF THE BEST OUTCOME IS SIMPLY THE RECOGNITION THAT YOUR ASPIRATION IS ATTAINABLE. IN EVERY ACCOMPLISHMENT AND IN EVERY ACHIEVEMENT, THERE ARE MANY WORTHY AND MERITORIOUS DEGREES BESIDES THE HIGHEST, AND IF YOU AIM FOR THE APEX, YOU ARE NEARLY ALWAYS GUARANTEED TO REACH AT LEAST HALFWAY. FOR HE WHO REACHES FOR THE STARS IS CERTAIN TO AT LEAST REACH THE LEVEL OF THE MOON.

4

MASTER, YOUR EVOLUTION IS YOUR GRADUAL UNFOLDING, OR GROWTH, INTO A HIGHER FORM OF EXISTENCE. FOR THE GOOD OF YOUR KINGDOM, YOU MUST MAKE YOUR (AND YOUR KINGDOM'S) EVOLUTION YOUR PRINCIPAL AND PRIMARY CONCERN. YOUR EVOLUTION SHALL INVARIABLY CORRELATE PRECISELY WITH YOUR ACQUISITION OF **KNOWLEDGE** AND **UNDERSTANDING**. THE UNIVERSE SHALL NOT ONLY SHOW ITS FAVOR TO HE WHO EVOLVES, BUT IT SHALL ALSO BRING YOU EXACTLY THAT WHICH YOU NEED IN ORDER TO EVOLVE. HOWEVER, BECAUSE YOUR WILL IS FREE, IT IS ONLY ONCE YOU MAKE THE CONSCIOUS DECISION TO MOVE FORWARD, THAT LIFE SHALL SHIFT IN ORDER TO SHOW YOU HOW.

INSIDE OF EVERYONE, THERE IS A SEED OF **POWER** WHOSE ABILITY TO GROW IS UNLIMITED. POTENTIALITY IS BOUNDLESS; THUS, YOUR OPPORTUNITY TO EVOLVE SHALL NEVER END. WHILE CHANGE IS INEVITABLE, EVOLUTION IS A CHOICE THAT YOU MUST KNOWINGLY AND CONTINUALLY MAKE. IT IS ONLY THE DEDICATION OF YOURSELF TO A VISION THAT SHALL ALLOW YOU TO BE SWEPT UP INTO THE ETERNAL COSMIC RIVER OF EVOLUTION. IF YOU REMAIN FOCUSED UPON THIS VISION, YOU SHALL BE CARRIED ALONG UNTO THE FRINGES OF ETERNITY. FOR YOUR VISION IS YOUR LINK TO IMMORTALITY.

5

MASTER, WHAT SEPARATES A GREAT KING FROM AN ORDINARY MAN IS NOT TALENT OR RESOURCES, BUT A VISION. A GREAT **KING** HAS THE ABILITY TO LOOK AT WHAT EVERYONE ELSE IS LOOKING AT, AND YET SEE WHAT NO ONE ELSE IS ABLE TO SEE. ALTHOUGH THOSE WITH VISION SHALL BE THE SAVIORS OF THEIR KINGDOM, THE DISADVANTAGE OF BEING A VISIONARY IS THAT VERY FEW SHALL UNDERSTAND YOU.

6

MASTER, YOU SHALL BECOME THE VISION THAT YOU HONOR IN YOUR THOUGHTS AND THE IDEAL WHICH YOU EXALT WITHIN YOUR HEART. HE WHO HARBORS A RESPLENDENT VISION AND AN ILLUSTRIOUS IDEAL SHALL ONE DAY REALIZE IT. YOUR IDEAL IS THE AUGURY OF WHAT YOU SHALL ONE DAY BECOME, AND YOUR VISION IS THE PROGNOSTICATION OF WHAT YOU SHALL ONE DAY REVEAL TO THE WORLD. A **KING** NEVER SHIES AWAY FROM AN ADVENTURE. FOR IT IS BY ADVENTUROUS SPIRITS ONLY THAT

VISIONS ARE REALIZED.

7

MASTER, TO HE WHO HAS NOT A VISION, EVEN THE BEST ADVICE IS WORTHLESS. YOUR VISION IS THE BEARER OF YOUR **UNDERSTANDING.** TRUE HAPPINESS SHALL ONLY COME TO YOU WHEN YOU GAIN A CLEAR VISION OF WHO YOU TRULY ARE. YOU ARE **THE TRUTH**, MY SON. YOU ARE A **KING.** TRANSCRIBE THIS UPON THE VERY PARCHMENT OF YOUR SOUL. FOR YOUR REALITY SHALL ALWAYS SUPPORT THE VISION YOU HAVE OF YOURSELF.

8

MASTER, YOU SHALL ONLY MASTER YOUR LIFE WHEN THE VOICE INSIDE OF YOU BECOMES MORE ZEALOUS AND SCREAMS WITH MORE IMPETUOSITY THAN THE JUDGMENTS OF THOSE OUTSIDE OF YOU. IT IS FOR THIS REASON THAT YOU MUST BECOME YOUR OWN WORST CRITIC AND MOST SEVERE CENSOR. IF YOU REFUSE TO FLEE FROM THE PAIN OF SELF-CRUCIFIXION, YOU SHALL NEVER FAIL TO ACHIEVE THE VISION UPON WHICH YOUR HEART IS SET.

9

MASTER, THE FIRST STEP IN BECOMING GREAT, THE STEP THAT SHALL MAKE EVERYTHING ELSE FALL INTO ITS PROPER PLACE, IS THE ATTAINMENT OF A LUCID, DETAILED, AND PURPOSEFUL VISION. FOR IT IS THE **KNOWLEDGE** OF EXACTLY WHAT IT IS THAT YOU WISH TO ACHIEVE THAT SHALL BE THE SPARK WHICH SHALL IGNITE THE SUBLIME FLAMES OF GREATNESS THAT LIE SMOLDERING

WITHIN YOU. YOUR VISION AND REALITY YEARN TO COME TOGETHER. YOU MUST AID THEM IN THIS TASK BY CONSCIOUS CHANNELING YOUR ENERGY INTO YOUR VISION DAILY, BUILDING UPON IT, AND LEARNING TO MAKE ALL OF THE SEPARATE COMPONENTS OF YOUR LIFE WORK TOWARD THE FULFILLMENT OF YOUR VISION. IT IS ONLY ON THE PATH TO ACTUALIZING YOUR VISION THAT YOU SHALL BE INTRODUCED TO THE **WISDOM** AND **STRENGTH** THAT HE WHO RULES MUST HAVE.

10

MASTER, IT IS VITAL THAT YOU HOLD ON TO AND BELIEVE IN THE POSSIBILITY OF YOUR VISION EVEN BEFORE IT HAS COME INTO FRUITION. FOR EVEN BEFORE IT MANIFESTS ITSELF ON THIS PHYSICAL PLANE, REST ASSURED, MY SON, IT EXISTS. JUST AS AN AUTHOR SEES THE END OF HIS STORY AT ITS BEGINNING AND TOLERATES NO DEVIATION, SO TOO MUST YOU SEE THE DESTINATION TO WHICH YOUR VISION SHALL LEAD YOU AND ALLOW NOTHING TO STEER YOU AWAY FROM THIS GLORIOUS CONCLUSION. WHAT SHALL ENSURE THAT YOU REACH YOUR GOAL IS THE FORMATION OF A CLEAR PLAN. THIS IS THE KEY TO SUCCESS IN ANY ENDEAVOR. WHILE IT IS DIFFICULT TO PREDICT EXACTLY WHAT THE LONG-TERM CONSEQUENCES OF ACTUALIZING YOUR VISION SHALL BE, THE MORE EARNESTLY AND CORRECTLY YOU SCRUTINIZE THE POTENTIAL POSSIBILITIES, AND PLAN FOR THEM, THE MORE YOU SHALL BE ABLE TO REMAIN COOL, COMPOSED, AND RATIONAL WHEN DISCONCERTING CIRCUMSTANCES ARISE, AS THEY INVARIABLY SHALL. DON'T JUST PLAN TO THE END OF YOUR ENTERPRISES. PLAN PAST THEM TO THEIR AFTERMATH. NOT ONLY IS THIS THE SUREST WAY TO CREATE SOMETHING THAT SHALL LAST, BUT THE CLEARER AND

FARTHER SEEING YOUR VISION IS, THE EASIER YOUR EMOTIONS SHALL BE TO CONTROL. UNDER NO CIRCUMSTANCE AND FOR NO REASON SHOULD YOU EVER ALLOW NEGATIVE EMOTIONS TO CAUSE YOU TO STRAY AWAY FROM THE PATH TO NOBILITY. THE ENJOYMENT OF WHAT YOU ARE DOING, COMBINED WITH A VISION THAT YOU ARE WORKING TOWARD, SHALL BECOME THE MOST POWERFUL FORCE IN THE UNIVERSE KNOWN AS ENTHUSIASM. ENTHUSIASM IS THE **POWER** THAT SHALL TRANSFER THE MENTAL BLUEPRINT OF YOUR VISION INTO THE PHYSICAL REALM MOST EFFECTIVELY.

11

MASTER, FOR YOU TO ACHIEVE GREATNESS, IT IS A MUST THAT AT ALL TIMES YOU KEEP YOUR HIGHEST VISION FOR YOUR KINGDOM IN THE FORE OF YOUR THOUGHTS, AND IN EVERY SITUATION THAT YOU FIND YOURSELF IN, SEEK THE HIGHEST OUTCOME ACCORDING TO THAT VISION. IT IS ONLY BY DEVOTING YOURSELF TO YOUR VISION THAT YOU SHALL BE ABLE TO ALIGN YOURSELF WITH THE HIGHEST POTENTIAL THAT YOU WERE BORN TO MANIFEST. WHAT SHALL ELEVATE YOU ABOVE ALL OTHERS IS THE ABILITY TO FOCUS TO THE EXTENT THAT YOU ARE ABLE TO EXTEND YOUR VISIONS AND PLANS OVER SUCH LONG PERIODS OF TIME THAT THOSE AROUND YOU SHALL NOT EVEN REALIZE THAT YOU HAVE A PLAN IN MIND UNLESS YOU TELL THEM. WHEN YOU ACQUIRE LONG-TERM OBJECTIVES, THEY SHALL GIVE DIRECTION TO ALL YOUR ENERGIES. CONSEQUENTIAL AND CRUCIAL DECISIONS SHALL BECOME EASIER TO MAKE. IF SOME DAZZLING DISTRACTION THREATENS TO SEDUCE YOU AND LURE YOU AWAY FROM YOUR AMBITION, YOU SHALL BE ABLE TO RESIST IT. FOR YOUR EYES SHALL BE FOCUSED UPON THE ATTAINMENT OF YOUR VISION AND

NOTHING ELSE. REMAIN FOCUSED UPON YOUR VISION AND IF IT EVER STRUGGLES TO UNFOLD, PLACE NO BLAME. RATHER, EXAMINE YOUR MIND SO THAT YOU MAY COME TO SEE HOW YOU YOURSELF ARE HAMPERING ITS UNFOLDMENT.

12

MASTER, WHATEVER IS COMING IS ON ITS WAY. FOR DESTINY IS A GUEST THAT CAN NEVER BE TURNED AWAY. BEHIND THE SEEMINGLY HAPHAZARD SERIES OF CHANGES AND EVENTS WHICH OCCUR IN LIFE LIES CONCEALED A GRAND ORDER AND UNFOLDING PURPOSE. THERE ARE NO ADVENTITIOUS EVENTS IN LIFE, NOR ARE THERE OCCURRENCES OR PHENOMENA THAT EXIST BY AND FOR THEMSELVES IN ISOLATION. REST ASSURED, MY SON, AS THE SNOW FALLS, EACH FLAKE LANDS IN THE PERFECT PLACE. NOTHING IN THE COSMOS IS RANDOM. THE VERY WORD COSMOS ITSELF MEANS THE ORDERED UNIVERSE. THERE IS ONLY ONE UNIVERSE AND EACH EVENT THAT TAKES PLACE WITHIN IT IS INTERCONNECTED AND HAS ITS NECESSARY AND ESSENTIAL PLACE AND FUNCTION WITHIN THE WHOLE. THE CAUSES OF EVEN THE MOST INFINITESIMAL OCCURRENCES ARE PRACTICALLY INFINITE AND CONNECTED WITH THE TOTALITY OF THE COSMOS IN WAYS THAT ARE TOO COMPLEX FOR THE MIND TO GRASP.

13

MASTER, YOU ARE AN ETERNALLY BLOOMING FLOWER THAT IS FOREVER EVOLVING. YOUR LIFE SHALL ALWAYS UNFOLD ACCORDING TO WHAT IS BEST AND MOST EVOLUTIONARY FOR YOU. IT IS YOUR DESTINY TO EVOLVE. THE SOONER YOU REALIZE THAT A COSMIC PLAN FOR YOUR EVOLUTION IS

UNFOLDING, THE SOONER YOU SHALL BE ABLE TO STEP BACK AND APPRECIATE LIFE FOR THE INEFFABLE WONDER THAT IT IS. DESTINY IS NOT A MATTER OF CHANCE BUT A MATTER OF CHOICE. ONCE YOU MAKE THE CHOICE OF WHAT YOUR DESTINY SHALL BE, THE UNIVERSE HAS NO CHOICE BUT TO ACCOMMODATE YOUR DECISION. YOU ARE THE ARCHITECT OF YOUR OWN FUTURE CIRCUMSTANCES AND THE AUTHOR OF YOUR OWN STORY. YOU ARE A **KING**. YOUR DESTINY AND THE LEGACY THAT YOU SHALL LEAVE THE WORLD ARE ONE AND THE SAME. THE FIRST STEP IN ESTABLISHING YOUR LEGACY IS TO CONTEMPLATE AND ASCERTAIN THE DIRECTION THAT YOUR SKILLS AND TALENTS ARE PUSHING YOU AND DETERMINE EXACTLY WHAT IT IS THAT YOU ARE DESTINED TO ACHIEVE. YOU MUST ENVISION YOURSELF BRINGING YOUR DESTINY TO FRUITION IN ILLUSTRIOUS DETAIL. WHAT HAS DISTINGUISHED ALL THOSE THAT HAVE BEEN GREAT THROUGHOUT THE ANNALS OF HISTORY ARE THE EXACT, DETAILED, AND PRECISE VISIONS THAT THEY MEDITATED UPON INCESSANTLY, VISUALIZING THEM CLEARLY UNTIL THEY BECAME REALITY. YOUR DESTINY IS YOUR DESTINATION. IF YOU REMAIN AWARE OF THE DIRECTION IN WHICH YOU ARE HEADED, YOU SHALL REACH IT GRACEFULLY. BUT NEVER LOSE HEART IF YOU EVER FEEL LOST AND INCAPABLE OF DECIPHERING THE RIDDLE OF YOUR OWN DESTINY. FOR LIFE IS SUCH AN INTRICATE LABYRINTH THAT SOMETIMES A MAN FINDS HIS DESTINY ON THE VERY PATH THAT HE TOOK TO AVOID IT.

14

MASTER, SMALL OPPORTUNITIES ARE THE BEGINNINGS OF GREAT ENTERPRISES. HOWEVER, BECAUSE OPPORTUNITY SHALL WAIT FOR NO MAN, IT IS ONLY THOSE BLESSED WITH THE VISION TO

RECOGNIZE THESE OPPORTUNITIES FOR WHAT THEY ARE AND THE DETERMINATION NECESSARY TO UTILIZE THEM THAT SHALL HAVE THE **POWER** TO ELEVATE THEMSELVES TO THE HEIGHTS OF **DIGNITY** AND **HONOR**. COURAGE, RESOLUTION, AND FOCUS ARE REQUIRED TO RENDER USEFUL THE GOLDEN GIFT OF OPPORTUNITY. THEREFORE, REGRET AND BLAME ARE DESERVED BY ALL THOSE WHO REFUSE TO SUMMON THESE THINGS FROM INSIDE THEMSELVES. FOR ALL THAT IT TAKES TO SUMMON THESE THINGS FROM INSIDE YOURSELF IS THE DECISION TO DO SO. A GREAT OPPORTUNITY SHALL BE WORTH TO YOU EXACTLY WHAT YOUR COURAGE, RESOLUTION, AND FOCUS ENABLE YOU TO MAKE OF IT. COURAGE, RESOLUTION, AND FOCUS ARE THE MAGNETS THAT SHALL DRAW ALL OPPORTUNITY TO YOU. OPPORTUNITY SHALL STALK ALL THOSE WHO POSSESS THE COURAGE, RESOLUTION, AND FOCUS NECESSARY TO RECOGNIZE AND EMBRACE HER. BE THANKFUL FOR EVERY OPPORTUNITY TO SERVE YOUR KINGDOM THAT IS LAID BEFORE YOU. FOR YOUR ABILITY TO SERVE YOUR KINGDOM IS WHAT SHALL MAKE YOU **KING**. YOU ARE WHAT YOU CHOOSE TO BE. YOU CAN EITHER CHOOSE TO BECOME **THE GREATEST KING THAT HAS EVER LIVED,** OR YOU CAN LET THE OPPORTUNITY PASS THAT STANDS BEFORE YOU. WHATEVER DECISION THAT YOU MAKE, MY ONLY REQUEST, MASTER, IS THAT YOU ARE THE ONE THAT MAKES YOUR OWN.

15

MASTER, THE ONLY TYPE OF SUCCESS THAT SHALL ENDURE FOR ANY SIGNIFICANT AMOUNT OF TIME IS THAT SUCCESS WHICH IS BUILT UP GRADUALLY AND SLOWLY. THAT WHICH SHALL GIVE YOU THE **STRENGTH** TO BEAR THE MONOTONOUS DUBIETY WHICH SHALL INVARIABLY ACCOMPANY ANY ENDEAVOR OF THIS

TYPE IS **FAITH**. **FAITH** IS THE INNER CERTAINTY THAT CHANGE CAN AND INEVITABLY SHALL OCCUR. **FAITH** IS THE **KNOWLEDGE** THAT YOU ARE **POWER**. IT IS THE **WISDOM** THAT WHISPERS TO YOU ASSERTIVELY DURING YOUR MOMENTS OF DOUBT TO REMIND YOU THAT EVERYTHING IS INDEED GOING IN PRECISELY THE FASHION THAT IT MUST IN ORDER FOR YOUR DESTINY TO BE FULFILLED. **STRENGTH** IS BORN OF CONFIDENCE, AND CONFIDENCE IS BORN OF **FAITH**. THE MEASURE OF A MAN'S **STRENGTH** LIES IN HIS ABILITY TO ENDURE. THE MEASURE OF HIS **FAITH** IS THE MEASURE OF THE PAIN THAT HE IS WILLING TO ENDURE IN ORDER TO REALIZE HIS VISION.

MY SON, REMAIN FOREVER FAITHFUL TO YOURSELF AND YOUR VISION. FOR IT IS THE **FAITH** THAT SOMEONE HAS IN SOMETHING THAT SHALL GIVE THAT THING ITS **POWER**. IT IS YOUR DUTY AS **KING** TO HAVE **FAITH** THAT THERE IS GOOD IN YOUR KINGDOM AND THAT IT IS WORTH FIGHTING FOR. IT IS OF THE UTMOST IMPORTANCE FOR THE GOOD OF YOUR KINGDOM THAT YOU **HONOR** THIS DUTY TO THE HIGHEST OF YOUR CAPABILITIES. THE FATE OF YOUR KINGDOM REST PRECARIOUSLY BALANCED UPON THE EDGE OF A KNIFE. IF YOU STRAY BUT A LITTLE FROM THE PATH OF **THE TRUTH**, ALL SHALL BE LOST TO THE RUIN OF ALL THOSE THAT INHABIT YOUR REALM. HOWEVER, **FAITH** SHALL KEEP YOU FOREVER UPRIGHT AS LONG AS YOU REMAIN ON THE PATH. THE FIRST REQUIREMENT OF **FAITH** IS ACTION. **FAITH**, WHICH IS THE ART OF BELIEVING BY DOING, ONLY EXISTS SO LONG AS IT IS BEING USED. TO HAVE A VISION AND NOT ACT UPON IT IS TO POSSESS NO **FAITH** IN THAT VISION, AND THUS NO POSSIBILITY OF EVER FULFILLING IT. IT IS ONLY THE MARRIAGE OF YOUR **FAITH** TO ACTION THAT

SHALL PRODUCE ENTHUSIASM, WHICH IS THE **POWER** BEHIND ALL OF LIFE'S CREATIONS.

16

MASTER, IF YOU WOULD SHUT THE GATES OF FEAR BEHIND YOU, THE GATES OF **FAITH** SHALL OPEN TO YOU AND YOU SHALL BE FREE TO ENTER THE CELESTIAL ABODE OF VICTORY IN ANY ENDEAVOR THAT YOU DEVOTE YOURSELF TO. **FAITH** AND FEAR ARE TWO ENEMIES THAT SHALL NEVER ASSENT TO INHABIT THE SAME SPACE AT THE SAME TIME. **FAITH** IS **THE TRUTH**. FEAR IS A LIE. YOUR **FAITH** IS YOUR **STRENGTH** AND THE REQUISITE FOR ANY GLORY THAT YOU HOPE TO ATTAIN. **FAITH** IS THE FOUNDATION OF PEACE AND HARMONY. IT IS **FAITH** THAT SHALL ENABLE YOU TO SEE **THE TRUTH**. ALTHOUGH UNTRAVELED ROADS CAN BE DIFFICULT AND ARE OFTEN DANGEROUS, OFTENTIMES, THEY ARE THOROUGHFARES TO GREATNESS.

PEOPLE SHALL ALWAYS SEEK OUT THE COMPANIONSHIP AND COUNSEL OF HE WHO POSSESSES **FAITH** AND A VISION. FOR IT IS THEIR HOPE THAT PERHAPS AN INKLING OF THAT WHICH DRIVES HIM SHALL BE ABSORBED BY THEM, AND THEY TOO SHALL ATTAIN THE PROFOUND SECRETS OF **POWER**. ALWAYS STRIVE TO INSPIRE AWE IN THE HEARTS OF YOUR PEOPLE, MY SON. FOR THEIR AWE SHALL **POWER** THEIR **FAITH**, AND THEIR **FAITH** IN YOU SHALL YIELD TO YOU THE UNCONQUERABLE **STRENGTH** NECESSARY TO ACCOMPLISH ANYTHING POSSIBLE. AS THE TREES DEPEND UPON THE RAIN, SUN, AND SOIL FOR THEIR SUSTENANCE, SO DOES YOUR **FAITH** DEPEND UPON THE **WISDOM** AND **UNDERSTANDING** OF WHO YOU TRULY

ARE. YOU ARE **THE TRUTH**. ALWAYS HAVE **FAITH** IN, AND FOCUS UPON, **THE TRUTH**. FOCUS AND **FAITH** ARE AT THE ROOT OF ALL ACHIEVEMENT. **FAITH** IS THE GENERATOR THAT SHALL **POWER** YOUR RESOLUTIONS. FOCUS IS THE INSTRUMENT WITH WHICH YOU MAY HARNESS, GUIDE, AND DIRECT THE FLOW OF THE ENERGY AVAILABLE TO YOU INTO THE DIRECTION THAT YOUR VISION DICTATES. ON YOUR JOURNEY TO THE THRONE, YOUR VISION MUST BE YOUR GUIDING LIGHT. FOR YOUR VISION IS THE ONLY LIGHT ABLE TO ILLUMINATE YOUR PATH TO RENOWN. IT IS ONLY ONCE ONE STOPS WALKING IN DARKNESS THAT THEY SHALL CEASE TO BE BLIND.

17

MASTER, FROM THE VERY MOMENT THAT YOU CAME INTO THIS WORLD, YOUR TIME IS THE ONLY THING THAT IS TRULY YOUR OWN. TIME IS THE ONLY CURRENCY THAT YOU SHALL EVER IN REALITY POSSESS. HOW YOU SPEND IT SHALL DEFINE WHO YOU BECOME. TIME IS YOUR GREATEST WEAPON, MASTER. IF YOU WOULD BUT KEEP IN MIND PATIENTLY A LONG-TERM VISION, THERE IS NO FORCE ON THE EARTH THAT SHALL BE ABLE TO PREVENT YOU FROM ATTAINING YOUR HOPE. AS YOU JOURNEY EVER ONWARD OVER THE SANDS OF TIME IN THE DESERT OF PHYSICAL EXISTENCE, IF YOU DESIRE TO ATTAIN GREATNESS, YOU MUST MAKE **THE TRUTH** THE STAR THAT GUIDES YOU TO THE OASIS OF YOUR HEART'S DESIRE.

18

MASTER, A **KING** HAS NO SPARE TIME. A **KING** IS SUBJECT TO THE CALL OF DUTY AT ALL TIMES. THE TIME THAT A **KING**

POSSESSES OUGHT TO BE SPENT BUILDING UP HIS KINGDOM. DUE TO THE INEVITABILITY OF CHANGE, ALL FORMER GLORIES ARE, AND SHALL ALWAYS BE QUICKLY COVERED AND HIDDEN BY THAT WHICH FOLLOWS. THUS, IF FOR ONE MOMENT YOU CEASE TO INCREASE THE GREATNESS OF YOUR KINGDOM, YOU OPEN THE POSSIBILITY FOR ITS DEMISE. NEVER ALLOW YOURSELF TO BECOME VEXED WITH CHANGE. FOR THERE IS NOTHING DEARER TO LIFE, NOR MORE VITAL TO THE COSMOS THAN CHANGE. IN FACT, THERE IS NOTHING THAT HAS EVER HAPPENED OR EVER SHALL HAPPEN WITHOUT IT. WASTE NOT YOUR TIME ON FRIVOLITY AND FLUFF. FOR BETWEEN THE VAST EXPANSE OF TIME BEFORE BIRTH AND THE INFINITE ABYSS THAT SHALL FOLLOW DEATH LIES THE BLINK OF THE EYE THAT IS YOUR TIME HERE IN THIS WORLD. TIME IS ONE OF THE EASIEST THINGS TO LOSE, AND TIME LOST IS SOMETHING THAT IS NEVER AGAIN REGAINED.

PROCRASTINATION IS THE KILLER OF DREAMS AND THE MURDERER OF VISIONS. NEVER ALLOW THIS VILE ADVERSARY TO SEDUCE YOU INTO FOLLOWING ITS WAYS. TIME IS A **DIVINE** FORCE THAT POSSESSES THE ABILITY TO HEAL THE WOUNDS OF FAILURE, DISAPPOINTMENT, REGRET, RIGHT ALL WRONGS, AND TURN ALL ERRORS INTO ADVANTAGES. HOWEVER, IT SHALL ONLY FAVOR THOSE WHO SIDE AGAINST PROCRASTINATION AND MARCH VALIANTLY DAILY TOWARDS THE ATTAINMENT OF A DEFINITE OBJECTIVE. YOUR MEASURE OF RESPECT FOR TIME SHALL PROVE TO BE OPPORTUNITY'S AND SUCCESS'S MEASURE OF RESPECT FOR YOU.

19

Master, the most important relationship that you ever shall have in life is your relationship with the present moment. It is the present moment and the present moment only that has the **POWER** to deliver unto you your glorious destiny. Yesterday is gone forever, Master. It shall never return. However, it is always possible to make up for time lost by making the most of today. The past is a guest that shall never again reappear and give testimony against your words. Thus, you shall always have the freedom to refashion and retranslate it into a form that is useful to you in the present, and serviceable to your vision of the future. Never fear that which eternity shall bring to you in the future, nor lament that which it has delivered to you in the past. For all that you have done or that has happened, and all that you shall do or that shall happen, exists only in your imagination and is therefore unreal. Only that which you are doing and is taking place now has reality. **LOVE** your past and cherish it always, my son. Without loving your past, it is impossible to **LOVE** who you are today. It is because of your past that you are great. It is because of your past that you are **KING**. To bear any resentment towards any event that has occurred within your past is to resent your kingship today. It is impossible to build the future while avenging the past. Everything leads to sorrow when one refuses to forgive yesterday.

20

MASTER, IT IS A REQUISITE OF HE WHO HOPES TO ATTAIN SUCCESS THAT HE HAVE **FAITH** IN HIMSELF AND CEASE TO LOOK OUTSIDE OF HIMSELF FOR APPROVAL AND FULFILLMENT FROM OTHERS. YOU MUST ALWAYS BE WILLING TO WALK ALONE. THE KEY TO ACCOMPLISHMENT LIES BURIED IN THE PURSUIT OF YOUR OWN VISIONS AND THE SEEKING OF YOUR OWN DESTINY, NOT THOSE WHICH THE OUTSIDE WORLD SEEKS TO THRUST UPON YOU. EVEN IF EVERYONE ELSE DOUBTS YOUR **POWER** TO LIVE THE LIFE THAT YOU INTEND TO LIVE AND ACCOMPLISH THAT WHICH YOU INTEND TO ACCOMPLISH, YOU MUST NEVER ALLOW THEIR SKEPTICISM TO DISTURB YOU OR BEGUILE YOU INTO DEPARTING FROM THE ROAD THAT SHALL LEAD YOU DIRECTLY TO GLORY. TO SEEK TO TRAVEL THE PATH OF TRUE GREATNESS IS TO DARE TO VENTURE DOWN AN ARDUOUS AND DEMANDING PATH THAT VERY FEW SHALL UNDERSTAND AND EVEN FEWER SHALL CHOOSE FOR THEMSELVES. HAVE COURAGE AND TAKE SOLACE IN THE FACT THAT THOSE WHO TRULY CARE FOR YOU SHALL NEVER FORSAKE OR ABANDON YOU. WHATEVER THAT DOES NOT **HONOR** YOUR QUEST FOR GREATNESS AND ASSIST YOU ALONG YOUR PATH TO MAGNIFICENCE ONLY DEPRIVES ITSELF OF YOUR LIGHT.

21

MASTER, EVERYTHING THAT HAS EVER OCCURRED IN YOUR LIFE HAS BEEN THE UNFOLDING OF YOUR DESTINY TO YOURSELF. YOU MUST NEVER LOSE HEART AT THE MISINTERPRETATIONS OF YOUR ACTIONS FROM OTHERS. YOUR DESTINY IS YOURS AND YOURS ALONE. THOSE IN HISTORY WHO HAVE ATTAINED THE **DIGNITY** OF GREATNESS HAVE ONLY RARELY BEEN

UNDERSTOOD DURING THEIR ASCENT TO MAJESTY. NEVER LOOK AROUND IN SEARCH OF THAT WHICH GUIDES OTHERS, BUT RATHER FOCUS ENTIRELY UPON WHERE IT IS THAT THE LIGHT OF YOUR OWN GREATNESS IS LEADING YOU. EACH PERSON POSSESSES THEIR OWN LIGHT AND THEIR OWN MINDS WHICH ALLOW THEM TO FOLLOW THIS LIGHT. WASTE NO TIME GAZING AFTER THE LIGHTS OF OTHERS. INSTEAD, KEEP YOUR EYES ON THE STRAIGHT PATH AHEAD. SEEK ONLY TO BE GUIDED IN THE DIRECTION THAT YOUR OWN NOBILITY SEEKS TO STEER YOU. MAINTAIN THE ABILITY TO IGNORE THE CONVENTIONAL **WISDOM** WHICH SAYS WHAT YOU SHOULD OR SHOULD NOT BE DOING. JUST BECAUSE THINGS MAY MAKE SENSE TO OTHERS, IT DOES NOT NECESSARILY MEAN THAT THOSE THINGS BEAR ANY RELATION TO YOUR VISION AND DESTINY. BECAUSE A **KING** MUST BE WISE AND PATIENT ENOUGH TO PLOT MANY STEPS AHEAD OF HIS NEXT MOVE, THE PATH TO HIS DESTINATION, ESPECIALLY IN MATTERS OF GREAT IMPORTANCE, SHALL INVARIABLY BE INDIRECT. IT IS THIS INDIRECTION THAT SHALL BE THE REASON THAT YOUR ACTIONS MAY APPEAR STRANGE AND CAUSE CONFUSION TO ENTER THE MINDS OF THOSE WHO HAVE NOTHING BETTER TO DO THAN WATCH AND CRITICIZE YOU. EVENTUALLY YOU SHALL COME TO FIND THAT THERE IS NO GREATER AGENT OF SECURITY FOR YOU AND YOUR PLANS THAN THIS PERPLEXITY IN THE MINDS OF THE WATCHERS AND CRITICS. FOR THE LESS OTHERS UNDERSTAND YOU, THE LESS LIKELY IT IS THAT THEY SHALL BE ABLE TO HINDER YOUR AMBITIONS. LIKE A STORM AT SEA, THE DOUBTS, AND CRITICISMS OF THOSE AROUND YOU CAN COME UNEXPECTEDLY FROM ANY POINT OF THE COMPASS. TO CHANGE THE COURSE OF YOUR VESSEL WITH EACH GUST OF WIND SHALL ONLY CAUSE YOU TO LOSE YOUR WAY AND BECOME LOST.

As **KING**, you must waste not your time worrying about the vain hot air which others blow from their mouths, but instead concentrate upon your ship, the skill and **STRENGTH** that you possess, the course you have plotted, and your determination to reach your destination. Let nothing else concern you. Those who never succeed themselves are quite often the first to tell someone else how. When you listen to the opinions of and take the advice of unsuccessful people concerning matters of your own success, you are certain to get the worst of the bargain. A true **KING** shall always assume responsibility for the outcome in whatever situation he finds himself in.

22

Master, your life is pure potential, until you make the decision to shape it into something with the **POWER** of your will. Your will is the pen with which you shall compose the narrative of your life. In order to attain the honorable appellation of greatness, it is necessary that you develop the relentless and implacable will to become something far greater than what you currently are. To become anything in this world, including great, you must first decide what it is that you wish to be and then do whatever it takes to become that. You shall receive anything in this world that you desire as long as you are willing to pay the price to obtain it. One does not become great simply by sitting still and wishing to be so, nor has anyone's vision ever been made manifest simply by talking about it. The wish to be great shall amount

TO NOTHING WITHOUT THE WISH TO WORK FOR GREATNESS. ONE DOES NOT RISE TO GREATNESS BECAUSE OF AN OPPORTUNITY. GREATNESS ARISES IN A PERSON BECAUSE OF THE WORK THEY HAVE PUT IN PREPARATION FOR AN OPPORTUNITY. IF YOU WOULD CONTINUALLY WORK AND WALK IN THE DIRECTION THAT FULFILLMENT OF YOUR VISION DEMANDS, IT IS INEVITABLE THAT IT SHALL MANIFEST AS REALITY. IN TIME, THOSE THINGS TOWARD WHICH YOU MOVE SHALL COME TO BE. WHILE ALL ACHIEVEMENT BEGINS WITH A THOUGHT, ACHIEVEMENTS ARE ONLY ACCOMPLISHED THROUGH WORK. WORK IS THE LIAISON BETWEEN YOUR ASPIRATIONS AND THEIR CONSUMMATION. GREATNESS IS A CERTAINTY IF ONLY YOU WOULD BECOME INFATUATED WITH HARD WORK AND TAKE THE TIME TO LEARN HOW TO BEAR THE INCONVENIENCES, DIFFICULTIES, AND ANNOYANCES OF LIFE WITH INTERMINABLE PATIENCE. NEVER DESPAIR AT THE DIFFICULTY OF THIS TASK. JUST LIKE ANY SKILL, IT TAKES STAGES OF DEVELOPMENT TO MASTER. THAT WHICH YOU PERSIST IN DOING SHALL EVENTUALLY BECOME EASIER, NOT BECAUSE THE NATURE OF THE TASK HAS CHANGED, BUT BECAUSE YOUR ABILITIES HAVE INCREASED. THE BUILDING OF EVEN THE GREATEST OF CASTLES IN THE MOST GLORIOUS OF KINGDOMS BEGAN WITH THE LAYING OF A SINGLE STONE. TO DAILY BUILD UPON YOUR SMALL TRIUMPHS, SUCCESSES, AND ADVANCEMENTS DURING THE ACQUISITION OF ANY NEW SKILL IS TO OBTAIN ONE TREASURE AFTER ANOTHER. IN TIME, YOU SHALL BECOME FABULOUSLY WEALTHY WITHOUT EVEN REALIZING HOW IT CAME ABOUT. BECAUSE DEATH COMES TO ALL UNEXPECTED, AND ALL OF MEN'S DAYS ARE NUMBERED, IT IS CRUCIAL THAT YOU ALWAYS STRIVE TO GET AS MUCH DONE IN THE PURSUIT OF YOUR VISION IN THE SHORTEST AMOUNT OF TIME POSSIBLE. MY SON, THE WORLD DESPERATELY NEEDS YOUR VISION TO BECOME ONE WITH

THE REST OF REALITY.

23

MASTER, WHILE THERE IS NOTHING SO COMMON AS THE WISH TO BE GREAT, THERE IS NOTHING SO RARE AS THE MAN WHO TRULY BECOMES SO. WHILE ALL SAY THAT THEY WISH TO BE GREAT, VERY FEW ARE WILLING TO PAY THE PRICE NECESSARY TO ATTAIN THIS STATUS. NEVER ALLOW YOURSELF TO BE LIKE THOSE WHO YEARN FOR GREATNESS, WISH TO DO EVERYTHING GREAT, WANT TO RECEIVE PRAISE FOR BEING GREAT, AND YET FLINCH AT AND COWER FROM THE AMOUNT OF CONTINUOUS GREAT EFFORT IT TAKES TO PRODUCE GREAT RESULTS. IT IS ONLY BY DOING SOMETHING CONSTANTLY, FAITHFULLY, AND WITH GREAT STEADFASTNESS THAT YOU SHALL BE ABLE TO ACCOMPLISH SOMETHING THAT IS GREAT AND WORTH PRAISING. WHATSOEVER YOU UNDERTAKE AND WISH TO CARRY ON TO A GLORIOUS CONCLUSION, YOU MUST IMBUE WITH THE RADIANT LIGHT OF YOUR DETERMINATION AND COMMITMENT. THE MORE ENERGY YOU DEVOTE TO ANY ENDEAVOR, THE GREATER SHALL BE THE REWARD THAT YOU DERIVE FROM IT. ALWAYS AIM FOR GREATNESS. IT IS ONLY GREAT AIMS THAT ARE CAPABLE OF AROUSING GREAT ENERGIES. WHEN YOU COMMIT YOURSELF ENTHUSIASTICALLY TO SOME GOAL, THE MORE ENERGY YOU GIVE, THE MORE YOU SHALL HAVE TO GIVE. FOR ENTHUSIASM HAS THE POWER TO REPLENISH ITSELF. SET YOUR SIGHTS UPON AND PLACE YOUR RESOLVE IN THE ACCOMPLISHMENT OF YOUR OWN HOPES AND VISIONS, AND YOU SHALL UNDOUBTEDLY ATTAIN SUCCESS. FOR MEN DO BEST THAT WHICH THEY WISH TO DO. YOU SHALL NEVER NEED NOR SHOULD YOU EVER REQUEST THE PERMISSION OF ANOTHER TO USE YOUR ENERGY IN THE

MEANINGFUL PURSUIT OF YOUR OWN VISION. TO BELIEVE OTHERWISE IS TO DEPEND UPON ANOTHER FOR YOUR OWN SUCCESS. THIS IS ONE THING THAT A **KING** MUST NEVER DO. DESIRE GREATNESS ABOVE ALL ELSE. WITHOUT FAIL, A MAN OF GREAT ACHIEVEMENT IS ALSO A MAN THAT HAS A STRONG DESIRE TO BE GREAT. IF A MAN TRULY DESIRES A THING, HE SHALL FIND A WAY TO GET IT. IF HE DOES NOT TRULY DESIRE A THING AND IS INSTEAD LYING TO BOTH HIMSELF AND THE WORLD CONCERNING HIS DESIRES, HE SHALL FIND AN EXCUSE NOT TO. THE MAN WHO FINDS AN EXCUSE IS NO **KING**. THE GREATEST MOTIVE BEHIND ANY MAN'S ENTERPRISES IS THE DESIRE FOR THE PERSONAL FREEDOM THAT ONE INVARIABLY ACHIEVES IN GREATNESS. ONLY A **KING** IS TRULY FREE. FOR ONLY A **KING** IS TRULY GREAT. IF YOU CAN FIND NO WAY TO ATTAIN GREATNESS, THERE IS NONE THAT SHALL DO THIS FOR YOU. YOU MUST LEARN TO VIEW ALL OF YOUR POSSIBLE ACTIONS IN ONE OF TWO WAYS. THOSE THAT SHALL LEAD YOU TO THE ATTAINMENT OF THE CROWN OF GREATNESS AND THOSE THAT SHALL LEAD YOU TO THE PROCUREMENT OF THE SHACKLES OF MEDIOCRITY.

24

MASTER, NEVER ALLOW YOURSELF TO BE TRICKED INTO BELIEVING THAT LIFE IS AN ARBITRARY SEQUENCE OF RANDOM EVENTS. LIFE IS A LOGICAL PROGRESSION IN WHICH WHAT FOLLOWS ONE MOMENT ALWAYS BEARS SOME RELATION TO THAT WHICH CAME BEFORE. THE LAW OF CAUSE AND EFFECT RULES THE ENTIRE UNIVERSE. THERE IS NOTHING THAT ESCAPES THIS LAW. BECAUSE THERE ARE MANY PLANES OF CAUSATION, THERE ARE SOME CAUSES THAT MAY GO UNNOTICED, BUT THERE IS NO SUCH THING AS LUCK. LUCK IS MERELY A NAME GIVEN TO UNRECOGNIZED CAUSE

AND EFFECT. THAT WHICH SOME CALL LUCK CAN BE CREATED BY YOU IN THE PURSUIT OF YOUR VISION BY CRITICALLY EXAMINING CIRCUMSTANCES IN DEPTH, SOAKING UP AS MUCH DATA AND AS MANY PARTICULARS AS YOU CAN, AND BASED UPON THAT WHICH YOU HAVE OBSERVED, FORMULATING A FREE-FLOWING STRATEGY FOR THE ATTAINMENT OF YOUR DESIRES THAT SHALL PLACE YOU IN POSITIONS THAT AFFORD YOU THE GREATEST AMOUNT OF OPTIONS. IN ANY ENDEAVOR THAT YOU UNDERTAKE, CARRY IT OUT TO THE END. THEN, RESOLVE YOURSELF TO END WHATEVER IT IS THAT YOU COMMENCE WELL.

25

MASTER, CONTRARY TO THE OPINION OF THE VULGAR MASSES, VERY RARELY, IF EVER, SHALL THE PATH OF EASE LEAD TO GREATNESS. IT IS HARDSHIP AND ADVERSITY, THE VERY THINGS THAT MOST HATE, THAT SHALL BESTOW UPON YOU THE STRENGTH NECESSARY TO REACH THE EXALTED PINNACLES WHERE GREATNESS MAKES HER HOME. IT IS THROUGH AFFLICTIONS AND TROUBLES THAT FORCE ONE TO GROW SO THAT THEY MAY SURVIVE THOSE VERY THINGS WHICH TROUBLE AND AFFLICT THEM. THIS INNER GROWTH IS THE REWARD FOR ENDURING ADVERSITIES. IT IS SYNCHRONOUS WITH THE OUTER GREATNESS THAT ENVELOPS ALL WHO HAVE OVERCOME THE CALAMITIES AND EVILS THAT HAVE STOOD IN THEIR PATH ON THEIR WAY TO ACTUALIZING THEIR VISIONS. THERE IS NOTHING MORE VITAL TO THE MANIFESTATION OF YOUR MAGNIFICENCE THAN INNER GROWTH. THUS, YOU MUST NOT ALLOW YOURSELF TO SUBSTITUTE THE ILLUSION OF EXTERNAL REWARDS FOR THE REALITY OF INNER GROWTH. DO NOT ALLOW YOURSELF TO HATE THE STRUGGLE. IT IS THOSE WHO HAVE HAD THE GREATEST

STRUGGLES THAT HAVE GONE ON TO ACTUALIZE THE GREATEST VISIONS.

EVERY EXPERIENCE THAT YOU GO THROUGH IS MERELY THE TURNING OF A NEW PAGE IN THE BOOK OF YOUR EVOLUTION. IF YOU ARE DELAYED IN THE REALIZATION OF YOUR VISION OR YOUR WORK DOES NOT SEEM TO BE COMING ALONG AS QUICKLY AS YOU MAY WISH, YOU MUST NOT ALLOW YOURSELF TO BECOME DISCOURAGED AT THIS. INSTEAD, BE GRATEFUL AND APPRECIATE THAT YOU ARE BEING PREPARED AND TRAINED FOR A GREATER INITIATION THAN YOU HAD ORIGINALLY PLANNED UPON. THERE IS NO GREAT OR EVEN GOOD ACCOMPLISHMENT THAT HAS EVER BEEN ACHIEVED WITHOUT PATIENT PREPARATION. EVERY MAN WHO HAS OR IS PREPARED TO RISK HIS LIFE IN THE PURSUIT OF HIS VISION KNOWS THAT COMFORT IS WORTHLESS, AND A MAN WHO IS TOO AFRAID TO RISK HIS COMFORT IN THE PURSUIT OF HIS VISION HAS A WORTHLESS LIFE. RISK IS A PART OF SUCCESS. YOU SHALL NEVER SUCCEED IF YOU ARE RELUCTANT TO RISK FAILURE. IF YOU WOULD PURPOSELY CONTEMPLATE YOUR VISION AND THEN MAKE THIS VISION THE UNDERLYING THOUGHT TO ALL OF YOUR WORDS AND ACTIONS, YOU SHALL ENTER THE RANKS OF THOSE GREATS THROUGHOUT HISTORY WHO ONLY SAW FAILURE AS AN EXPEDIENT MEANS TO ACCOMPLISHMENT AND HAD THE **POWER** TO MAKE ALL CIRCUMSTANCES SERVE THEM. YOU SHALL HAVE NO THOUGHTS BESIDES THOUGHTS OF **STRENGTH**, WHICH SHALL ALLOW YOU TO ATTEMPT ENDEAVORS FEARLESSLY AND ACCOMPLISH WHATEVER YOU UNDERTAKE MASTERFULLY. YOU MUST TRAIN YOURSELF TO BE MORE ENCOURAGED BY AND FOCUS MORE UPON YOUR SUCCESSES, THAN YOU ARE DISCOURAGED BY AND FOCUSED UPON YOUR FAILURES. AS YOUR CONFIDENCE AND ASSURANCE ARE FED AND

NOURISHED BY YOUR PREVIOUS SUCCESSES, YOU SHALL LEARN TO RATIONALIZE AND LEARN FROM YOUR PREVIOUS FAILURES TOTALLY AND COMPLETELY. IT IS THEN THAT YOU SHALL BEGIN TO SOAR WITH THE EAGLES, HIGH ABOVE THE DULL MULTITUDE, AMONGST THE LOFTY PEAKS OF GREATNESS. YOU SHALL BECOME AS A GIANT AMONGST THE TIMID MASSES WHO ARE TOO AFRAID AND DISTRACTED EVEN TO HAVE A DREAM, MUCH LESS ACT UPON ONE.

EVERY MISHAP, EVERY TRIAL, HAS WITHIN IT THE POTENTIAL FOR A FAR GREATER ADVANTAGE. YOU NEED ONLY HAVE THE **FAITH** IN YOUR OWN ABILITIES TO BE ABLE TO SEE IT. IT IS ONLY THE **FAITH** THAT YOU HAVE IN YOURSELF THAT SHALL GIVE YOU THE **POWER** TO CONVERT ADVERSE TIMES AND TEMPORARY DEFEATS INTO FORCES THAT SHALL WORK FOR THE BENEFIT OF YOUR KINGDOM. NEVER FEAR A PROBLEM. FOR EVEN THOSE PROBLEMS THAT APPEAR TO BE UNSOLVABLE ARE DISGUISED OPPORTUNITIES TO DISPLAY YOUR GREATNESS. NEVER FEAR A CRITIC. A MAN WHO TAKES THE TIME TO CRITICIZE THE VISION OF ANOTHER IS MERELY A COWARD THAT IS TOO AFRAID TO TAKE THE TIME TO FOCUS UPON A VISION FOR HIMSELF. IF YOU WERE ACTUALLY ABLE TO SEE EXACTLY JUST WHAT IT IS THAT RULES AND HOLDS **POWER** OVER THESE CRITICS AND GAIN AN **UNDERSTANDING** OF WHAT IT IS THAT MOTIVATES THEM TO CRITICIZE YOUR VISION, YOU SHALL SEE JUST HOW TERRIFIED THEY TRULY ARE AND GAIN AN **UNDERSTANDING** OF WHAT POOR CRITICS THEY ARE OF THEMSELVES. FAR FROM FEARING THEM, YOU SHALL BEGIN TO PITY AND DEVELOP COMPASSION FOR THEM, AND THEY TOO SHALL ADD FUEL TO THE FLAMES OF YOUR GREATNESS.

26

MASTER, THE BEGINNINGS OF ALL EVENTS SIMULTANEOUSLY CONTAIN THEIR ENDINGS AS WELL. JUST AS NO GOOD, STRONG TREE SHALL EVER HAVE BAD WEAK ROOTS, NO VENTURE OF TRUE GREATNESS SHALL EVER BEGIN WITH INIQUITOUS INTENTIONS. IF YOU BE GOOD AND SEEK GOOD, GOODNESS SHALL BE DRAWN TO YOU AS STEEL IS DRAWN TO A MAGNET. ALTHOUGH THE TRUE MEANING OF LIFE MAY BE ULTIMATELY UNKNOWABLE, REST ASSURED, MY SON, YOU SHALL MAKE NO MISTAKE IN LIVING UP TO THE BEST THAT IS IN YOU. THE MORE YOU FOCUS UPON THE GOODNESS IN YOURSELF, IN OTHERS, AND IN THE WORLD ITSELF, THE MORE SMOOTHLY THINGS SHALL FLOW AND THE MORE EASILY THINGS SHALL COME TO YOU. CONVERSELY, WHEN YOU FOCUS UPON WHAT YOU PERCEIVE AS BAD IN YOURSELF, OTHERS, AND IN THE WORLD, BECAUSE YOU HAVE CUT YOURSELF OFF FROM THE GOODNESS OF THE UNIVERSE, YOU SHALL RECEIVE NO HELP FROM IT, AND MYRIAD OBSTACLES AND NEGATIVITIES SHALL BE PLACED IN YOUR PATH. ONE THING THAT IS GUARANTEED TO CURTAIL YOUR SUCCESS IS THE RESENTMENT OF ANOTHER'S SUCCESS. IN ORDER TO ATTRACT SUCCESS TO YOURSELF, IT IS ESSENTIAL THAT YOU WELCOME, SALUTE, AND APPRECIATE IT WHENEVER AND WHEREVER YOU MAY SEE IT. NEVER BE LIKE THOSE WHO TRY TO PREVENT OTHERS FROM SUCCEEDING BECAUSE THEY BELIEVE THAT ANOTHER'S SUCCESS MAY DIMINISH THEIR OWN IN SOME TYPE OF FASHION. IT IS NOT NECESSARY FOR OTHERS TO FAIL IN ORDER THAT YOU MAY SUCCEED. THE APOTHEOSIS OF ACCOMPLISHMENT IS THE ACT OF REACHING YOUR GOAL RIGHTEOUSLY. TO MOVE IN EVEN THE SLIGHTEST AMOUNT TOWARDS YOUR GOAL BY DOING AN INJUSTICE TO ANOTHER IS A MOST CONTEMPTIBLE AND WRETCHED FAILURE.

LEARN TO FIND JOY AND CONTENTMENT IN DOING JUSTLY WHATEVER TASKS THE PURSUIT OF YOUR VISION PLACES IN FRONT OF YOU. EMBRACE WHATEVER RESULTS THESE ACTIONS BRING TO YOU. IF YOU DO THIS, SUCCESS SHALL BECOME YOUR COMPANION ON WHATEVER PATH YOU CHOOSE TO WALK. ANYTHING THAT YOU ENJOY DOING, ACTIVELY LINKS YOU TO THE **POWER** BEHIND ALL OF CREATION. YOUR LEVEL OF SUCCESS DEPENDS ENTIRELY UPON YOUR CONNECTION TO THAT JOY WHICH RESIDES WITHIN YOU. JOY COMES NOT FROM WHAT YOU DO OR THE POSSESSIONS THAT YOU OWN, BUT RATHER IT FLOWS INTO THAT WHAT YOU DO AND THOSE THINGS THAT YOU OWN. JOY FLOWS INTO THIS WORLD FROM WITHIN YOU AND THE EXPERIENCE OF JOY IS THE MOST IMPORTANT EXPERIENCE THAT YOU COULD EVER HAVE. WITHOUT THE JOY THAT PEOPLE BRING INTO THIS WORLD, THIS WORLD WOULD HAVE NO JOY. PEOPLE TRY TO FILL UP THEIR LIVES WITH MATERIAL OBJECTS WHEN THEY CAN NO LONGER FEEL THE JOY THAT THEY HAVE WITHIN THEMSELVES.

THE IGNORANT BELIEVE THAT THE MORE THINGS THEY HAVE THE MORE THEY ARE. SUCCESS SHALL ONLY CONSENT TO ATTEND THE ORDER THAT HARMONIOUS ACTION BRINGS ABOUT. A VISION WITHOUT ACTION IS MERELY A FRIVOLOUS DREAM AND SHALL AMOUNT TO NOTHING BESIDES DISAPPOINTMENT. A WEAK MAN THINKS OF COUNTLESS THINGS, BUT BECAUSE HE LACKS FORTITUDE AND RESOLVE, HE SHALL ACT UPON NONE OF THEM. BECAUSE HE REFUSES TO ACT, HE SHALL REMAIN ENSLAVED TO HIS VERY OWN WEAKNESS AND DEPENDENCY. THAT WHICH YOU DO TODAY CREATES EVERY TOMORROW; THEREFORE, THOSE THAT DO NOTHING TODAY SHALL HAVE NOTHING TOMORROW BESIDES EXCUSES. ANYTHING OF MAGNITUDE, DURABILITY, AND MERIT GROWS SLOWLY. THUS, PATIENCE IN ANY ENTERPRISE OF

GREATNESS IS A REQUISITE. PATIENCE AND INITIATIVE ARE THE ONLY THINGS IN THIS WORLD THAT YOU CANNOT DO WITHOUT IF YOU ASPIRE FOR GREATNESS. QUITE OFTEN, PEOPLE ALLOW THE MAGNITUDE OF THEIR OWN GLORIOUS VISIONS TO OVERWHELM AND DISCOURAGE THEM FROM BELIEVING IN THE POSSIBILITY OF THEIR VISION'S ACTUALIZATION. THEY ALLOW THIS DISBELIEF TO ROB THEM OF THEIR INITIATIVE AND THEY TAKE NOT A STEP TOWARD THE ACTUALIZATION OF THEIR VISION, NOT REALIZING THAT TAKING THAT FIRST STEP, NO MATTER HOW INSIGNIFICANT IT MAY SEEM, IS THE KEY TO MAKING THEIR VISION REALIZABLE. YOU MUST BUILD UPON YOUR VISION ONE THOUGHT AND ONE ACTION AT A TIME. THUS, BUILDING ONE UPON ANOTHER UNTIL YOU REACH THE HEIGHTS OF GREATNESS THAT IS YOUR BIRTHRIGHT AS MY SON. IT IS ESPECIALLY IMPORTANT THAT AS A **KING**, YOU ALWAYS KEEP THE CLEAREST POSSIBLE SENSE OF YOUR VISION IN YOUR MIND. AT ALL TIMES, KEEP YOUR FOCUS UPON ITS ACTUALIZATION. TO DO OTHERWISE IS TO DO NOTHING BUT ENSURE YOUR OWN FAILURE.

27

MASTER, ONE THING IN LIFE THAT YOU SHALL SOON COME TO SEE IS THAT THOSE PEOPLE WHO HAVE THE MOST **POWER** SHALL ALWAYS HAVE A PURPOSE. FOR IT IS A MAN'S PURPOSE THAT GIVES HIM HIS **POWER**. NEVER CHASE MONEY AS SO MANY MAKE THE MISTAKE OF DOING, BUT INSTEAD PURSUE **POWER** AND PURPOSE. MONEY AND MATERIAL POSSESSIONS ARE AS NOTHING WHEN COMPARED TO **POWER** AND PURPOSE. WITH **POWER**, THE INFLUENCE THAT YOU POSSESS SHALL ENSURE THAT YOU ARE ABLE TO ACQUIRE ALL THAT YOU MAY NEED OR DESIRE, AND IT IS PURPOSE THAT GIVES YOUR LIFE INSPIRATION.

IT IS NEVER WISE TO FOCUS UPON THE PAST, MY SON. IT IS ALWAYS BETTER TO SWIM FORWARD WITH THE CURRENT IN THE RIVER OF TIME THAN IT IS TO ATTEMPT TO SWIM BACKWARDS AGAINST IT. FOR NOT ONLY IS THIS IMPOSSIBLE BUT THE PAIN THAT YOU INFLICT UPON YOURSELF AND OTHERS BY THE ATTEMPT SHALL SURELY BRING RUIN UPON YOUR KINGDOM. BECAUSE IT IS THE VERY NATURE OF PURPOSE TO KEEP YOU FOREVER FACING FORWARD AND MOVING TOWARDS IT, WITHOUT A DOUBT, A LIFE DIRECTED TOWARDS AN AIM SHALL ALWAYS BE A GREATER AND MORE HONORABLE LIFE THAN AN AIMLESS ONE. IT IS SOLELY THE ETCHING OF A GRAND PURPOSE UPON YOUR HEART AND THE MAKING OF THIS PURPOSE BOTH THE FOCAL POINT OF YOUR CONTEMPLATIONS AND YOUR SUPREME DUTY THAT SHALL PAVE FOR YOU THE ROYAL ROAD TO GLORIOUS RENOWN.

PURPOSE IS THE GREATEST PART OF VALOR, MY SON, AND IT IS ONLY WHEN YOU COURAGEOUSLY UNITE YOUR MIND TO YOUR PURPOSE THAT YOUR THOUGHTS SHALL BE TRANSFORMED INTO A FANTASTICAL, CREATIVE FORCE THAT SHALL ENABLE YOU TO BECOME SOMETHING MIGHTIER AND MORE EXALTED THAN A MERE MORTAL. IT IS ONLY THOSE WHO HAVE NO CENTRALIZING PURPOSE IN THEIR LIFE THAT EXHIBIT THE DEBILITATING CHARACTERISTICS OF SELF-PITY, IRRESOLUTION, AND ANXIETY, WHICH ARE ALL INDICATORS OF WEAKNESS. IT IS ONLY ONCE YOUR LIFE HAS BEEN IMPREGNATED WITH THE SEED OF PURPOSE, THAT YOU SHALL BE ABLE TO BECOME TRULY POWERFUL. AN AIMLESS AND PURPOSELESS MAN IS A MAN THAT SHALL ALWAYS BE UNPREPARED FOR THE CHALLENGES THAT LIFE SHALL INEVITABLY THRUST UPON HIM. IT IS ONLY WHEN YOU KNOW EXACTLY WHERE IT IS THAT YOU WISH TO GO THAT YOU SHALL BE ABLE TO PREPARE YOURSELF DELIBERATELY, CAREFULLY, AND ADEQUATELY

FOR YOUR JOURNEY. THE MAN WHO KNOWS HIS DESTINATION AND IS RESOLVED AND DETERMINED TO GET THERE SHALL ALWAYS RECEIVE AID ON HIS PILGRIMAGE. WHENEVER YOU DECIDE TO COMMENCE ANY TYPE OF ENTERPRISE, YOU MUST FOCUS EVERYTHING THAT YOU HAVE WITHIN YOU UPON THE ONE AIM IN VIEW. FOR AIMLESSNESS IS A HORRIBLE VICE THAT SHALL ONLY LEAD YOU TO DEBACLE AND PERDITION.

28

MASTER, YOU ARE A **KING**, AND EVERY TRUE **KING** HAS A MISSION TO FULFILL RATHER THAN A MERE STATION TO OCCUPY. WHILE ORDINARY MEN HAVE DREAMS, **KINGS** HAVE PURPOSES. IT IS BECAUSE OF THEIR PURPOSE THAT **KINGS** ARE ABLE TO RISE ABOVE MISFORTUNES, WHILE LESSER MEN ARE BROKEN, SUBDUED, AND DOMINATED BY THEM. AS A **KING**, YOU HAVE A VERY UNIQUE AND SPECIFIC PART TO PLAY IN THE EVOLUTION OF THE GREATER WHOLE OF WHICH YOU ARE A PART. EVERY **KING** HAS HIS OWN SPECIFIC MISSION IN THIS LIFE. THEREFORE, NO **KING** CAN BE REPLACED, NOR CAN HIS LIFE BE REPEATED. THE TASK OF EVERY **KING** IS AS UNIQUE AS THE FINGERPRINTS THAT ADORN HIS FINGERS. IT IS ESSENTIAL THAT YOU EXAMINE THE CIRCUMSTANCES OF YOUR LIFE SO THAT YOU MAY BE ABLE TO DISCERN THE TRUE NATURE OF YOUR PURPOSE AND CONTRIVE A WAY TO BEST USE YOUR CIRCUMSTANCES, BOTH THE POSITIVE AND THE NEGATIVE, TO PUSH YOU TO YOUR PURPOSE'S COMPLETION. YOUR PURPOSE IS WHAT YOU AND ONLY YOU DETERMINE IT TO BE, AND YOUR LIFE'S MISSION IS WHATEVER YOU SAY THAT IT IS. ASSIGNING TO YOURSELF A LIFE MISSION SHALL BOTH INSPIRE AND GUIDE YOU. WHEN YOU BECOME INSPIRED BY A GREAT PURPOSE, EVERYTHING IN THE UNIVERSE SHALL BEGIN TO AIDE, ASSIST, AND

GUIDE YOU TOWARD THE COMPLETION OF YOUR TASKS. YOU SHALL BEGIN TO RELINQUISH AND LIBERATE YOURSELF FROM THE FRIVOLITIES OF LIFE. ANYTHING THAT IS NOT SERVING YOUR PURPOSE HAS NO PLACE IN YOUR KINGDOM. THOSE WHO CAN ONLY SEE AS FAR AS THEIR NEXT STRUGGLE FOR SURVIVAL SHALL NEVER BE ABLE TO ENJOY LIFE. IT IS ONLY ONCE YOU RISE ABOVE MERE SURVIVAL THAT THE TRANSCENDENCY THAT COMES HAND IN HAND WITH PURPOSE SHALL BECOME ABLE TO BE OF PARAMOUNT IMPORTANCE IN YOUR LIFE.

NEVER ALLOW THE FEAR OF FAILURE TO PREVENT YOU FROM PURSUING YOUR PURPOSE, MY SON. FOR EVEN IF YOU FAIL TO ACCOMPLISH THE PURPOSE THAT YOU HAVE ENGRAVED UPON YOUR HEART, THE **STRENGTH** OF CHARACTER THAT YOU GAIN IN THE PROCESS SHALL BE THE TRUEST MEASURE OF YOUR SUCCESS.

29

MASTER, EVEN YOUR ENEMIES CAN AID YOU IN THE FORMULATION AND DEFINITION OF YOUR PURPOSE. THE MORE CLEARLY AND CONCLUSIVELY YOU ARE ABLE TO RECOGNIZE WHO AND WHAT YOU DO NOT WISH TO BE, THE MORE DEFINITE YOUR SENSE OF IDENTITY AND PURPOSE SHALL BECOME. JUST AS THE OPPOSITE POLES ON A MAGNET CREATE THE FORCE THAT CAUSES MOTION TO OCCUR, SO TOO CAN YOUR ENEMIES, WHICH ARE MERELY YOUR OPPOSITES IN THE UNIVERSE, FILL YOU WITH PURPOSE AND DIRECTION. IT IS A FACT OF HUMAN NATURE THAT MOST PEOPLE NEED AN ENEMY IN ORDER TO FEEL A SENSE OF PURPOSE. PEOPLE ARE MUCH EASIER TO LEAD WHEN THEY HAVE A SENSE OF PURPOSE. WITHOUT A SENSE OF PURPOSE, THE PEOPLE

IN YOUR KINGDOM SHALL RESORT TO HOPELESSNESS.
THEREFORE, THERE SHALL BE TIMES WHEN YOU MUST INVENT AN
ENEMY IN ORDER TO LEAD YOUR PEOPLE IN THE DIRECTION THAT
YOU WISH THEM TO GO.

30

**MASTER, YOUR LIFE IS A WORK OF ART THAT YOU YOURSELF ARE
IN CHARGE OF CREATING.** LIFE IS AN ART AND **KINGS** ARE ITS
VIRTUOSOS. FOR A **KING** IS SIMPLY ONE WHO HAS MASTERED
THE ART OF LIFE. TO MAKE YOUR LIFE THE WAY THAT YOU WISH
IT TO BE, YOU MUST ACTIVELY AND INTENTIONALLY CULTIVATE
CREATIVITY. IF YOU WOULD MAKE NEVER-ENDING CREATIVITY
YOUR GOAL, THERE SHALL BE NO LIMIT TO THAT WHICH YOU MAY
ACCOMPLISH. IF EVER YOU FIND YOURSELF ENSNARED IN A
SITUATION THAT DOES NOT ALLOW YOU TO EXPAND CREATIVELY,
IT IS IMPERATIVE THAT YOU LEAVE THAT SITUATION EXPEDITIOUSLY
FOR ONE THAT DOES. FOR TO STAY IN THAT SITUATION IS TO
MURDER YOUR POTENTIAL FOR GROWTH. NEVER OVERLY
CONCERN YOURSELF WITH THE CREATED. YOU LIVE IN CREATION
AND ARE CONSTANTLY CREATING. OR, IN OTHER WORDS, NEVER
OVERLY CONCERN YOURSELF WITH THE PAST. FOR YOU LIVE IN
THE PRESENT AND ARE CONSTANTLY SHAPING YOUR FUTURE.

BOOK THREE

1

MASTER, MEN DEFINE THEMSELVES BY THE CHOICES THEY
MAKE. EVERY CHOICE THAT YOU MAKE SHAPES YOU AND CAUSES
YOU TO GROW AND EVOLVE IN A PARTICULAR DIRECTION. THERE
IS ONLY ONE LIFE. ALL ARE FREE TO SHAPE IT IN WHATEVER
FASHION THAT THEY SEE FIT. EVERYONE HAS BEEN BLESSED WITH
THE GIFT OF CHOICE. THIS GIFT IS BESTOWED UPON ALL THE
VERY MOMENT THAT THEY ARE CONCEIVED. ALTHOUGH
CIRCUMSTANCES AND ABILITY MAY VARY, THE POSSIBILITY OF FREE
WILL DOES NOT. INDECISION IS THE SILENT MURDERER OF
MILLIONS OF VISIONS AND ASPIRATIONS DAILY. EVEN TO MAKE A
WRONG CHOICE IS BETTER THAN MAKING NO CHOICE AT ALL. A
KING, WITHOUT FAIL, POSSESSES THAT RAREST OF COURAGE
THAT IS FOUND ONLY IN THE GREATEST OF MEN WHICH COMPELS
THEM ALWAYS TO GO FORWARD. IT IS THE MAN WHO STANDS AT
THE FORK IN THE ROAD AND HAS NOT THE **STRENGTH** TO
DECIDE UPON A DIRECTION THAT SHALL NEVER GET ANYWHERE.
A RESOLVED, DETERMINED, AND DECISIVE MAN CANNOT BE
STOPPED FROM ACHIEVING HIS GOALS AND AMBITIONS. BUT AN
IRRESOLUTE, FAITHLESS, AND INDECISIVE MAN SHALL NEVER EVEN
BEGIN TO START PURSUING HIS DREAMS.

2

MASTER, EVERYTHING IN EXISTENCE IS BUT A PART OF A UNIFIED
WHOLE. THERE IS NO CHOICE THAT YOU SHALL EVER MAKE, NO
MATTER HOW LARGE OR SMALL, WHICH SHALL NOT AFFECT
EVERYTHING ELSE. IT IS FOR THIS EXACT REASON THAT YOU MUST

NEVER ALLOW YOURSELF TO DESPAIR. FOR YOU ARE POSSESSED OF SUCH GREAT POWER THAT EVERY DECISION THAT YOU MAKE MOVES THE ENTIRE UNIVERSE. IN ANY SITUATION THAT YOU MAY FIND YOURSELF IN, THERE ARE ALWAYS MULTIPLE POSSIBILITIES WHICH YOU MAY CHOOSE FROM. MULTIPLE CHOICES THAT YOU CAN MAKE SHALL BE ABLE TO GUIDE YOU TO VICTORY OVER THAT WHICH VEXES AND AFFLICTS YOU. HOWEVER, YOU SHALL ONLY BE ABLE TO SEE THESE POSSIBILITIES IF YOU ARE WILLING TO KEEP YOUR EYES OPEN FOR THEM. IT IS CRUCIAL THAT YOU MAINTAIN THE ABILITY TO GAUGE EACH NEW SITUATION THAT YOU FIND YOURSELF IN CRITICALLY, ACCURATELY, AND ACT ACCORDINGLY.

3

MASTER, THE TIMES ARE NOT FOR YOU TO CHOOSE. YOUR CHOICE LIES WITH WHAT YOU SHALL DO WITH THE TIME THAT YOU HAVE BEEN GIVEN. IT SHALL SAVE YOU MUCH PAIN IF WHEN THE TIME COMES FOR YOU TO MAKE A CHOICE, YOU CONSIDER ALL THE POSSIBLE OUTCOMES OF THAT CHOICE AND NOT JUST THOSE THAT YOU DESIRE. GOOD CHOICES ATTRACT GOOD RESULTS AND PLACE YOU IN SUCH A POSITION OF GOODNESS THAT IT IS A SIMPLE MATTER TO MAKE ANOTHER GOOD CHOICE. THE WIND SHALL ONLY FAVOR YOUR SAIL WHEN YOU RESOLUTELY CHOOSE A DIRECTION. IT IS ALWAYS WITHIN YOUR **POWER** TO PROSPER. YOU NEED ONLY TO CHOOSE YOUR PATH WISELY AND HAVE THE **STRENGTH** AND **FAITH** NECESSARY TO THINK AND ACT IN ACCORDANCE WITH THE CHOICE. ALL OF THE CHOICES YOU HAVE MADE IN YOUR LIFE AND EVERYTHING YOU HAVE DECIDED ABOUT YOURSELF ARE PLAYING OUT IN THIS VERY MOMENT BEFORE YOUR VERY EYES.

4

Master, all men are born to live and die, each according to the same rules. Never fail to believe that you can do what any other man has done before you. You are whatever you choose to be. Thus, you must never allow another to determine your value. If you allow another to decide your worth, you shall forever be mired in insignificance. It is a particular peculiarity of human nature that although most cherish themselves more than they do others, the majority of people in this world value others' opinions of them more than they value their own opinions of themselves. You must never allow a defeat or setback to cause you to lower your estimation of yourself if you hope ever to attain your desires. Every defeat or setback which you meet shall mark a decisive point in your life. It is only when you face failure that you shall come face-to-face with the choice of renewing confidence in yourself. Thus, learn from your errors so that you would not be mastered by your mistakes or dwell in doubt.

5

Master, you and only you are responsible for all the good and bad in your life. Never allow tradition to be the determining factor in any of your choices. Tradition has the diabolical **POWER** to rob you of your freedom of choice and disguise your enslavement to it as your duty. The future is a living thing that can

NEVER BE TRULY KNOWN WITH COMPLETE CERTAINTY. FOR IT RIPPLES WITH CHANGE WHENEVER YOU USE YOUR FREE WILL TO MAKE A CHOICE. THE DECISIONS OF YOUR PRESENT ARE THE ARCHITECTS OF YOUR FUTURE. IT IS THE WISE **KING** THAT CHOOSES TO FOCUS MORE UPON HIS FUTURE THAN HE DOES HIS PAST. IT IS BY CHOOSING TO FOCUS UPON THE PAST THAT YOU SHALL PREVENT LIFE FROM RENEWING ITSELF INTO SOMETHING MIRACULOUS. THE FUTURE IS NOT A STRAIGHTFORWARD PATH PURPOSELY FASHIONED BY THE WAYFARER ON THAT PATH. THE FUTURE IS A COMPOSITION OF YOUR THOUGHTS AND ACTIONS IN THE PRESENT, WITH THE CHOICES OF EACH MOMENT PIECING THEM TOGETHER IN ORDER TO CONSTRUCT YOUR FUTURE. THERE SHALL COME A TIME IN THE LIFE OF EVERY **KING** WHEN A DECISION THAT HE MAKES SHALL CARVE THE PATH TO HIS DESTINY. IT IS AT THIS CROSSROADS, WITHOUT HIM KNOWING WHAT LIES AHEAD, THAT HE MUST MAKE A CHOICE THAT SHALL INFLUENCE ALL THE EVENTS IN HIS LIFE TO FOLLOW. AS THE DRAMA OF YOUR LIFE UNFOLDS, IT MAY BE PERHAPS THE SIMPLEST OF EVENTS WHICH CONTAIN WITHIN THEM THE CHOICE THAT PROVES TO BE THE PIVOTAL POINT AROUND WHICH YOUR FUTURE DESTINY REVOLVES. LIVE EACH AND EVERY MOMENT IN THE BEST POSSIBLE MANNER. TO DO SO IS TO LIVE A LIFE WITHOUT REGRET WHICH IS THE KEY TO THE ACCEPTANCE OF AN INEVITABLE DEATH. NO GREAT **KING** EVER HAS REGRETS. FOR ONE COULD NEVER HAVE GOTTEN TO WHERE HE IS WITHOUT CHOOSING TO COME THE WAY THAT HE CAME.

6

MASTER, THERE IS A REVERSE SIDE TO EVERY SHIELD AND A FLIP SIDE TO EVERY COIN. THE PHYSICAL WORLD IS LOCKED

PERPETUALLY IN A WAR BETWEEN EVOLUTION AND DEGENERATION, IMPROVEMENT, AND DECLINE. THIS IS THE EBB AND FLOW OF THE UNIVERSE. THE CHOICE BETWEEN ALIGNING YOURSELF WITH EVOLUTION OR DEGENERATION IS A CONSTANT ONE THAT YOU MUST CONTINUALLY MAKE AT EVERY MOMENT. THE OPTION OF STANDING STILL DOES NOT EXIST. IF YOU CHOOSE DAILY TO ALLY YOURSELF WITH EVOLUTION, YOU SHALL EVOLVE FOR AN ENTIRE LIFETIME AND MOST ASSUREDLY ATTAIN GREATNESS. BECOMING GREAT COMES DOWN TO A SERIES OF CHOICES THAT YOU MUST MAKE IN WHICH YOU REFUSE TO CHOOSE TIME AND AGAIN THAT WHICH IS BENEATH GREATNESS. BECAUSE YOU PROJECT YOUR PERSONAL BELIEFS ONTO EVERY SITUATION, FEELING GREAT IS ALWAYS YOUR CHOICE. THE MAN WHO WOULD FEEL AND ACHIEVE MEDIOCRITY CHOOSES TO SACRIFICE LITTLE, WHILE THE MAN WHO WOULD FEEL AND ACHIEVE GREATNESS SHALL SACRIFICE ALL THAT HE HAS. NATURE HAS NOT, NOR SHALL SHE EVER, SET SUCH LIMITS ON HUMAN EPITHETS THAT A MAN MAY NOT ASCEND FROM ONE TO ANOTHER. A MAN MERELY HAS TO ACHIEVE THE DIGNITY THAT GOES ALONG WITH A TITLE IN ORDER TO PROVE HIMSELF WORTHY OF THAT TITLE. THIS IS WELL WITHIN ANY MAN'S **POWER** TO DO. FOR EVEN THOSE WHO HAVE NOT BEEN GENEROUSLY ENDOWED BY NATURE ARE ABLE, THROUGH GREAT EFFORT AND CARE, TO POLISH, AND TO A GREAT EXTENT, AMEND THEIR NATURAL INSUFFICIENCIES IN ANY AREA.

7

MASTER, THERE'S ONLY ONE UNIVERSE. THERE IS ONLY ONE LIFE. ALL ARE CONNECTED AND ULTIMATELY ALL PATHS ARE CONNECTED TO ALL OTHER PATHS. AS **KING**, IT FALLS UPON YOUR SHOULDERS TO BE THE GUIDING LIGHT OF BENEVOLENT

ALTRUISM TO ALL THOSE IN YOUR KINGDOM WHO WALK THE NOBLE PATH OF LIFE. THE HEART OF A **KING** IS FORGED, NOT ONLY IN THOSE MOMENTS OF INTREPIDITY WHEN HE MUST TAKE A COURAGEOUS STAND AGAINST GREAT ODDS OR OPPOSITION, BUT ALSO IN THOSE OFTEN UNOBSERVED MOMENTS WHEN HE MAKES THE HEROIC DECISION TO PUT OTHERS BEFORE HIMSELF. THE CHOICES YOU MAKE DETERMINE WHETHER OR NOT YOU ARE WORTHY TO SIT ON THE THRONE AND PLACE THE CROWN UPON YOUR HEAD. AS **KING**, YOU ARE THE CENTER OF YOUR KINGDOM. IT IS OF SUPREME IMPORTANCE THAT YOU BECOME THE HEARER OF ALL THAT TRANSPIRES IN IT. IN ORDER TO HEAR, IT IS ONLY NECESSARY THAT YOU LISTEN. IN ORDER TO LISTEN, YOU MUST FIRST CHOOSE TO LISTEN. AS **KING**, IT IS VITAL AND IMPERATIVE THAT YOU MAKE THIS CHOICE. FOR THE FAILURE TO LISTEN IS NONE OTHER THAN THE FAILURE TO PAY ATTENTION. AND THIS IS A CHOICE THAT SHALL RESULT IN THE RUIN OF YOUR KINGDOM. ALTHOUGH IT IS YOUR DUTY TO SERVE AND ASSIST THOSE UNDER YOUR INFLUENCE, YOU SHALL NEVER BE ABLE TO ASSIST ANY WHO IS UNWILLING TO HELP THEMSELVES. FOR ALTHOUGH YOU MAY **LOVE** THEM ABOVE ALL ELSE, IT IS IMPOSSIBLE TO HELP A PERSON UNLESS THAT PERSON IS WILLING TO BE HELPED.

8

MASTER, A KING IS MADE A KING BY HIS CHOICES AND BY THE AGREEMENTS THAT HE MAKES WITH LIFE. LEARN TO SEE AND UTILIZE EVEN THE MOST TRIVIAL EVERYDAY OCCURRENCE AS A MEANS OF OBTAINING THE **WISDOM, UNDERSTANDING,** AND **POWER** REQUISITE TO RULE EFFECTIVELY. TRUE FREEDOM IS HAVING THE ABILITY TO CHOOSE

HOW EVERYTHING THAT TIME BRINGS BEFORE YOU SHALL BE USED FOR THE BENEFIT OF YOUR KINGDOM. ONLY UNGRATEFUL CHILDREN COMPLAIN AND RAIL AGAINST ANY CIRCUMSTANCE WHICH **DIVINE** LIFE PRESENTS TO THEM. A **KING** IS AN INDEPENDENT FORCE THAT DEPENDS UPON NO CIRCUMSTANCE TO BE OTHER THAN WHAT IT IS. A **KING** DOES NOT WISH FOR ANY CIRCUMSTANCE TO BE OTHER THAN ITSELF. FOR A **KING** HAS THE **WISDOM** NECESSARY TO BE ABLE TO USE ANY MATERIAL WHICH A SITUATION MAY BRING TO HIM FOR THE ADVANCEMENT OF HIS GOALS. IN EVERY MAN'S LIFE, IF HE WISHES TO RULE, THERE SHALL COME A TIME WHEN HE MUST SLAY THE BOY WITHIN HIMSELF, SO THAT THE **KING** INSIDE HIM MAY BE BORN. FOR IT TAKES A MAN TO RULE.

BOOK FOUR

1

MASTER, THERE'S NO STRONGER BREASTPLATE THAN A PURE HEART UNTAINTED. VIRTUE IS PRUDENCE AND THE **KNOWLEDGE** OF HOW TO CHOOSE THAT WHICH IS EXCELLENT. VICE, ON THE OTHER HAND, IS IMPRUDENCE AND THE IGNORANCE WHICH LEADS MEN INTO ERRONEOUS JUDGMENTS. MEN DO NOT CHOOSE EVIL INTENTIONALLY BUT ARE DECEIVED BY THEIR IGNORANCE INTO CHOOSING EVIL THINGS WHICH BEAR A CERTAIN SEMBLANCE OF GOOD. IT IS ONLY THE LIGHT OF VIRTUE THAT IS CAPABLE OF BANISHING ALL DARKNESS FROM YOUR KINGDOM. HE WHO FILLS HIMSELF WITH THE LIGHT OF VIRTUE SHALL BE ABLE TO DISSIPATE ALL DARKNESS WITH HIS PRESENCE. AS A **KING**, YOU ARE THE LAMP OF NOBILITY WHICH ILLUMINATES YOUR KINGDOM AND FREES IT FROM THE DARKNESS OF IGNORANCE. IT IS IGNORANCE THAT MAKES UNITY IMPOSSIBLE. IT IS THE LIGHT OF YOUR VIRTUE THAT SHALL BRING FORTH **UNDERSTANDING**. YOUR **UNDERSTANDING** THAT SHALL BRING FORTH **LOVE**. YOUR **LOVE** THAT SHALL BRING FORTH PATIENCE. AND IT IS YOUR PATIENCE THAT SHALL ALLOW UNITY TO FLOURISH THROUGHOUT YOUR REALM. YOUR KINGDOM IS A REFLECTION OF THE LIGHT THAT SHINES FORTH FROM WITHIN YOU.

2

MASTER, THE UNIVERSE ITSELF HELPS THOSE WHO ARE WORTHY AND VIRTUOUS AND IMPEDES THOSE WHO ARE WICKED AND ACRIMONIOUS. ALTHOUGH LIFE AND DESTINY ARE INDEED TO BE

CONQUERED, THEY SHALL ONLY YIELD TO THOSE WHO SEEK TO CONQUER THEM WITH VIRTUOUS FORCES. THE ONLY TRUE RICHES IN THIS WORLD ARE VIRTUES. EARTHLY RICHES AND MATERIAL POSSESSIONS ARE MERELY A REFLECTION OF THESE. THE GREATER AND MORE COPIOUS SPIRITUAL RICHES ARE, THE MORE ADVANTAGEOUS THEY WILL BE. OFTENTIMES, RICHES WITHOUT RICHES OF VIRTUE OF THE SPIRIT WILL BE A GREATER LIABILITY THAN AN ASSET. FOR WITH AN ABUNDANCE OF MATERIAL WEALTH COMES AN ABUNDANCE OF THOSE WHO WOULD ROB YOU OF IT BY WAY OF FORCE, DECEPTION, OR FRAUD. VERY OFTEN, WHEN MEN ARE ENJOYING EASE AND PROSPERITY AND FORTUNE ARE SMILING UPON THEM, THEY BECOME CORRUPTED BY THE VERY SAME PLEASURES THAT THEIR ABUNDANCE HAS BROUGHT THEM. FAR MORE IMPORTANT THAN MATERIAL OPULENCE ARE THOSE VIRTUES THAT ARE CONDUCIVE TO MORAL EXCELLENCE. THE ONLY RICHES THAT YOU MUST EVER GREEDILY STRIVE TO ACCUMULATE ARE THE PRECIOUS JEWELS OF TEMPERANCE, **STRENGTH, LOVE**, HARMONY, AND HAPPINESS. FOR THESE ARE THE RICHES THAT MAKE YOU TRULY AFFLUENT.

3

MASTER, WHILE THE POTENTIALITY FOR VIRTUE IS ROOTED DEEP WITHIN EVERY MAN'S SOUL, IT SHALL FAIL TO DEVELOP TO HIS FULL POTENTIAL UNLESS IT IS EXERCISED REGULARLY. IF VIRTUE WAS AS NATURAL TO MEN AS MOISTURE IS TO WATER, THEN MEN CAN NEVER BECOME ACCUSTOMED TO INIQUITY. INIQUITY IS NOT NATURAL TO MEN IN THIS WAY. FOR IF IT WERE, THEN MEN CAN NEVER BECOME VIRTUOUS. INDEED, MEN ARE CAPABLE OF BECOMING INIQUITOUS, VIRTUOUS, AND HABITUATED TO THE ONE OR THE OTHER THROUGH THE BEHAVIOR THAT THEY ADAPT.

4

MASTER, YOU MUST MAKE IT A HABIT TO FOCUS UPON THE
EXCELLENCE OF THE WORLD. BE NOT LIKE THOSE MISERABLE
SOULS WHOSE SOLE PURPOSE IN LIFE IS TO SEEK OUT THE FAULTS
OF THE WORLD. THOSE WHO ARE EXCELLENT DO NOT LOOK FOR
FAULTS. IN ALL OF YOUR ACTIONS, YOU SHOULD BE INSPIRED BY
AND STRIVE TO EXPRESS VIRTUE. THE SYMMETRICAL STRUCTURE
OF A STRONG, BEAUTIFUL CHARACTER IS BUILT UP AND SHAPED BY
INDIVIDUAL ACTS OF VIRTUE. IT IS ONLY ONCE YOUR ACTIONS
ARE PURE AND VIRTUOUS THAT ALL CIRCUMSTANCES AROUND YOU
SHALL SETTLE INTO THEIR OWN PERFECT PLACE ON THEIR OWN
ACCORD. TO BE A GREAT **KING**, THE CHARACTER THAT YOU
MUST CONSTRUCT AND FASHION FOR YOURSELF MUST BE ONE
BASED UPON THE PRINCIPLES OF INVINCIBLE **STRENGTH**,
VALOR, MODESTY, JUSTICE, LOYALTY, COURTESY, COMPASSION,
AND DEVOTEDNESS. WHEN IT COMES TO THE WAY THAT YOU
APPLY THESE VIRTUES TO YOUR THOUGHTS AND ACTIONS IN THE
WORLD, IT IS BEST TO EMULATE THE BOXER RATHER THAN THE
SWORDSMAN. FOR THE BOXER, INDEPENDENT OF ALL OBJECTS
FOREIGN TO HIMSELF, IS ALWAYS ARMED AND NEEDS ONLY TO
MAKE A FIST IF HE WISHES TO ENGAGE AN OPPONENT, WHEREAS
THE SWORDSMAN IS DEPENDENT UPON A SWORD WHICH HE IS
OBLIGED TO PICK UP WHEN THREATENED ONLY TO SET IT DOWN
AGAIN WHEN THE THREAT IS GONE.

5

MASTER, ALTHOUGH HEAVEN INDEED HAS NO FAVORITES, IT
SHALL ALWAYS SIDE WITH HE WHO IS PURE OF HEART. JUST AS
THE AIM OF EVERY GOOD PHYSICIAN SHOULD BE TO MAKE HIS

PATIENTS HEALTHY AND FREE FROM DISEASE, THE AIM OF EVERY GOOD **KING** SHOULD BE TO MAKE HIS PEOPLE VIRTUOUS AND FREE FROM IGNORANCE. THE RULE OF A **KING** CAN ONLY BE SAID TO BE GOOD WHEN IT ENCOURAGES THE PEOPLE TO STRIVE TO KNOW, UNDERSTAND, AND EXERCISE VIRTUE. IT IS ONLY BY SOWING VIRTUE IN THE GARDEN OF YOUR SOUL THAT YOU SHALL BE ABLE TO GATHER A HARVEST OF FAULTLESS, MERITORIOUS, AND NOBLE BEHAVIOR. NEVER ALLOW YOURSELF TO FORGET THAT "WHEREVER LIFE IS POSSIBLE, IT IS POSSIBLE TO LIVE"[19] VIRTUOUSLY.

6

MASTER, JUST US NOTHING CAN COME FROM ORANGE TREES EXCEPT ORANGES, VIRTUES BEGET ONLY VIRTUE, AND VICES BEGET ONLY VICE. NOTHING CAN MANIFEST IN AN EFFECT THAT IS NOT ALSO PRESENT IN THE CAUSE.

7

MASTER, NEGATIVITY IS NEVER INTELLIGENT. TRULY GOOD THINGS COME ONLY TO THOSE WHO THEMSELVES ARE GOOD. EVERY RIGHTEOUS PERSON SHALL BE REWARDED. DUE TO THE **DIVINE** LAW OF CAUSE AND EFFECT, EVERY MAN SHALL EVENTUALLY RECEIVE THAT WHICH THEY TRULY DESERVE. TRUE HAPPINESS IS FOUND ONLY IN THE DOING OF WHAT IS RIGHT. ONLY THE PRESENCE OF A GOOD **KING** SHALL GIVE THE PEOPLE THE HOPE AND COURAGE TO TRUST IN GOODNESS. THERE IS NO FAKING GOODNESS, MY SON, AND IT IS FOOLISH TO ENDEAVOR TO DO SO. FOR THE EYES BETRAY THE QUALITIES OF GOODNESS,

---

[19] Marcus Aurelius, Roman Emperor. Written between 170-180 AD.

SINCERITY, AND KINDLINESS, AND THEY CANNOT BE COUNTERFEITED OR DISGUISED. ONE OF THE MOST IMPORTANT INDICATORS OF A GOOD PERSON IS THE HABIT OF ATTENDING TO SMALL THINGS AND OF GENUINELY APPRECIATING SMALL COURTESIES. TO SHOW INSOLENCE OR DISPLAY ARROGANCE IN MATTERS OF GREAT IMPORTANCE, IN WHICH ALL ARE WATCHING, IS TO INVITE SCORN UPON YOURSELF FROM THOSE THAT WITNESS YOUR BEHAVIOR. IT IS ONLY THE TRULY GOOD MAN THAT SHALL BEHAVE WITH THE SAME GOODNESS AND CONSIDERATION WHETHER HE IS SEEN BY A THOUSAND WITNESSES OR NONE. FOR IT IS ONLY THE TRULY GOOD MAN THAT UNDERSTANDS THAT LIFE ITSELF IS AN EVER-PRESENT WITNESS, WITNESSING THROUGH HIS VERY EYES, ALL OF HIS THOUGHTS AND ACTIONS, NO MATTER HOW SEEMINGLY SMALL OR INSIGNIFICANT.

8

MASTER, JUST AS INTELLECTUAL VIRTUE (KNOWLEDGE) GROWS AND IS PERFECTED BY THE TEACHING OF IT, MORAL VIRTUE (GOODNESS) GROWS AND IS PERFECTED BY THE PRACTICE OF IT. GOODNESS IS LIKE A DAINTY FLOWER SPROUTING IN AN ARID DESERT. UNLESS YOU CARE FOR IT AND WATCH OVER IT FAITHFULLY, IT SHALL WITHER AND DIE OVERNIGHT. ALL KINGDOMS THAT HAVE CARRIED THE TITLE OF GREAT HAVE ALSO CARRIED THE APPELLATION OF BEAUTIFUL. JUST AS ONE CANNOT HAVE A CIRCLE WITHOUT A CENTER, ONE CANNOT HAVE BEAUTY WITHOUT GOODNESS. NO MATTER HOW DARK LIFE MAY GET, ALWAYS KEEP IN MIND THAT THE SUN SHINES ALWAYS EVEN AT NIGHT. ALWAYS REMAIN FAITHFUL TO THE LIGHT OF GOODNESS. TO THE PURE AND GOOD, ALL THINGS ARE PURE AND GOOD. BUT, TO THE BASE AND EVIL, ALL THINGS ARE BASE AND EVIL. BE

CAREFUL IN THE GUISE YOU ASSUME WHEN GOING AMONGST THE VULGAR. FOR THE VULGAR **LOVE** NOTHING MORE THAN TO ACCUSE VIRTUE AND GOODNESS OF BEING THEIR OPPOSITES.

9

BEAUTY IS THE SUPREME AND PREEMINENT ADORNMENT OF ALL THINGS. TRUE BEAUTY IS THE MOST SACRED THING IN EXISTENCE, SO TO CALL ANYTHING BEAUTIFUL IS TO BESTOW UPON IT THE HIGHEST PRAISE POSSIBLE. BEAUTY DISPELS THE DARKNESS OF THE WORLD AND WITH HEAVENLY **POWER**, GRANTS VICTORY TO THE **DIVINE** OVER THE CRASSNESS OF MATERIAL NATURE. THERE'S ALWAYS SOMETHING BEAUTIFUL TO BE FOUND IF ONLY YOU WOULD LOOK FOR IT. YOU SHALL ONLY LIVE AND ENJOY THE VITALITY OF LIFE TO THE DEGREE THAT YOU ARE SENSITIVE TO THE BEAUTY OF THOSE THINGS AROUND YOU. IT IS YOUR ABILITY TO SEE BEAUTY IN ALL CIRCUMSTANCES THAT SHALL GIVE YOUR LIFE MEANING. ALL THAT WE PERCEIVE IS A REFLECTION OF THAT WHICH LIES WITHIN US. THE WORLD IS ONLY BEAUTIFUL TO THOSE WHO ARE BEAUTIFUL THEMSELVES. WHEN BUILDING YOUR KINGDOM, YOU MUST CONTEMPLATE CONTINUALLY BEAUTIFUL THOUGHTS OF **LOVE**, LIFE, AND KINDNESS. IT IS ONLY BY RADIATING BEAUTY FROM YOUR OWN BEING THAT YOU SHALL ALIGN YOUR PEOPLE WITH BEAUTY.

BEAUTY IS GOODNESS AND THE TRUE **LOVE** OF BEAUTY IS ALWAYS GOOD. NO MATTER WHAT THINGS YOU MAY STUDY, YOU SHALL ALWAYS FIND THAT THOSE THINGS WHICH ARE GOOD AND USEFUL ARE ALSO GRACED WITH BEAUTY. THINK OF THE BEAUTIFUL ELEGANCE OF THE STRIPES WHICH THE ZEBRA WEARS UPON ITS HIDE. HOW USEFUL THESE STRIPES ARE IN AIDING THIS

NOBLE CREATURE TO ESCAPE THE FEROCIOUS LION WHICH HUNTS IT. THINK OF THE BEAUTIFUL GRANDEUR OF THE SPAN OF A MIGHTY EAGLE'S WINGS. HOW SERVICEABLE THEY ARE IN ITS FLIGHT. THINK OF THE LONG, MAJESTIC, AND BEAUTIFUL STRIDES OF A RUNNING CHEETAH. HOW EFFICACIOUS THESE STRIDES ARE IN ALLOWING THIS PRINCELY CAT TO REACH SPEEDS UNREACHABLE BY ANY OTHER ANIMAL THAT RUNS ON LAND. INDEED, MY SON, **I AM** CERTAIN THAT IF YOU WERE TO EXAMINE ANY NUMBER OF EXAMPLES SUCH AS THESE, YOU WOULD SEE UNERRINGLY THAT TRUE BEAUTY AND UTILITY IN FACT GO HAND IN HAND.

IT IS A MOST ABOMINABLE OCCURRENCE WHEN AN EVIL SPIRIT DWELLS WITHIN A BEAUTIFUL BODY. IT IS ONE OF THE GREATEST TRAVESTIES OF HUMANITY THAT, IN SOME, THEIR BEAUTY MAKES THEM PROUD, THEIR PRIDE MAKES THEM CRUEL, AND THEIR CRUELTY MAKES THEM UGLY. IT IS ONLY WHEN THE POSSESSOR OF BEAUTY COMBINES THIS BEAUTY WITH MODESTY, GRACE, AND POISE THAT THEY BECOME NATURALLY REGAL AND TRULY DESERVING OF THE **HONOR** THEIR BEAUTY NATURALLY BESTOWS UPON THEM.

10

MASTER, ALL THOSE THAT HAVE WALKED THE PATH OF TRUE GREATNESS HAVE ALWAYS BEEN ACCOMPANIED BY GENEROSITY AND KINDNESS. THE POSSESSION OF GRACE MAKES A PERSON PLEASING. MERCY AND GOODNESS SHALL FOREVER PRESERVE YOU SO LONG AS YOU UPHOLD YOUR THRONE WITH LOVINGKINDNESS. ALWAYS STRIVE TO BE SEEN AS CLEMENT AND COMPASSIONATE RATHER THAN CRUEL AND VENOMOUS. THERE IS NOTHING

WHICH CAN HAPPEN TO YOU THAT CAN RESTRICT YOU FROM BEING JUST OR SELF-CONTROLLED. TO BE KIND IS ALWAYS WITHIN YOUR **POWER**. NO ONE HAS IT IN THEIR **POWER** TO TURN YOU FROM THE PATH OF REASON AND GOOD JUDGMENT, NOR THE ABILITY TO PREVENT YOU FROM BEING MAGNANIMOUS. THERE IS NO **POWER** THAT THEY POSSESS WHICH IS ABLE TO STOP YOU FROM BEHAVING BENEVOLENTLY. IT IS NOT THOSE QUALITIES OF IRRITABILITY, PETULANCE, OR CONTENTIOUSNESS THAT GIVE EVIDENCE OF **STRENGTH**, FORTITUDE, AND **POWER**, BUT THOSE OF COURTESY, KINDNESS, AND RESPECT. IT IS THESE QUALITIES, BECAUSE THEY ARE MANLIER, THAT ARE MORE NATURAL TO, AND MORE APPROPRIATE TO BE EXHIBITED BY THE SPECIES OF MAN CALLED **KING**.

11

MASTER, KINDNESS, AS LONG AS IT IS GENUINE, IS BOTH IRRESISTIBLE AND UNCONQUERABLE. EVEN THE MOST HAUGHTY AND INSOLENT MAN HAS NO CHOICE BUT TO BOW BEFORE ONE WHO IS RELENTLESSLY AND IMPLACABLY COURTEOUS AND KIND. HE WHO HAS A CONGENIAL AND SWEET PERSONALITY HAS THE **POWER** TO GET ALMOST ANYONE TO BEHAVE TOWARDS HIM AS HE WISHES THEM TO BEHAVE. THE MOST EFFECTIVE WAY TO ENLIST THE AID OF OTHERS TOWARDS ACHIEVING ALL THAT YOU DESIRE TO ACHIEVE IS TO BE SUCH A MAGNANIMOUS SPIRIT THAT PEOPLE WANT TO HELP YOU AND DO THINGS FOR YOU. YOU MUST ALWAYS BE KIND TO OTHERS SO THAT YOU MAY RECEIVE KINDNESS IN RETURN. KINDNESS GIVEN IS KINDNESS RECEIVED. KINDNESS EXTENDED, RECEIVED, OR EVEN OBSERVED SHALL BENEFICIALLY IMPACT THE LIFE OF ALL INVOLVED. UNKIND

THOUGHTS SHALL ALWAYS WEAKEN A KINGDOM. KIND THOUGHTS SHALL ALWAYS STRENGTHEN ONE.

12

MASTER, ANGER, AND HATRED ARE THE CONDITIONS OF THE MIND THAT REPRODUCE UGLINESS IN YOUR LIFE AND CAUSE ALL AROUND YOU TO SUFFER PAIN. NEVER BELIEVE THAT BEING ANGRY OR HAVING A BAD TEMPER SOMEHOW ARE POSITIVE ATTRIBUTES. YOUR GENTLENESS SHALL FORCE PEOPLE TO MOVE IN YOUR DIRECTION MUCH MORE OFTEN THAN YOUR FORCE SHALL MOVE OTHERS TO TREAT YOU WITH GENTLENESS. THE MAN WHO RESPONDS TO THE NEXT MAN WITH KINDNESS IS A MAN THAT IS CONSIDERATE OF THE FUTURE. FOR IT IS IN THE FUTURE THAT HE SHALL HAVE HELP WHEN ADVERSITY COMES DOWN UPON HIM. IT IS EASY TO BE KIND AND GRACIOUS WHEN YOU ARE BEING TREATED WELL AND ADORED, BUT IT IS A TOTALLY DIFFERENT MATTER WHEN YOU ARE BEING SCORNED AND THE WORLD HOLDS YOU IN CONTEMPT. ALWAYS BEAR IN MIND THE MOST EFFECTIVE ANTIBODY AGAINST RUDE BEHAVIOR IS GENTLENESS.

THE TRUE MEASURE OF THE HEART OF ANY **KING** IS DETERMINED BY THE AMOUNT OF UNKINDNESS THAT HE HAS REPAID WITH KINDNESS. ALTHOUGH REVENGE DOES INDEED OFTEN CAUSE ONE TO FEEL HAPPY AND STRONG, THOSE THAT ARE HAPPY AND STRONG ARE NEVER VENGEFUL. MORE THAN ANYONE ELSE, YOU MUST BE KIND TO UNKIND AND PETTY PEOPLE. FOR PETTY, UNKIND PEOPLE ARE THE PEOPLE THAT NEED KINDNESS THE MOST. NEVER ALLOW ANYTHING TO PLEASE YOU MORE THAN BEING MAGNANIMOUS, FREE, POISED, GRACEFUL, AND DEVOUT. A MAGNANIMOUS **KING** IS NOT ONLY PLEASANT AND AT EASE IN

HIS DEALINGS WITH OTHERS, BUT HIS VERY BEING IS CHARACTERIZED BY FRIENDLINESS AND CONTENTMENT. WHILE MAGNANIMITY, THE DEFINING VIRTUE OF A **KING**, MAY ENHANCE AND AUGMENT ALL OF YOUR OTHER VIRTUES, IT CANNOT EXIST ALONE. FOR ANYONE LACKING THE OTHER VIRTUES SHALL NEVER BE MAGNANIMOUS.

13

MASTER, GREAT **KINGS** ARE KNOWN FOR THEIR NOBLE COURTESY, THEIR MAGNANIMITY, THEIR COURAGE, THEIR POISE, AND THEIR KIND SPIRIT. YOUR **POWER** AMONGST YOUR PEOPLE SHALL, IN A VERY LARGE PART, RESIDE IN THE BRILLIANCE OF YOUR CHARM. A MAN'S GREATNESS IS MEASURED BY HIS MANNERS. THE GREATER HIS COURTESY, THE GREATER SHALL BE HIS RENOWN, HIS FAME, AND HIS GLORY. THOSE THAT ARE POLITE AND COURTEOUS ENJOY THE FRIENDSHIPS OF MANY PEOPLE. ELEGANCE AND STYLE SHALL WIN OUT OVER VULGARITY ON EACH AND EVERY OCCASION. COURTESY IS AN IRRESISTIBLE FORCE WITH WHICH YOU MAY DISARM ANY ENEMY OR ANTAGONIST. WHAT HEAT IS TO ICE, POLITENESS IS TO HUMAN NATURE. TWO THINGS THAT YOU MUST NEVER ALLOW YOURSELF TO FORGET, MY SON, ARE THAT A GRATEFUL DOG IS WORTH MORE THAN AN UNGRATEFUL MAN, AND WHERESOEVER COURTESY AND COMMON SENSE VENTURE, TACTFULNESS SHALL NEVER BE FAR BEHIND.

14

MASTER, SELF-DOUBT, AND HUMILITY ARE NOT THE SAME THING. WHILE HUMILITY DESERVES **HONOR**, RESPECT, AND SHALL

ALWAYS STEER YOU TO EMINENCE, A LOW OPINION OF YOURSELF SHALL ALWAYS LEAD YOU TO DESECRATION AND EVIL. TO BE CONFIDENT IS TO HAVE IMMENSE **POWER**. FOR SELF-CONFIDENCE AND MENTAL **STRENGTH** ARE ONE AND THE SAME. CONFIDENCE IS ASKING YOURSELF FOR AN ANSWER AND EXPECTING THAT ANSWER TO BE CORRECT. HE WHO HAS GENUINE AND SINCERE CONFIDENCE IN HIMSELF SHALL ALSO, WITHOUT FAIL, POSSESS SOUND CHARACTER. FOR THESE THINGS GO HAND IN HAND. GREAT **STRENGTH** AND CONFIDENCE LIE IN DISCIPLINE AND SELF-CONTROL. ONLY THE MAN WHO HAS THE **STRENGTH** TO CONTROL AND DISCIPLINE HIMSELF SHALL HAVE THE CONFIDENCE TO MEET AND TRIUMPH OVER WHATSOEVER LIFE MAY FLING AT HIM. JUST AS AN OAK TREE CAN ONLY GROW FROM AN ACORN, **STRENGTH** CAN ONLY GROW FROM WEAKNESS. JUST AS AN ADULT CAN ONLY GROW FROM A CHILD, EXPERIENCE CAN ONLY GROW FROM INEXPERIENCE. A GREAT PART OF COURAGE IS THE COURAGE OF HAVING DONE A THING BEFORE. EXPERIENCE BRINGS ALONG WITH IT, SELF-RELIANCE. THUS, **STRENGTH** ITSELF IS BUILT FROM EXPERIENCE. THE TRUE **STRENGTH** OF CONFIDENCE STEMS FROM A **LOVE** THAT IS CERTAIN AND SELF-SUFFICIENT WITHIN ONESELF. WHILE THE FALSE **STRENGTH** THAT IS ARROGANCE STEMS FROM BUILDING A WALL OF FEAR AND SELF-DEFENSIVENESS AROUND ONESELF, THE MAN WHO LIVES MIRED IN ARROGANCE IS A MAN WHO BUILDS HIMSELF AN ABODE OF GARBAGE AND CALLS IT A FORTRESS.

15

MASTER, CONFIDENCE, FEARLESSNESS, AND SELF-RELIANCE ARE PERHAPS MORE IMPORTANT IN TIMES OF PEACE AND REPOSE THAN

THEY ARE IN ADVERSITY. As **KING**, THERE IS NOTHING MORE REQUISITE TO YOUR ACQUISITION OF **POWER** THAN THESE QUALITIES. CONFIDENCE, FEARLESSNESS, AND SELF-RELIANCE ARE THE DEATH OF THE HORRIBLE DISEASE OF DEPENDENCY. THERE IS NOTHING WORSE THAN SUFFERING FROM THE AFFLICTION OF DEPENDENCY. FOR DEPENDENCY SHALL MAKE YOU VULNERABLE TO THOSE TREACHEROUS ADVERSARIES OF THE MIND, KNOWN AS BETRAYAL, DISAPPOINTMENT, AND FRUSTRATION. A **KING** MUST REFRAIN FROM INDULGING IN ANY OF THESE CONDITIONS AT ALL COST.

16

MASTER, COURAGE IS THE GREATEST **POWER** OF ALL. ALL DARKNESS FLEES IN THE LIGHT OF COURAGE. BRAVERY IS ALWAYS RESPECTED EVEN IN AN ENEMY. INSTEAD OF SEEKING TO ENJOY THE BENEFITS THAT THE TIMES OR OTHERS MAY BRING YOU, ALWAYS SEEK TO ENJOY THE BENEFITS OF YOUR OWN **WISDOM** AND VALOR. WHILE THOSE WHO BY WISE AND VALOROUS WAYS BECOME **KING** MAY ACQUIRE THEIR KINGDOMS WITH GREAT DIFFICULTY, BECAUSE OF THE FOUNDATION THEY HAVE LAID WITH THEIR PRUDENCE AND COURAGE, THEY SHALL BE ABLE TO MAINTAIN AND KEEP THEIR KINGDOMS WITH GREAT EASE. IF YOU CAN LEAD AND ARE A MAN OF GALLANTRY THAT IS UNDISMAYED IN ADVERSE TIMES, WITH THE FORCE OF YOUR RESOLUTION AND DETERMINATION, YOU SHALL KEEP YOUR PEOPLE ENCOURAGED AND FILLED WITH ENTHUSIASM. YOU SHALL NEVER FIND YOURSELF DECEIVED IN THEM; AND THEY, BECAUSE OF THEIR ADORATION OF YOU, SHALL FOREVER KEEP THE CROWN UPON YOUR HEAD AND THE SCEPTER OF **POWER** WITHIN YOUR FIST. DO NOT FEAR THE HARDSHIPS THAT YOUR ASCENSION TO THE

THRONE MAY THRUST UPON YOU. FOR LIKE GOLD IN THE FIRE, A TRUE **KING'S** SHINING QUALITIES OF VALOR AND VIRTUE SHALL BE MOST REFINED AND COME FORTH MOST BRILLIANTLY AMIDST THE TURBULENT STORMS OF FORTUNE.

17

MASTER, THERE IS NOTHING MORE POWERFUL OR MORE DANGEROUS THAN AN HONEST, SINCERE MAN OF INTEGRITY. IT IS ONLY THROUGH THE VIRTUE OF INTEGRITY THAT ONE SHALL BE ABLE TO GAIN THE CONFIDENCE AND **FAITH** OF OTHERS. INTEGRITY IS THE RAREST OF JEWELS FOUND ONLY IN THE HEARTS OF A SELECT FEW. IT IS THE ONE ESSENTIAL REQUIREMENT OF ALL GENUINE AND PROPER RELATIONSHIPS. WITHOUT FAIL, INTEGRITY SHALL ENGRAVE ITSELF UPON EVERY WORD THAT ONE UTTERS, UPON EVERY DEED THAT ONE COMMITS, AND UPON EVERY THOUGHT THAT ONE THINKS TO SUCH AN EXTENT THAT EVEN ONE WHO IS NOT EXPERIENCED IN THE ANALYSIS OF HUMAN NATURE SHALL BE ABLE TO DETECT ITS PRESENCE. AT ALL COST, YOU MUST AVOID DOING, SAYING, OR EVEN THINKING ANYTHING THAT CARRIES THE VILE TAINT OF HYPOCRISY. A HYPOCRITICAL PERSON SHALL EXPOSE THIS DESPICABLE WEAKNESS OF THEIR CHARACTER IN THE TONE OF THEIR VOICE, THE EXPRESSIONS ON THEIR FACE, THE NATURE OF THEIR CONVERSATIONS, THEIR CHOICE OF ASSOCIATES, AND EVEN IN THE MANNER OF ASSISTANCE THAT THEY PROVIDE. WHEREVER INSINCERITY, DISHONESTY, AND HYPOCRISY EXIST, CONFIDENCE AND **FAITH** SHALL NEVER RESIDE. FOR THESE THINGS MIX LIKE OIL AND WATER. BEFORE YOU CAN BE HONEST AND SINCERE WITH OTHERS, YOU MUST FIRST HONESTLY AND SINCERELY BELIEVE IN

YOURSELF. HE WHO HAS NO **FAITH** IN HIMSELF SHALL NEVER BE SINCERE AND UPRIGHT IN HIS DEALINGS WITH OTHERS.

18

MASTER, WHILE FEALTY SHALL BRING ONE **LOVE** AND VALOR SHALL BRING ONE **HONOR**, DISLOYALTY AND COWARDICE SHALL BRING ONE NAUGHT BUT HUMILIATION AND DISGRACE. TO APPEAR AS ANYTHING BESIDES COURAGEOUS, ENTERPRISING, HONORABLE, AND LOYAL IS TO BOTH INCUR AND BE DESERVING OF THE GRAVEST CENSURE AND REPROOF. THERE IS GREAT **HONOR** TO BE FOUND IN LOYALTY, MY SON. THUS, YOU MUST ALWAYS BE SURE THAT THE PRESENCE OF YOUR CHARACTER ALWAYS PRESENTS THE EVIDENCE OF COMPLETE LOYALTY AND AN HONORABLE, UNDAUNTED SPIRIT. THE **STRENGTH** OF A KINGDOM, JUST LIKE THE **STRENGTH** OF AN ARMY, DEPENDS UPON THIS LOYALTY AND **HONOR**. NEVER DISHONOR AND ABASE YOURSELF BY ALLOWING OPPORTUNITY TO CONTROL YOUR LOYALTY. FOR YOUR FOLLOWERS SHALL FOREVER **LOVE** YOU IF YOU ARE LOYAL AND VALUE **HONOR** ABOVE ALL ELSE.

19

MASTER, BEING A GREAT AND NOBLE **KING** SHALL ALWAYS GIVE YOU SOMETHING TO LIVE UP TO. THE PEOPLE SHALL ALWAYS WATCH, MEASURE, AND DEPEND UPON THEIR **KING**. THEREFORE, LET NOTHING BE A GREATER MOTIVATING **POWER** TO YOU THAN YOUR SENSE OF **HONOR** AND **DIGNITY**. IN GIVING IN TO FEAR, DEPRAVITY, ANGER, OR DISCOURAGEMENT, AND LOSING YOUR COMPOSURE, MAJESTY, AND POISE ON ACCOUNT OF THESE THINGS, YOU DISGRACE NOT ONLY YOURSELF,

BUT ALL THOSE THAT BELIEVE IN YOU AS WELL. A MAN WHO HAS NO **HONOR** SHALL DISHONOR EVERYONE THAT HE COMES INTO CONTACT WITH. FOR A MAN WITH NO **HONOR** ONLY VIEWS OTHER PEOPLE AS A MEANS TO RAISE HIS OWN STATUS AND STATURE IN THE EYES OF THE WORLD. IT IS IMPOSSIBLE TO TRULY **HONOR** SOMEONE IF YOU ARE USING THEM MERELY AS A MEANS OF ENHANCING YOUR IMAGE IN THE MINDS OF OTHERS. YOU SHALL NEVER BE ABLE TO TRULY COMPREHEND YOUR OWN GREATNESS UNLESS YOU ARE ABLE TO SEE, ACKNOWLEDGE, AND **HONOR** THAT SAME GREATNESS IN OTHERS. IT IS ALWAYS A GOOD IDEA TO ASSUME AND ACT UPON THE ASSUMPTION THAT OTHERS ARE MEN OF **HONOR** UNLESS THEY SHOW YOU OTHERWISE. FOR YOU SHALL ATTRACT **HONOR** UNTO YOURSELF IF THAT IS HOW YOU MAKE A HABIT OF REGARDING THOSE WITH WHOM YOU MUST HAVE DEALINGS.

20

MASTER, OF ALL THE RESPONSIBILITIES THAT FALL TO A KING, THE MOST IMPORTANT OF THEM ALL IS JUSTICE. THE PRESENCE OF A JUST **KING** INSTILLS A SENSE OF PURPOSE IN HIS PEOPLE. WITHOUT JUSTICE, THERE CAN BE NO MORALITY IN A KINGDOM. BECAUSE JUSTICE, THAT PURE INCORRUPTIBLE ALLY OF MODESTY AND GOODNESS, TEACHES ONE WHAT TO DO, WHAT SHOULD BE DONE, AND TO ABSTAIN FROM WHAT IT IS WRONG, IT CAN VERILY BE SAID THAT JUSTICE IS THE QUEEN OF ALL VIRTUES. WHEN A RULER IS JUST, IT IS AN **HONOR** TO **HONOR** HIS DECREES. WITH ALL THE **POWER** THAT YOU POSSESS IN YOUR HEART, YOU MUST DRIVE TO BANISH FROM YOUR MIND ALL DELIBERATIONS AND CONSIDERATIONS WHICH DO NOT INCLUDE PROBITY, GOODWILL, LIBERTY, AND RECTITUDE. YOUR OWN

FREEDOM AND WELL-BEING SHALL BE IN DIRECT PROPORTION TO YOUR HARMONY WITH JUSTICE. FOR THE UNIVERSE ITSELF SHALL ENFOLD YOU IN THE PROTECTIVE LIGHT OF RIGHTEOUSNESS IF YOU WOULD PERFORM ALL YOUR INTERACTIONS WITH OTHERS WITH LOVE, RESPECT, AND CONSIDERATION.

21

MASTER, ONE SHOULD NEVER EXPECT JUSTICE FROM A MAN WITH AN EMPTY STOMACH. FOR IT IS IMPOSSIBLE TO BE JUST WHEN YOU ARE DISTRACTED BY LESSER THINGS THAN JUSTICE. TO AVOID SUFFERING LOSS OR TO SEEK GAIN AT THE EXPENSE OF OTHERS IS THE VERY ESSENCE OF INJUSTICE. IT SHALL ALWAYS BE SEEN THAT THE GREATEST OBSTRUCTION TO JUSTICE COMES ALWAYS FROM THE EXECUTOR'S CONCERNS OVER HIS OWN PERSONAL INTEREST. MY SON, INJUSTICE OCCURS SIMPLY BECAUSE MOST PEOPLE LACK THE INNER STRENGTH AND COURAGE THAT COME WITH SPIRITUAL AND MENTAL MATURITY. NEVER FEAR TO WITHSTAND THE PAIN THAT COMES FROM INVOKING THE WRATH OF JUSTICE UPON YOURSELF.

22

MASTER, NEVER SAY THAT YOU SHALL REPAY TOMORROW WHAT YOU HAVE THE CAPABILITY OF REPAYING TODAY. FOR JUSTICE DELAYED TOO LONG IS JUSTICE DENIED. BECAUSE MOST ARE UNABLE TO MAKE THAT WHICH IS JUST, RIGHTEOUS, AND GOOD WITHIN THEMSELVES STRONG, THEY MAKE THAT WHICH IS WICKED, WEAK, AND UNRIGHTEOUS WITHIN THEMSELVES JUST. TO BECOME UNJUST IS TO BECOME VINDICTIVE, AND AS A RESULT, HATED BY THOSE WHOM YOU WOULD RULE. FOR THE VINDICTIVE

ARE THOSE WHO WOULD USE A HAMMER WHEN A FEATHER WOULD SUFFICE. ALWAYS MAKE MERCY AND PATIENCE KEY COMPONENTS OF YOUR JUSTICE. FOR PEOPLE DO NOT DO WRONG INTENTIONALLY.

23

MASTER, THE HANDS OF THE KING ARE THE HANDS OF A HEALER, AND IT IS THUS THAT THE RIGHTFUL KING SHALL BE MADE KNOWN. FORGIVENESS AND COMPASSION ARE TWO OF THE MAIN INGREDIENTS OF WISDOM. IT IS THE CAPACITY FOR COMPASSION AND FORGIVENESS THAT A KING EXHIBITS THAT SHALL DETERMINE THE HEALTH AND WELL-BEING OF HIS KINGDOM. IT IS IMPOSSIBLE FOR THE IGNORANT NOT TO COMMIT ACTS OF IGNORANCE, AND TO HOPE FOR THE IMPOSSIBLE IS IGNORANT IN AND OF ITSELF. FORGIVENESS AND COMPASSION FOR OTHERS SHALL ARISE NATURALLY WITHIN YOU ONCE YOU COME TO THE REALIZATION THAT ALL PEOPLE SUFFER FROM THE AILMENT OF IGNORANCE, SOME MORE STRONGLY THAN OTHERS. FORGIVENESS IS THE CHAUFFEUR THAT SHALL TRANSPORT YOU FROM THE PAIN OF A HURTFUL PAST TO THE GLORY OF A MAGNIFICENT FUTURE. TO BE ABLE TO FORGIVE ANOTHER IS TO POSSESS THE ABILITY TO SEE PAST THE UGLINESS OF THE IGNORANCE THAT THEY ARE EXHIBITING AND DISCERN THE BEAUTY WITHIN THEM THAT IS THEIR TRUE ESSENCE. FORGIVE AND BE COMPASSIONATE TOWARDS EVEN THE PROUD AND THE ARROGANT, MY SON. FOR THE PROUD AND THE ARROGANT ONLY DISPLAY PRIDE AND ARROGANCE BECAUSE THEY ARE AFRAID THAT IF THEY DO NOT, THE WORLD SHALL SEE HOW WEAK AND IMPOTENT THEY TRULY ARE. THE CIVILITY AND GREATNESS OF A KING IS JUDGED NOT BY THE FORGIVENESS AND COMPASSION

THAT HE DISPLAYS FOR HIS FRIENDS, BUT BY THE FORGIVENESS AND COMPASSION THAT HE BESTOWS UPON HIS ENEMIES.

24

MASTER, WISDOM IS ALWAYS FOUND IN PATIENCE. THOSE WHO HAVE NO PATIENCE ARE FOOLS, FOR THOSE WHO HAVE NO PATIENCE HAVE NO VISION. PATIENCE IS THE ALMIGHTY, SUPREME VIRTUE AND CHIEF CHARACTERISTIC OF THE POWERFUL. IMPATIENCE, THE CHIEF HINDRANCE TO ATTAINING TRUE **POWER** AND GLORY, IS THE PRINCIPAL CAUSE OF THE IMPOTENCE OF THE INEPT. IT TAKES PATIENCE AND DETERMINATION TO ATTAIN LEVELS OF IMMINENT DISTINCTION IN LIFE, MY SON. DILIGENCE IS NAUGHT BUT CONCENTRATED PATIENCE. ALL THINGS THAT YOU MAY HOPE TO ACCOMPLISH COME FURNISHED WITH THEIR OWN INNER SCHEDULE. IF YOU WOULD JUST HAVE PATIENCE, TIME ITSELF SHALL SUBMIT TO YOUR DESIRES.

THE MAN WHO WORSHIPS **DIVINE** PATIENCE SHALL ALWAYS HAVE TIME AS HIS ALLY. HE WHO POSSESSES PATIENCE, HUMILITY'S FAVORITE COMPANION, SHALL HAVE A MIND AS CALM AS THE DEPTHS OF THE OCEAN AND AS STABLE AS A MOUNTAIN. A MAN WITH NO PATIENCE SHALL HAVE A MIND AS FICKLE AS THE WIND AND SHALL BECOME UNSETTLED BY EVEN THE TINIEST OBSTACLES AND SETBACKS. TO EXERCISE PATIENCE IS TO GIVE SOMETHING ITS DUE RESPECT AND TO PERMIT IT TO DEVELOP IN ITS OWN TIME AND AT ITS OWN PACE. PATIENCE IS SIMPLY THE ABILITY TO ALLOW CIRCUMSTANCES TO UNFOLD IN A MORE SPLENDID MANNER THAN YOU WERE ABLE TO FORESEE. TO BE PATIENT IS TO LIVE EVERY MOMENT WITH THE

UNDERSTANDING THAT THERE IS SOMETHING AWESOME WAITING FOR YOU IN EACH ONE.

IT IS THE WISE MAN WHO GLORIFIES AND REVERES MIGHTY PATIENCE AND MISTRUSTS HASTE. A WISE MAN UNDERSTANDS THAT ALL FRUSTRATION AND FAILURES ARE ROOTED IN IMPATIENCE. IF YOU ARE TO BE A TRULY GREAT **KING** IN THE ARMOURY OF YOUR VIRTUES, YOU MUST MAKE HUMILITY YOUR SWORD AND PATIENCE YOUR PROTECTIVE SHIELD. THE MORE IMPORTANT ONE'S POSITION AND THE GREATER THEIR INFLUENCE, THE GREATER IS THE NECESSITY THAT THEY POSSESS PATIENCE AND HUMILITY.

25

MASTER, IT IS ONLY THOSE SOULS THAT ARE GENEROUS THAT SHALL EVER BE ABLE TO ATTAIN THE DISTINCTION OF GREATNESS. TO BECOME BELOVED BY ALL YOUR PEOPLE, IT IS A MUST THAT YOU EXCEED ALL OF YOUR CONTEMPORARIES IN MUNIFICENCE AND PRUDENCE, AND LIKE THE SUN POSSESS A GIVING NATURE THAT IMPARTS LIFE TO ALL THOSE UPON WHOM IT SHINES. NO ONE MAKES ENEMIES BY BEING GENEROUS. IT IS ONLY BY GIVING THAT YOU SHALL FIND TRUE JOY AND ATTRACT GENUINE LOYALTY. IT IS IMPOSSIBLE TO RECEIVE THAT WHICH YOU DO NOT GIVE. FOR OUTFLOW DETERMINES INFLOW. IN FACT, THE VERY LAWS OF THE COSMOS ARE SO SITUATED THAT THE MORE ONE GIVES, THE MORE ONE SHALL RECEIVE. GENEROSITY IS THE COMMON COURSE WHEN ONE FEELS A PART OF THE WHOLE AND NOT SEPARATE FROM IT. ON YOUR WAY TO GAINING A KINGDOM, IT IS OF THE UTMOST IMPORTANCE THAT YOU BE CONSIDERED LIBERAL. IF SOMEONE ASKS SOMETHING OF YOU, THANK THEM. FOR THAT

PERSON IS AIDING YOU IN YOUR JOURNEY TO GREATNESS BY PROVIDING YOU WITH THE OPPORTUNITY TO DISPLAY YOUR GENEROSITY TO THE UNIVERSE. WHEN YOU SHOW GENEROSITY, IT IS ALWAYS BEST TO MAKE A POINT OF MAKING YOUR GENEROSITY AS PERSONAL AS POSSIBLE. IT IS MORE VITAL TO BE GENEROUS WITH YOUR TIME, PRAISE, APPRECIATION, COUNSEL, AND ADVICE, THAN IT IS TO BE GENEROUS WITH MONEY AND MATERIAL THINGS. NEVER BELIEVE THOSE VULGAR PESSIMISTS WHO ATTEMPT TO CONVINCE YOU THAT YOUR GENEROSITY SHALL AVAIL YOU NOT AND MAKE IT A POINT TO VALIDATE THEIR OPINIONS BY POINTING OUT TO YOU WHEN YOUR GENEROSITY GOES UNAPPRECIATED. FOR WHILE AT TIMES YOUR GENEROSITY SHALL APPEAR TO DO YOU NO GOOD, AT OTHER TIMES, IT SHALL REPAY YOU DOUBLE.

26

MASTER, JUST AS ALL WHO WRITE CANNOT ALL BE JUSTLY CALLED POETS, ALL WHO GIVE CANNOT ALL BE JUSTLY CALLED GENEROUS. THERE ARE THOSE WHO GIVE WITH INTENTIONS TO MANIPULATE, AND THERE ARE THOSE WHO GIVE ONLY BECAUSE THEY EXPECT TO BE GIVING SOMETHING IN RETURN. NEVER NUMBER YOURSELF AMONG THESE, MY SON. FOR IF YOU GIVE EXPECTING A REWARD FOR YOUR GIVING, THEN THAT EXPECTATION SHALL DIMINISH THE REWARDS THAT YOU RECEIVE FROM YOUR GENEROSITY. IT IS THE MAN WHO HATES COVETOUSNESS THAT SHALL PROLONG HIS DAYS. TO THE ONE WHO ALWAYS STRIVES TO GIVE, SHALL COME THE FULLNESS OF LIFE. BUT TO THE ONE WHO ALWAYS STRIVES TO TAKE, ONLY AN EMPTY HAND SHALL COME TO HIM. SELFISHNESS AND GREED SHALL SHRIVEL UP THOSE SOULS WHICH THEY INHABIT AND MAKE THEM SMALL AND UGLY. THE SELFISH,

GREEDY MAN SHALL NOT ONLY TURN HIS BACK ON OTHER PEOPLE'S NEEDS, BUT HE SHALL NEVER BE SATISFIED WITH WHAT HE HIMSELF POSSESSES. MONEY IS OF NO USE TO THE SELFISH, STINGY MAN. FOR TO ACCUMULATE WEALTH HE SHALL DENY EVEN HIMSELF. INDEED, THERE'S NO MAN WORSE OFF THAN A SELFISH MISER. FOR MISERLINESS IS A VICE THAT BRINGS ALONG WITH IT ITS OWN PUNISHMENT.

27

MASTER, A KING WHO LACKS UNDERSTANDING IS MERELY AN OPPRESSOR. UNDERSTANDING IS THE FOUNDATION OF ALL HARMONY. UNDERSTANDING IS A SKILL, AND LIKE ALL SKILLS, IT MUST BE PRACTICED UNTO PERFECTION. AS KING, IT IS VITAL THAT YOU UNDERSTAND AS MUCH AS POSSIBLE. THE MORE YOU UNDERSTAND, THE MORE YOU SHALL BE ABLE TO RECONCILE AND RELATE. YOU ARE THE SOURCE OF YOUR OWN UNDERSTANDING. THEREFORE, YOU HAVE THE POWER TO SHIFT YOUR RELATIONSHIP WITH ANYTHING OUTSIDE OF YOURSELF, WITHIN YOURSELF. IT IS IN YOUR UNDERSTANDING THAT ALL EVIL AND HARM, AS WELL AS ALL GOOD AND BENEFIT HAVE THEIR DWELLING. THUS, IT IS ONLY YOUR UNDERSTANDING THAT IS RESPONSIBLE FOR THESE THINGS IN YOUR LIFE. YOUR UNDERSTANDING IS THE PAINT WITH WHICH YOU COLOR THE ENTIRE PICTURE OF YOUR REALITY.

28

MASTER, IT IS POSSIBLE FOR A MAN TO KNOW A GREAT DEAL, AND YET UNDERSTAND VERY LITTLE. WHEREVER ONE SEES HUMILITY,

UNDERSTANDING IS PRESENT ALSO. FOR UNDERSTANDING COMES ONLY THROUGH HUMILITY. IT IS ONLY ONCE YOU ARE HUMBLE ENOUGH TO ADMIT THAT YOU DO NOT UNDERSTAND SOMETHING THAT YOUR QUEST FOR UNDERSTANDING CAN BEGIN. WISDOM ARISES NATURALLY ONCE ONE BEGINS TO SEEK UNDERSTANDING. IN FACT, BECAUSE THE LIPS OF WISDOM ARE CLOSED EXCEPT TO THE EARS OF UNDERSTANDING, UNDERSTANDING IS THE REQUISITE TO THE ATTAINMENT OF ALL WISDOM. IF YOU SEEK ALWAYS FIRST TO UNDERSTAND BEFORE YOU SEEK TO BE UNDERSTOOD, YOU SHALL BE RECOMPENSED MIGHTILY. THE MORE ATTENTION YOU PAY TO THINGS, THE MORE THOSE THINGS SHALL REWARD YOU WITH THE MIGHTY POWER OF THEIR UNDERSTANDING. AS A KING, YOU MUST NEVER MAKE YOUR UNDERSTANDING A PRIVATE POSSESSION THAT YOU REFUSE TO SHARE WITH OTHERS, NOR SHOULD YOU EVER SHUT OUT UNDERSTANDING FROM YOUR LIFE. FOR TO REFUSE TO SHARE YOUR UNDERSTANDING WITH THE WORLD IS TO DENY THE WORLD YOUR LIGHT, AND TO SHUT OUT UNDERSTANDING FROM YOUR LIFE IS TO BECOME A VICTIM TO THE WORLD.

29

MASTER, JUST AS WHERE THERE IS NO LIGHT, THERE IS NOT SIGHT, WHERE THERE IS NO KNOWLEDGE, THERE CAN BE NO UNDERSTANDING. KNOWLEDGE, WHICH IS A MAN'S AWARENESS OF HIS OPTIONS, SHALL ALWAYS BEAR FRUIT FOR THE KING WHO POSSESSES IT. IN ORDER TO BE A TRUE KING, IT IS A MUST THAT YOU ACQUIRE KINGLY

KNOWLEDGE. JUST AS THE MIND USES THE BODY AS AN INSTRUMENT TO CARRY OUT ITS DESIGNS, SO TOO DOES KNOWLEDGE USE THE MIND TO CARRY OUT ITS DESIGNS. THE MAN WHO LACKS KNOWLEDGE SHALL EASILY FALL INTO VICE. FOR THE WICKEDNESS OF A MAN IS THE DIRECT RESULT OF HIS IGNORANCE. THE NOBLENESS OF A KING IS A DIRECT RESULT OF HIS KNOWLEDGE. IGNORANCE CREATES SEPARATION AND DISUNITY. SEPARATION AND DISUNITY CREATE PAIN. WHILE IGNORANCE DIVIDES, KNOWLEDGE EMBRACES AND UNITES. IGNORANCE IS A QUALITY WHICH NOT ONLY MUST YOU SHUN AT EVERY OPPORTUNITY, BUT UNDER NO CIRCUMSTANCE MUST YOU EVER BOAST OF HAVING. FOR AN IGNORANT MAN IS A FOOL WHO HAS NEVER EVEN THOUGHT ABOUT THOSE THINGS OF WHICH HE IS MOST CERTAIN.

30

MASTER, KNOWLEDGE IS THE MATERIAL WHICH YOUR ATTENTION SHALL USE TO CONSTRUCT YOUR KINGDOM. BECAUSE IT IS MORE FITTING FOR A KING TO BE EDUCATED THAN IT IS FOR ANYONE ELSE, YOU MUST MAKE YOURSELF INTO A MORE THAN AVERAGE SCHOLAR. LEARNING SHALL MAKE YOU KNOWLEDGEABLE, ELOQUENT, SELF-ASSURED, AND GRACEFUL, NO MATTER WITH WHOM YOU ARE INTERACTING. CURIOSITY SHALL ALWAYS BE THE BEST SEEKER OF KNOWLEDGE. FOR KNOWLEDGE OF ANYTHING IS UNABLE TO EMERGE BY ANY OTHER MEANS BESIDES THE DESIRE TO KNOW.

31

MASTER, TO HAVE ALL THE KNOWLEDGE IN THE WORLD IS USELESS IF A MAN HAS NOT THE WISDOM TO APPLY IT CORRECTLY. BECAUSE KNOWLEDGE, LIKE WEALTH IS INTENDED FOR INTELLIGENT USE, THE POSSESSION OF KNOWLEDGE WITHOUT INTELLIGENT UTILIZATION AND EXPRESSION IN ACTION IS AKIN TO SQUANDERING PRECIOUS METALS. KNOWLEDGE WITHOUT WISDOM IS A VAIN AND FOOLISH THING WHICH SHALL BRING NO REAL BENEFIT TO ITS POSSESSOR. ALWAYS EXPRESS INTELLIGENTLY INTO ACTION ANY KNOWLEDGE THAT YOU HAVE GAINED. THE KING WHO LACKS WISDOM SHALL USE HIS KNOWLEDGE AS A WEAPON AND IT SHALL BRING ABOUT DESTRUCTION, WHILE THE WISE KING SHALL USE HIS KNOWLEDGE AS A TOOL, AND IT SHALL BRING ABOUT CONSTRUCTION. BE CAREFUL TO LISTEN AND BE AWARE OF THE WORDS THAT COME BOTH FROM YOUR MOUTH AND THE MOUTHS OF OTHERS. FOR THE WAY A MAN USES HIS WORDS IS THE TELLING FACTOR IN HOW HE SHALL USE HIS KNOWLEDGE.

32

MASTER, IN ORDER TO RULE EFFECTIVELY, IT IS NECESSARY THAT YOU ACQUIRE WISDOM. FOR WISDOM IS THE GUIDING LIGHT OF ALL THE OTHER VIRTUES. IN ALL YOUR DAYS, SEEK WISDOM, MY SON. IT IS A MOST DESPICABLE THING WHEN THE MEN WHO MUST BE LED ARE WISER THAN THOSE WHO MUST LEAD THEM. IT IS THE WISE ONLY WHO ARE ABLE TO ESPY AND DISCERN ACCURATELY THE HIDDEN POISON THAT LIES SECRETLY CONCEALED IN ALL THE AFFAIRS.

THE PRESENCE OF A WISE **KING** UNIFIES HIS KINGDOM. A WISE **KING** VIEWS HIS OBEDIENCE TO THE HIGHER CALL OF RIGHTEOUSNESS AS AN **HONOR** NOT AN INDIGNITY. A **KING** THAT IS WISE RULES, NOT BY BESTIAL FORCE, BUT BY **UNDERSTANDING**, CHARISMA, RESPECT, AND THE ABILITY TO COMBINE ALL OF HIS PEOPLE'S DIFFERENT, DIVERGENT MOTIVATIONS AND VISIONS INTO ONE VISION AND MOTIVATION BY WHICH THE ENTIRE KINGDOM IS BENEFITED. PLACE YOUR HEART IN THE HANDS OF **WISDOM**, MY SON, SO THAT **WISDOM** MAY GUIDE AND TURN IT WHEREVER SHE SEES FIT. TO TRULY BECOME **KING**, YOU MUST DIE TO YOUR LEARNED HABITUAL WAYS OF KNOWING, SO THAT YOU MAY BE ABLE TO BE RESURRECTED INTO THE MALLEABLE NESCIENCE THAT IS THE VERY ESSENCE OF **WISDOM**.

33

MASTER, IT IS ONLY WHEN **WISDOM** IS SHOWN THAT IT MAKES ITSELF KNOWN. THE **WISDOM** OF A **KING** IS PROVED BY HIS ACTIONS AND DISCLOSED BY HIS WORDS. **WISDOM** AND RIGHT ACTION ARE THE EXACT SAME THING. BECAUSE INFLUENTIAL PEOPLE APPRECIATE GOOD SENSE, IF YOU SPEAK WISELY, YOU SHALL GET AHEAD IN THIS WORLD. EVERY GREAT PERSON RECOGNIZES **WISDOM** AND SHALL BESTOW **HONOR** UPON ALL WHO SHOW IT. IN ANY ENDEAVOR, VICTORY SHALL BE ESCORTED BY **WISDOM**, COURAGE, AND PERSEVERANCE. IF YOU CONTEMPLATE AND ARE DELIBERATELY CAREFUL UPON THE DEPENDABILITY OF **WISDOM** IN EVERY SITUATION, YOU SHALL SOON COME TO REALIZE THAT THERE IS NOTHING MORE FIT FOR A **KING** TO POSSESS THAN THIS **DIVINE** HEAVENLY ATTRIBUTE.

34

MASTER, IN ORDER TO ATTAIN WISDOM, YOU MUST TRAIN YOURSELF TO SEE EVERY PERSON THAT YOU MEET AND EVERY EVENT WHICH OCCURS IN YOUR LIFE AS A TEACHER. THE WISE MAN TREASURES STILLNESS. TO BE PEACEFUL, QUIET, AND RECEPTIVE IS TO ALLOW WISDOM TO FLOW THROUGH YOUR ENTIRE BEING. IT IS ONLY ONCE THE EARS OF THE STUDENT ARE READY TO HEAR THAT THE LIPS OF WISDOM SHALL COME. IF YOU ARE WILLING TO LISTEN AND LEARN TO ACKNOWLEDGE AND APPRECIATE WISDOM WHENEVER YOU HEAR IT, YOU SHALL SOON GROW WISE YOURSELF AND YOU AND YOUR WORDS SHALL BECOME A SOURCE OF WISDOM FOR OTHERS. STRIVE TO MAKE YOUR FRIENDSHIPS ONLY WITH THE WISE OR WITH THOSE WHO ARE WISHING TO BE SO. FOR IT IS ONLY BY SUCH ASSOCIATIONS THAT YOU SHALL ATTAIN THE MIGHTY CURRENCY OF GREATNESS. THE WISE NOT ONLY RECOGNIZE THE VOICE OF WISDOM, BUT THEY ALSO OBEY HER EVERY COMMAND. TO RELY UPON WISDOM FOR SUPPORT IS NEVER TO KNOW DISGRACE. ARM YOURSELF WITH WISDOM SO THAT YOU MAY BE ABLE TO ASCERTAIN ACCURATELY THAT HAPPY MEDIUM BETWEEN THE TWO EXTREMES FOUND IN EVERY SITUATION, WHICH IS THE VIRTUE. THE FOOLISH SHALL NEVER EVEN DESIRE WISDOM. WISDOM IS A GIFT THAT IS DESIRED BY, AND THUS GIVEN ONLY TO THE WISE. BECAUSE WISDOM IS RARE, IN ORDER TO ACQUIRE GREAT WISDOM, YOU MUST BE ABLE TO HANDLE BEING THOUGHT OF AS A FOOL OR WORSE. WISDOM ADOPTS AND BECOMES THE MOTHER OF ALL THOSE WHO SEARCH HER OUT AND SHE SHALL RAISE ALL OF HER ADOPTED CHILDREN TO GREATNESS. HE WHO STUDIES WISDOM AND HER WAYS SHALL SOON LEARN ALL OF HER SECRETS.

35

Master, food only looks good to a hungry man. When you have **WISDOM** that another person knows that they need, you must always give it to them. However, when another person knows not yet that they need your **WISDOM**, you must keep it to yourself. To the ignorant, **WISDOM** is as useless as a ruined house. A wise **KING** stores his treasures in heaven. A fool attempts to store his on Earth. To be wise amongst fools is often a dangerous endeavor. To be sane amongst lunatics is oftentimes the height of lunacy. Attempting to teach or explain something to a fool is like trying to wake an exhausted man out of a deep sleep. A fool causes a lifetime of grief. The wise are wise because they admit and correct their mistakes as soon as they recognize them. Fools are fools because they refuse to recognize their mistakes. All a fool is concerned with is foolishness, unaware that even if one knew all there was to know about foolishness, this would not make one wise. A fool cannot help but show his foolishness. For a fool who tries to keep his foolishness inside is like a woman in labor trying to keep the baby inside. It is the wise only that consider the consequences of their words. While a wise person refuses to speak until exactly the right moment, a fool refuses to be quiet even in the wrong moment. Fools say whatever come to their minds, while the wise select very carefully the words which start their voice. Never tell a fool a secret, Master. For a secret in the mouth of a fool is like a thorn in the finger.

36

MASTER, IT IS ONLY RARELY THAT WISDOM DOES NOT WAIT UPON AGE. ALTHOUGH NATURE REFUSES TO GIVE ALL OF HER GIFTS AT ONE TIME, SHE SHALL COMPENSATE YOU FOR THE LOSS OF YOUR YOUTH WITH THE GAINING OF EXPERIENCE'S FAITHFUL COMPANION, WISDOM. AS YOUR YOUTH AND PHYSICAL STRENGTH DECLINE, YOUR UNDERSTANDING AND KNOWLEDGE SHALL INCREASE. GROWING OLD IS SIMPLY A MEANS OF MATURING AND ACCUMULATING GREATER PRUDENCE AND INTELLIGENCE. IF YOU LEARN TO VALUE WISDOM IN YOUR YOUTH, SHE SHALL NOT ABANDON YOU WHEN YOU GROW OLD. CHASE NOT RICHES, MY SON, AND DO NOT OVERLY CONCERN YOURSELF WITH WEALTH. THE POOR MAN THAT IS WISE SHALL SOON BE THOUGHT OF AS SOMEONE GREAT. A POOR MAN'S WISDOM LIFTS HIS HEAD HIGH AND SETS HIM AMONGST POWERFUL MEN.

WISDOM COMBINED WITH DISCIPLINE FOSTERS FOCUS AND PATIENCE. THE MAN THAT IS WISE IS CAREFUL IN ALL THAT HE DOES. SIMPLICITY FOLLOWS WISDOM, JUST AS WETNESS FOLLOWS THE RAIN. HAPPY IS THE PERSON WHO USES GOOD SENSE AND IS CONCERNED WITH WISDOM. WHILE THE HAPPINESS OF THOSE WHO WISH TO BE FAMOUS AND POPULAR DEPENDS UPON OTHERS, THE HAPPINESS OF THE WISE GROWS OUT OF THEIR OWN FREE ACTS. YOUR MOST VALUABLE ASSET, WHICH IS TIME CAN ONLY BE CONSIDERED VALUABLE IN TRUTH IF YOU INVEST IT WITH WISDOM. EVEN DARK TIMES ARE VALUABLE, MY SON, FOR THERE IS WISDOM FOUND IN EVERY WOUND. ALWAYS HAVE FAITH IN WISDOM. ONCE YOU PROCLAIM YOUR LOVE FOR HER, IT IS MADNESS TO FEAR HER LEAVING

YOU. **WISDOM** COMES TO THE WISE MAN IN EVERY SINGLE BREATH.

37

MASTER, THERE'S NOTHING AT ALL ROYAL ABOUT PETULANCE. ANGER CANCELS GOOD JUDGMENT AND BLOCKS SUCCESS. ANGER IS THE GAOLER OF THOUGHT AND THE CRIPPLER OF ABILITIES. WHEN A **KING** IS CONFRONTED WITH A PROBLEM, HE KEEPS HIS POISE AND ATTEMPTS TO GRACEFULLY REACH A SOLUTION BY GARNERING FACTS BEARING UPON THE QUANDARY. THOSE WHO DO NOT HAVE THE **WISDOM** OF A **KING** WHEN CONFRONTED BY THE SAME PROBLEM ARE OVERWHELMED BY NEGATIVE FEELINGS LIKE ANGER OR DESPAIR. EVEN THE MIGHTIEST WARRIOR HAS NO **STRENGTH** COMPARED TO THE MAN THAT IS ABLE TO CONTROL HIS ANGER. **WISDOM** IS ONLY A COMPANION TO THOSE WHO ARE PEACEFUL IN SPIRIT.

38

MASTER, THE MORE LOVING, PEACEFUL, AND HARMONIOUS YOU BECOME, THE GREATER SHALL BE YOUR ACHIEVEMENTS, INFLUENCE, AND **POWER.** THE **KING** WHO HAS ACHIEVED WITHIN HIMSELF THE ABILITY TO RELATE TO ALL OF LIFE WITH POISE SHALL ETERNALLY BE USEFUL. FOR HIS COUNSEL SHALL ALWAYS BE **UNDERSTANDING** AND WISE. TO REMAIN COMPOSED AND POISED WHILE WAITING FOR ADVERSITY AND DISORDER TO DISAPPEAR IS THE ART OF SELF-POSSESSION. SUPREME **WISDOM** CANNOT MANIFEST ITSELF IN A SPIRIT WHOSE TEMPER CAN BE UNSETTLED AND MADE AGITATED BY THE EXTREMES OF EVIL TO WHICH SOME MEN MAY GO. CALMNESS

AND **WISDOM** ARE THE TOOLS MOST NEEDED IN ORDER TO ACT WITH TACT AND GRACE. OMNIPOTENT SELF-CONTROL IS ATTAINED ONLY THROUGH THE EXERCISE OF ONE'S REASON AND THE PERSISTENT APPLICATION OF SELF-DISCIPLINE. THE MOST BEAUTIFUL JEWEL OF **WISDOM**, CALMNESS, IS THE RESULT OF AN ABOVE-AVERAGE **KNOWLEDGE** OF THE LAWS OF LIFE, AND TEDIOUS, PATIENT EFFORT IN SELF-CONTROL. ITS PRESENCE IN A MAN IS AN INDICATION OF GREAT **UNDERSTANDING**. THE POWERFUL, CALM MAN IS ALWAYS LOVED AND REVERED. HE IS LIKE A LIFE-GIVING OASIS IN A THIRSTY LAND OR A SHELTERING REFUGE IN A TUMULTUOUS TEMPEST. GREAT CALM IN A MAN BESPEAKS GREAT **POWER** IN A MAN. THE LESS CALM YOU ARE, THE LESS FOCUSED YOU ARE.

39

MASTER, WHEN THE SPIRIT OF A KING IS ATTUNED TO SERENITY, IT BECOMES READILY RECEPTIVE TO TRUE BRAVERY. THIS, IN TURN, MAKES IT INTREPID, UNASSAILABLE, AND IMPERVIOUS TO SUFFERING. SERENITY INFUSES THE MIND WITH A POWERFUL INFLUENCE THAT GUIDES IT INTO HONORABLE WAYS AND INFORMS IT IN ALL RESPECTS WITH SUCH AN UNSHAKABLE PLACIDITY THAT IT IS IN ALL THINGS READY TO RESPOND COMPLETELY TO **WISDOM** AND FOLLOW HER WHEREVER SHE MAY LEAD WITH THE UTMOST SUBMISSIVE DOCILITY, LIKE YOUNG DUCKLINGS WALKING ALONGSIDE THEIR MOTHER STOPPING WHEN SHE DOES AND MOVING ONLY IN RESPONSE TO HER WISHES.

HE WHO HAS SELF-RESTRAINT IS LIKE THE **KING** WHO FIGHTS VALIANTLY, AND WHO, WHEN THE ENEMY IS STRONG AND POWERFUL, CONQUERS ALL THE SAME, BUT NOT WITHOUT GREAT DIFFICULTY AND DANGER. HOWEVER, HE WHO HAS SERENITY IS

LIKE THE **KING** WHO CONQUERS AND RULES WITHOUT ANY OPPOSITION WHATSOEVER. LIKE A WARRIOR **KING** IN TIME OF CIVIL WAR, ALMIGHTY SERENITY ANNIHILATES SEDITIOUS ENEMIES WITHIN AND HANDS OVER TO **UNDERSTANDING** THE SCEPTER OF ABSOLUTE **POWER**. THE PRESENCE OF A SERENE **KING** INSTILLS A SENSE OF SERENITY INTO HIS KINGDOM. IF YOU ARE CONTENT, ALL THINGS SHALL COME TO YOU. NOTHING COMES TO THE MAN WHO CHASES EVERYTHING, BUT EVERYTHING COMES TO THE MAN WHO CHASES SERENITY.

40

MASTER, EVERY MAN WANTS RESPECT. THUS, IF YOU ALWAYS HAVE RESPECT, YOU SHALL ALWAYS HAVE WHAT ALL MEN WANT. RESPECT IS A BOUNDARY THAT A **KING** SHOULD NEVER CROSS. ALL THE CONFLICT THAT EXISTS IN THE WORLD IS DUE TO LACK OF RESPECT. RESPECT IS THE COMPLETE ACCEPTANCE OF EVERYTHING THAT EXISTS JUST THE WAY THAT IT IS, NOT THE WAY THAT YOU WISH IT TO BE. ALWAYS RESPECT YOUR PEOPLE, MY SON. IT IS THE VERY PEOPLE THAT YOU MUST RULE WITH RESPECT THAT MAKE YOU THEIR **KING**. THE **KING** THAT SHALL RULE MOST EFFECTIVELY SHALL ALWAYS HAVE THE HUMILITY AND REVERENCE TO RECOGNIZE HIS OWN LIMITATIONS AND APPRECIATE THE WEALTH OF RESOURCES THAT ARE MADE AVAILABLE THROUGH DEALING WITH THE HEARTS AND MINDS OF THOSE IN HIS KINGDOM. YOUR KINGDOM SHALL BECOME ETHEREAL ONLY WHEN YOU MAKE THE DECISION TO RESPECT IT COMPLETELY.

41

MASTER, WISDOM SHALL NEVER CONSENT TO BEFRIEND A CONCEITED MAN, NOR SHALL SHE DARE ENTER INTO THE MIND OF A LIAR. HUBRIS IS THE MOST TREACHEROUS COMPANION THAT A KING COULD EVER HAVE. FOR BY MAKING VAIN LIARS OUT OF ALL MEN, IT IS CAPABLE OF MAKING A FOOL OUT OF EVEN THE GREATEST OF MEN. NEVER ALLOW THE PURITY OF YOUR WISDOM TO BECOME OBSCURED BY THE MURKINESS OF YOUR PRIDE. PRIDE IS A FOUNTAIN WHICH SPEWS FORTH VILE POISON. WHOEVER PERSISTS IN DRINKING HER PUTRID WATERS SHALL SOON PERISH. WHILE TRUE SUCCESS BEGINS WITH HUMILITY, FAILURE BEGINS WITH ARROGANT STUBBORNNESS. STUBBORNNESS BRINGS ONLY MISFORTUNE AND CALAMITY. THEREFORE, A STUBBORN MAN SHALL ALWAYS BE BURDENED WITH TROUBLES. WHILE SIMPLICITY AND HUMILITY ARE THE ALLIES OF WISDOM, PRIDE AND POMPOSITY ARE THE CONFEDERATES OF IGNORANCE. HE WHO IS ARROGANT IS ALSO IGNORANT AS WELL. FOR IF HE WEREN'T, ARROGANCE WOULD NOT BE HIS CHOSEN WAY OF LIFE.

42

MASTER, TO THE WISE, SELF-ESTEEM AND HUMILITY ARE THE EXACT SAME THING. ARROGANCE IS A SURE INDICATOR OF INSECURITY AND IS THE VERY OPPOSITE OF NOBILITY. VANITY HAS BEEN THE RUIN OF MANY WORTHY ENDEAVORS. FEROCIOUS ARROGANCE IS OFTEN CONCEALED BY HUMBLE MEEKNESS AND PRIDE OFTENTIMES IS COVERED UP BY PURITY. THE MALEVOLENT PRIDE THAT MAKES A SHOW OF VIRTUOUS PIETY IS THE MOST PERVERSE PRIDE OF ALL. MONUMENTS OF GLORIOUS PRIDE WILL

SOON BECOME MEMORIALS OF TERRIBLE FOLLY. NO **KING** HAD EVER A POINT OF PRIDE THAT WAS NOT INJURIOUS TO HIS KINGDOM. THOSE WHOM HEAVEN WOULD DESTROY; IT FIRST MAKES PROUD. THE THRONES OF THE ARROGANT ARE SOON OVERTURNED. ALL ARROGANCE SUFFERS A FALL AND FACES DISGRACE. TO VIEW THE WORLD THROUGH THE LENS OF ARROGANCE IS TO VIEW THE HEAVENS THROUGH THE WRONG END OF THE TELESCOPE. IF YOU WERE TO LOOK AT THE WORLD THROUGH THE EYES OF AN INSOLENT AND SNOBBISH MAN, ALL YOU WOULD SEE IN YOUR LIFE IS MISERY. BEWARE OF ENVY, MY SON. FOR ENVY IS THE OFFSPRING OF PRIDE, AND IF YOU ENTERTAIN IT IN YOUR HEART, IT SHALL LEAD TO HATRED AND REVENGE ON THE INNOCENT. IT IS WHEN YOU HAVE ALL THAT YOU WANT THAT YOU MUST THINK WHAT IT WOULD BE LIKE TO BE HUNGRY AND POOR. FOR THINGS ARE ABLE TO CHANGE IN A SINGLE MOMENT.

43

MASTER, HUMILITY IS THE GREATEST VIRTUE OF THEM ALL. HUMILITY IS THE SOUL'S TRIUMPH OVER THE FOOLISHNESS OF VANITY. HUMILITY IS INSEPARABLE FROM **UNDERSTANDING**. A LACK OF HUMILITY IS A SURE SIGN OF A LACK OF **UNDERSTANDING**. HE WHO HAS A LOT OF **UNDERSTANDING** IS ALWAYS HUMBLE. HUMILITY ADDED TO ANY SITUATION RESULTS IN **UNDERSTANDING**. IT IS ONLY AN EMPTY MIND THAT FLOATS PROUDLY AMONGST THE CLOUDS. THE MIND THAT IS FULL OF **UNDERSTANDING** BOWS LOW TO THE GROUND. THERE CAN BE NO **HONOR** WITHOUT HUMILITY. FOR THERE ARE NO HEIGHTS THAT CAN BE REACHED WITHOUT FIRST BEING LOW. HUMILITY IS

STRENGTH THAT HAS DISGUISED ITSELF AS WEAKNESS, WHILE ARROGANCE IS WEAKNESS PRETENDING TO BE STRENGTH. A WILLINGNESS TO ADMIT A MISTAKE IS IN ITSELF A SIGN OF IMMENSE STRENGTH. IT IS A TRULY BRAVE MAN THAT ACKNOWLEDGES THE STRENGTHS AND VIRTUES OF OTHERS. HUMILITY OF HEART SHALL ATTRACT MORE SINCERE LOYALTY AND LOVE THAN ALL THE JEWELS IN THE WORLD. EVEN IF YOU ARE OTHERWISE PERFECT, YOU SHALL FAIL IF YOU LACK HUMILITY.

A KING IS ALWAYS HUMBLE AND PERPETUALLY IN A STATE OF GRATITUDE. MERCY SHALL ONLY COME TO AN INDIVIDUAL AFTER HE HAS PARTNERED HIMSELF WITH HUMILITY. HUMILITY IS ESSENTIAL TO THE OUTCOME OF WHETHER OR NOT A MAN SHALL MAKE A GREAT KING. THE GREATER YOU ARE, THE MORE YOU MUST HUMBLE YOURSELF. SUCCESS WITHOUT HUMILITY OF HEART SHALL BE BOTH TEMPORARY AND UNSATISFYING. THE HUMILITY OF A KING COMES FROM HIS UNDERSTANDING THAT HE HAS NO NEED TO PROVE OR ASSERT HIMSELF IN ANY SITUATION. FOR BY BEING OF A RARE, NOBLE, AND MAGNANIMOUS CHARACTER, HE KNOWS THAT HE SHALL ALWAYS DESERVE MUCH MORE THAN HE RECEIVES.

44

MASTER, SILENCE IS THE LANGUAGE OF THE DIVINE. ONLY A FOOL WOULD TELL THE WORLD THE EXTENT OF HIS POWER. IT IS ALWAYS MUCH BETTER AND MORE LIBERATING TO MOVE QUIET AND UNDETECTED. HUMILITY IN AND OF ITSELF IS NOT ENOUGH TO MAKE A MAN GREAT. HOWEVER, WHEN THAT HUMILITY IS ACCOMPANIED BY GENUINE VALOR AND AUTHENTIC CAPABILITIES, IT DOES GREAT CREDIT TO THE KING WHO

POSSESSES IT. ALTHOUGH HUMILITY MAY BE SILENT, PRAISEWORTHY DEEDS SPEAK FOR THEMSELVES AND ARE FAR MORE ADMIRAL WHEN ACCOMPANIED BY HUMILITY THAN WHEN ACCOMPANIED BY ARROGANCE AND BOASTFULNESS. HUMILITY IS MOST IMPRESSIVE IN HE WHO IS CAPABLE AND COURAGEOUS. GREATNESS IN A MAN IS MAGNIFIED BY HIS HUMILITY, AND HUMILITY IN A MAN IS ENHANCED AND MADE MORE APPARENT ON ACCOUNT OF HIS GREATNESS. IT IS ALWAYS THOSE WHO ARE BELIEVED TO BE BOTH WORTHY AND HUMBLE THAT ARE ESTEEMED AND VENERATED THE HIGHEST. NO MATTER HOW GREAT HIS ATTAINMENT AND WONDROUS ARE HIS ACHIEVEMENTS, HE THAT IS TRULY WISE IS BUT LITTLE IN HIS OWN EYES. FOR HE UNDERSTANDS THAT EVEN THE HIGHEST OF EARTHLY ACHIEVEMENTS AND ATTAINMENTS ARE AS NOTHING IN THE FACE OF INFINITE ETERNITY. SEEK NOT PRAISE, AND SEARCH NOT FOR APPROVAL OR APPLAUSE. FOR JUST AS PRAISE ADDS NOTHING TO TRUE BEAUTY MAKING IT NEITHER BETTER OR WORSE, SO TOO SHALL PRAISE NEITHER MAKE YOU BETTER OR WORSE.

45

IT IS YOUR DUTY AS KING TO BE AN INSPIRATION TO YOUR PEOPLE BY BECOMING A LIVING STANDARD OF EXCELLENCE. IN ORDER TO INSPIRE OTHERS TO GREATNESS, YOU MUST FIRST BECOME INSPIRED BY YOUR OWN GREATNESS. ALL OF THE INTELLIGENCE, WISDOM, AND GOODNESS THAT YOU REQUIRE IN ORDER TO CONSTRUCT A KINGDOM OF WONDROUS MAGNIFICENCE IS ALREADY INSIDE YOU. YOU WERE BORN FULL OF POTENTIAL, FULL OF POWER, FULL OF GREATNESS, AND THESE THINGS STILL EXIST AND SHALL FOREVER EXIST WITHIN YOU. THE VIRTUE OF GREATNESS IS AN EXCELLENT ADORNMENT. LIKE ALL

THINGS VALUABLE, GREATNESS HAS A PRICE, AND THAT PRICE IS RESPONSIBILITY. IF YOU ARE WILLING TO PAY THE PRICE OF RESPONSIBILITY, YOU SHALL BE THE SAVIOR OF YOU AND YOUR KINGDOM. NOTHING GREAT HAS EVER BEEN ACHIEVED WITHOUT ENTHUSIASM. TRUST CAN ALWAYS BE PLACED IN HARD WORK, PERSEVERANCE, AND DETERMINATION.

46

MASTER, SUCCESS IS THE RESULT OF ONE'S EFFORTS TO PERSONIFY EXCELLENCE. YOU MUST LEARN TO SEE YOURSELF AS THE WISDOM AND LIGHT YOUR PEOPLE SEEK, THE HAPPINESS AND GOODNESS THEY DESIRE, THE LOVE AND COMPASSION THEY CRAVE, AND THE ABUNDANCE AND PROSPERITY THEY DESERVE. BECAUSE PROSPERITY AND SUCCESS OFTEN INVITE SLOTH AND INDOLENCE, YOU MUST AT ALL TIMES BE WATCHFUL AND PREPARED TO CONQUER THESE ATTENDANT VICES.

47

MASTER, GREATNESS OCCURS WHEN YOU CONTINUALLY EXCEED EXPECTATIONS. EXPERTISE AND IMPRESSIVE RÉSUMÉS MATTER FAR LESS IN BECOMING A GREAT KING THAN DO CHARACTER AND THE CAPACITY TO SERVE AND SACRIFICE. CHARACTER REVEALS ITSELF IN WHAT A MAN CHOOSES TO DO WHEN THERE IS NO OBLIGATION OR OUTSIDE COMPULSION. AS YOUR CHARACTER GROWS IN STRENGTH, WISDOM, AND HUMILITY, YOUR KINGDOM SHALL GROW IN PROPORTION TO THESE THINGS. FRET NOT OVER WHERE YOU WERE BORN OR THE HISTORY OF YOUR FAMILY. THESE THINGS IN THEMSELVES HAVE NOT THE ABILITY TO HINDER YOU FROM BEING GREAT. THE FINEST GIFTS OF

NATURE ARE QUITE OFTEN FOUND IN PERSONS OF VERY HUMBLE FAMILIES. A UNIVERSAL CHARACTERISTIC OF GREATNESS IS HUMILITY. FOR THE GREAT UNDERSTAND THAT THEIR GIFTS COME FROM A HIGHER **POWER**. NEVER FORGET, IT IS NOT NECESSARY THAT YOU HAVE A DEGREE IN ORDER TO HAVE THE QUALITIES OF A **KING**.

48

MASTER, POWERFUL MEN TEND TO BE INTENSE AND PENSIVE. THE GREATNESS OF A MAN IS FOUND NOT IN A SINGLE ACT, BUT RATHER IN THE COLLECTION OF HABITS THAT HE POSSESSES. IN ORDER TO ACHIEVE GREATNESS, YOU MUST NEVER ALLOW YOURSELF TO BECOME SPITEFUL, CRAVING, SUSPICIOUS, OR PEDANTIC. YOU MUST MURDER ALL OF THE CAPRICIOUSNESS, FRIVOLOUSNESS, MEAN-SPIRITEDNESS, AND IRRESOLUTION THAT YOU HAVE INSIDE YOU. TO BE CONSIDERED TO BE ANY OF THESE THINGS IS TO BE HELD IN CONTEMPT. IN ALL OF YOUR ACTS, YOU MUST DISPLAY THE TRAITS OF COURAGE, GRAVITY, AND FORTITUDE. THESE ARE THE VIRTUES THAT SHALL CAUSE YOU TO BE HELD IN AWE. IF YOU WOULD BE JUST, TEMPERATE, STRONG, WISE, MUNIFICENT, AND CLEMENT, YOU SHALL EARN GLORY AND FAVOR BOTH IN HEAVEN AND ON EARTH. THROUGH GRACE, YOU SHALL ACQUIRE THAT HEROIC VIRTUE, WHICH SHALL RAISE YOU ABOVE THE HINDRANCES THAT PLAGUE THE MASSES AND MAKE YOU CAPABLE OF BEING REGARDED AS AN EXTRAORDINARY MAN.

THE UNIVERSE DELIGHTS IN AND PROTECTS, NOT THOSE **KINGS** WHO WISH TO IMITATE THE MIGHT OF NATURE BY DISPLAYING THEIR GREAT **POWER** AND MAKING THEMSELVES FEARED BY MEN, BUT THOSE WHO WITH THE **POWER** THAT

THEY WIELD, STRIVE TO RESEMBLE NATURE IN BENEVOLENCE AND **WISDOM.** THESE DUTIFUL SERVANTS STRIVE VICTORIOUSLY TO WORK AND DISTRIBUTE FOR THE GOODNESS OF THEIR KINGDOM THE AWESOME **DIVINE** GIFTS AND BENEFITS WHICH NATURE HAS BESTOWED UPON THEM. IT IS YOUR OWN INTEGRITY AND DETERMINATIONS THAT YOU MUST MAKE YOUR STANDARD OF RIGHTNESS AND NOT SOME EXTERNAL PRECEPT. A **KING** MUST FOREVER REMAIN MORE INDEBTED TO THE STRICTNESS OF HIS OWN OPINIONS AND JUDGMENTS OF HIMSELF THAN TO THE OPINIONS AND JUDGMENTS THAT OTHERS THRUST UPON HIM.

49

MASTER, THE THREE THINGS THAT INTELLIGENT MEN LOOK FOR IN THOSE THEY WOULD FOLLOW ARE A STRONG WILL, INTELLIGENCE, AND A HEART FILLED WITH COMPASSION. INTELLIGENT MEN UNDERSTAND THAT INTERNAL FACTORS, NOT EXTERNAL, THAT ARE THE MOST CRUCIAL IN ASSESSING AND EVALUATING THE GREATNESS OF ANOTHER HUMAN BEING. IT IS NOT WEALTH, POPULARITY, OR SOCIAL STATUS, BUT SINCERITY, GENEROSITY, HONESTY, SIMPLICITY, AND HUMILITY, ALL QUALITIES THAT ARE WITHIN EASY REACH OF EVERY SOUL, THAT ARE THE TRUE INDICATORS OF ONE'S ELEVATION. JEALOUSY, THAT MOST IGNOBLE OF VICES, IS A COMMON AFFLICTION AMONGST LESSER MEN. IT IS DUE ENTIRELY TO A LACK OF RESPECT. ANY WHO IS JEALOUS OF ANOTHER IS SO BECAUSE THEY HAVE NO RESPECT FOR THEMSELVES AND THEIR OWN ABILITIES. THERE IS NOTHING WHICH ANOTHER MAY ACCOMPLISH THAT YOU MAY NOT. RESPECT ALLOWS ONE TO SEE THINGS AS THEY TRULY ARE. THUS, IT MUST TAKE PRECEDENCE IN ALL THINGS. THERE CAN BE NO GREATNESS WITHOUT RESPECT.

50

MASTER, A NOBLE HEART SHALL ALWAYS BE FOUND IN THE MAN WHO PERSEVERES. A TRULY NOBLE PERSON IS ONE THAT IS FULLY AWARE THAT HE IS PERFORMING A PART IN THE **DIVINE** HISTORICAL DRAMA KNOWN AS THE HISTORY OF THE UNIVERSE. NOBILITY IS A BRIGHT LIGHT THAT NOT ONLY MAKES CLEAR AND VISIBLE TO YOU WHAT SHOULD AND SHOULD NOT BE DONE, BUT ALSO INSPIRES YOU TO HIGH PERFORMANCE BY INSTILLING WITHIN YOU A HOPE OF VENERATION AND A FEAR OF DISHONOR. BECAUSE THEY DO NOT HAVE THE BRILLIANCE OF NOBILITY IN THEIR POSSESSION, ORDINARY MEN LACK THE HOPE OF BEING VENERATED AND CARE NOT IN THE LEAST ABOUT DISHONOR. THOSE WHO LACK NOBILITY ARE UNLIKELY TO STRENGTHEN AND INCREASE THE KINGDOMS IN WHICH THEY DWELL. FOR THOSE WITHOUT NOBILITY DO NOT BELIEVE THAT THEY ARE BOUND TO SURPASS WHAT WAS ACHIEVED BY THEIR FORBEARERS, OR EVEN TO ATTAIN THEIR LEVEL OF ACHIEVEMENT. THE NOBLE SHALL ALWAYS INCREASE AND EXPAND THE KINGDOMS IN WHICH THEY ARE FOUND. FOR THE NOBLE, IT IS REPREHENSIBLE NOT TO ATTAIN AT LEAST THE STANDARD SET BY THEIR ANCESTORS. TRUE NOBILITY SHALL NEVER BE FOUND IN BEING BETTER THAN SOMEONE ELSE. IT SHALL ONLY BE FOUND IN BEING BETTER THAN YOU USED TO BE.

BOOK FIVE

1

MASTER, YOU MUST NEVER ALLOW YOURSELF TO FALTER IN YOUR STEPS, FOR IT IS THE PATH OF THE KING THAT LIES BEFORE YOUR FEET. YOU WERE SINGLED OUT TO BE A KING BY A DIVINE DETERMINATION THAT WAS MADE AT THE COMMENCEMENT OF TIME. BECAUSE YOU HAVE A VERY SIGNIFICANT PART TO PLAY IN THE DIVINE DRAMA OF EXISTENCE, IT IS OF THE UTMOST IMPORTANCE THAT YOU TRANSCEND THE EVANESCENCE AND INSIGNIFICANCE OF ORDINARY HUMAN EXISTENCE SO THAT YOU MAY REACH A NEW AND HIGHER STATE OF DIGNITY AND MAJESTY. A KING ACTS AS A KING BECAUSE HE IS A KING, AND A KING IS A KING BECAUSE HE ACTS AS A KING. THE WAY THAT YOU CONDUCT YOURSELF SHALL ALWAYS DETERMINE HOW THE UNIVERSE SHALL TREAT YOU. THE GREATEST OF KINGS ARE NOT CROWNED BY OTHERS, BUT RATHER BY THEIR OWN WAYS AND ACTIONS. ELEVATE YOURSELF ABOVE THE MASSES. IT IS YOU, NOT THEY, THAT HAVE BEEN SINGLED OUT FOR GREATNESS. ALWAYS GIVE YOUR PEOPLE SOMETHING TO BELIEVE IN AND FOLLOW. A KING IS INSPIRATION ITSELF. MAKE ALL OF YOUR THOUGHTS ETHEREAL AND SUBLIME SO THAT YOUR DEEDS MAY BE LOFTY AND ALL OF YOUR ACTIONS MAY BE WORTHY OF A KING. IN ALL YOUR DOINGS, SHOW THE WORLD THAT YOU DESERVE TO BE KING. CONDUCT YOURSELF IN SUCH A REGAL AND GRACEFUL MANNER THAT IT SHOWS ALL THOSE WHOM YOU WOULD RULE THAT IT IS IN THEIR BEST INTEREST FOR YOU TO DO SO. NO MATTER WHAT THE CIRCUMSTANCES MAY BE, A TRUE KING ALWAYS DISPLAYS ROYAL DIGNITY AND NOBLE GRACE.

2

MASTER, HE WHO REPEATEDLY HAS THE NEED TO TELL OTHERS THAT HE IS KING IS NO TRUE KING AT ALL. BEFORE YOU SEEK THE TITLE OF KING, YOU MUST FIRST SEEK THE CHARACTER OF A KING. THE CHARACTER OF A KING SHALL ALWAYS COMBINE IN BEAUTIFUL MEASURE, GRAVITY WITH CHARM. A KING DOES WHATEVER NEEDS TO BE DONE WITHOUT MAKING A FUSS ABOUT IT. IN HIS HEART, A TRUE KING SHALL BE RELUCTANT TO TAKE THE THRONE, BUT HE SHALL ALWAYS BE WILLING TO DO SO ON THE BEHALF OF THOSE WHO DWELL IN THE REALM. CHARACTER IS NOT SOMETHING THAT CAN BE COUNTERFEITED OR HID. IF YOU REHEARSE AN ACT THAT YOU NEVER MEANT THE AUDIENCE TO SEE, SOONER OR LATER THEY SHALL SEE IT. AS KING, YOU ARE THE SEED FROM WHICH YOUR KINGDOM SHALL SPROUT. ALWAYS RULE AS YOU MUST FOR YOUR KINGDOM TO BE GREAT.

3

MASTER, THE FIRST STEP IN LEARNING HOW TO RULE IS LEARNING TO RULE YOURSELF. A GREAT KING IS A KING WHO ALWAYS MAINTAINS THE ABILITY TO GOVERN HIMSELF. A GREAT KING IS ASTUTE IN THE MANAGEMENT OF HIS AFFAIRS, EXHIBITS GREAT SKILL AND EXCELLENT JUDGMENT IN THE UTILIZATION OF HIS RESOURCES, AND ALWAYS SHOWS PRUDENCE AND CIRCUMSPECTION DURING STORMS OF ADVERSITY. BECAUSE HE HAS THE PATIENCE OF SOMEONE WHO IS ALREADY ON TOP, A GREAT KING ALWAYS ACTS WITH GRACE UNDER FIRE. IF YOU DO NOT DISCIPLINE YOURSELF TO ACT WITH REASON, EVERYONE ELSE SHALL PAY THE PRICE OF YOUR PASSION.

4

MASTER, LEADERSHIP IS SIMPLY ONE DOING THE CORRECT THINGS. IT IS NO SHAME OR DISGRACE FOR A **KING** TO APPEASE A MAN WHEN IT WAS THE **KING** HIMSELF WHO FIRST GAVE OFFENCE. A **KING** MUST NEVER RELINQUISH THE **DIGNITY** OF HIS RANK UNDER ANY CIRCUMSTANCE. HE MUST MAKE HIMSELF A LIVING EXAMPLE OF CIVILITY AND GRACE, WHILE MAINTAINING HIS INDEPENDENCE AT THE SAME TIME. IT IS ONLY BY MAINTAINING YOUR INDEPENDENCE THAT YOU SHALL BE ABLE TO RULE. FOR ONCE THOSE YOU SEEK TO RULE FEEL THAT THEY POSSESS YOU, YOU SHALL LOSE ALL **POWER** TO RULE THEM. ALTHOUGH YOU MUST ALWAYS MAINTAIN YOUR INDEPENDENCE, YOU MUST NEVER DISCONNECT FROM YOUR PEOPLE. FOR TO ISOLATE YOURSELF FROM YOUR PEOPLE IS TO INSULT THEM AND GIVE THEM REASON FOR INSURRECTION AND MUTINY.

5

MASTER, A TRUE **KING** RULES SO THAT HE MAY BE A SLAVE TO HIS PEOPLE AND HAVE THE OPPORTUNITY TO GIVE HIS LIFE TO HIS KINGDOM. THE FINEST **KINGS** ARE THOSE THAT LISTEN MORE THAN THEY TALK. MAKE YOUR RULE SWEET AND SERENE LIKE THAT OF A LOVING FATHER OVER A GOOD SON. A GOOD **KING** SHOULD ALWAYS DO EVERYTHING IN HIS **POWER** TO MAKE HIS KINGDOM LIKE THE KINGDOM OF HEAVEN FOR THE SAKE OF ALL THOSE WHO ABIDE IN HIS DOMAIN.

6

MASTER, IF AN ACTION IS NOT RIGHTEOUS, IT IS NOT RIGHT FOR A KING TO DO IT. NEVER PROFESS TO BE A GREAT EATER OR DRINKER OF LIQUOR, MY SON, AND REFRAIN FROM INDULGING IN BAD HABITS, OR FROM BEING DISGUSTING AND DISSOLUTE IN YOUR MANNER OF LIVING. TO DO THESE THINGS WOULD BE TO ACT LIKE A PEASANT WHO STINKS OF INELEGANCE AND VULGARITY FROM A MILE AWAY. IT IS NOT ALWAYS FITTING FOR A KING TO CAUSE LAUGHTER. ALTHOUGH IT MAY SEEM THAT STUPID ACTING FOOLS, DRUNKARDS, CLOWNS, OR BUFFOONS MAY BE IN HIGH DEMAND ON ACCOUNT OF THEIR COMEDIC VALUE, THEY MERIT NEITHER THE TITLE NOR DIGNITY OF KING. THE WAY A KING ACTS AND BEHAVES ACTS AS A GUIDE AND MODEL FOR HIS PEOPLE. HIS CONDUCT NECESSARILY GOVERNS THE CONDUCT OF ALL. THE MOST CONVINCING PROOF THAT A KING IS GOOD IS WHEN HIS PEOPLE ARE GOOD.

7

MASTER, SILENCE IS A KING'S BEST FRIEND. A SILENT TONGUE SHALL NEVER BETRAY ITS OWNER. THE WISEST OF KINGS CONCEAL THEMSELVES IN THE UNFATHOMABILITY OF SILENCE SO THAT NO ONE MAY BE ABLE TO OBSERVE THEIR THOUGHTS. THAT WHICH CANNOT BE OBSERVED OR TOUCHED CAN NEVER BE STOPPED. BY BEING PROFOUNDLY QUIET, YOU AUTOMATICALLY PLACE OTHERS IN THE SUBORDINATE POSITION OF TRYING TO DECIPHER YOUR MYSTERY. THOSE THAT ARE GRAVELY TACITURN SHALL ALWAYS ELICIT THE RESPECT WHICH SURROUNDS ANYTHING UNKNOWN AND DRAW AWE UPON THEMSELVES. IN ORDER TO INCREASE THE ANTICIPATION OF YOUR PROCLAMATION, REFUSE TO

PROCLAIM YOURSELF IMMEDIATELY. TO AROUSE VENERATION, INFUSE ALL OF YOUR CONDUCT AND ACTIVITIES WITH MYSTERY. BY HOLDING YOURSELF BACK IN SOCIAL SITUATIONS AND KEEPING SILENT, YOU SHALL RADIATE AN AURA OF CLANDESTINE **POWER** THAT PEOPLE SHALL AUGMENT AND MAGNIFY IN THEIR EXCESSIVE ATTEMPTS TO INTERPRET YOU. IT IS ALWAYS BEST TO WEAR THE COSTUME OF UNREADABLE TACITURNITY. IT IS BEHIND THIS DISGUISE THAT ALL SORTS OF PLANS MAY BE MADE WITHOUT BEING DETECTED.

8

MASTER, TO KEEP YOUR SILENCE IS TO KEEP YOUR DIGNITY. TO AVOID IDLE TALK IS TO AVOID TROUBLE. THE MAN WHO HAS THE **UNDERSTANDING** TO REMAIN QUIET UNTIL THE CORRECT TIME TO SPEAK SHALL SOON GAIN A REPUTATION FOR HAVING GOOD SENSE. EVEN A FAVOR ACCOMPANIED BY SILENCE AND DISCRETION HAS MUCH GREATER **POWER** TO INFLUENCE OTHERS THAN ONE THAT IS DONE NOISILY WITH THE INTENTION OF DRAWING ATTENTION TO ITSELF. WORDS ARE SACRED. THEREFORE, YOU MUST NEVER RELEASE THEM CARELESSLY. NEVER SAY ANYTHING THAT IS NOT WORTH THE TIME TO SAY. THE LESS YOU SAY, THE MORE DEEPLY PROFOUND AND POWERFUL YOU SHALL APPEAR. ONE OF THE BEST HABITS THAT YOU COULD HAVE IS THE HABIT OF TALKING VERY LITTLE. ALL WORDS ARE CHILDISH AND VAIN UNLESS THEY ARE CONCERNED WITH SOME SUBJECT OF IMPORTANCE. GREAT RULERS RARELY SPEAK, SO THAT ALL OF THEIR WORDS MAY BE VALUABLE. JUST AS A DOG IS NOT CONSIDERED A GOOD DOG BECAUSE IT IS GOOD AT BARKING, A **KING** SHALL NEVER BE CONSIDERED TO BE A GOOD **KING** BECAUSE HE IS GOOD AT TALKING. THE MORE ONE TALKS, THE

MORE SECRETS THEY ARE LIKELY TO REVEAL, BOTH ABOUT THEMSELVES AND OTHERS. IT IS WISE TO KEEP SECRET THAT EXTENT OF YOUR **KNOWLEDGE** AND ABILITIES. ALWAYS BE WILLING TO ALLOW SECRETS TO DIE UPON YOUR LIPS. FOR TO REPEAT SECRETS IS TO HAVE REGRETS. A SECRET IS JUST LIKE A BIRD THAT YEARNS TO BE FREE. IF YOU RELEASE IT FROM ITS CAGE, IT SHALL FLY AWAY AND SING ITS SONG EVERYWHERE. GOSSIP CAN TRAVEL THROUGH EVEN THE TINIEST CRACK IN THE MOST SECURE OF FORTRESSES.

9

MASTER, IN THE SAME SITUATION, AN INTELLIGENT PERSON SHALL SMILE QUIETLY, WHILE A FOOL ROARS WITH LAUGHTER. A FOOL HAS NO APPRECIATION FOR THE VALUE OF SILENCE. IF YOU WOULD BUT WATCH OVER YOUR WORDS, YOUR WORDS SHALL WATCH OVER YOU IN RETURN. ABOVE ALL ELSE, A **KING** MUST GUARD HIS TONGUE. A SLIP OF THE TONGUE IS WORSE THAN A SLIP AND FALL ON ICE. RESTRAINT SHALL DO WONDERS TO BEAUTIFY YOUR SPEECH. THE MORE A MAN SAYS, THE MORE LIKELY A MAN IS TO SAY SOMETHING FOOLISH. IT IS MORE DAMAGING FOR A **KING** TO SAY FOOLISH THINGS THAN IT IS FOR HIM TO DO THEM. THOSE WHO OPEN THEIR MOUTHS TOO MUCH PLACE THEMSELVES AT THE MERCY OF THOSE WHO HEAR THEM. NO ONE LIKES A PERSON WHO TALKS TOO LONG AND REFUSES TO GIVE OTHERS A CHANCE TO SPEAK. IN SOCIAL SITUATIONS, YOU MUST LEARN TO INTERJECT YOUR PERSONALITY ONLY WHEN IT IS NECESSARY. TO RESTRAIN YOUR TONGUE IS TO COMPEL THOSE AROUND YOU TO REVEAL THEIR MOTIVATIONS. THE MORE A MAN TRIES TO IMPRESS OTHERS WITH WORDS, THE MORE HE SHALL SAY. THE MORE WORDS A MAN SAYS, THE LESS IN

CONTROL HE SHALL SEEM. THE LESS IN CONTROL A MAN SEEMS, THE LESS HE LOOKS LIKE A **KING**. THE LESS A MAN LOOKS LIKE A **KING**, THE MORE COMMON THE WORLD SHALL TREAT HIM.

10

MASTER, A GREAT **KING** MUST ALWAYS BE WILLING TO BE LITTLE. HE WHO EXALTS HIMSELF SHALL BE HUMBLED, AND HE WHO HUMBLES HIMSELF SHALL BE EXALTED. THE HUMBLE MAN IS ALWAYS WILLING TO LISTEN. LISTENING IS A TREMENDOUS GIFT WHICH ANYONE CAN GIVE. THE APPEARANCE OF A SYMPATHETIC EAR SHALL ENTICE ANYONE TO TALK. WONDERFUL THINGS HAPPEN IN THE WORLD WHEN PEOPLE LISTEN. ONE CAN ONLY HEAR THINGS BY LISTENING.

11

MASTER, YOU SHALL ALWAYS BE ABLE TO TELL A PERSON'S CHARACTER BY LISTENING TO THE WAY THAT HE EMPLOYS LANGUAGE. ALWAYS MEASURE THE WORDS THAT YOU DESIRE TO SPEAK WITH THE VIRTUES OF COURTESY AND SINCERITY. WHETHER IT BE PURPOSELY OR UNINTENTIONALLY, YOU PAINT A PORTRAIT OF YOUR CHARACTER TO THE MINDS OF YOUR LISTENERS WITH EVERY UTTERANCE THAT YOU MAKE. A PERSON WHO CANNOT CONTROL THEIR WORDS SHOWS THAT THEY CANNOT CONTROL THEMSELVES. THE MAN WHO SPEAKS RASHLY AND RECKLESSLY SHALL EITHER BE FEARED, HATED, OR BOTH, BY ALL WHOM HE ENCOUNTERS. IT SHALL NEVER BENEFIT A **KING** TO BE FEARED OR HATED BY HIS PEOPLE. ALWAYS SPEAK CONSIDERATELY AND WISELY, OR ELSE REMAIN SILENT.

12

MASTER, AN INTELLIGENT **KING** SHALL NEVER MAKE STUPID THREATS. IT IS A COMMON THING FOR A DOG TO HOWL AT THE MOON. IF THE MOON WERE TO HOWL AT THE DOG, THE MOON WOULD BE FORGOTTEN, AND EVERYONE WOULD WORSHIP THE DOG. NEVER SHOW THAT YOU TOOK NOTICE OF AN INSULTING TONE OR LACK OF RESPECT. NO WISE **KING** SHALL EVER ALLOW HIMSELF TO BE SEEN IN AN UNCONTROLLABLE RAGE. A **KING** UNDERSTANDS THAT THE USE OF THREATS IS THE MOST FOOLISH KIND OF EXPOSURE, AND UNLEASHING BLIND ANGER WITHOUT FORETHOUGHT IS THE MOST PERILOUS INDULGENCE THAT A **KING** COULD PARTAKE IN. ABSTAIN FROM THREATS AND ACRIMONIOUS LANGUAGE. ONLY A FOOL WOULD SHOW HIS CARDS WHEN THE GAME HAS JUST BEGUN. RANCOROUS DESECRATION SHALL TAKE NOTHING FROM THE **STRENGTH** OF YOUR ADVERSARY. ON THE CONTRARY, HARSH AND INJURIOUS WORDS SHALL ONLY MAKE YOUR ENEMY MORE CAUTIOUS AND INFLAME HIS HATRED TO SUCH A POINT THAT HE CONSIDERS NOTHING MORE DILIGENTLY THAN HOW TO BRING DESTRUCTION TO THE SOURCE OF THE ABUSE. IT IS NEVER AN INTELLIGENT THING TO SAY OR TELL ANYONE ANYTHING THAT YOU DO NOT WANT TO BE USED AGAINST YOU. THERE IS NEVER ANYTHING TO BE GAINED FROM INSULTING A PERSON UNNECESSARILY. YOU CAN NEVER BE COMPLETELY SURE WHO THE PERSON YOU ARE DEALING WITH SHALL BE IN THE FUTURE.

13

Master, a KING ought always to be faultless and irreproachable with his speech. Speak only with integrity, graciousness, and sincerity. Those that use their words impeccably shall never betray themselves. The quickest way to create an emotional disturbance is through words. As KING, you shall never have an acceptable excuse for the rash and careless use of words which may insult or offend others. In regards to your conversation, you ought to take great care never to be so sharp, biting, and sarcastic that you earn a reputation for cruelty. Never with your tongue should you attack without cause or with flagrant malevolence those that are extremely powerful, those who are weak and defenseless, those who were irrefutably depraved, or especially those whom you LOVE and know that you are not offend. To attack the extremely powerful would be extremely unwise. To attack the weak and defenseless would be malevolently malicious. To attack the irrefutably depraved would be a waste of time. To attack those whom you LOVE and know you ought not to offend would be plain stupid. Just one word thoughtlessly spoken is able to destroy the opportunity of a lifetime. Never allow your loquacity to consume you to the degree that you become inelegant because you are not paying attention to the kind of people that you are talking to, the place where you are speaking, or to the rules of gravity and modesty that a KING ought always to observe.

14

MASTER, IT IS ONLY BY PRESENTING SOMEONE WITH AN ARGUMENT VERY QUIETLY WITHOUT AGGRESSION, AND WITHOUT RAISING YOUR TONE, THAT YOU DO NOT SEEM TO CHALLENGE THEIR DIGNITY OR INTEGRITY. EVERY MAN BELIEVES HE IS RIGHT, AND WORDS ARE RARELY ABLE TO CONVINCE HIM OTHERWISE. THE REASONING OF AN ARGUER IS WASTED, FOR IT FALLS UPON EARS THAT REFUSE TO LISTEN. NEVER ARGUE OVER TRIVIAL INSIGNIFICANT THINGS. EVEN IF YOU DO WIN SUCH A DEBATE, NOT ONLY SHALL YOU HAVE GAINED NO REAL ADVANTAGE, BUT YOU WOULD HAVE WASTED YOUR TIME. IT IS NATURAL TO WANT TO PERSUADE OTHERS BY IMPOSING YOUR WILL UPON THEM WITH ARGUMENTS. UNDERSTAND THAT THIS TACTIC SHALL INVARIABLY WORK AGAINST ALL WHO ATTEMPT TO UTILIZE IT. NEVER ARGUE WITH THE LOQUACIOUS. THIS IS LIKE THROWING DRY WOOD UPON AN ALREADY BLAZING CONFLAGRATION. DO NOT INTERRUPT ANOTHER WHILE HE IS SPEAKING. IT IS ONLY BY NOT INTERRUPTING SOMEONE THAT YOU SHALL BE ABLE TO PROPERLY RESPOND TO THEM. BE EVER READY TO LISTEN AND ALWAYS BE SURE TO TAKE YOUR TIME IN ANSWERING WHEN SOMEONE PRESENTS YOU WITH AN ARGUMENT. ONLY ANSWER IF YOU KNOW WHAT TO SAY, AND IF YOU DON'T KNOW WHAT TO SAY, REMAIN QUIET. WORDS CAN BRING FORTH HONOR, AS WELL AS DISGRACE. THE WORDS YOU ALLOW TO COME FORTH FROM YOUR MOUTH CAN RUIN YOU. THE MOST EFFECTIVE WAY TO DEAL WITH ANY POLEMICAL ATTACK IS TO DON THE COSTUME OF SILENCE. FOR SILENCE GIVES AN ATTACKER NOTHING TO ATTACK.

15

Master, always do your best to refuse public applause. It is not wise to call too much attention to your actions. The appearance of superiority over others is a vain, trivial thing compared to the reality of it. Modest humility shall always be preferable to arrogant haughtiness. It shall always be best to talk less about your own achievements and accomplishments than it shall be to discuss the accomplishments and achievements of others. By expressing humble admiration and respect for the light of others, you bring attention to your own light. It is always more powerful to be reticent concerning your powers than loquacious about them. No matter how great your skills and talents may be, doubts about the extent of your abilities shall arouse much more esteem and awe than precise KNOWLEDGE of them. To be honored by all, you must never allow the depths of your genius to be realized. While a great KING may allow others to glimpse the capabilities and faculties that he possesses, he never allows others to fully know them.

16

Master, the more you are seen and heard from, the more common you shall appear. The more common you appear, the less majesty you shall be able to radiate. He who is seen too much, draws upon himself the scorn and disdain that accrue to all things common. He who liberates himself from the crowd and makes his presence a rare

DAYLIGHT DRAWS UPON HIMSELF THE RESPECT AND **HONOR** OF ALL THINGS ROYAL. LIKE RAIN, GREATNESS IS ONLY APPRECIATED IN ITS ABSENCE. THE LONGER THE DAYS OF HEAT AND DROUGHT, THE MORE THE RAIN IS HOPED FOR AND DESIRED. THE LONGER THE DAYS OF WETNESS, THE MORE THE WATER IS HELD IN CONTEMPT AND IS WISHED AWAY. IT IS ALWAYS BETTER TO DO THINGS QUIETLY AND WITH GRACE THAN IT IS TO DO THEM IN ANY OTHER FASHION. LEARN TO MAKE YOUR AID TO OTHERS SUBTLE INSTEAD OF OSTENTATIOUS, THEN YOUR RECOMPENSE SHALL ALWAYS BE GRATIFYING AND POWERFUL.

17

MASTER, OF ALL PEOPLE, EMOTIONAL PEOPLE ARE THE EASIEST TO DECEIVE. WITHOUT CONTROL OF YOUR EMOTIONS, YOU SHALL NEVER BE ABLE TO RULE EFFECTIVELY. AS **KING**, YOU ARE THE REPRESENTATIVE OF THE **DIVINE** ORDER WHICH HAS BEEN SENT FORTH FROM THE HEAVENS. THE ONLY THING THAT CAN COME FROM A DESTRUCTIVE ATTITUDE IS DESTRUCTION. RAGE SHALL DO MORE HARM THAN THAT WHICH WAS THE CAUSE OF THE ANGER IN THE FIRST PLACE. IT IS BY SHOWING A CALM AND UNRUFFLED EXTERIOR IN THE FACE OF UNPLEASANTNESS THAT YOU SHALL PUT THOSE AROUND YOU AT EASE. EVERY ACTION THAT YOU PERFORM, YOU MUST IMBUE WITH GRACIOUSNESS. WITHOUT THE FLAVOR OF GRACE, ANY EXCELLENT QUALITIES, OR ATTRIBUTES THAT YOU MAY HAPPEN TO POSSESS SHALL BE WORTHLESS. WHEN GRACIOUSNESS IS THE ADORNMENT THAT GUIDES, INFORMS, AND ACCOMPANIES ALL OF YOUR ACTIONS, TO ALL, IT SHALL BE APPARENT THAT YOU ARE CLEARLY WORTHY OF THE COMPANIONSHIP, FAVOR, AND GRACE OF THE GREAT. A GRACIOUS **KING** NEVER SHOWS THAT SOMETHING HAS

AFFECTED HIM OR THAT HE IS OFFENDED. IT IS TYPICAL OF A
GRACIOUS **KING** NOT TO LOSE HIS TEMPER, NO MATTER
WHATSOEVER MAY BEFALL HIM. A GRACIOUS **KING**
UNDERSTANDS THAT TO SHOW CHAGRIN IS TO SHOW THE
UNIVERSE THAT YOU HAVE LOST THE **POWER** TO FASHION
CIRCUMSTANCES WITH YOUR WILL. A GREAT **KING** WOULD
NEVER DISPLAY THIS TYPE OF WEAKNESS. VEXATION AND
PETULANCE ARE NOT INDICATORS OF **STRENGTH** AS SOME
BELIEVE BUT ARE TESTIMONIES TO ONE'S IMPOTENCE. HE WHO
POSSESSES SUCH LITTLE SELF-CONTROL THAT HE WOULD RESORT
TO EXHIBITING FITS OF BAD TEMPER IN ORDER TO GET HIS WAY,
IS FAR FROM BEING WORTHY OF THE CROWN.

18

MASTER, IN ORDER TO BE A TRULY GREAT **KING**, THERE ARE
FOUR ESSENTIAL THINGS THAT YOU MUST LEARN. YOU MUST
LEARN TO CHECK, RESTRAIN, AND BRIDLE YOUR ARROGANCE.
YOU MUST LEARN TO RISE ABOVE BOTH PLEASURE AND PAIN. YOU
MUST LEARN TO IGNORE FLATTERY. AND ABOVE ALL, YOU MUST
LEARN HOW TO NOT ONLY KEEP FROM BEING UPSET WITH THE
IGNORANT BUT TO GIVE THEM A HELPING HAND. THE WORLD IS
FULL OF IGNORANT PEOPLE, MY SON. IT IS FULL OF THOSE WHO
ARE UNGRATEFUL, IMPATIENT, FICKLE, AND INSINCERE. WHEN
DEALING WITH PEOPLE OF THIS NATURE, THINK OF THEM AS YOU
WOULD A SMALL, SPOILED CHILD. THIS WAY YOU SHALL BE ABLE
TO DETACH YOURSELF FROM THEIR IGNORANT ACTIONS AND
ATTITUDES, STRENGTHEN YOURSELF, AND MAINTAIN YOUR
EMOTIONAL BALANCE. THIS IS A MOST IMPORTANT THING FOR A
KING TO DO. FOR IT IS IGNORANCE WITHIN YOURSELF IF YOU
REACT TO IGNORANCE IN ANOTHER. TO REACT CONSTANTLY TO

THE IGNORANT ACTIONS OF AN IGNORANT PERSON IS TO GIVE IGNORANCE CONTROL OVER BOTH OF YOU AND YOUR KINGDOM. THE ABILITY TO REMAIN FOCUSED IN THE FACE OF IGNORANCE IS ONE OF THE MOST VITAL SKILLS THAT A **KING** MUST POSSESS.

19

MASTER, DO NOT ALLOW YOURSELF TO BECOME OVERLY DISCONCERTED IF SOMEONE DOES SOMETHING THAT TRESPASSES AGAINST YOUR SENSIBILITIES AND OFFENDS YOU. FOR WHAT THAT PERSON DID WAS EITHER RIGHT OR WRONG. IF WHAT THEY DID WAS RIGHT, YOU HAVE NO CALL TO BE OFFENDED. IF WHAT THEY DID WAS WRONG, THEN OBVIOUSLY THEY ACTED FROM IGNORANCE AND ARE HELPLESS BEFORE THE COMPULSIONS THAT COME FROM THEIR OWN FOOLISH NATURE. NEVER TAKE ANYTHING PERSONALLY. PEOPLE ARE FOREVER PROJECTING THEIR BELIEFS UPON THE SCREEN OF THE OUTSIDE WORLD. NOTHING OTHERS SAY OR DO IS BECAUSE OF YOU. WHAT THEY SAY OR DO IS MERELY A PROJECTION OF THEIR OWN REALITY AND VISION FOR THEMSELVES. THEIR JUDGMENTS AND OPINIONS OF YOU HAVE NO VALIDITY WHATSOEVER UNLESS YOU VALIDATE THEM. YOU SHALL NEVER BE ABLE TO CONTROL WHETHER OR NOT ANOTHER DERIDES YOU. THE ONLY THING THAT YOU CAN DO IS TO MAKE SURE YOU DO OR SAY NOTHING THAT IS WORTHY OF DERISION. WHILE LESSER MEN FEEL INSULTED AND NURSE THEIR GRIEVANCES, A GREAT **KING** IS SO MATURE A MAN THAT HE NEVER TAKES INSULT AT A SLIGHT OR BECOMES RESENTFUL AND REFUSES A PROFITABLE OFFER BECAUSE OF ONE. YOUR ABILITY TO KEEP POSSESSION OF YOUR SERENITY IN THE FACE OF IGNORANCE IS WHAT SHALL MAKE YOU **KING**.

20

MASTER, THE STIFFEST TREE IS THE ONE MOST EASIEST FELLED. To let things be is far from the worst of life's maxims. Uncontrolled rage shall do naught but bring about your downfall. A man only loses his temper and becomes enraged about anything when he forgets that everything which occurs serves the purpose of the totality of creation. Another's ignorance is none of your business. The cause of that which upsets you has always taken place in the universe, shall always take place within the universe, and even now, at this precise moment, is taking place somewhere within the universe.

It is a grave error for a **KING** to be oversensitive and become infuriated in the face of criticism. Although it may be difficult, it is crucial that you learn the skill of taking criticism without taking offense. Another's opinion of you is none of your concern, and only a fool would get in an argument over something that is none of their concern. Allow people their petty judgments and opinions of you. Never allow them to make you defensive. To display defensiveness is to display weakness and show the world that you do not deserve the throne. Never allow yourself to become angry, frustrated, or terrified during a crisis. Anger, frustration, and terror shall ruin your poise, and undermine your ability to think clearly enough to lead. In a crisis, remain patient and keep yourself encouraged even in the face of apparent disaster. Until you can avoid feeling anger, frustration, or terror, you must always be heedful about how you express these subversive

EMOTIONS. NEVER ALLOW THEM TO INFLUENCE YOUR PLANS IN ANY WAY. IF YOU SOMETIMES FAIL TO BEHAVE AS YOUR ROYAL NATURE DICTATES, NEVER DESPISE, LOSE PATIENCE, OR GIVE UP ON YOURSELF. INSTEAD, AFTER EACH SETBACK THAT OVERCOMES YOU, RETURN TO YOUR ROYAL NATURE AND BE CONTENT IF THE MAJORITY OF YOUR ACTS ARE WORTHY OF A **KING**.

21

MASTER, IN TIMES OF DISORDER, YOU MUST REMAIN SUPREMELY FOCUSED TO THE EXTENT THAT TO THE COMMON OBSERVER IT APPEARS THAT YOUR **STRENGTH** COMES FROM AN UNWORLDLY SOURCE. THERE IS NO WORSE FATE FOR A **KING** THAN TO GET THROWN INTO THE FURIOUS CHAOS OF HYSTERIA. ALWAYS EXPECT THE UNEXPECTED. A TRUE **KING** NEVER ALLOWS HIMSELF TO BE CAUGHT OFF GUARD. THERE IS NEVER AN EXCUSE FOR BEING UNPREPARED. ALWAYS LEAVE ROOM FOR THE UNEXPECTED TO APPEAR SO THAT WHEN IT DOES, IT SHALL UPSET NOTHING. LET THERE BE NOTHING MORE IMPORTANT TO YOU THAN THE DOING OF THAT WITH YOUR KINGLY NATURE DICTATES AND THE ENDURANCE OF WHATEVER LIFE DELIVERS TO YOU IN THE PRESENT MOMENT. TO DO THIS IS TO ACCEPT LIFE AS IT IS. IT IS ONLY BY ACCEPTING LIFE AS IT IS THAT YOU SHOULD BE ABLE TO EXPLOIT EACH MOMENT IN ORDER TO GAIN THE MOST OUT OF EVERY SITUATION THAT YOU FIND YOURSELF PLACED IN. WHILE YOU SHALL NEVER BE ABLE TO CONTROL THE CONDITIONS OF THE SEA, YOU SHALL ALWAYS BE ABLE TO CONTROL THE DIRECTION OF YOUR OWN SHIP. ALTHOUGH YOU MAY NOT BE ABLE TO CONTROL AN OUTCOME TO A SITUATION, YOU MUST ALWAYS CONTROL YOUR RESPONSE TO THE OUTCOME OF ANY SITUATION. CIRCUMSTANCES NEVER REPEAT THEMSELVES EXACTLY. TRAIN

YOURSELF TO RESPOND TO CIRCUMSTANCES AS THEY OCCUR. RESPONDING AND ADAPTING TO EACH NEW CIRCUMSTANCE REQUIRES YOU TO SEE THE EVENTS WHICH OCCUR IN YOUR LIFE WITH YOUR OWN EYES AND MAINTAIN THE ABILITY TO IGNORE THE ADVICE WHICH OTHERS MAY ATTEMPT TO THRUST UPON YOU. IT IS ULTIMATELY YOU WHO MUST DECIDE HOW YOU MUST CHOOSE TO RESPOND TO EACH NEW SITUATION.

22

MASTER, HE WHO POSSESSES THE PERFECT CHARACTER LIVES EACH MOMENT AS IF IT WERE HIS LAST, WITHOUT PRETENDING TO BE OTHER THAN WHAT HE IS. NEITHER WAIL WITH THE GRIEF STRICKEN, NOR QUAKE WITH THE FEARFUL. IN ALL SITUATIONS, LEARN TO DO ALL THAT YOU CAN DO AND ACCEPT THE REST. IT IS FAR EASIER TO RUN INTO PERIL BY ATTEMPTING TO SWIM AGAINST THE CURRENT OF THE RIVER, THAN IT IS TO GO WITH THE FLOW. ALL DISAPPOINTMENT IS ROOTED IN EXPECTATION. EXPECTATIONS ARE MERELY ONE'S ATTEMPT TO CONTROL THE FUTURE, WHICH IS UNCONTROLLABLE. RATHER THAN PLACING EXPECTATIONS UPON LIFE, MUCH BETTER IS IT TO BE OPEN TO IT, AND WELCOME TO ANYTHING WHICH MAY OCCUR. THERE IS NO CIRCUMSTANCE THAT SHALL EVER BE ABLE TO HINDER YOU FROM BEHAVING AS A **KING** SHOULD. A **KING** THINKS SUBJECTIVELY, BEHAVES COURTEOUSLY, AND FEELS EASY ABOUT CIRCUMSTANCES OUTSIDE OF HIS CONTROL. THOSE WHO TRY TO CONTROL THINGS OUTSIDE OF THEIR CONTROL SOON BURN THEMSELVES OUT, LOSE THEIR SENSE OF DIRECTION, AND BECOME OUT OF CONTROL THEMSELVES. YOU HAVE ONLY THE **POWER** TO CONTROL YOURSELF AND IT IS NOT YOUR RESPONSIBILITY TO DO WHAT YOU LACK THE **POWER** TO DO. IN ORDER TO RULE

AS YOU MUST, YOU MUST ALLOW REALITY TO BECOME ACCEPTABLE TO YOU AS IT IS, AND NOT AS YOU TRY TO FORCE IT TO BE.

23

MASTER, GRACIOUSNESS IS THE MARK OF A **KING.** WHEN YOU ACHIEVE YOUR ACCOMPLISHMENTS GRACIOUSLY, PEOPLE SHALL NATURALLY ASSUME THAT YOUR SKILL MUST BE GREATER THAN WHAT YOU ARE EXHIBITING. FOR GRACIOUSNESS MAKES ONLOOKERS BELIEVE THAT A PERSON WHO PERFORMS SO WELL, SO ELEGANTLY, SO TACTFULLY, AND SO EFFORTLESSLY MUST INDEED POSSESS EVEN GREATER SKILL THAT HE IS SHOWING, AND IF HE TOOK GREATER PAINS AND EFFORT, HE WOULD PERFORM EVEN BETTER. IN WHATEVER YOU DO, STAY CLEAR OF HAUGHTY PRETENTIOUSNESS AS IF IT WERE A DANGEROUS WILD BEAST. PRACTICE A CERTAIN GRACIOUSNESS IN ALL THINGS THAT CONCEAL ALL AFFECTATION AND CAUSE WHATEVER YOU SAY OR DO TO SEEM UNCONTRIVED AND EFFORTLESS. THIS SHALL EVOKE RESPECT AND ADMIRATION IN YOUR PEOPLE AND NO SOUL SHALL BE ABLE TO FATHOM THE BOUNDS OF YOUR MAGNIFICENCE.

AS THE **DIVINE** IS MUCH TOO GRACIOUS EVER TO INDULGE IN THE VANITY OF REVEALING HER SECRETS OF **POWER**, SO TOO MUST YOU NEVER REVEAL THE CRAFT BEHIND YOURS. HE WHO IMITATES THE GRACIOUSNESS OF THE **DIVINE** APPROXIMATES ITS INFINITE POTENCY.

ALWAYS RESEARCH AND REHEARSE INCESSANTLY BEFORE ANY ACTION THAT YOU MUST PERFORM IN PUBLIC, BUT NEVER EXPOSE THE TOIL AND TRAVAIL THAT LIE BEHIND YOUR POISE. IF YOU KEEP THE MYSTERY OF YOUR TALENTS TO YOURSELF, YOU SHALL APPEAR TO HAVE THE **POWER** OF HEAVEN ON YOUR SIDE.

Although your performances may be outstanding, always have the graciousness to never let it be thought that you have spent much time or trouble on them. It is essential that you be well briefed and prepared for everything you may have to do or say, while at the same time giving the impression that all of your actions are spontaneous. When you know the praises you receive on account of your excellence are deserved, you ought never to assent to them too openly, but instead disclaim them modestly and let it be known by all, without voicing it, that your accomplishments merely serve as ornaments to the gracious greatness of your soul. In this way, you shall avoid the vice of haughty pretentiousness, and even your model achievements shall appear great. To seek and pursue praise and acclaim from outside of yourself betrays a lack of control over your own mind, and thus over circumstances. Remain forever gracious and behave with the **KNOWLEDGE** that because of your greatness all things shall come to you eventually.

24

Master, if you desire the best that the world has to offer, you must always resolve to offer the world your best. It is your own conduct that shall determine the degree of regard and consideration that others manifest towards you. As **KING**, it is of the utmost importance that you always present yourself in a respectable manner. The masses shall always have an overwhelming desire to believe in something, my son. You must strive to become

THE FOCAL POINT OF THEIR DESIRES BY BECOMING WORTHY OF THEIR BELIEF. THE **KING** WHO REFUSES TO BE GREAT DOES A GREAT DISSERVICE TO HIS KINGDOM. WITH YOUR EVERY ACT, YOU SHALL SHOW BOTH YOURSELF AND OTHERS WHO YOU ARE. IF YOU ARE HIGHLY REGARDED, YOU SHALL NEVER BE EASILY PLOTTED AGAINST. HOWEVER, WHEN YOUR PEOPLE HAVE NO RESPECT FOR YOU AND BEAR HATRED TOWARDS YOU, YOU SHALL NEVER BE SAFE AMONGST THEM. YOU SHALL NEVER BE ESTEEMED MORE HIGHLY THAN WHEN EVERYONE SEES THAT YOU EXEMPLIFY EXCELLENCE.

ALWAYS STRIVE TO PUT EVERY EFFORT AND DILIGENCE INTO EXCEEDING AND SURPASSING THE AVERAGE STANDARD IN EVERYTHING THAT YOU DO, IF ONLY JUST A LITTLE BIT, SO THAT TO ALL, YOU SHALL ALWAYS BE RECOGNIZED AS A SUPERIOR EXAMPLE OF A MAN. IF YOU ARE TO EARN THAT UNIVERSALLY DISTINGUISHED RENOWN THAT ALL MEN COVET, YOU MUST ACCOMPANY YOUR EVERY ACTION WITH THAT FINE JUDGMENT AND DISCRETION WHICH SHALL NEVER ALLOW YOU TO TAKE PART IN ANY SORT OF FOOLISHNESS. ALWAYS LEAD FROM THE FRONT OF THE PACK, NEVER FROM THE BACK. LET YOUR PEOPLE SEE YOU IN THE TRENCHES MAKING SACRIFICES FOR THE GOOD OF YOUR KINGDOM. THIS SHALL FILL YOUR PEOPLE WITH THE DESIRE TO EMULATE YOU AND WIN YOUR FAVOR. IT IS BY SHARING YOUR BLESSINGS, EXPERIENCES, AND OPPORTUNITIES WITH OTHERS THAT YOU SHALL BE ABLE TO ATTAIN NOT ONLY EVERLASTING PROSPERITY AND AFFLUENCE, BUT ALSO THE RESPECT AND REGARD OF ALL WHO KNOW OF YOU. STRIVE TO TURN YOURSELF INTO A SYMBOL OF NOBLE REGALITY. BY DOING SO, YOU SHALL AMPLIFY ALL OF YOUR ACTIONS, MAKING THEM, AND THUS YOURSELF LARGER THAN LIFE. HOWEVER, IN ALL MATTERS, YOU MUST BE DISCREET, JUDICIOUS, AND MATURE ENOUGH NOT TO

EXAGGERATE YOUR ABILITIES IN ANY WAY. VERY OFTEN, IN SEEKING TO WIN PRAISE BY WAY OF EXAGGERATION, ONE OFTEN WINS SHAME. THOSE WHO ARE HIGHLY RESPECTED ARE FOR THE MOST PART EXTREMELY MODEST. IF YOU CONDUCT ALL YOUR AFFAIRS WITH HUMILITY, YOU SHALL BE ADORED MORE THAN A GENEROUS GIVER OF GIFTS. HOWEVER, WHILE MEEKNESS IS INDEED A PRAISEWORTHY QUALITY TO HAVE, YOU MUST ALWAYS PAY HEED TO THE ROYAL MAJESTY THAT BEFITS YOUR RANK, AND NEVER ALLOW YOUR AUTHORITY TO BE DIMINISHED IN THE SLIGHTEST BY LOWERING YOURSELF TOO FAR. IT TAKES FOREVER TO BUILD A GOOD REPUTATION, BUT ONLY A SECOND TO BLOW IT AWAY. ONCE THE REPUTATION OF A **KING** HAS BEEN STAINED THROUGH COWARDICE, ARROGANCE, OR SOME OTHER DISGRACEFUL BEHAVIOR, EVEN IF ONLY ONCE, IT SHALL ALWAYS REMAIN DEFILED IN THE EYES OF THE WORLD.

25

MASTER, THE BEST WAY TO RECEIVE FAVOR FROM THE GREAT IS NOT TO PURSUE OR SEEK IT, BUT TO DESERVE IT. THE WORLD SHALL NEVER ACCEPT YOU UNTIL YOU FIRST ACCEPT YOURSELF. YOU SHALL NEVER BE COMFORTABLE IF YOU LACK YOUR OWN APPROVAL. NO ONE SHALL EVER ADMIRE A MAN WHO BEGS OTHERS FOR ADMIRATION. THOSE THAT RECEIVE THE MOST LAUDATION ARE THOSE WHO ARE MOST UNCONCERNED ABOUT IT. RESPECT YOURSELF BEFORE YOU SEEK TO GAIN RESPECT FROM OTHERS. NO ONE SHALL EVER RESPECT A PERSON WHO HAS NO RESPECT FOR THEMSELVES. VALUE LIES WITHIN YOU; THEREFORE, IT SHALL ALWAYS BE WITHIN YOUR **POWER** TO SET YOUR OWN PRICE. WHENEVER SOMEONE ASKS YOU TO SET YOUR OWN PRICE, IT IS ALWAYS BETTER TO ASK FOR TOO MUCH THAN TOO LITTLE.

IN ORDER TO RAISE YOUR PRICE, A VALUABLE ART TO MASTER IS THE ART OF WITHDRAWAL. THE ART OF WITHDRAWAL IS THE ART OF MAKING YOURSELF SCARCE. THAT WHICH IS SCARCE SHALL ALWAYS SEEM TO BE MORE VALUABLE. USED CORRECTLY, WITHDRAWAL SHALL GAIN YOU **HONOR**, AND THE LONGING FOR YOUR PRESENCE THAT IT AROUSES SHALL CAUSE YOU TO BE HIGHLY ESTEEMED. NEVER ATTACH TOO MUCH IMPORTANCE TO THE PRAISE OF OTHERS, ESPECIALLY THOSE WHO CAN'T EVEN FIND REASON TO PRAISE THEMSELVES. PRAISE IS A FICKLE GOD, AND IT IS ABLE TO TURN INTO CONDEMNATION IN AN INSTANT. NEVER FEEL OBLIGATED TO ANSWER TO ANY MAN FOR WHO YOU ARE OR WHAT YOU DO, AND NEVER FEEL AS IF YOU MUST HIDE WHO YOU ARE OR WHAT YOU DO. ALTHOUGH YOU MAY BE SO AWESOME THAT EVERYONE IS AMAZED AT YOUR TALENTS AND **KNOWLEDGE**, AND YOU AT NO ONE ELSE'S, NEVER SHOULD YOU EXHIBIT THAT ARROGANT CRUEL INDIFFERENCE WHICH PROHIBITS YOU FROM SHOWING ADMIRATION FOR WHAT OTHERS ACCOMPLISH BECAUSE YOU FEEL THAT YOU YOURSELF COULD DO FAR BETTER. INSTEAD, ALWAYS PRAISE THE ACHIEVEMENTS OF OTHERS WITH GREAT KINDNESS AND GOODWILL. FOR THE PEOPLE WHO DISPLAY THAT VAIN, INHUMANE PASSIVITY THAT REFUSES TO ACKNOWLEDGE THE LIGHT OF OTHERS, DO SO AS TO SUGGEST THAT NOT ONLY IS THERE NO ONE THEIR EQUAL, BUT THERE IS NO ONE WHO IS EVEN CAPABLE OF APPRECIATING THE PROFUNDITY OF THEIR **KNOWLEDGE**. EVEN IF YOU DO THINK YOURSELF A MAN TO BE ADMIRED, AND BY A LONG MEASURE SUPERIOR TO ALL, YOU MUST NEVER BE SO VAIN AND FOOLISH AS TO REVEAL THAT YOU FEEL THIS WAY.

26

Master, you can elevate yourself to any station that you desire, simply by preparing yourself to be able to do whatever that station requires. Never be afraid of expressing those qualities that set you apart and draw attention to you. To stand apart from the general mediocrity is the very definition of greatness. He who renders more and better service than which he agrees to perform shall soon be **KING**. Any fool can make a promise. What marks a **KING**, is the ability to deliver on his promises. Do not be stubborn and contentious like some who have the annoying habit of dissenting to every opinion that they hear, spitefully, and without hesitation. Avoid foolish haughtiness and try never to be the bearer of evil tidings. Never be careless in saying things that may offend. Rather, use your words to bring joy to hearts and smiles to faces. Never be a vain, lying gossiper nor a falling sycophant. Be modest, reserved, grave, and above all, observant.

A true **KING** is a man of such a noble disposition that even when he is sure that he is not being observed, seen, or recognized by anyone, he avoids doing anything, no matter how trivial, for which he would receive dishonor. Never mumble, my son. For a **KING** must either speak up or shut up. The spontaneous and valorous are admired by all, but the constrained and cowardly by none. The more spontaneous and bold you appear, the more respect you shall garner. That which is familiar is always held in contempt. Those whose actions

ARE EASILY PREDICTED DESCRIBE THEMSELVES TO THE WORLD AS COMMON AND SUBORDINATE. IT IS ONLY BY ADAPTING YOUR STYLE TO THE MOMENT THAT YOU SHALL BE ABLE TO AVOID THE DANGEROUS PITFALLS OF FAMILIARITY. OVERSTAYING YOUR WELCOME AND BORING PEOPLE WITH YOUR PRESENCE DEMONSTRATE THE ULTIMATE FAILINGS FOR A **KING**. THE PEOPLE SHOULD ALWAYS DESIRE MORE OF THE PRESENCE OF THE **KING**, NOT LESS OF IT.

TO SECURE THE GOODWILL OF THE PEOPLE WHOM YOU SERVE, YOU MUST LEARN TO DEVELOP THE SKILL WHICH ALLOWS YOU TO PRAISE WITHOUT OVERDOING IT, THE HUMILITY WHICH ALLOWS YOU TO POSSESS GREAT **KNOWLEDGE** AND TALENT WITHOUT SHOWING OFF, AND THE ABILITY TO ORDER YOUR WHOLE LIFE SO THAT YOU MAY, WITHOUT EXCITING ENVY, MODESTLY EXHIBIT YOUR GOOD QUALITIES NO MATTER WITH WHOM YOU MAY BE ASSOCIATED. IT IS CERTAINLY RIGHT TO EXHIBIT THOSE THINGS THAT YOU DO WELL. JUST AS IT IS WRONG TO SEEK FALSE GLORY FOR WHAT IS NOT DESERVED, SO ALSO IS IT WRONG TO CHEAT YOURSELF OF DUE **HONOR**.

27

MASTER, HE WHO ALWAYS AIMS HIS ACTIONS TOWARD THE COMMON GOOD AND WELL-BEING OF HIS KINGDOM AS A WHOLE SHALL BE GREAT THROUGHOUT HIS ENTIRE LIFE. IN ALL THAT YOU DO, MAKE YOUR PRIMARY OBJECTIVES TO LIVE IN HARMONY WITH AND BENEFIT YOUR KINGDOM. WHEN YOU DO EVERYTHING FOR THE PROFIT OF YOUR KINGDOM AND NOT SIMPLY FOR YOUR OWN PERSONAL PROFIT, IT SHALL BE A SIMPLE MATTER TO BECOME A GREAT **KING**. HE WHO RENDERS THE

GREATEST SERVICE TO HIS KINGDOM UNCOVERS THE GREATEST OPPORTUNITIES OF BENEFIT FOR HIMSELF. THE WISEST ACTIONS SHALL ALWAYS BE THOSE THAT THAT ARE APPROPRIATE AND IN HARMONY WITH THE WHOLE. ACTS SUCH AS THESE SHALL ALWAYS BE ADVANTAGEOUS TO BOTH THE **KING** AND THE KINGDOM.

28

MASTER, NO SONG SOUNDS SWEETER TO THE EARS OF MEN THAN PRAISE. THERE IS NOTHING THAT MEN'S EARS ARE GREEDIER FOR. BE GRACIOUS IN VICTORY, AS WELL AS IN DEFEAT. IN SOCIAL SITUATIONS, BE MODEST, DIFFIDENT, AND RESERVED, RATHER THAN EAGER AND FORWARD. BE FOREVER ON GUARD AGAINST ASSUMING THAT YOU KNOW WHAT YOU DO NOT KNOW. ALWAYS GIVE THE APPEARANCE THAT YOU YOURSELF THINK NOTHING OF YOUR ACCOMPLISHMENTS. BECAUSE OF YOUR MAGNIFICENCE, YOUR HUMILITY SHALL CAUSE OTHERS TO THINK HIGHLY OF YOU. NEVER TAKE DELIGHT IN APPEARING MALICIOUSLY VINDICTIVE OR SPITEFUL, OR IN UTTERING CRITICISMS AND QUIPS MERELY TO TEASE AND WOUND ANOTHER. TO DO ANY OF THESE THINGS IS TO RISK PERILOUS ENMITIES WHICH A **KING** MUST HAVE AS FEW OF AS POSSIBLE. FAVOR FROM A GREAT MAN, ESPECIALLY WHEN IT IS GRANTED WITHOUT BEING ASKED FOR AND ACCEPTED MODESTLY, SHALL GREATLY ENHANCE THE REPUTATION OF THE ONE WHO IS SEEN TO BE RECEIVING IT. NEVER HELP SOMEONE AND REPRIMAND THEM AT THE SAME TIME, AS DO SOME WHO USE GENEROSITY MERELY AS A MEANS OF ELEVATING THEIR STATUS IN THE EYES OF OTHERS. ONCE YOU HAVE DONE A GOOD DEED AND ANOTHER HAS BENEFITED FROM IT, IT IS A VAIN THING TO ASK FOR A REWARD IN REPUTATION, COMPENSATION, OR RECOMPENSE. THOSE WHO EXHIBIT THIS IMMODEST BEHAVIOR

USUALLY CONFINE THEIR EXPRESSIONS OF ESTEEM TO THE RICH AND POWERFUL ALONE. NEVER FORGET, THE POOR AND WEAK OF TODAY MAY BECOME THE RICH AND POWERFUL OF TOMORROW.

29

MASTER, IF YOU LIVE AS A FOOL, YOU SHALL COME TO A FOOL'S END. NEVER INDULGE IN HABITS WHICH RENDER YOUR MIND EFFEMINATE AND SO CAUSE YOU TO FEAR DEATH, OR ANY HARDSHIP. IT IS IMPERATIVE THAT YOU CONTROL YOUR BEHAVIOR NO MATTER WHAT THOUGHTS MAY PASS THROUGH YOU. EVERY MAN IS WHO HE IS AND WHERE HE IS BECAUSE OF THE HABITS WHICH HE HAS ACQUIRED. GOOD HABITS ARE STRENGTHENERS OF BOTH THE MIND AND THE SOUL. IT IS OF THE UTMOST IMPORTANCE THAT A **KING** CULTIVATES AS MANY GOOD HABITS AS POSSIBLE. BREAK FROM THE HABITS WHICH TRADITION HAS THRUST UPON YOU AND MAKE USE OF THEM OR NOT ACCORDING TO NECESSITY.

OFTENTIMES HOW ONE OUGHT TO LIVE IS SO FAR DISTANT FROM HOW ONE "OUGHT" TO LIVE THAT THE **KING** WHO OVERLOOKS WHAT SHOULD BE DONE IN FAVOR OF WHAT TRADITION DECREES SHOULD BE DONE SOONER BRINGS ABOUT HIS OWN RUIN THAN EFFECTS HIS OWN PRESERVATION. HE WHO WISHES TO BASE HIS ENTIRE CONDUCT UPON HIS THOUGHTS OF TRADITION SHALL SOON MEET WITH THAT WHICH SHALL DESTROY HIM AMONGST SO MUCH THAT IS EVER CHANGING. IF YOU HAPPEN TO MAKE A MISTAKE, AS ALL MEN EVENTUALLY DO, NEVER FEAR ACCEPTING THE RESPONSIBILITY FOR IT, AND UNDER NO CIRCUMSTANCES ARE YOU TO TRY TO SHIFT THAT RESPONSIBILITY TO ANOTHER.

30

MASTER, YOU SHALL ABUSE AND WRONG YOURSELF GREATLY IF EVER YOU WEAR A MASK OF SINCERITY AND SPEAK HYPOCRISY TO YOUR PEOPLE. WHAT MOST DAMAGES THE SPIRIT IN ANY KINGDOM IS THE FEELING THAT THE **KING** IS A HYPOCRITE. IF EVER YOU MUST ACT, NEVER ACT TENTATIVELY, UNWILLINGLY, SELFISHLY, OR IMPULSIVELY. NEVER ALLOW ANY MORTAL MAN TO BEND YOU TO THEIR WILL UNLESS YOU YOURSELF WISH IT TO BE SO. TRY NOT TO INDULGE IN ANYTHING THAT MAY SOMEDAY FORCE YOU TO BREAK YOUR WORD, LOSE RESPECT FOR YOURSELF, PRETEND TO BE SOMETHING OTHER THAN WHAT YOU ARE, OR HATE, SUSPECT, OR CURSE ANOTHER. NEVER LUST AFTER THAT WHICH YOU WOULD BE ASHAMED TO OPENLY ADMIT THAT YOU DESIRE. NEVER ALLOW ANOTHER TO IMPOSE THEIR BELIEFS CONCERNING YOU UPON YOU. FOR TO DO SO IS TO HAVE A LIFE THAT IS NOT WORTH LIVING.

31

MASTER, BECAUSE THERE ARE FAULTS PARTICULAR TO BOTH THE OLD AND THE YOUNG, A YOUNG **KING**, AS WELL AS AN OLD ONE, MUST BE AWARE OF AND CONSCIOUSLY SEEK TO OVERCOME THEIR SHORTCOMING WITH RESPECT TO THEIR AGES. IN A YOUNG **KING**, A SERIOUS AND SOBER YOUTHFULNESS IS THE MOST PRAISEWORTHY SINCE IT TEMPERS AND CORRECTS THE FRIVOLOUS CARELESSNESS, WHICH IS THE CHARACTERISTIC VICE OF THAT TIME OF LIFE. A YOUNG **KING** SHOULD BE GRAVE, SERIOUS, AND RESERVED IN HIS SPEECH, WHILE AT THE SAME TIME, POISED AND FREE FROM THOSE ARROGANT VAIN WAYS THAT ARE SO COMMON AT THAT AGE. A YOUNG **KING** WHO POSSESSES

THESE TRAITS SHALL APPEAR TO POSSESS A CERTAIN INDESCRIBABLE GREATNESS THAT OTHERS LACK. THIS IS OF THE UTMOST IMPORTANCE. A YOUNG **KING** MUST BE STRONG, AND A RELAXED ATTITUDE OF THIS KIND IS THE INDICATOR OF THE MOST IMPRESSIVE **STRENGTH** SINCE IT ARISES NOT FROM PASSION, BUT FROM DELIBERATION, AND IS UNDERSTOOD TO BE RULED BY **WISDOM** RATHER THAN EMOTION. THIS TYPE OF **STRENGTH**, WHICH IS EXCLUSIVELY FOUND IN GREAT MEN, IS DISPLAYED BY THOSE ANIMALS WHICH ARE THE MOST NOBLE AND POWERFUL, SUCH AS THE **KING** OF THE JUNGLE, THE LION, THE **KING** COBRA, AND THE **KING** OF THE AIR, THE EAGLE. THE POSSESSOR OF THIS TYPE OF **STRENGTH** ATTACKS WITH SUDDEN IMPETUOUS MOVEMENT WITHOUT WORDS OR SHOW OF PASSION WHATSOEVER, ERUPTING SUDDENLY IN A FOCUSED EXPLOSION LIKE THE BLAST OF A GUN.

WHEN YOU BECOME AN OLD **KING**, BE ON YOUR GUARD AGAINST PRAISING YOURSELF TOO MUCH, BUT TAKE FULL ADVANTAGE OF, AND MAKE USE OF, ALL THE **WISDOM** AND **KNOWLEDGE** THAT YOU HAVE ACQUIRED THROUGH YOUR LONG EXPERIENCE. AN OLD **KING** SHOULD BE LIKE AN ORACLE TO WHOM ALL TURN FOR COUNSEL, BECAUSE HE SPEAKS GOOD SENSE WITH GRACE AND **DIGNITY**, AND ACCOMPANIES THE SERIOUSNESS OF HIS ADMONITIONS WITH A CERTAIN ENTERTAINING, YET MEASURED SENSE OF HUMOR. TO POSSESS THESE TRAITS AS AN OLD **KING** IS TO BE WELCOMED AND CONSIDERED GOOD COMPANY BY ALL, AND TO ALWAYS BE OF GREAT WORTH IN MATTERS OF IMPORTANCE.

32

MASTER, TO RECEIVE AND NOT GIVE BACK IS TO INCUR A DEBT WITH LIFE. WHENEVER YOU RECEIVE ANYTHING FROM ANYONE, ALWAYS IF POSSIBLE TRY TO GIVE BACK MORE THAN YOU RECEIVE. IF YOU DESIRE TO PAY BACK ANY WRONGS THAT YOU HAVE RECEIVED, MAKE YOUR GREATEST **WISDOM** LIE IN YOUR ABILITY TO CONCEAL THE CUNNING WHICH IS A NECESSITY IN ALL MATTERS OF REVENGE. HOWEVER, MY SON, FOR YOUR OWN SAKE, I STRONGLY RECOMMEND THAT THE ONLY PEOPLE THAT YOU SEEK TO GET EVEN WITH ARE THOSE WHO HAVE AIDED YOU ALONG YOUR PATH. WHEN YOU HOLD ONTO RESENTMENTS, YOU MAKE YOURSELF PETTY. WITH A BOND MIGHTIER THAN STEEL, YOU BIND YOURSELF TO THE VERY THING THAT CAUSED YOU PAIN. IT IS COMMON AND PREDICTABLE FOR A WEAK MAN TO HOLD ONTO GRUDGES, OR TO BECOME ENVIOUS OF ANOTHER. NEVER ALLOW YOURSELF TO APPEAR COMMON AND PREDICTABLE. FLY EXPEDITIOUSLY FROM ALL FEELINGS OF RESENTMENT, AND WITH ALL YOUR MIGHT, EXPEL ALL TRACES OF ENVY FROM YOUR HEART.

33

MASTER, NEVER BELIEVE YOURSELF TO BE IMPERVIOUS TO JUSTICE. THERE IS SOMETHING THAT ABIDES BEHIND THE THRONE THAT IS GREATER THAN THE CROWN ITSELF. RIGHT CAN BE ESTABLISHED BY NO OTHER MEANS THAN RIGHT. IN ANY QUARREL, FOR NEITHER **LOVE** NOR GAIN, MUST YOU EVER FIGHT ON THE SIDE THAT IS NOT JUST AND RIGHTEOUS. IT IS AN ABOMINATION FOR A **KING** TO COMMIT WICKEDNESS. A THRONE CAN ONLY BE TRULY ESTABLISHED UPON A FOUNDATION OF RIGHTEOUSNESS. IF YOU WOULD ACT RIGHTEOUSLY, YOUR ENTIRE KINGDOM SHALL

REJOICE IN YOUR EMINENCE. IF YOU ARE WICKED, YOUR ENTIRE KINGDOM SHALL DESPAIR IN YOUR SHAME. A **KING** WHO DOES NOT STRIVE TO LIVE RIGHTEOUSLY SHALL NEVER HAVE RIGHTEOUSNESS AMONGST HIS PEOPLE. IT IS THE WISE **KING** THAT PULLS THE WEEDS OF WICKEDNESS FROM THE SOIL OF HIS OWN HEART AND PLANTS THE GOLDEN SEEDS OF GOODNESS WITHIN HIS SOUL. INSTEAD OF INCESSANTLY PEERING INTO THE DARKNESS OF ANOTHER'S CHARACTER, ALWAYS SEEK TO RUN TOWARDS THE LIGHT OF YOUR OWN.

34

MASTER, WHATEVER YOU HAVE DONE, YOU SURELY SHALL HAVE TO ACCEPT ITS REACTION SOMETIMES. IT IS ESSENTIAL AS **KING** THAT YOU SOW JUSTICE TO ALL MEN, SO THAT YOU MAY BE ABLE TO REAP IT FROM THE UNIVERSE. **DIVINE** LAW REQUIRES THAT YOU WANT NOT FOR OTHERS WHAT YOU DO NOT WISH FOR YOURSELF. ALWAYS JUDGE THE POOR WITH MERCY AND **UNDERSTANDING** SO THAT YOUR THRONE MAY BE ESTABLISHED FOREVER. BECAUSE MORE PEOPLE ARE CHANGED BY AN ACT OF MERCY THAN BY YEARS OF PUNISHMENT, YOU MUST GRANT MERCY TO ALL THOSE THAT TRULY DESERVE IT.

35

MASTER, ALWAYS HOLD YOURSELF IN CHECK LONG ENOUGH TO VIEW THE WHOLE BEFORE YOU REACT OR ATTEMPT TO GIVE ASSISTANCE IN ANY SITUATION. WITHOUT CAREFUL OBSERVATION, MORE EVIL THAN GOOD SHALL INEVITABLY BE THE RESULT OF YOUR ACTIONS. AS **KING**, DIVINATION ADORNS

YOUR LIPS. FOR THAT WHICH YOU SAY SHALL COME TO PASS. THEREFORE, YOU MUST NEVER ALLOW YOUR MOUTH TO TRANSGRESS IN JUDGMENT NOR MUST YOU EVER ACT CONTRARY TO THE DEMANDS OF JUSTICE. NEVER JUDGE ANOTHER BECAUSE OF SLANDER. WHAT PEOPLE SAY ABOUT OTHERS OR THEMSELVES MATTERS NOT. FOR PEOPLE SHALL SEE ANYTHING. WHILE WORDS MAY AND OFTEN DO LIE, DEEDS NEVER SHALL. CAREFULLY WEIGH EACH MAN'S CHARACTER AND ACTIONS BEFORE FORMULATING YOUR OWN ESTIMATE OF HIM. REFINE YOUR **POWER** OF DISCERNMENT TO SUCH A DEGREE THAT YOU SHALL NEVER PRESUME ANYTHING OF ANYONE UNLESS YOU ARE CERTAIN THAT IT IS TRUE.

36

MASTER, NEVER CONDEMN A MAN FOR FALLING VICTIM TO TEMPTATION. IF YOUR BROTHER FALLS, YOU MUST NEVER BOAST YOURSELF ABOVE HIM. FOR YOU KNOW NOT IF YOU WOULD HAVE BEEN ABLE TO WITHSTAND THE SAME TEMPTATIONS. IT IS VERY DIFFICULT FOR A STARVING MAN TO SLAP THE HAND THAT FEEDS HIM. WHENEVER YOU NOTICE THAT SOMEONE ELSE HAS GONE ASTRAY, IMMEDIATELY THINK BACK TO WHEN YOU YOURSELF HAVE TAKEN MONEY, FAME, OR SOME OTHER INSIGNIFICANT THING AND ESTEEMED IT AS THE HIGHEST GOOD, AND IN DOING SO, WENT ASTRAY YOURSELF. INSTEAD OF SETTING YOUR HEART UPON BEING THE JUDGE OF ANOTHER'S CHARACTER, PUT AN END TO ALL OF THE INJUSTICE WITHIN YOURSELF. YOU HAVE NOT THE RIGHT TO JUDGE OTHERS IN TERMS OF YOUR OWN CUSTOMS, HOWEVER PROUD YOU MAY BE OF THEM. TO HOLD OTHERS IN CONTEMPT BECAUSE THEY DO NOT OBSERVE YOUR PARTICULAR CUSTOMS IS THE HEIGHT OF BARBARITY. TO DEFINE ANOTHER WITH

NEGATIVE JUDGMENTS IS TO SEVERELY HANDICAP YOURSELF. ONE ONLY DOES VIOLENCE TO THEMSELVES WHENEVER THEY SCORN ANOTHER. NEVER PARTICIPATE IN GRATUITOUS FAULT-FINDING. WHENEVER YOU PUT ANOTHER DOWN, YOU DOWN YOURSELF. YOU SHALL NATURALLY TREAT THOSE WHO HAVE DONE WRONG MORE GENTLY IF YOU MAKE IT A POINT TO REMEMBER THAT NO ONE KNOWINGLY CHOOSES TO ACT WITHOUT **WISDOM**, JUSTICE, OR COMPASSION. IF YOU WISH TO SPEAK OUT AGAINST WRONGDOING, SPEAK WHAT SEEMS TO YOU TO BE THE MOST JUST, WITHOUT BEING RUDE, ARROGANT, OR PRETENTIOUS ABOUT IT. YOU SHALL NOT DIE IF YOU CEASE JUDGING OTHERS. ON THE CONTRARY, YOU SHALL FULLY COME TO LIFE. IT IS ESSENTIAL THAT YOU LEARN TO SEE THROUGH ALL OF THE PHONY CONCEPTUAL LABELS THAT THE WORLD HAS PLACED UPON BOTH YOURSELF AND OTHERS, SO THAT YOU MAY BE ABLE TO SEE THE SAME "**BEING**" PRESENT IN EVERY HUMAN BEING.

37

MASTER, BE CAREFUL NEVER TO RULE WITH TOO MUCH SEVERITY, NOR WITH TOO MUCH TOLERANCE. TO RULE TOO SEVERELY IS TO BECOME HATED BY YOUR PEOPLE AND TO CAUSE SEDITION, CONSPIRACY, AND A MILLION AND ONE OTHER EVILS TO BE BORN. TO RULE TOO TOLERANTLY IS TO BECOME DESPISED AND ENCOURAGES A DISSOLUTE WAY OF LIFE IN YOUR KINGDOM. AS LONG AS YOU'RE ABLE TO KEEP YOUR PEOPLE UNITED AND FAITHFUL, FEAR NOT ACQUIRING THE APPELLATION OF CRUEL. HE WHO DOES NOT CHASTISE OFFENDERS IN A WAY THAT PUTS IT OUT OF THEIR **POWER** TO OFFEND AGAIN, SHALL PROVE TO BE BOTH UNWISE AND TRIFLING AS A **KING**. TO BE SEEN AS CRUEL BY THOSE WHO INTEND TO VIOLATE YOUR KINGDOM IS MUCH

MORE MERCIFUL THAN TO BE LIKE THOSE WHO, THROUGH TOO MUCH TOLERANCE, ALLOW SEVERE DISORDERS TO ARISE IN THEIR REALMS.

38

MASTER, IF INSTEAD OF CRITICIZING REALITY, YOU ACCEPT IT, YOU SHALL ENTER INTO CONSCIOUS ALIGNMENT WITH PERFECTION. ACCEPTANCE SHALL ALWAYS BE BETTER THAN CRITICISM. TO COMPLAIN OR LAMENT ABOUT ANYTHING IS TO LABEL THE UNIVERSE INADEQUATE. RID YOURSELF OF THE TERRIBLE HABIT OF BLAME. SINCE FATE ISN'T CAPABLE OF DOING WRONG, EITHER VOLUNTARILY OR INVOLUNTARILY, IT IS THE UTMOST FOLLY TO BLAME FATE FOR YOUR ILLS. IT IS MALICIOUS TO BLAME YOUR FELLOWMEN, FOR THEIR WRONGS ALL STEM FROM IGNORANCE. NEITHER SLANDER NOR REVILE, AND IF YOU ARE INCAPABLE OF PRAISE, YOU MUST NOT CONDEMN. GOSSIP STRENGTHENS THE IGNORANCE OF THE PERSON GOSSIPING THROUGH THE INSINUATED YET IMAGINED SUPERIORITY THAT IS PRESENT EACH TIME THEY APPLY NEGATIVE JUDGMENTS TO ANYONE. PEOPLE ONLY CONDEMN OR MALICIOUSLY CRITICIZE OTHERS WHEN THEY ARE INSECURE AND NEED TO FEEL BIGGER AND SUPERIOR TO THE TARGET OF THEIR CRITICISM. AT ALL COST, REFRAIN FROM SLANDER AND GOSSIP. IT IS LUDICROUS TO NOT AVOID GOSSIPING ABOUT SOMEONE OR DOING ANY WRONG TO ANOTHER, WHICH YOU HAVE THE **POWER** TO DO, WHILE AT THE SAME TIME WISHING TO AVOID BEING GOSSIPED ABOUT OR BEING DONE SOME OTHER EVIL BY OTHERS, WHOSE ACTIONS YOU HAVE NO CONTROL OVER. IF YOU ARE ABLE TO BE PERSUADED BY ANYTHING, BE PERSUADED ONLY BY ARGUMENTS THAT ARE BASED UPON JUSTICE AND THE COMMON GOOD. NEVER ALLOW

YOURSELF TO BE PERSUADED BY GOSSIP OR BY WHAT APPEALS EXCLUSIVELY TO YOUR TASTE FOR PLEASURE OR POPULARITY.

39

MASTER, NOTHING BRINGS A KING MORE HONOR THAN TO ESTABLISH LAWS AND ORDINANCES THAT SHALL ENABLE HIS PEOPLE TO LIVE SAFE AND DIGNIFIED LIVES IN PEACE. WHEN SUCH THINGS ARE FOUNDED UPON PRINCIPLES OF WISDOM AND UNDERSTANDING, HE WHO ESTABLISHED THEM SHALL ALWAYS BE REVERED AND ADMIRED ABOVE ALL. TO RULE YOUR KINGDOM WISELY AND JUSTLY, IT IS NECESSARY THAT YOU STRIVE TO TRULY BE WISE AND JUST. A KING CAN ONLY RULE HIS KINGDOM BY THE SAME LAWS BY WHICH HE GOVERNS HIMSELF.

40

MASTER, YOUR CHARACTER SHALL BE EITHER YOUR GREATEST ASSET OR YOUR GREATEST LIABILITY. NEVER WISH TO BE ANYTHING BESIDES THAT WHICH YOU ARE, WHICH IS KING. ALWAYS STRIVE TO BE THIS FULLY. YOU SHALL BE MOST POWERFUL AND MOST EFFECTIVE ONLY WHEN YOU ARE BEING YOURSELF COMPLETELY. UNSOCIABLE MANNERS ARE ALWAYS A MOST DEPLORABLE THING. NO MATTER WHAT THE CIRCUMSTANCE, YOU MUST ALWAYS CONDUCT YOURSELF IN A DIGNIFIED AND HONORABLE MANNER. A MAN'S HABITS AND MANNERS PROVIDE THE KEY CLUES TO DETERMINING THE QUALITY OF MAN THAT HE IS. IN ALL OF YOUR AFFAIRS, DISPLAY COURTESY, DECISIVENESS, INDIFFERENCE TO POMP AND

OSTENTATION, INDUSTRIOUSNESS, AND POISE. STRIVE IN EVERY ENCOUNTER, ESPECIALLY FIRST ENCOUNTERS, TO GIVE AN EXCELLENT IMPRESSION OF YOURSELF. YOUR REPUTATION, WHICH IS FORMED BY THE IMPRESSIONS THAT YOU GIVE OTHERS OF YOURSELF, AROUSES SUCH A FEELING OF EITHER AFFECTION OR LOATHING IN THOSE WHO HEAR OF IT, THAT IT IS FOR THE MOST PART THE BASIS UPON WHICH YOU SHALL BE JUDGED. BECAUSE OF THEIR EFFECT UPON YOUR REPUTATION, YOU SHOULD PAY PARTICULAR ATTENTION TO YOUR LOCUTIONS, YOUR MANNERISMS, AND ESPECIALLY THE WAY YOU DRESS. FOR THESE ARE THE MAIN FACTORS THAT DETERMINE HOW THE WORLD PERCEIVES YOU. AFTER DECIDING WHAT TYPE OF MAN YOU WISH TO BE, YOU SHOULD DRESS ACCORDINGLY SO THAT YOUR ATTIRE MAY HELP YOU TO BE TAKEN AS SUCH, EVEN BY THOSE WHO HAVE NEVER HEARD YOU SPEAK OR SEEN YOU PERFORM ANY ACT WHATSOEVER.

41

MASTER, A KING MUST ALWAYS RETAIN THE PRIVILEGE OF LAUGHING WHENEVER HE PLEASES. RADIATE CONFIDENCE, MY SON, NEVER ARROGANCE OR DISDAIN. ALWAYS PRESENT YOURSELF AS CHEERFUL WITH A CALM SENSE OF PURPOSE. ALLOW YOUR ENTIRE MANNER TO GIVE EVIDENCE OF THAT COMPOSURE AND RESOLUTION PECULIAR TO THOSE WHO ARE ACCUSTOMED TO FACING AND CONQUERING THEIR FEARS. FOR THE SAKE OF YOUR FOLLOWERS, NEVER ALLOW YOURSELF TO BE SEEN AGONIZING OVER ANYTHING. YOU SHALL BE RESPECTED MOST HIGHLY IF YOU LIVE AMONGST YOUR PEOPLE IN SUCH A FASHION THAT NO UNEXPECTED CIRCUMSTANCE OR CONDITION, WHETHER THEY BE ADVANTAGEOUS OR FOR WOE, CAUSES YOU TO ALTER YOUR ROYAL

DEMEANOR. BECAUSE OSTENTATION AND POMP, ESPECIALLY WHEN SEEN ON A DAILY BASIS, SHALL ATTRACT MORE HATRED AND HOSTILITY THAN SHALL GRAVITY, MODERATION, AND HUMILITY, YOU SHOULD ALWAYS ACT A LITTLE MORE HUMBLE THAN YOUR STANDING REQUIRES.

AT ALL COST, AVOID ACQUIRING THE NAME OF LIAR OR LOUDMOUTH BRAGGART. IN YOUR DAILY TALKS, BE CAREFUL NOT TO STRAY FROM **THE TRUTH** OR TELL TOO OFTEN THOSE TRUTHS THAT ARE SO FANTASTICAL AS TO HAVE THE SEMBLANCE OF FALSEHOOD. DO NOT ACCEPT TO READILY RECEIVE THE PRAISES AND ESTEEM WHICH ARE OFFERED TO YOU. INSTEAD, WHILE HUMBLY DECLINING, SHOW AT THE SAME TIME THAT YOU VALUE THEM HIGHLY. GRACIOUSLY REFUSE THEM IN SUCH A MANNER THAT YOU INSPIRE THOSE OFFERING THEM TO YOU. THE MORE MODEST RESISTANCE IS SHOWN IN ACCEPTING PRAISE AND ESTEEM, THE PERSON WHO IS SHOWERING THEM UPON, WITH GREATER TENACITY, SHALL THINK THAT THEY ARE RESPECTED, AND THE GREATER THE **HONOR** THAT THEY ARE BESTOWING UPON YOU SHALL SEEM. THERE IS NOTHING MORE DANGEROUS THAN APPEARING SMARTER THAN THE NEXT PERSON. ALWAYS MAKE IT A POINT TO CLOAK YOUR CLEVERNESS WITH HUMILITY AND NEVER BE LIKE THOSE WHO, THROUGH THEIR VAIN AND INSECURE ARROGANCE, OFFEND ALL BY ALWAYS MAKING A POMPOUS SHOW OF THE TRIFLING **KNOWLEDGE** WHICH THEY HAVE COME TO POSSESS.

42

MASTER, IT IS OF THE UTMOST IMPORTANCE THAT YOU BECOME AS GREAT AS YOU ARE ABLE TO BECOME. NEVER ALLOW YOUR EYES

TO SHOW FEAR OR NERVES. MAKE IT YOUR FOREMOST OBJECTIVE TO ALWAYS EXCEED EXPECTATIONS. YOU SHALL ALWAYS BE REWARDED FOR THOSE ACTIONS THAT REVEAL A SENSE OF SACRIFICE AND DEVOTION. FOR THE GOOD OF YOUR PEOPLE, THERE SHALL BE TIMES WHEN YOU MUST MAKE A PRUDENT SHOW OF THE SACRIFICES THAT YOU HAVE MADE FOR THEM. TO LABOR AT WHAT YOU ARE DOING AND THEN TO MAKE A HUGE OSTENTATIOUS FUSS OVER THE LABOR SHOWS AN EXTREME LACK OF GRACE AND CAUSES ALL THAT YOU HAVE DONE, NO MATTER HOW GREAT, TO BE SPITEFULLY DISCOUNTED AND MALICIOUSLY DISREGARDED. IF YOU WOULD REMAIN UNCEASINGLY GRACIOUS, PEOPLE SHALL ALWAYS COME TO YOU. THEY SHALL SEE IT AS BOTH A DIGNIFIED AND HONORABLE THING TO BE HELD IN HIGH REGARD BY YOU. THE MORE YOUR REPUTATION FOR GRACIOUSNESS GROWS AND BECOMES WELL-KNOWN, THE MORE THOSE SHALL COME WHO SEEK TO BASK IN THE **DIVINE** LIGHT OF YOUR ROYAL GOODNESS.

FAME, WHICH IS NOTHING MORE THAN THE FUTURE GOSSIP OF OTHERS, IS SOMETHING THAT YOU MUST NEVER BETRAY YOUR PRINCIPLES FOR. THE IMAGE THAT YOU OUGHT ALWAYS TO CONVEY OF YOURSELF IS THAT OF A CONCILIATORY MAN OF PEACE WHO, ALTHOUGH NEVER AFRAID AND EXTREMELY CAPABLE, ONLY RELUCTANTLY GOES TO WAR. SOMETIMES THE BRAVEST PEOPLE ARE THOSE WHO DO NOT MIND LOOKING LIKE COWARDS. NEVER ALLOW YOURSELF TO BE LAZY IN YOUR ACTIONS, CONFUSED IN YOUR CONVERSATION, OR AIMLESS IN YOUR THOUGHTS. FOR TO DO ANY OF THESE THINGS IS TO BRING RUIN UPON YOURSELF.

43

MASTER, ALL KINGS WERE CREATED FOR THE WORLD SO THAT THEY MAY HELP ALL THOSE THAT DESERVE HELP, AND IF POSSIBLE RESTRAIN THEM FROM HARMING ONE ANOTHER. THE GREATEST IN ANY GROUP SHOULD ALWAYS BE A SERVANT TO ALL THE REST. IT SHALL NEVER BE DIFFICULT FOR A GOOD KING TO KEEP THE HEARTS OF HIS PEOPLE LOYAL AND STEADFAST FROM BEGINNING TO END AS LONG AS HE DOES NOT FAIL TO SUPPORT AND AID THEM IN THEIR TRIBULATIONS. IT IS THE WISE KING THAT SEEKS TO GAIN HELP BY HELPING OTHERS. IT IS THE FOOLISH KING WHO SEEKS TO GAIN HELP BY THE USE OF THREATS OR FORCE. THE WISE KING UNDERSTANDS THAT THE USE OF FORCE AS A MEANS OF COERCION SHALL ONLY STRENGTHEN PEOPLE'S RESISTANCE TO HIS INFLUENCE. BECAUSE IT IS IMPOSSIBLE TO HURT OR HELP ANOTHER WITHOUT DOING THE SAME TO YOURSELF, IT IS FOOLISH NOT TO HELP OTHERS WHEN BY DOING SO, YOU HELP YOURSELF. IT IS A VAIN AND CRUEL THING TO PROVIDE PEOPLE WITH WATER DURING THE RAINY SEASON AND IGNORE THEIR THIRST DURING A TIME OF DROUGHT. NEVER TURN YOUR BACK ON A POOR PERSON OR GIVE HIM ANY REASON TO CURSE YOU. YOU MUSTN'T ADD TO THE TROUBLES OF SOMEONE WHO IS ALREADY DESPERATE. IT SHALL NEVER BE WISE FOR A KING TO GIVE A HUNGRY MAN REASON TO RESENT HIM. WHEN YOU DO GIVE, NEVER ALLOW HURTFUL WORDS TO ACCOMPANY YOUR GIFT. FOR NO ONE APPRECIATES A GIFT THAT SOMEONE RESENTS GIVING.

44

MASTER, THE MAN WHO INTERFERES IN A QUARREL NOT OF HIS

OWN, IS AS FOOLISH AS A MAN WHO GRABS A STRANGE DOG BY THE EARS. IF YOU SEE ONE FOOL MEDDLING IN THE SQUABBLES OF ANOTHER, YOU MUST TAKE GREAT CARE TO ENSURE THAT YOU ARE NOT THE SECOND. IT IS A GRAVE MISTAKE FOR A **KING** TO ALLOW OTHERS TO DRAG HIM INTO THEIR TRIVIAL AND TRIFLING DEBATES AND DISPUTES. A WISE **KING** KNOWS THAT EACH MOMENT HE SPENDS DROWNING IN THE PETTY ILLS OF OTHERS SHALL SUBTRACT FROM HIS **POWER**. BY MAINTAINING INTERNALLY HIS FREEDOM AND INDEPENDENCE FROM THEIR NEEDINESS, HE PLACES HIMSELF IN A POSITION OF RESPECT AND **STRENGTH** FROM WHICH HE SHALL BE BETTER ABLE TO AID AND ASSIST.

45

MASTER, IT IS CRUCIAL THAT YOU LEARN TO PAY CLOSE ATTENTION TO THE CHARACTERISTICS AND PECULIARITIES OF THOSE WITH WHOM YOU MUST INTERACT AND BEHAVE ACCORDINGLY. AS **KING**, IT SHALL BE OF THE UTMOST NECESSITY THAT YOU BE ABLE TO ACCOMMODATE YOUR CONDUCT TO DEALING WITH A WIDE VARIETY OF PEOPLE. GUIDED BY **WISDOM**, YOU MUST DISCERN THE DIFFERENCES BETWEEN ONE MAN AND ANOTHER AND ALTER YOUR MANNER ACCORDING TO THE NATURE OF THOSE WITH WHOM YOU WISH TO HAVE DEALINGS. NO MATTER WITH WHOM YOU ARE DEALING, YOU SHALL ALWAYS BE FAR MORE ESTEEMED AND VENERATED IF YOU ARE HUMBLE, SAYING LITTLE AND BOASTING HARDLY EVER, THAN IF YOU ARE FOREVER SINGING YOUR OWN PRAISES. WHETHER YOU ARE SPEAKING TO THE WEALTHIEST **KING**, OR TO THE MOST DESTITUTE MENDICANT, ALWAYS MAKE YOUR SPEECH SIMPLE, RESPECTFUL, AND FAR FROM PRETENTIOUS. AS **KING**, IT IS

ESSENTIAL THAT YOU SPEAK YOUR TRUTH QUIETLY BUT CLEARLY. BE RECEPTIVE TO EVEN THE LOWLIEST CONSTITUENTS IN YOUR KINGDOM. FOR THEY TOO HAVE A STORY. AVOID WITH EQUAL CAUTION AGAINST BOTH OFFENDING OTHERS, AS WELL AS LOSING PATIENCE WITH THEM. IN YOUR DISCOURSES WITH OTHERS, BE ELOQUENT, AS WELL AS FORTHRIGHT. LEARN TO CONCENTRATE INTENTLY UPON EXACTLY WHAT THOSE AROUND YOU ARE SAYING, SO THAT YOU MAY BE ABLE TO ENTER AS DEEPLY AS POSSIBLE INTO THE MIND OF EACH SPEAKER, AND THUS MAKE ALL OF YOUR DETERMINATIONS CONCERNING THEM WISE. FIND THE COURAGE TO ASK QUESTIONS AND EXPRESS WHAT YOU REALLY DESIRE TO EXPRESS, SO THAT YOU MAY COMMUNICATE WITH OTHERS AS CLEARLY AS POSSIBLE AND AVOID MAKING ASSUMPTIONS. ASSUMPTION IS THE FATHER TO ALL MISUNDERSTANDING. WHEN COMMUNICATING WITH YOUR PEOPLE, ALWAYS BEAR IN MIND THAT THE BEST WAY TO MOTIVATE THEM SHALL ALWAYS BE THROUGH EMOTION, RATHER THAN LOGIC OR REASON. THROUGH AN APPEAL TO THEIR HEART, RATHER THAN TO THEIR MIND. TO REFLECT BACK TO ANOTHER THEIR INNERMOST FEELINGS AND THOUGHTS IS TO CAPTURE THEIR HEART AND DISARM THEM. THE FEELING OF BEING HARMONIOUSLY REFLECTED IN THE OUTSIDE WORLD IS PERHAPS THE MOST POTENT SEDUCER OF MEN. MOST PEOPLE SHALL RESPOND MORE FREELY TO A REQUEST FROM ONE THEY CALL FRIEND THAN AN ORDER FROM ONE THEY CALL STRANGER.

46

MASTER, THE EASIEST WAY TO ATTAIN POWER IS TO BECOME A SOURCE OF PLEASURE FOR THOSE AROUND YOU. IT IS OF THE UTMOST IMPORTANCE TO HAVE THE PEOPLE FRIENDLY TOWARDS

YOU. WITHOUT THIS, YOU SHALL NEVER HAVE SECURITY IN YOUR ADVERSITY. THE PROBLEM FROM HATRED COMES WHEN YOU FAIL TO RECOGNIZE IT UNTIL IT IS TOO LATE. NEVER NAIVELY ACCEPT THE FACADE THAT THOSE AROUND YOU MAY PRESENT. READ BETWEEN THE LINES OF THE ACTIONS THAT THEY COMMIT. IF YOU CANNOT AVOID BEING HATED BY SOMEONE, YOU OUGHT TO AVOID BEING DESPISED BY THE MAJORITY. IF YOU CANNOT ACCOMPLISH THIS, THEN YOU MUST ENDEAVOR WITH THE UTMOST DILIGENCE TO AVOID THE HATRED OF THE MOST POWERFUL. A **KING** BECOMES HATED BY HIS PEOPLE WHEN HE IS FOUND TO BE A RAPACIOUS VIOLATOR OF THE PROPERTY OR **HONOR** OF HIS FOLLOWERS. WHEN NEITHER THEIR PROPERTY NOR THEIR **HONOR** IS TOUCHED, THE MAJORITY OF MEN LIVE CONTENTED. HOWEVER, WHEN A MAN IS DEPRIVED OF THAT WHICH HE CONSIDERS IMPORTANT AND USEFUL, HE SHALL NEVER FORGET HIS DESIRE FOR VENGEANCE. EVERY TRIVIAL OCCURRENCE SHALL BRING THE MEMORY OF HIS LOSS TO THE FORE OF HIS THOUGHTS, AND TRIVIAL OCCURRENCES RECUR PERPETUALLY. IT IS NOT WHAT IS GIVEN THAT SHALL MAKE A RULER ODIOUS, BUT RATHER THAT WHICH IS USURPED.

BY ENCROACHING UPON ANOTHER'S INTERESTS, YOU SHALL RUIN YOUR OWN. IT IS A WEAK **KING** WHO WOULD RATHER PLUNDER HIS FOLLOWERS THAN ENRICH THEM. AVOID PRIDE AND HAUGHTINESS AS YOU WOULD A POISONOUS SNAKE. ALTHOUGH PRIDE AND HAUGHTINESS IN THEMSELVES MAY DO PEOPLE NO HARM, THE PEOPLE SHALL NEVERTHELESS HOLD IN HATRED AND CONTEMPT ANY PERSON THAT EXHIBITS THESE CHARACTERISTICS. WHILE IT MAY BE TRUE THAT IN THE PRESENCE OF AN ENEMY YOU SHOULD BE FEROCIOUS, ROUGH, AND PERHAPS A TAD BIT BELLICOSE, EVERYWHERE ELSE YOU MUST

BE GENTLE, MODEST, RETICENT, AND ANXIOUS. ABOVE ALL, AVOID DISPLAYING THAT OUTRAGEOUS OSTENTATION WHICH ALWAYS AROUSES LOATHING AND DISGUST IN ALL THOSE WHO BEAR WITNESS TO IT. IT IS WISE TO BE GENTLE WITH LIONS AND TIGERS IF YOU WISH TO TAME THEM. WHEN YOU ARE TRULY GREAT AND DESERVING OF THE THRONE, THE MORE PEOPLE BELIEVE THAT YOU ARE AVERSE TO USURPING AUTHORITY OVER THEM, THE READIER THEY SHALL BE TO SURRENDER THEMSELVES INTO YOUR HANDS. PEOPLE SHALL ALWAYS FEAR YOUR GREATNESS LESS WHEN THEY FIND YOU ACTING TOWARDS THEM WITH KIND CONSIDERATION, RATHER THAN VAIN EGOTISM. THE INTEREST OF THE **KING** AND THE INTEREST OF HIS PEOPLE SHOULD BE ONE AND THE SAME. IT SHALL NEVER BE IN THE BEST INTEREST OF A **KING** TO HURT OR OFFEND THOSE WHO ARE IN A POSITION TO HARM HIM. IT IS ESSENTIAL THAT YOU DEVELOP, NOT ONLY THE ABILITY TO BE ALL THINGS TO ALL MEN, BUT ALSO THE ABILITY TO DO SO WITH A SMILE.

47

MASTER, IT SHALL ALWAYS BE BETTER FOR YOU TO SUFFER FROM THE AFFLICTION OF LONELINESS THAN IT SHALL BE FOR YOU TO ASSOCIATE INTIMATELY WITH THOSE WHOSE MINDS ARE CONTAMINATED WITH THOUGHTS OF FAILURE, ANXIETY, OR FOOLISHNESS. STRIVE TO AVOID LOUD AND AGGRESSIVE PEOPLE. AVOID MAKING A HABIT OF VISITING STUPID PEOPLE OR SPENDING A LOT OF TIME TALKING TO THEM. PEOPLE LIKE THIS ARE GREAT VEXATIONS TO THE SPIRIT. TO AVOID THEIR PRESENCE IS TO NOT ONLY AVOID BEING POLLUTED BY THE NEGATIVITY, BUT ALSO TO BE UNTROUBLED OR WORN DOWN BY THEIR FOLLY. FAR MORE HARM IS CAUSED WHEN A **KING** IS TOO TRUSTFUL OF THE

COUNSEL OF OTHERS THAN WHEN HE IS DISTRUSTFUL OF THEM, WHICH INDEED IS NOT ONLY SOMETIMES HARMLESS, BUT OFTEN BRINGS ADVANTAGE. HOWEVER, IN THIS MATTER, AS WELL AS IN ALL, A **KING** MUST EXERCISE DISCRETION SO THAT HE MAY INTELLIGENTLY DISCERN WHO IS WORTHY OF CREDENCE AND WHO IS NOT. YOU SHOULD NEVER SEEK COUNSEL FROM UNPRODUCTIVE PEOPLE. IT IS USELESS TO DISCUSS YOUR PROBLEMS WITH SOMEONE INCAPABLE OF CONTRIBUTING TO THE SOLUTION. SEEK THE ADVICE OF THE WISE AND MAKE YOURSELF A FREQUENT INQUIRER OF THEIR **WISDOM**, AND AFTERWARDS A PATIENT LISTENER CONCERNING THAT WHICH YOU HAVE INQUIRED AFTER.[20] IN ALL THAT YOU INQUIRE OF THEM, MAKE IT PERFECTLY CLEAR THAT YOU DESIRE NOTHING LESS THAN **THE TRUTH**. EVEN THOUGH IT IS OF THE UTMOST IMPORTANCE THAT YOU HEAR AND RESPECT THE OPINIONS OF THOSE WHOM YOU CONSIDER INTELLIGENT AND WISE, WHEN MAKING DECISIONS OF GREAT CONSEQUENCE, A TRULY WISE AND INTELLIGENT **KING** SHALL ALWAYS MAKE HIS OWN DECISIONS.

48

MASTER, IT IS ONE OF THE GREATEST TRAGEDIES OF MAN THAT WHEN SOMEONE RICH SAYS SOMETHING ASININE OR DOES SOMETHING FOOLISH THERE SHALL BE MANY PEOPLE WHO SHALL ATTEMPT TO COVER UP FOR HIM AND EXPLAIN AWAY EVEN THOSE THINGS WHICH HE HIMSELF KNOWS THAT HE NEVER SHOULD HAVE DONE OR SAID, WHEREAS WHEN A POOR MAN MAKES A MISTAKE, ALL HE SHALL HEAR IS DISPARAGEMENT AND RIDICULE, AND EVEN IF HE SPEAKS WITH GOOD SENSE ONLY A FEW SHALL

---

[20] Niccolo Machiavelli: The Prince (thefreelibrary.com)

EVEN LISTEN. IT IS BOTH A GRAVE MISTAKE AND A GREAT WRONG TO REFUSE TO **HONOR** AN INTELLIGENT PERSON SIMPLY BECAUSE THEY ARE POOR. JUST AS A MASTER MASON WOULD NEVER ENDANGER HIS REPUTATION OR THE QUALITY OF HIS WORK BY USING INFERIOR EQUIPMENT TO CONSTRUCT THE STRUCTURES THAT HE DESIRES TO BUILD, A **KING** MUST NEVER ATTEMPT TO CONSTRUCT THE EDIFICE OF HIS KINGDOM WITH ANYTHING LESS THAN HIS VERY BEST TOOLS. IN FORMING YOUR KINGDOM, SURROUND YOURSELF EXCLUSIVELY WITH THOSE WHO ARE GRACIOUS, SAGACIOUS, AND DISCREET.

TO BE ROYAL, YOU MUST SURROUND YOURSELF WITH NOBLE THINGS. SHINE THE LIGHT OF YOUR FAVOR UPON THE GOOD AND WISE, AND IF IT IS NECESSARY TO BE WRATHFUL, ALLOW YOUR WRATH TO FALL ONLY UPON THE BROWS AND BACKS OF THOSE WHO FOOLISHLY BRING SHAME. ALWAYS SHOW YOURSELF TO BE A PATRON OF TALENT, SKILL, AND INGENUITY. **HONOR** THE MASTERLY IN EVERY ART. AS **KING**, IT IS YOUR DUTY TO BE THE FIRST TO SHOW SINCERE REGARD FOR THOSE WHO ARE SEEKING TO MASTER OR HAVE MASTERED A PARTICULAR SKILL OR SUBJECT, SO THAT EACH OF THESE PERSONS MAY RECEIVE THE RESPECT AND VENERATION THAT IS THEIR DUE. A TRUE **KING** SHALL ALWAYS MAKE LIPS THAT SPEAK **THE TRUTH** HIS RAPTURE AND SHOW PREFERENCE FOR THOSE WHO SPEAK WHAT IS RIGHT. GIVE THOSE WHOM YOU SURROUND YOURSELF WITH THE LIBERTY AND CONFIDENCE TO SPEAK **THE TRUTH** TO YOU ON ANYTHING ABOUT WHICH YOU INQUIRE. CAREFULLY LISTEN TO THEIR THOUGHTS AND COMPOSE YOURSELF IN A MANNER THAT MAKES IT CLEAR THAT THE MORE FREELY THEY SPEAK, THE MORE THEY SHALL BE PREFERRED. AFTER HEARING EVERYTHING THAT THEY HAVE TO OFFER, YOU MUST FORM YOUR OWN CONCLUSIONS

ON MATTERS AND BE STEADFAST IN YOUR RESOLUTIONS.

49

MASTER, HE WHO BEHAVES GRACIOUSLY SHALL ATTRACT GRACIOUSNESS FROM OTHERS. AS FAR AS POSSIBLE WITHOUT COMPROMISING YOUR NOBLE AND GENTEEL NATURE, STRIVE TO BE ON GOOD TERMS WITH ALL PERSONS. YOUR MOST FORMIDABLE WEAPON IN THE ACCOMPLISHMENT OF THIS SHALL ALWAYS BE YOUR **POWER** TO INSPIRE A SENSE OF WELL-BEING IN YOUR COMPANY. WHEN YOU ARE ABLE TO CONVINCE A PERSON THAT THEIR WELFARE IS OF THE GREATEST IMPORTANCE TO YOU, YOU SHALL GAIN THEIR HEART AND CAUSE THEM TO TRUST AND BELIEVE MORE IN YOU THAN THEY DO THEMSELVES. TRUST AND BELIEF ARE THE HIGHEST FORMS OF HUMAN MOTIVATION. THEY BRING OUT THE VERY BEST IN THOSE TO WHOM THEY ARE GIVEN. HE WHO CAN NEVER PERSUADE HIMSELF TO BELIEVE IN OR TRUST ANYTHING COMPLETELY, SHALL NEVER BE TRUSTED OR BELIEVED IN COMPLETELY.

WHEN YOU SHOW CARE AND CONCERN FOR OTHERS, MALEVOLENCE DISSOLVES, AND **LOVE**, PEACE, AND HARMONY GROW IN ITS STEAD. ALWAYS ALLOW YOUR GREATNESS TO BE ACCOMPANIED BY A CERTAIN WARM-HEARTED AMICABILITY, A GRACIOUS AMIABILITY, AND AN ACCOMPLISHED HUMANITY WHICH DISCREETLY FAVORS BOTH FRIENDS AND STRANGERS IN VARYING DEGREES, EACH ACCORDING TO THEIR MERIT. IT IS ONLY BY ATTENDING TO THOSE WITH WHOM YOU MUST HAVE DEALINGS THAT YOU SHALL BE ABLE TO ACCURATELY DISCERN THEIR WAYS OF THINKING, AND TAILOR YOUR WORDS AND ACTIONS TO WHAT YOU KNOW SHALL CHARM AND DELIGHT THEM. THIS IS OF THE

UTMOST IMPORTANCE, MY SON, FOR A **KING** MUST TUNE HIMSELF SO PERFECTLY TO THOSE AROUND HIM THAT THEY TAKE MORE DELIGHT IN HIS COMPANY THAN ANYTHING HE HAS TO OFFER. BECAUSE HARMONIOUS COOPERATION IS A PRICELESS ASSET WHICH CAN ONLY BE ACQUIRED IN PROPORTION TO THE AMOUNT THAT IS GIVEN, IT IS ESSENTIAL THAT YOU GAIN THE ABILITY TO SYMPATHIZE WITH ANOTHER'S WAY OF DOING THINGS AND ADAPT YOURSELF TO HARMONIOUS CONCERT WITH THE WAYS AND ATTITUDES OF OTHERS.

IN ORDER TO GAIN THE FULLEST COOPERATION OF ALL THOSE WITHIN YOUR KINGDOM, YOU MUST LEARN TO RELATE YOURSELF TO EACH PERSON ACCORDING TO THAT PERSON'S PERSONALITY. THE GREATEST COMPLIMENT THAT YOU CAN PAY TO ANOTHER AND THE SUREST WAY TO ANOTHER'S HEART IS TO CONCENTRATE YOUR ATTENTION UPON THAT PERSON'S PERSONAL INTEREST. IF YOU WOULD STRIVE TO OBTAIN THE GOOD GRACES OF AN EMINENT AND GREAT MAN, YOU MUST ALWAYS COME BEFORE HIM WITH THOSE THINGS WHICH HE HOLDS MOST PRECIOUS AND IN WHICH YOU SEE HIM TAKE THE MOST DELIGHT. LEARN TO SEE THE LIGHT IN OTHERS AND TREAT THEM AS IF THAT IS ALL THAT YOU SEE. WHENEVER POSSIBLE, LEAVE AFFAIRS OF REPROACH TO THE MANAGEMENT OF OTHERS AND KEEP THOSE OF GRACE IN YOUR OWN HANDS. IF YOU TREAT A MAN ACCORDING TO HOW HE IS, THEN THAT MAN SHALL REMAIN EXACTLY AS HE IS. BUT IF YOU TREAT A MAN AS HE SHOULD BE, THEN THAT MAN SHALL BECOME AS HE SHOULD BE. ALWAYS MAKE IT A POINT TO FIND SOMETHING TO APPRECIATE IN OTHERS AND HAVE A WILLINGNESS TO COMMUNICATE IT WITH THEM. A **KING** SHALL ALWAYS MAKE EVERYONE WITH WHOM HE INTERACTS FEEL THE INNER GLOW WHICH COMES FROM BEING APPRECIATED. THE PLEASURE

THAT YOU GIVE OTHERS MUST NEVER BE LESS THAN THAT WHICH YOU RECEIVE.

50

MASTER, ALL PEOPLE, BOTH THOSE THAT ARE INTELLIGENT AND FOOLISH, HAVE A TENDENCY TO BUILD THEIR HOPES AROUND PROMISES. WHILE A PROMISE IS A CLOUD THAT SHIELDS ONE FROM THE SUN ON A HOT SCORCHING DAY, THE FULFILLMENT OF A PROMISE IS THE RAIN THAT BRINGS FORTH LIFE. THE MAN WHO DOES NOT KEEP HIS PROMISES TO HIS PEOPLE CAN NEVER JUSTLY BE CALLED **KING**. EVERY SEED OF FAVOR THAT YOU SOW TOWARDS OTHERS SHALL MULTIPLY ITSELF AND YOU SHALL RECEIVE ITS HARVEST IN OVERWHELMING ABUNDANCE. THE DENIAL OF A FAVOR, ESPECIALLY FAVOR TO A TRUE FRIEND IS A MALICIOUS ACT. FOR FAVORS FROM FRIENDS ARE NOT LIGHTLY ASKED, AND SO CANNOT BE LIGHTLY REFUSED. YOU CANNOT SAY NO TO THE PEOPLE THAT YOU TRULY **LOVE** TOO OFTEN. BUT WHEN YOU MUST, YOU MUST MAKE IT SO THAT THEY THEMSELVES SAY NO TO WHATEVER IT IS THAT THEY REQUESTED. GRATITUDE IS THE LEAST LASTING OF ALL VIRTUES. THUS, YOUR FAVORS TO YOUR PEOPLE MUST ALWAYS BE CONTINUALLY REPLENISHED. IF SOMEONE DOES YOU A FAVOR, YOU MUST ALWAYS MAKE IT A POINT TO SHOW YOUR GRATITUDE TANGIBLY.

51

MASTER, WHATEVER YOU ARE, SO ALSO SHALL THE MEN BELOW YOU BE. THE BEHAVIOR OF THE **KING** IS EXTREMELY CONTAGIOUS. WHEN A **KING** IS A BULLY AND LIVES BY THE RULE OF BRUTE FORCE, HIS PEOPLE SHALL BECOME BULLIES ALSO.

WHEN HE PLACES GREAT VALUE UPON STATUS, HE CAUSES HIS PEOPLE TO COMPETE AND BRINGS LOSS TO HIS KINGDOM. TO RULE YOUR PEOPLE MOST EFFECTIVELY, YOU MUST SPEAK AS IF YOU ARE BELOW THEM AND REFRAIN FROM MEDDLING EXCESSIVELY IN THEIR LIVES. TO MEDDLE EXCESSIVELY IN THE AFFAIRS OF YOUR PEOPLE IS TO CAUSE THEM TO BECOME REBELLIOUS, RESTLESS, AND DISTURBED. TO KNOW AND UNDERSTAND YOUR OWN HEART, ABOVE ALL, SHALL CAUSE YOUR PEOPLE TO BE GENUINE, SIMPLE, AND PURE. CIVILIZATION IS THE DOMESTICATION OF MAN. IT IS YOUR COURAGE AND AUDACITY THAT SHALL SET YOU APART FROM THE TIMID SHEEP-LIKE MASSES. THE HEAD CAN NEVER TRAVEL WITHOUT THE FEET. THUS, YOU MUST ALWAYS SEEK TO ENDEAR YOURSELF TO THOSE WHO HOLD EVEN THE LOWLIEST POSITION IN YOUR KINGDOM. THE WIDER YOUR SUPPORT BASE, THE STRONGER SHALL BE YOUR **POWER**. HUMOR THE CROWD AND DO NOT NEGLECT THEIR CONSIDERATIONS. FOR THIS IS THEIR JUST REWARD FOR THE ESTEEM THAT THEY SHALL BESTOW UPON YOU. NEVER BEHAVE LIKE THOSE WHO COMMIT THE GRAVE ERROR OF FLAUNTING THEIR INFATUATION WITH A CULTURE THAT IS NOT THEIR OWN. TO DO THIS PROJECTS SCORN, CONTEMPT, AND ARROGANCE TOWARDS YOUR PEOPLE AND SEPARATES YOU FROM THEM. ALTHOUGH IT IS TRUE THAT YOU MUST RESPECT THE PEOPLE AND ALWAYS BEAR IN MIND THEIR SENTIMENTS, YOU MUST TAKE GREAT CARE TO NEVER RELY UPON THE MULTITUDE OR THEIR OPINIONS TOO FAR. FOR IN THEIR DISTRESS AND TIMES OF ILL, THEY SHALL BE SURE TO FORSAKE YOU.

52

MASTER, A WISE **KING** ALWAYS KEEPS WATCH. FOR A WISE **KING** KNOWS AND UNDERSTANDS THAT EVIL IS FOREVER

AWAITING THE OPPORTUNITY TO ENTER A KINGDOM. IN YOUR LIFE, THERE SHALL BE MANY OCCASIONS WHEN EVIL FORCES ATTEMPT TO GAIN CONTROL OF YOUR KINGDOM. THUS, YOU MUST ALWAYS BE BOTH ABLE AND WILLING TO WIELD THE SWORD IF NECESSARY, EVEN IF YOU ARE A POET AT HEART. A GOOD **KING** MUST BE A GREAT WARRIOR. FOR HE SHALL HAVE TO BATTLE BOTH ASSAULT WITHOUT AND SEDITION FROM WITHIN. JUST BECAUSE A PERSON WANTS SOMETHING FROM YOU DOES NOT MEAN THAT YOU HAVE TO GIVE THEM WHAT THEY WANT. IT IS A **KING'S** BUSINESS TO PREVENT BLOODSHED IF HE CAN. NOT TO PROVOKE IT. THE ONLY ADEQUATE REASON FOR QUARRELING IS IF THE OTHER PARTY BEGINS IT. FOR IT IS AT THAT TIME THAT A SORT OF DUTY TO STOP IT FALLS UPON YOUR SHOULDERS. HOWEVER, IT IS ALWAYS BEST THAT WRONGS BE ADDRESSED BY REASON RATHER THAN BY FORCE. IT IS FAR EASIER TO AVOID A QUARREL THAN IT IS TO EMERGE VICTORIOUS FROM ONE. IF SOMEONE HATES YOU, THAT IS THEIR OWN BUSINESS. YOUR ONLY TASK IS TO SHOW THE MISTAKES IN THAT PERSON'S THINKING BY BEING ALWAYS GENTLE, POISED, AND WELL-DISPOSED TOWARDS EVERYONE. WHEN YOU FIND YOURSELF DEALING WITH A RUDE PERSON, WITHOUT EMBARRASSING THEM IN FRONT OF OTHERS, AND IN A ROUNDABOUT FASHION, DISCREETLY BRING TO THEIR ATTENTION THAT EVEN DOLPHINS, ELEPHANTS, OR ANY OTHER ANIMALS THAT ARE NATURALLY COMMUNAL DO NOT BEHAVE IN SUCH AN UGLY MANNER.

DO NOT ALLOW YOURSELF TO FEEL FOR MISANTHROPES WHAT THEY FEEL FOR THEIR FELLOW MAN. NEVER HOLD THE SAME VIEWS AS THE PERSON WHO HARMS OR WISHES HARM UPON YOU. IN FACT, ENCOURAGE THEM AND WISH THEM PROSPERITY IN ALL OF THEIR ENDEAVORS. BECAUSE NO ONE KNOWS WHAT KIND OF

DISASTER HIS GOOD FORTUNE MAY BRING, IT IS A MOST FOOLISH THING TO BE JEALOUS OR RESENTFUL OF AN EVIL MAN'S SUCCESS. NO GOOD SHALL COME TO THE WICKED MAN NOR SHALL ANY GOOD COME TO THOSE WHO AID AND COMFORT HIM IN HIS WICKEDNESS. EACH GOOD THING THAT ONE DOES FOR THE WICKED SHALL BRING TWICE AS MUCH DISTRESS IN RETURN. HOWEVER, BEFORE YOU ACCUSE SOMEONE OF BEING WICKED BECAUSE OF THEIR DECEIT, OR EVIL BECAUSE OF THEIR INGRATITUDE, ACCUSE YOURSELF OF BEING FOOLISH ENOUGH TO TRUST A LIAR OR WICKED ENOUGH TO DO A GOOD DEED WITH STRINGS ATTACHED. IF YOU DO THIS, IT IS ALMOST CERTAIN THAT YOU SHALL CEASE TO ACCUSE.

<h1 style="text-align:center">53</h1>

MASTER, EVEN THOUGH THERE SHALL BE OCCASIONS WHEN CIVILIZATION IMPOSES INJURIES UPON YOU THAT YOU MUST ENDURE, IF YOU WOULD REMAIN HUMBLE AND PATIENT, THERE SHALL INEVITABLY COME A TIME WHEN YOU SHALL BE ABLE TO EXACT REVENGE EVEN ON THE MOST POWERFUL. A GREAT **KING** MUST NEVER FLAUNT AN INJURY INFLICTED BY AN ENEMY. IN SITUATIONS OF CONFLICT, YOU MUST REFRAIN FROM SHOWING YOUR ANGER IN ANY WAY. SLANDER IS MERELY AN ASSASSINATION ATTEMPT OF A COWARD. NEVER FALL INTO THE TRAP OF QUARRELING WITH ONE WHO DISPARAGES YOU. NEVER TAKE THEIR CONDEMNATIONS TO HEART. A GOOD WORD CONCERNING SOMEONE THAT SPEAKS EVIL OF YOU IS THE ONLY ACCEPTABLE RESPONSE FOR A **KING**. IN THE FACE OF AN ENEMY WEAK ENOUGH TO LOSE CONTROL OF THEIR TONGUE, YOU SHALL EXACT YOUR MOST FANTASTIC REVENGE BY SIMPLY REMAINING INDIFFERENT TO THEIR ATTACKS AND IGNORING THEIR TRIFLING

PRESENCE, NEITHER RIDICULING THEM, NOR REJOICING OPENLY OVER THEIR REVEALED FEEBLENESS. WHILE THIS MAY INFURIATE AND DISTURB THEM, THERE SHALL BE NOTHING THAT THEY SHALL BE ABLE TO DO ABOUT IT. THERE IS NOTHING SO EXASPERATING, AND THUS SO DEBILITATING AS A MAN WHO IS ABLE TO KEEP HIS POISE AS OTHERS ARE LOSING THEIRS. BY BLOCKING YOUR HATERS FROM YOUR CONSIDERATIONS, YOU ALLOW THEM TO BURN IN THEIR OWN HELL. WHEN YOUR DETRACTORS WANT TO, BUT CANNOT FIGURE OUT WHAT YOU ARE DOING, THEY SHALL IMPRISON THEMSELVES IN A WRETCHED STATE OF INCERTITUDE AND DREAD. NO MATTER THE EXTENT OF THE MALEVOLENCE THAT YOUR ENEMIES ATTACK YOU WITH, OR HOW MUCH PAIN THEY MAY CAUSE YOU, SMILE. FOR WHEN DEALING WITH EVIL MEN, EVEN A GOOD HONEST MAN MUST LIE SOMETIMES. A SMILING FACE IS ABLE TO DEFEAT EVEN THE CRUELEST OF ANTAGONISTS. HE WHO SMILES FREQUENTLY IS ABLE TO DISARM HIS FOES WITHOUT UTTERING A SINGLE SYLLABLE. MOST PEOPLE FIND IT DIFFICULT NOT TO BE OPEN WITH ONE WHO SMILES CONSTANTLY WHEN HE SPEAKS. A SMILING, FRIENDLY EXTERIOR COMBINED WITH A GRACEFUL, DISCREET MANNER SHALL ENABLE YOU TO SECRETLY GATHER INFORMATION ON ANYONE, EVEN THOSE WHO HAVE DECLARED THEMSELVES YOUR ENEMIES. IT IS BECAUSE A LAMB IS SPLENDIDLY SUBMISSIVE AND GENTLE THAT THE WOLF WEARING THE DISGUISE OF A LAMB IS ABLE TO MOVE UNDETECTED.

54

MASTER, THERE SHALL BE TIMES WHEN THE GREATEST AND MOST HIGH WISDOM SHALL LIE IN APPEARING NOT TO BE WISE AT ALL. HE IS NO FOOL WHO POSES AS A FOOL. FOR WHILE A WISE

MAN IS CAPABLE OF PLAYING A FOOL, A FOOL SHALL NEVER BE ABLE TO PLAY A WISE MAN. A **KING** MUST NEVER BE IGNORANT, BUT ALWAYS CAPABLE OF CONVINCING OTHERS THAT HE IS SO. ALWAYS BE ALERT AND WATCHFUL. FOR IN THIS WORLD, THERE EXISTS EVEN HONORABLE MEN WHO SPEND THEIR ENTIRE LIVES PREPARING FOR ONE SUPREME ACT OF TREACHERY. NEVER TRUST WHAT A PERSON TELLS YOU FROM THEIR KNEES. ALWAYS BE WARY WHEN PEOPLE SEEM TO SHARE YOUR SENTIMENTS AND OPINIONS EXACTLY. FOR THEY MAY BE MERELY MIRRORING YOU IN ORDER TO ENTRANCE YOU. THOSE THAT ARE THE BEST AT THE GAME OF DECEPTION UNDERSTAND THAT THE BEST WAY TO DECEIVE A MAN IS TO PLAY UPON THOSE INSECURITIES WHICH HE POSSESSES. THUS, YOU MUST NEVER ALLOW YOURSELF TO BE FOOLED BY A PERSON WHO PRAISES YOU EXCESSIVELY. FOR THEY MAY BE DISTRACTING YOU AS THEY PLOT, SCHEME, AND SHARPEN THEIR KNIVES BEHIND YOUR BACK. NEVER UNDERESTIMATE ANYONE, NO MATTER HOW MIGHTY YOU MAY BECOME. FOR THERE IS A MONGOOSE FOR EVERY **KING** COBRA AND TEN HYENAS FOR EVERY LION.

55

MASTER, A MAN SHALL NEVER BECOME **KING** IF HE DOES NOT DEVELOP THE ABILITY TO SEE THINGS EXACTLY AS THEY ARE, AND TO DO THINGS EXACTLY AS THEY MUST BE DONE. IT IS IMPOSSIBLE FOR A PERSON TO EVOLVE UNLESS THEY FIRST DISSOLVE THE PERSON THAT THEY WERE. EACH AND EVERY DAY A BRAND NEW WORLD IS BORN. IF YOU COMMIT YOURSELF TO BEING REBORN EACH DAY, YOU SHALL EXPERIENCE A NEW WORLD WITH EACH SUNRISE. ADAPTATION IS NEVER ACHIEVED ONCE AND FOR ALL. THERE IS NOTHING ABOUT LIFE THAT IS STATIC AND

UNCHANGING. THE CONSTANT FLOW OF TIME SHALL AGAIN AND AGAIN DEMAND FROM YOU FRESH ADAPTATION. IT SHALL ALWAYS BE BEST TO BEND AND SWAY WITH THE WINDS OF TIME, RATHER THAN ATTEMPTING TO STAND FIXED AND IMMOBILE AGAINST THEM. THE MAN WHO REFUSES TO CHANGE SHALL BECOME BRITTLE, AND LIFE SHALL SOON HIT HIM WITH SOMETHING WHICH SHALL SHATTER HIM.

56

MASTER, THERE IS NOTHING YOU SHALL DO THAT SHALL NOT AFFECT EVERYTHING ELSE. KINGS WERE DESIGNED TO ACT, NOT TO BE ACTED UPON. WHILE THE COMMON MAN REACTS TO CIRCUMSTANCES, THE GREAT KING CREATES CIRCUMSTANCES FOR HIMSELF. YOUR RESPONSE TO THE PRESENT MOMENT SHALL BECOME YOUR FUTURE. FOR THE FUTURE IS MERELY THE EFFECT OF CAUSES SOWN NOW. IF YOU MAKE THE BEST OF EACH MOMENT, EVERY DAY SHALL BECOME THE GREATEST AND MOST WONDER FILLED DAY OF YOUR ENTIRE LIFE. WHAT MOST OFTEN BRINGS PEOPLE MISERY AND PREVENTS THEM FROM ADVANCING IS THEIR OBSESSIVE FOCUS UPON THEIR WOEFUL PAST. YOU MUST LET GO OF YOUR THOUGHTS CONCERNING YOUR UNHAPPY PAST AND FORCE YOURSELF TO FOCUS UPON THE PRESENT MOMENT. WHAT IS PAST HAS BEEN LEFT BEHIND. THE FUTURE HAS NOT YET COME. YOU SHOULD NEVER CHASE AFTER THE PAST, NOR PLACE EXPECTATIONS ON THE FUTURE. INSTEAD, YOU MUST ARDENTLY DO WHAT YOU SHOULD DO TODAY. FOR ONE NEVER KNOWS IF DEATH SHALL COME TOMORROW. IT IS IMPOSSIBLE TO LIVE WELL IN THE PRESENT, WHILE WORRYING CONSTANTLY ABOUT THE PAST AND FUTURE.

57

MASTER, TRAIN YOURSELF TO SEE OPPORTUNITY MORE QUICKLY THAN YOU PERCEIVE THE FAULTS OF OTHERS. ONE OF THE MOST FOOLISH ENDEAVORS THAT YOU CAN UNDERTAKE IS TO WASTE YOUR TIME WORRYING ABOUT WHAT OTHERS ARE DOING OR THINKING. WHAT OTHERS MAY DO OR THINK IS OF THE UTMOST IRRELEVANCE COMPARED TO WHAT YOU YOURSELF ARE DOING AND THINKING. TO PUT JUDGMENT BEHIND YOU IS TO END UP AHEAD. WHEN YOU DO NOT JUDGE OTHERS, THERE IS NO ONE IN THE WORLD THAT SHALL BE WORTHY TO JUDGE YOU. JUST AS A MIRROR REFLECTS WHATSOEVER IS PLACED BEFORE IT WITHOUT DISTORTION OR JUDGMENT, SO TOO MUST YOU ACCEPT AND REFLECT THAT WHICH COMES INTO YOUR LIFE WITHOUT JUDGMENT. IT IS BY JUDGING OTHERS THAT YOU LIMIT YOURSELF. THAT WHICH YOU HABITUALLY LOOK FOR IN OTHERS, YOU SHALL EVENTUALLY FIND REFLECTED IN YOUR OWN CHARACTER. THE HABIT OF LOOKING FOR THE GOOD IN OTHERS AND HELPING THEM TO SEE THIS GOOD IN THEMSELVES SHALL INEVITABLY LEAD TO THE FURTHER DEVELOPMENT OF GOOD IN YOURSELF. FOR TO HELP ANOTHER CROSS THE RIVER IS TO REACH THE OTHER SIDE AS WELL.

58

MASTER, EVEN A KING MUST KNOW WHEN TO TAKE HIS LEAVE AND LET THINGS GO. LEARN TO BEHAVE, SPEAK, AND THINK LIKE A MAN THAT IS PREPARED TO DEPART THIS WORLD WITH HIS VERY NEXT BREATH. YOU CAN LIVE NO LIFE OTHER THAN THAT WHICH YOU SHALL SOMEDAY LOSE, AND ONLY YOU SHALL LOSE THE LIFE THAT YOU ARE LIVING NOW. THE MAN WHO IS ABLE TO BECOME

TOTALLY DISPASSIONATE AND DETACHED FROM THE THINGS OF THIS WORLD SHALL FIND **WISDOM** AND WEALTH SITTING AT HIS FEET WAITING TO SERVE HIM. ALWAYS STRIVE WITH ALL YOUR **POWER** TO RECEIVE THINGS WITHOUT CONCEIT, AND TO RELEASE THEM WITHOUT A STRUGGLE. SO LONG AS YOU CLING AND ATTACH YOURSELF TO ANYTHING, YOU SHALL NEVER BE FREE. A WISE **KING** SHALL ALWAYS STRIVE TO RID HIMSELF OF ALL ATTACHMENTS. FOR A WISE **KING** SHALL ALWAYS VALUE THE REALITY OF FREEDOM OVER THE ILLUSION OF SECURITY. EVERYTHING IN THE UNIVERSE DESIRES FREEDOM. ANYTHING THAT YOU CHASE SHALL HESITATE TO COME TO YOU OR FLEE FROM YOU. EVERYTHING THAT YOU HAVE IMPRISONED BY BECOMING ATTACHED TO IT, SHALL TRY TO ESCAPE FROM YOU. HOWEVER, WHEN YOU DO NOT CLING TO ANYTHING, AND WHEN YOU DO NOT CHASE AFTER THINGS, EVERYTHING THAT YOU DESIRE SHALL COME AND REMAIN WITH YOU. LEARN TO SEE ALL THE THINGS OF THIS WORLD AS SMOKE AND NOTHINGNESS. ALL THINGS CHANGE, AND ONCE A THING CHANGES, IT CEASES TO EXIST AS WHAT IT APPEARED TO BE FOR THE REST OF ETERNITY. RATHER THAN ASKING HOW TO OBTAIN A THING, ASK INSTEAD HOW TO KEEP YOURSELF FROM LUSTING AFTER A THING. LEARN TO JUDGE THE COST OF THINGS, NOT ONLY IN TERMS OF MONEY, BUT ALSO IN TERMS OF THE TIME AND PEACE OF MIND THAT SHALL BE SPENT ACQUIRING THEM. THE MORE YOU WANT SOMETHING, THE MORE YOU MUST EXAMINE WHAT GETTING IT SHALL COST YOU TOTALLY.

59

MASTER, YOUR NOBLENESS IS EXPRESSED THROUGH WHAT YOU DO. YOUR CHARACTER IS FORGED BY YOUR ACTIONS. EACH AND

EVERY MOMENT THAT YOU LIVE SHALL PROVIDE YOU WITH THE OPPORTUNITY TO PRACTICE THE ART OF BEING A GREAT **KING**. ALWAYS SEEK TO DO GOOD NOW, RATHER THAN BECOME GOOD LATER. THE TRULY BLESSED PERSON CREATES THEIR OWN BLESSEDNESS THROUGH GOOD HABITS OF THE SOUL, GOOD INTENTIONS, AND GOOD DEEDS. THOSE PERSONS THAT ARE BOUND BY THEIR DEPRAVED INCLINATIONS SHALL FIND ALL OF THEIR AMBITIONS IMPEDED ACCORDINGLY. ALWAYS HOLD TO WHAT IS GOOD AND NEVER SEEK TO GAIN GRACE AND FAVOR THROUGH EVIL METHODS, OR BY INIQUITOUS MEANS. HE WHO WISHES TO BE GOOD NEEDS NO MORE TO BE SO THAN THE AMBITION ITSELF. HE WHO HAS REACHED THE STAGE IN HIS LIFE WHERE HE WANTS NOTHING MORE ZEALOUSLY THAN TO BE GOOD SHALL HAVE NO DIFFICULTIES WHATSOEVER LEARNING ALL THAT IS NECESSARY TO BE SO. IT IS ONLY THOSE WHO FEEL THAT THEY ARE DESTITUTE, INFERIOR, OR DEFICIENT IN SOME WAY THAT BELIEVE THAT IT IS BETTER TO BE GOOD AT "THINGS" THAN IT IS TO BE GOOD IN GENERAL.

INSTEAD OF ATTEMPTING TO FIND WAYS TO EARN PRAISE FOR WHAT YOU ACCOMPLISH, YOU SHOULD ATTEMPT TO FIND WAYS OF EARNING PRAISE FOR BEING A GOOD PERSON. NOT ONLY MUST YOU BE GOOD, BUT YOU MUST STRIVE TO MAKE OTHERS GOOD AS WELL, MUCH LIKE THE SET SQUARE USED BY MASONS WHICH IS RIGHT AND EXACT, AND ALSO MAKES RIGHT AND EXACT EVERYTHING TO WHICH IT IS APPLIED. THE DOING OF A GOOD DEED SHALL ALWAYS BE ITS OWN REWARD. FOR GREATNESS IS ATTAINED BY PLACING ONE GOOD DEED AFTER ANOTHER AND STANDING THEM SO CLOSE TOGETHER THAT NOT EVEN THE SLIGHTEST CRACK IS ABLE TO BE SEEN BETWEEN THEM.

60

Master, it is only by acting regally and confident of your POWER that you shall make yourself worthy of the throne. If you wish to inspire regard and gain the admiration of your people, you must above all respect yourself. Desist and refrain from unseemly behavior out of respect for your own greatness rather than the restraint of any external POWER. Be prudent and magnanimous. Take care for the safety of your people and maintain good order in conducting and commanding them. Under no circumstance must you do any outrage, nor any cruel, spiteful, or wicked thing. On all occasions, you must fly from treason, untruthfulness, and dishonest dealings. Just as eloquent and excellent speech is not characteristic of one who possesses a foolish heart, malicious, acrimonious, deceitful lips are not characteristic of one who possesses the heart of a KING. Take the most extreme care never to let slip from your lips any utterance that is not altogether compassionate, conscientious, humane, reverent, and upright. In all situations, adorn your acts with the precious jewels of courtesy, courage, and loyalty. If something great must be said or done, my son, you must never deem yourself unworthy of saying or doing it.

61

Master, let only good things surround you, always keep your hands clean, and allow none of your proclamations

TO BE NEGATIVE. GIVE FORGIVENESS TO YOUR ENEMIES, TOLERANCE TO YOUR OPPONENTS, AND IN THE EXECUTION OF YOUR GLORIOUS DEEDS, ALWAYS BE INTREPID AND VALOROUS. BE COURTEOUS TO YOUR FRIENDS, MY SON, AND GIVE THEM YOUR HEART. GIVE YOUR CHILDREN A GOOD EXAMPLE. MAKE YOUR ELEGANCE NATURAL, AND ABOVE ALL ELSE GIVE YOUR MOTHER REASONS TO BE PROUD. BE MERCIFUL TO THE POOR, AND TO ALL MEN GIVE GOODWILL. TO YOURSELF, GIVE RESPECT, AND MAKE YOUR ELOQUENCE ADMIRABLE. IN ALL OF YOUR SAYINGS AND REPLIES, BE GENUINE AND MAKE YOUR CONVERSATION A SOURCE OF WEALTH. IF YOU DO ALL OF THESE THINGS, MY SON, YOUR MANNER SHALL BE SO CHARMING AND GRACIOUS THAT ANYONE WHO SPEAKS TO YOU OR MERELY SITS IN YOUR PRESENCE SHALL FEEL AN EVERLASTING AFFECTION FOR YOU.

62

MASTER, ONLY A POMPOUS IDIOT SEEKS TO BE SEEN AND CELEBRATED ALL DAY. TO INVITE HATRED WITHOUT ANY RESULTING ADVANTAGE IS UTTERLY FOOLISH. IT IS ESSENTIAL THAT YOU NEVER SHOW ANGER AT A SLIGHT, NEVER BOAST OF ANYTHING CONCERNING YOURSELF, AND AT ALL COST SHUN ANY SHOW OF PRIDE. EARN YOUR RESPECT WITH DEEDS AND NOT WORDS. NEVER BE THE ONE TO EXALT YOURSELF AND AUTOMATICALLY GO STAND IN THE PLACE OF THE GREAT. FOR IT SHALL ALWAYS BE BETTER TO BE HONORED AND TOLD TO STEP UP, THAN TO BE SHAMED AND TOLD TO STEP DOWN. A TRULY GREAT **KING** IS AN APPRECIATOR, RATHER THAN A DEPRECIATOR OF ALL THAT COMES INTO HIS LIFE. MAKE YOURSELF INTO A MAN OF SUCH HIGH CHARACTER THAT YOU RECEIVE EVERYONE, ALL WITH AN EQUAL SHARE OF **LOVE**, NO MATTER WHETHER THEY BE RICH

OR POOR, POWERFUL, OR POWERLESS. VIOLENCE IS THE PROOF OF ONE'S WEAKNESS. ALWAYS SHOW KINDNESS AND **UNDERSTANDING**. FOR EVERYONE THAT YOU KNOW IS FIGHTING A GREAT BATTLE WITHIN THEMSELVES.

63

MASTER, GREED IS A DISEASE WHICH DESTROYS ALL THAT ARE AFFLICTED BY IT. HE WHO IS A MISER SHALL ALWAYS BE A FOOL. NEVER HOLD YOUR HAND OPEN TO BORROW SOMETHING IF YOU ARE GOING TO SHUT IT WHEN IT COMES TIME TO PAY IT BACK. THE WISE MAN ALWAYS GIVES BEFORE HE TAKES. THE MORE YOU GIVE, THE MORE YOU SHALL GET FROM OTHERS. WHENEVER YOU GIVE SOMEONE SOMETHING, NEVER MAKE THE OTHER PERSON FEEL OBLIGATED TO YOU IN ANY WAY. WHEN YOU GIVE TO OTHERS WITHOUT EXPECTING ANYTHING IN RETURN, THINGS COME OF THEIR OWN ACCORD.

AS TREES BEND LOW WITH RIPENED FRUIT, AND CLOUDS HANG LOW WITH REFRESHING RAIN, SO TOO DOES A NOBLE **KING** BOW LOW WITH HUMBLE GRACIOUSNESS. FOR THIS IS THE WAY OF ALL GENEROUS THINGS. WHILE GENEROSITY IS INDEED A KINGLY TRAIT, BLIND **LOVE** SHALL SPOIL A PERSON. BE PRUDENT AND SHOW DISCRETION WHEN DISPLAYING YOUR GENEROSITY. THE MORE YOU GIVE TO THE UNGRACIOUS, THE MORE THEY SHALL BE UNGRATEFUL AND RESENTFUL OF WHAT THEIR PRIDE HAS CONVINCED THEM IS PATRONIZING CONDESCENSION. ALWAYS SHOW GRATITUDE AND NEVER COMPLAIN ABOUT A GIFT WHICH ANOTHER GIVES TO YOU. FOR A BENEFIT REPROACHED IS AN OFFENCE COMMITTED.

64

MASTER, A KINGDOM RULED BY A WISE KING GROWS WITH PROSPERITY. NEVER discount the wisdom of children. For a child's intelligence is much higher than its capacity to express itself. ALWAYS respect to the utmost your POWER of discernment, and never rely upon another to decide things for you. TO have too much respect for the UNDERSTANDING of others shall cause you to belittle your own. IT is of the utmost folly to dismiss the faithful sentinel of your own UNDERSTANDING from your gates. IN things dishonorable, you shall never be obligated to obey anyone. IF you ever find yourself in service to a wicked person, you should leave as soon as you become aware of this fact, so that you may be able to avoid the dreadful fate of all those who serve the wicked.

65

MASTER, NEVER UNDER ANY CIRCUMSTANCE MUST YOU EVER BE SATISFIED WITH YOUR OWN IGNORANCE. IT shall never be in your best interest to fraternize often with fools. ESPECIALLY those fools who consider themselves wise. FOLLY is a heavier burden than a large stone and it is far easier to carry a heavy load of dirt than it is to put up with a foolish person. WHILE even a stupid person is able to sit and listen, only those who are truly intelligent learn to listen well. NEVER discount even the slightest word what you may hear another utter as frivolous. THE GREATEST WISDOM is often found in small talk.

IN ORDER TO HEAR THE LESSONS OF LIFE, YOU MUST LEARN TO BE STILL AND LISTEN WITH THE EARS OF YOUR HEART. IF YOU EVER DECIDE TO STOP LEARNING, YOU SHALL SOON BEGIN TO FORGET ALL THAT YOU ALREADY KNOW. IT IS A MUST THAT AT ALL TIMES YOU BE BOTH EAGER AND PREPARED TO ACQUIRE **KNOWLEDGE**. THE MORE YOU SEE, UNDERSTAND, AND EXPERIENCE, THE GREATER YOUR KINGDOM SHALL BECOME. TO BE EVER-EXPANDING, WHICH MEANS TO BE CONTINUALLY GROWING INTELLECTUALLY, EMOTIONALLY, AND SPIRITUALLY IS TO LINK YOURSELF, AND THEREFORE YOUR KINGDOM, WITH INFINITY. A MAN MOVES FORWARD IN LIFE BY ASKING INTELLIGENT PEOPLE INTELLIGENT QUESTIONS. JUST AS BUTTERFLIES WING THEIR WAY AMONG THE PLANTS FLYING FROM ONE NECTAR FILLED FLOWER TO THE NEXT, SO TOO MUST YOU ACQUIRE **KNOWLEDGE** FROM THOSE WHO APPEAR TO HAVE IT AND ABSORB FROM EACH OF THEM THAT WHICH SEEMS MOST COMMENDABLE.

TO BECOME A GREAT **KING**, YOU MUST ALWAYS SEEK TO LEARN FROM ALL THAT YOU COME INTO CONTACT WITH. IN ADDITION TO YOUR NATURAL APTITUDE, YOU MUST MAKE EVERY ENDEAVOR TO LEARN FROM GOOD TEACHERS AND KEEP COMPANY WITH OUTSTANDING PERSONS, TAKING FROM EACH OF THEM THE BEST THAT THEY HAVE TO GIVE. IN DOING SO, YOU SHALL QUICKLY ATTAIN THE **DIGNITY** OF THE WISE. EVERY **KING** NEEDS A SAGE AND THE TEST OF YOUR HUMILITY SHALL BE HOW MUCH YOU ARE WILLING TO LISTEN TO THEIR **WISDOM**. NEVER SPURN THE DISCOURSES OF THE WISE. ACQUAINT YOURSELF THOROUGHLY WITH THEIR PROVERBS. IT IS FROM THE WISE THAT YOU SHALL ACQUIRE THE **WISDOM** WITH WHICH YOU MAY RULE YOUR KINGDOM WISELY.

66

Master, incessantly seek to expand your repertoire of skills and remain confident in your own discernment. In order to become a truly sovereign **POWER**, you must never overestimate others' abilities, nor underestimate your own. To dig for a fact shall always be a far more intelligent decision than to jump to a conclusion. If you would but seek **KNOWLEDGE**, you shall find it. He that knocks on the door of **UNDERSTANDING** shall have it opened for him. To bring success and **HONOR** to yourself, you must do right and study. For if you would but help yourself, others shall help you also. In order to exercise your intellect, you should read history, study, and learn from the actions of the illustrious **KINGS** of the past so that you may be able to use their greatness as a foundation upon which you may build your kingdom. Meditate upon how they handled themselves in times of adversity and scrutinize the causes of both their prosperities and despairs, keeping their glorious deeds always in mind to serve as a guiding light, which you may follow all the way to its source, which is magnificence itself. Many that have sat upon the throne have been possessed by their own sense of self-importance, and a few have fallen because they were seduced by their own distorted sense of pride. Never fall victim to the belief that your **KNOWLEDGE** makes you special, or your ability to see what others do not, makes you Superior. The greatest **KINGS** became so, not because they possessed more **KNOWLEDGE** than the rest, but because they had the ability to drop all of their

PRECONCEIVED NOTIONS, FOCUS INTENTLY UPON THE PRESENT MOMENT, AND BE EDUCATED BY THEIR PRESENT EXPERIENCE, WHICH IS THE BEST TEACHER OF ALL.

67

MASTER, FOR A KING TO BE CONSIDERED EXCELLENT, IT IS CRUCIAL THAT HE KNOWS HOW TO SPEAK WELL. THE TRICK IN MAKING OTHERS WANT TO LISTEN TO YOU LIES IN SAYING WHAT THEY DESIRE TO HEAR. FILL THEIR EARS WITH THAT WHICH IS PLEASANT TO THEM AND SPEAK WITH SUCH SIMPLE ELEGANCE THAT IT SEEMS LIKE NATURE HERSELF IS DRUGGING THEIR SENSIBILITIES WITH INTOXICATING SWEETNESS. ALWAYS MAKE YOUR WORDS A SPARK FOR ACTION, AND NOT MERE PASSIVE CONTEMPLATION. ONCE YOU HAVE PEOPLE'S ATTENTION, THE KEY TO HOLDING IT IS MAKING THEM FEEL STIRRED AND UPLIFTED. WHEN OPPORTUNITIES TO SPEAK PRESENT THEMSELVES, YOU MUST BE CAPABLE OF SPEAKING WITH SUCH **DIGNITY** AND **POWER** THAT YOU ARE ABLE TO AROUSE THE DEEPEST PASSIONS WITHIN YOUR LISTENERS' HEARTS, KINDLING AND STIRRING THEM AS THE NEED ARISES. SPEAK OUT FULLY AND FRANKLY WHILE AVOIDING TALKING NONSENSE OR DISPLAYING VANITY. MAKE ALL OF THE IDEAS THAT YOU CONVEY WITH YOUR WORDS BEAUTIFUL, WITTY, SHREWD, OR SOLEMN, EACH ACCORDING TO THEIR NECESSITY. WHEN YOU CHOOSE TO DISCUSS OBSCURE OR DIFFICULT MATTERS, WITHOUT APPEARING PEDANTIC, TAKE GREAT PAINS TO CLARIFY EVERY AMBIGUITY WHICH MAY APPEAR, AND FORMULATE YOUR IDEAS AND WORDS SO PRECISELY THAT YOU MAKE THEIR MEANING ABSOLUTELY PLAIN. TO SEPARATE INTELLIGENCE FROM YOUR WORDS IS LIKE DIVORCING THE SPIRIT FROM THE BODY. IN NEITHER CASE CAN

THIS BE DONE WITHOUT BRINGING ABOUT DEATH. IN YOUR SPEECH, LUCIDITY MUST ALWAYS WALK HAND IN HAND WITH INTELLIGENCE. ALWAYS MAKE THE MOST IMPORTANT INGREDIENT IN THE RECIPE OF YOUR SPEECH A THOROUGH **KNOWLEDGE** OF THE SUBJECT ON WHICH YOU ARE SPEAKING.

68

MASTER, A GOOD TEACHER SHALL ALWAYS BE A GOOD STUDENT. HE WHO TEACHES LEARNS. **KINGS** EXIST FOR THE SAKE OF THEIR FELLOW MAN. IF YOU CAN TEACH OTHERS TO BECOME BETTER, YOU MUST DO YOUR BEST TO DO SO. WHEREVER YOU GO, BRING PEACE AND LEARNING ALONG WITH YOU. IT SHALL NEVER BE FITTING FOR AN IGNORANT MAN TO EITHER TEACH OTHERS, OR TO RULE. IF YOU TRULY WISH TO BE **KING**, YOU MUST PUT EVERY CARE AND EFFORT FIRST INTO ACQUIRING **KNOWLEDGE**, AND THEN INTO INSCRIBING UPON YOUR HEART THE ORDINANCES OF **WISDOM** SO THAT DISCRETION SHALL BE INHERENT IN YOUR VERY NATURE. IT SHALL BE THEN THAT **UNDERSTANDING** SHALL ADMONISH AND SPEAK TO YOU WITHIN YOUR MIND AND RID YOU OF THE DISTURBANCES SUFFERED BY THOSE CONFUSED SOULS WHO ARE AFFLICTED BY THEIR IGNORANCE AND BLIND, PERVERSE DESIRES. WHEN TEACHING OTHERS, YOU MUST LEARN TO STUDY THE DISPOSITION OF YOUR PUPILS AND TEACH THEM ACCORDING TO THIS **KNOWLEDGE**, RATHER THAN BEING LIKE THOSE FOOLISH AND OBSTINATE FARMERS WHO INSIST UPON SOWING WHEAT IN GROUND FIT ONLY FOR CORN. BY THE **KNOWLEDGE** GAINED FROM THE OBSERVATION OF YOUR STUDENTS, YOU MUST DIRECT AND ASSIST THEM ALONG THE PATH TO WHICH THEY ARE INCLINED BY THEIR OWN INSTINCT, APTITUDE, AND BRILLIANCE.

In the introducing of new things and the wiping out of the old, usage shall always be more effective than explanation.

69

Master, there is nothing more important to people's vanity than their intelligence. Subtle suggestion shall often have more POWER to influence than conspicuous instruction. If you openly attempt to correct a person, oftentimes, that person shall grow insecure and resistant to your direction. People have their own ideas. They shall resent any attempt by you to persuade them that their ideas are mistaken. Many shall be offended by the very idea that you may know better than them. If you wish to communicate an important idea, never preach, or overtly reprove another. Instead, learn to plant impressions and insinuate suggestions. Allow them to connect the dots and come to the conclusion on their own. Such indirect communication, because it causes others to internalize the thoughts that you are trying to convey, and makes those thoughts seem to emerge from their own mind, has the POWER to penetrate undetected behind people's walls of obstinacy. Avoid conducting discussions as if you were a scholar talking to the less informed and inexperienced learners. Always encourage and welcome a free and unfettered exchange of ideas. The business of a teacher is to make ideas available, not to force or impose them upon people. When you force things upon others, you earn only displeasure and resistance.

70

MASTER, TRUE GREATNESS OF SPIRIT SPRINGS FROM A DELIBERATE DECISION AND FREE DETERMINATION TO SET HONOR AND DUTY ABOVE ALL. DUTY FLOWS UPHILL, AS WELL AS DOWN. SERVICE IS THE PRICE YOU MUST PAY FOR THE HONOR OF BEING KING. KINGSHIP MUST ALWAYS BE LOOKED UPON AS A DUTY AND NEVER A PRIVILEGE. A KING IS NEVER CHOSEN FOR THE PURPOSE OF TAKING CARE OF HIS OWN INTEREST, BUT TO SECURE THE WELL-BEING OF THOSE WHO CHOSE HIM. A KING RULES FOR THE BENEFIT OF HIS PEOPLE AND ALL WHO DEPEND UPON HIM. ALL ARE LOST IF YOU NEGLECT THEM, GOVERN THEM BY EMOTION, OR RULE THEM WITH A HARD, WILLFUL HEART. MAKE ALWAYS YOUR FIRST DUTY BE TO THOSE IN YOUR KINGDOM, MY SON. FOR AS THEIR LIVES ARE IN YOUR HANDS, YOU MUST ALWAYS LOOK TO THEIR BRIGHTEST FUTURE IN ALL THAT YOU DO. THE KING WHO REFUSES TO DO THIS FLEES FROM HIS DUTY, AND CONSEQUENTLY FLEES FROM THE THRONE. ANY KING WHO RUNS FROM HIS THRONE IS VERY CONFUSED INDEED. THAT WHICH YOU DO FOR YOURSELF SHALL DIE WITH YOU. BUT THAT WHICH YOU DO FOR YOUR KINGDOM SHALL ENDURE FOR ALL ETERNITY. PLACE THE KINGDOM ABOVE YOUR PRIDE, AND THE COMMUNITY ABOVE YOURSELF. ABSENT THIS HUMILITY, ANY KING, EVEN ONE THAT WAS ONCE NOBLE, SHALL PROVE TO BE NO LONGER A KING, BUT A TYRANT. JUST AS THE DIVINE MANIFESTED ITSELF AS LOVE IN ORDER TO BRING ORDER OUT OF CHAOS AND HARMONIZE THE NATURAL FORCES OF THE UNIVERSE AT THE BEGINNING OF CREATION, SO MUST A KING BECOME A MANIFESTATION OF DIVINE LOVE UPON THE EARTH, SO THAT HE MAY BE ABLE TO UNITE HIS PEOPLE IN HARMONY AND BRING ORDER TO HIS REALM.

ALTHOUGH OBEDIENCE MAY BE YOUR DUE, IT IS YOUR RESPONSIBILITY TO EARN LOYALTY AND DEVOTION. TO DO THIS, YOU MUST LEARN THE CHARACTER AND INCLINATIONS OF YOUR PEOPLE. REFLECT THE GREATNESS WHICH LIES WITHIN YOU. MAKE YOURSELF AVAILABLE WITH EASE TO ALL WHO HAVE A LEGITIMATE CLAIM ON ANY PORTION OF YOUR TIME. TAKE YOUR PLACE AS **KING** WITH A SERENE MANNER ABSENT ANY CONDESCENSION. JUST AS ANY TOOL, INSTRUMENT, OR VESSEL CAN ONLY BE CONSIDERED EXCELLENT IF IT PERFORMS WELL THAT TASK FOR WHICH IT WAS MADE, SO TOO CAN A **KING** ONLY BE CONSIDERED EXCELLENT IF HE PERFORMS WELL THAT TASK FOR WHICH HE WAS MADE. JUST AS THE NOSE, NOR THE TOES SHALL NEVER DEMAND ADDITIONAL COMPENSATION FOR PERFORMING THEIR DUTIES AND SERVING THE BODY, SO TOO MUST A **KING** NEVER DEMAND ADDITIONAL COMPENSATION FOR DOING HIS DUTY. THE **KNOWLEDGE** THAT IN YOUR DAY YOU DID YOUR DUTY AND LIVED UP TO THE ROYAL EXPECTATIONS OF YOURSELF IS IN ITSELF A MOST REWARDING EXPERIENCE AND MAGNIFICENT ACHIEVEMENT.

71

MASTER, IT IS YOUR OBLIGATION AS KING TO BE A LIGHT IN DARK PLACES EVEN WHEN ALL OTHER LIGHTS GO OUT. IN THE DARKEST MOMENTS OF YOUR PEOPLE, YOU MUST BE THE ONE TO HOLD THE LANTERN OF HOPE THAT SHALL GUIDE THEM BACK TO LIFE. TO PREPARE YOURSELF FOR LIFE IS TO PREPARE YOURSELF TO HANDLE ANY SITUATION THAT IT MAY BRING. IN ORDER TO BE GREAT, YOU MUST LEARN TO BEAR THE MANY DIVERSE CALAMITIES WHICH LIFE SHALL THRUST IN YOUR PATH WITH SUCH FORTITUDE THAT IT SHALL BE OBVIOUS TO ALL THAT, NOT ONLY CAN YOUR

WILL NEVER BE CRUSHED BY ADVERSITY, BUT ON THE CONTRARY, IT IS RAISED BY IT TO THE HEIGHTS OF THE TRUE **DIGNITY** AND UNIVERSAL RENOWN. THERE SHALL NEVER BE ANYTHING GAINED BY LAMENTING WHAT NEVER WAS. NEVER ALLOW ANY EARS TO EVER HEAR YOU COMPLAINING. NOT EVEN YOUR OWN. YOU SHALL BEGIN TO BE A TRUE **KING** ONLY ONCE YOU CEASE WHINING AND ACCUSING OTHERS OF BEING THE CAUSE OF YOUR CONDITION. FOR IT IS THEN THAT YOU SHALL CEASE STRUGGLING AGAINST CIRCUMSTANCES AND BEGIN TO USE THEM AS AIDS TO YOUR PROGRESS.

72

MASTER, A GREAT MAN NEVER TAKES PLEASURE OUT OF MAKING OTHERS FEEL INFERIOR. THE WORTH OF **POWER** LIES NOT IN ITS POSSESSION, BUT IN ITS USE. THE **KING** THAT USES HIS **POWER** FOR THE DETRIMENT OF OTHERS HAS FIXED HIS OWN DESTINY BY HIS OWN DEED. NEVER EXERCISE **POWER** SIMPLY BECAUSE IT COMES EASY TO YOUR HAND. THINGS SHOULD NOT BE DONE BECAUSE YOU ARE ABLE TO DO THEM, BUT RATHER BECAUSE YOU OUGHT TO DO THEM. DAILY, ASK YOURSELF WHAT GOOD CAN YOU DO FOR OTHERS WITH THE **POWER** THAT YOU POSSESS. THE MAIN REQUIREMENT OF **POWER** IS SELF-DISCIPLINE. IT IS ONLY THE IGNORANT IN THE WORLD WHO NEEDS OUTSIDE LEGISLATION TO RESTRAIN THEM. AS LONG AS YOU ARE IN CONTROL OF YOURSELF, IT SHALL BE IMPOSSIBLE FOR YOU TO BE CONTROLLED BY ANYONE ELSE, NOR SHALL YOU FEEL THE NEED TO CONTROL ANYONE ELSE.

73

Master, no true leader would ever set a pace too fast for his followers to keep up. No great **KING** would ever burden his followers with a greater load than they can carry. Courtesy is a savory spice. Commands seasoned with its flavor taste much sweeter and are much easier to digest than those given without it. Even a **KING** must learn to take commands. Those who know well how to follow shall soon learn how to command well, as well.

74

Master, slothful people are like excrement. Abhorrent, with everyone seeking to avoid them. Great notions die for lack of being acted upon. It is only by trying that you can succeed in anything. The only sure way to fail in anything is to not attempt. Your fate is yours alone. For your fate is a direct result of your own initiative or lack of it. He that can conceive an idea in his mind and dedicate his heart to it, shall achieve it in time. Rather than waiting for events to happen, you must cultivate the fire of personal initiative within yourself and cause the effects that you wish to see. While indeed nature shall give to a man that for which he works and shall never allow any form of labor to go uncompensated, nature shall never allow any man to get something without paying the full price for it. Whatsoever you do, you yourself shall become. Make it a part of your greatness that you profit from every experience. Follow the examples set by the great **KINGS** of the past and

IMITATE THOSE WHO HAVE REIGNED SUPREME. EVEN IF YOUR TALENTS DO NOT PROVE TO BE THEIR EQUAL, YOUR DEEDS SHALL AT LEAST BEAR SOME LIKENESS TO THEIRS. STRIVE TO MAKE YOUR DEEDS OF SUCH HIGH STANDARD THAT THEY SEEM TO BE BEYOND HUMAN NATURE. IT IS YOUR DISCIPLINE AND COMMITMENT TO ACHIEVING EXCELLENCE THAT SHALL DISTINGUISH YOU FROM ORDINARY MEN. A **KING** ADDS TO HIS SOCIETY IN WAYS THAT SHALL DEFINE THE LIVES OF ALL THOSE WHO SHALL FOLLOW HIM. EVERY DEED THAT YOU PERFORM, PERFORM WITH THIS TRUTH IN THE FORE OF YOUR MIND. DO NOTHING WITHOUT REGARD AS TO THE CONSEQUENCES. TO NOT PAY ATTENTION TO SMALL MATTERS IS TO BRING PERDITION UPON YOURSELF. DO NOTHING, NOT EVEN THE SMALLEST THING AS IF YOU CONSIDERED IT INSIGNIFICANT. DO NOTHING WITHOUT SOME END IN MIND AND MAKE THE COMMON GOOD THE ONLY END OF ALL THE ACTIONS THAT YOU PERFORM. ALL ENDEAVORS DIRECTED TOWARDS A PURELY SELFISH END CONTAIN WITHIN THEMSELVES THE GERMS OF THEIR VERY OWN CORRUPTION. ALTHOUGH IT IS INDEED TRUE THAT YOUR MIND SHOULD BE EVER ON THE STARS, IT IS EQUALLY TRUE THAT YOUR EYES MUST ALWAYS WATCH OVER YOUR STEPS.

75

MASTER, IN ALL ENDEAVORS, HASTE BREEDS DANGER. THERE ARE ONLY TWO PRINCIPLES THAT YOU MUST CONCERN YOURSELF WITH IN ANY ENTERPRISE THAT YOU DECIDE TO UNDERTAKE. AND THESE ARE MAKING THE PLAN AND STICKING TO THE PLAN. ANY ACCOMPLISHMENT THAT YOU HOPE TO ACHIEVE ON THIS EARTH HAS CERTAIN STEPS WHICH, WITHOUT LASHING OUT AT THAT WHICH MAY APPEAR TO OPPOSE YOU, OR BECOMING IRRITATED,

YOU MUST NOT ONLY FOLLOW, BUT REVERENCE. IT IS IN THIS WAY THAT YOU SHALL ADVANCE METHODICALLY TOWARDS THE FULFILLMENT OF YOUR AMBITIONS. ALTHOUGH FORTUNE, BECAUSE IT APPOINTS THE DETAIL OF CIRCUMSTANCE, MAY INDEED BE THE DIRECTOR OF HALF OF YOUR REALITY, IT STILL LEAVES YOU THE **POWER** TO DIRECT THE OTHER HALF, WHICH IS YOUR RESPONSE TO THOSE CIRCUMSTANCES. AS LONG AS YOU ALLOW FORTUNE TO DIRECT YOUR ACTIONS, AS WELL AS DETAIL YOUR CIRCUMSTANCES, YOU SHALL NEVER HAVE ANY **POWER** OVER YOUR LIFE. THERE IS AN ENDING FOUND IN ALL THINGS. IN ALL OF YOUR SCHEMES AND VENTURES, PLAN ALL THE WAY TO THEIR ENDING. MAKE THEIR CONCLUSIONS CRYSTAL CLEAR AND KEEP THE THOUGHTS OF THEIR CLOSURE CONSTANTLY IN MIND. THE **KING** WHO KEEPS HIS MIND EVER ON THE CONCLUSION OF HIS DESIGNS, RIDS HIMSELF OF ALL OF THE DOUBTS AND UNCERTAINTY WHICH CAUSE THE MAJORITY TO FAIL. THERE IS NO SATISFACTORY SUBSTITUTE FOR PLOTTING SEVERAL MOVES AHEAD AND PLANNING THE CONCLUSION OF AN ENTERPRISE. IF YOU CAREFULLY PLAN ALL THAT YOU DO, WHATEVER YOU DO SHALL TURN OUT RIGHT.

76

MASTER, A **KING** CANNOT AFFORD THE CAUTION OF COMMON MEN. A **KING** MUST EITHER CONQUER VALIANTLY OR DIE GLORIOUSLY. A **KING** MUST BE FORGIVEN IF HE PRESUMES TOO MUCH OF HIMSELF. FOR A **KING** WHO IS DESTINED TO ACHIEVE GREATNESS MUST NOT ONLY HAVE THE COURAGE TO DO GREAT THINGS, BUT ALSO THE UTMOST **FAITH** IN HIMSELF. THERE IS NOTHING THAT SHALL BESTOW UPON A **KING** AS MUCH RESPECT AND **HONOR** AS THE UNDERTAKING OF

AWESOME ENTERPRISES AND THE SETTING OF A HEROIC EXAMPLE. IN EVERY ACTION THAT YOU COMMIT, STRIVE TO ATTRACT UNTO YOURSELF THE REPUTATION OF BEING A REMARKABLY EXTRAORDINARY MAN. THOSE WHO SEEK TO ACHIEVE WONDROUS THINGS MUST SHOW NO MERCY TO EXCUSES FOR FAILURE. IT IS A MUST THAT YOU LEARN TO FORCE THE OPPORTUNITIES THAT YOU ENCOUNTER TO FIT THE NEEDS THAT YOU REQUIRE. GREAT DEEDS REQUIRE GREAT SACRIFICE. THERE SHALL BE NO ADVANCEMENT OR ACCOMPLISHMENT WHATSOEVER IF THERE IS NO SACRIFICE. YOUR SUCCESS SHALL DEPEND EXCLUSIVELY UPON THE MEASURE THAT YOU SACRIFICE YOUR INDOLENCE, FIX YOUR MIND UPON THE DEVELOPMENT OF YOUR PLANS, AND STRENGTHEN YOUR DETERMINATION. IN ORDER TO ACCOMPLISH SOME GREAT FEAT IN THIS LIFE, IT IS A MUST THAT YOU APPLY YOURSELF TO YOUR TASK WITH SUCH AN INTENSE FOCUS OF YOUR **POWER** THAT TO ARROGANT ONLOOKERS, WHO LIVE ONLY FOR THEIR ENTERTAINMENT, YOUR FOCUS APPEARS TO BE INSANITY. IN ALL VENTURES, A STAUNCH AND STEADY APPLICATION OF DILIGENCE SHALL ALWAYS PROVE IRRESISTIBLE. FOR THIS IS HOW TIME SUBDUES EVEN THE GREATEST POWERS OF THE UNIVERSE. TO BE DILIGENT, MY SON, IS TO MANEUVER THE CIRCUMSTANCES OF YOUR LIFE TO YOUR OWN ADVANTAGE. HE WHO IS PREPARED TO DIE IN ORDER TO ACCOMPLISH HIS GOALS, SHALL ALWAYS HAVE THE ADVANTAGE OVER HE THAT IS NOT. DO NOT DECLARE YOUR DESIGNS BEFOREHAND, BUT INSTEAD WATCH FOR EVERY OPPORTUNITY TO BRING THEM INTO FRUITION. EACH ACTION THAT YOU CHOOSE TO PERFORM, PERFORM WITH THE CONVICTION THAT WITH IT YOU SHALL EXCEL ALL OF YOUR PREVIOUS ONES. NEVER ALLOW YOURSELF TO BE SHAKEN BY SUCCESS OR FAILURE. FOR THE WINDS OF TIME SHALL BRING FORTH BOTH AS TRANSITORY STATES.

BOOK SIX

1

MASTER, WHERESOEVER LIFE MAY TAKE YOU ALONG YOUR JOURNEY, ALWAYS BEAR IN MIND YOUR DUTY TO BE A GOOD KING. IF WICKEDNESS MAKES YOU HAPPY, YOU ARE BOTH JUDGED AND CONDEMNED. YOU MUST NOT ONLY REFUSE TO DO WICKEDNESS BUT EVEN TO CELEBRATE IT. A KING FILLED WITH GOODNESS IS TO HIS PEOPLE WHAT RAIN AND SUNSHINE IS TO THE TREES. FOR HE CAUSES HIS PEOPLE TO GROW AND STAND TALL. A KING FILLED WITH WICKEDNESS IS LIKE A RAVENOUS TIGER OR RABID BEAR TO HIS PEOPLE, DOING NOTHING BUT DEVOURING AND DESTROYING THEIR WELL-BEING. IT CAN VERILY BE SAID THAT, WHILE THERE IS NOTHING SO ADVANTAGEOUS AND BENEFICIAL TO PEOPLE AS A GOOD KING, THERE IS NOTHING SO HARMFUL AND BANEFUL TO THEM AS A WICKED ONE. WHILE GOOD KINGS RULE NOT FOR THEMSELVES BUT FOR THEIR PEOPLE, WICKED KINGS COME TO FEAR THE VERY PEOPLE THAT THEY RULE. THE GREATER THE POWER THAT WICKEDNESS ENJOYS, THE MORE HARM IT SHALL BE ABLE TO DO. THE MORE POWER THAT A WICKED KING POSSESSES, THE MORE ENEMIES HE SHALL HAVE. THE GOOD KING BRINGS FORTH GOOD THINGS OUT OF THE GOODNESS THAT IS STORED UP IN HIS GOOD HEART. HE ATTRACTS GOOD THINGS TO HIMSELF BECAUSE OF THIS GOODNESS. IF YOU SLIP AND FALL INTO OIL, IT SHALL STICK TO YOUR CLOTHES AND MAKE THEM FILTHY. LIKEWISE IF YOU CONSTANTLY FRATERNIZE WITH THE WICKED, YOUR CHARACTER SHALL BE STAINED BY THEIRS. NEVER PUT YOURSELF IN A POSITION WHERE SOMEONE IS ABLE TO TRUTHFULLY DECLARE THAT YOU ARE NOT GOOD. IF YOU DO FIND YOURSELF IN SUCH A

POSITION, NEVER FORGET THAT THE **POWER** TO MAKE YOUR ACCUSER A LIAR LIES WITHIN YOUR POSSESSION.

2

MASTER, TO CONSTANTLY HAVE GOOD MOODS, GOOD INTENTIONS, AND GOOD CONDUCT IS TO HAVE GOOD FORTUNE. LIFE RELENTLESSLY INSISTS UPON AND FAVORS THAT WHICH BENEFITS THE WHOLE. THE UNJUST MAN DOES THE GRAVEST INJUSTICE TO HIMSELF. FOR HE MAKES HIMSELF BAD. THOSE WHO ENJOY EVIL SHALL HAVE IT AS A CONSTANT COMPANION INTO THEIR OLD AGE. THE **DIVINE** LAW IS ABSOLUTELY JUST, AND SHALL NEVER GIVE GOOD FOR EVIL, NOR EVIL FOR GOOD. NO LAW OF MAN CAN VOID **DIVINE** LAW. EVERY ACTION HAS A REACTION. JUST AS NO ONE SHALL FEEL SORROW FOR THE SNAKE CHARMER THAT IS BITTEN, NO ONE SHALL FEEL SORRY FOR HE THAT RUNS WITH THE WICKED, AND TRIPS AND FALLS.

3

MASTER, EVERY EVIL TO WHICH YOU DO NOT SUCCUMB SHALL BECOME YOUR BENEFACTOR. EVERYTHING THAT EXISTS IS FOR A PURPOSE. IT IS THE UNWISE ONLY THAT BELIEVE TO BE GREAT IS TO POSSESS ONLY ONE SIDE, THE SWEET, WITHOUT THE OTHER, THE BITTER. THERE WOULD BE NO UNIVERSE IF THERE WAS NO DARKNESS TO CONTEND WITH THE LIGHT. WHILE IT IS TRUE THAT GOOD IS BY NATURE BEAUTIFUL, AND EVIL IS BY NATURE UGLY, IT IS ONLY BECAUSE UGLINESS EXISTS THAT ONE IS ABLE TO RECOGNIZE BEAUTY. JUST AS THERE CAN BE NO HIGH WITHOUT A LOW, THERE COULD BE NO GOOD WITHOUT BAD. THE BRIGHTNESS OF THE MOON SHINES ALL THE BRIGHTER FOR THE

DARKNESS WHICH LIES BEHIND IT.

4

MASTER, BLAME NO MAN FOR SEEKING HIS OWN GOOD. NEVER ALLOW THE IGNORANCE OF OTHERS TO EXASPERATE YOU. EVERY QUALITY WHICH YOU ARE ABLE TO RECOGNIZE IN ANOTHER EXISTS ALSO WITHIN YOU. THIS IS THE SOLE REASON THAT YOU'RE ABLE TO RECOGNIZE IT. THE GREATER THE LIGHT IS, THE GREATER THE SHADOW SHALL BE. IN ORDER TO KNOW THE GOOD OF WHICH YOU ARE ABLE, YOU MUST FIRST COME TO ACKNOWLEDGE THE EVIL OF WHICH YOU ARE CAPABLE. YOUR BRIGHTEST LIGHT CAN ONLY SHINE ONCE YOU HAVE ACCEPTED YOUR DEEPEST DARKNESS. GOOD CONSISTS IN THE CULTIVATION OF A RIGHTEOUS ATTITUDE AND RIGHTEOUS ACTIONS. THERE LIES NO GOOD IN CONTEMPLATING OR PHILOSOPHIZING ABOUT WHAT A GOOD **KING** IS. GOOD LIES ONLY IN BECOMING ONE. ALLOW NO PREDICAMENT OR CIRCUMSTANCE WHATSOEVER TO DETER YOU FROM BECOMING GOOD. NO MATTER WHAT YOUR SITUATION IS, YOU SHALL NEVER FIND A SITUATION BETTER SUITED FOR THE PRACTICE OF KINGLY GOODNESS THAN THE ONE IN WHICH YOU NOW FIND YOURSELF.

5

MASTER, OFTENTIMES, THAT WHICH IS CALLED THE WORST EVIL BY SOME IS CONSIDERED TO BE THE GREATEST GOOD TO OTHERS. EVERYTHING IN LIFE IS RELATIVE. THE GREATEST EVIL CAN SPRING FROM THE DESIRE TO DO GOOD. INDEED, EVIL IS A FRUIT THAT UNEXPECTEDLY RIPENS WITHIN THE FLOWER OF THE GOOD INTENTIONS WHICH CONCEALED IT. EVIL EXERTS ITS **POWER**

BY MAKING THE DARKNESS SEEM LIKE THE LIGHT. PLEASURE IS THE BAIT WHICH INIQUITY USES TO LURE THE IGNORANT INTO EVIL'S LAIR. TIME PUSHES EVERYTHING BEFORE IT, AND IS ABLE TO BRING WITH IT GOOD, AS WELL AS EVIL, AND EVIL, AS WELL AS GOOD. IN THIS LIFE, YOU SHALL SOON DISCOVER THAT THERE ARE MANY THINGS WHICH MAY SEEM GOOD AT FIRST, BUT THEY ARE IN FACT EVIL, AND MANY WHICH AT FIRST MAY APPEAR EVIL, BUT ARE IN FACT GOOD. GOOD AND EVIL ARE BUT OPPOSITE POLES OF THE SAME FORCE. EVERY GOOD QUALITY HAS ITS DARK SHADOW. NOTHING GOOD CAN COME INTO THIS WORLD WITHOUT AT ONCE PRODUCING ITS CORRESPONDING EVIL. IN THE STORY OF EVERY HERO, YOU SHALL FIND A VILLAIN THAT REFLECTS HIM. EVIL IS THE OPPOSITE OF GOOD AND GOOD OF EVIL. THE ONE MUST ALWAYS BALANCE THE OTHER. IF ONE INCREASES OR DECREASES THE OTHER, ITS REQUISITE, COUNTERBALANCE SHALL DO THE SAME.

6

MASTER, ONE DOES NOT BECOME GOOD BY ACQUIRING GOODNESS, BUT RATHER BY COMING INTO CONTACT WITH THE GOODNESS THAT EXISTS ALREADY WITHIN THEMSELVES. THE IGNORANCE OF A DISEASE IS ITS MAIN CAUSE. THE AWARENESS OF THE DARKNESS WITHIN YOURSELF IS THE FIRST STEP TO ILLUMINATING IT. IT IS ONLY IN THE PRESENCE OF A DEDICATED COMMITMENT TO FACING YOUR DEMONS THAT THE WINDOW TO THE LIGHT OF YOUR TRUTH SHALL OPEN. YOUR POTENTIAL FOR GREATNESS SHALL ONLY EMERGE WHEN THE PROACTIVE EMBRACE OF YOUR LIGHT SURPASSES THE FEAR OF YOUR OWN DARKNESS. YOUR DARKNESS SHALL ONLY BE DISPERSED ONCE YOU OPEN YOUR HEART AND LET IN YOUR LIGHT. WHEN A ROOM IS DARK, ONLY A FOOL WOULD ATTEMPT TO SHOVEL OR SWEEP OUT THE DARKNESS INSTEAD OF MERELY OPENING THE CURTAIN AND

LETTING IN THE LIGHT.

7

MASTER, WHENEVER YOU SEE AN INSOLENT MAN, A VILLAIN, COWARD, OR LIAR, DO NOT BECOME UPSET. FOR IN THIS LIFE, IT IS IMPOSSIBLE FOR SUCH PEOPLE NOT TO EXIST. RATHER THAN BLAMING THE DARKNESS THAT YOU SEE IN OTHERS, ALLOW YOUR LIGHT TO SHINE SO THAT YOU MAY BE ABLE TO DISPEL IT. IF THE EVIL IN THIS WORLD IS TO BE DEFEATED, IT MUST COME THROUGH THE VICTORY OF RIGHTEOUSNESS WITHIN YOURSELF. THOSE WHO HAVE DEFEATED EVIL DID NOT DEFEAT IT BY FIGHTING IT, BUT BY TRANSCENDING IT. IT IS FUTILE TO FIGHT DARKNESS WITH DARKNESS, AND A FOOLISH THING TO ATTEMPT TO DEFEAT IGNORANCE BY ATTACKING IT. THOSE WHO MAKE IT THEIR MISSION TO DESTROY EVIL ARE VERY LIKELY TO TURN INTO THE VERY THING THAT THEY HOPE TO ANNIHILATE. TO FIGHT DARKNESS WITH DARKNESS SHALL ONLY INCREASE THE DARKNESS. TO ATTACK IGNORANCE IS TO BE DRAWN INTO IGNORANCE YOURSELF. DEAL WITH THOSE THAT ARE WICKED AND UNBALANCED, NOT WITH HATRED AND MALICE, BUT WITH JUSTICE AND THE **KNOWLEDGE** THAT EVIL SHOULD ALWAYS BOW BEFORE THE GOOD, AND THE WICKED SHALL INEVITABLY YIELD BEFORE THE RIGHTEOUS. NO MATTER HOW BLEAK THINGS MAY SEEM, MY SON, IT IS IMPERATIVE THAT YOU NEVER LOSE HOPE. FOR THERE ARE MORE FORCES AT WORK THAN EVIL IN THIS WORLD.

BOOK SEVEN

1

MASTER, THE GREATEST STEP THAT YOU CAN TAKE TO BECOME KING IS TO TAKE RESPONSIBILITY FOR THE CREATION OF YOURSELF AND YOUR KINGDOM. BECOMING THE CREATOR OF YOUR OWN REALITY IS MORE IMPORTANT THAN ANYTHING IN THE WORLD. YOU MUST NEVER ALLOW SOMEONE ELSE TO DICTATE WHO OR WHAT YOU SHALL BE. NO GOOD SHALL EVER COME OUT OF DIVIDED LEADERSHIP. BY CONTROLLING YOURSELF, YOU CONTROL THE ENTIRE WORLD. FOR THE WORLD IS WITHIN YOU, NOT THE OTHER WAY AROUND. A TRUE MASTER SHALL ONLY SEEK TO MASTER HIMSELF. HE WHO ACHIEVES SELF-MASTERY BECOMES THE MASTER OF EVERYTHING. TO TRULY RULE YOUR SPIRIT IS TO RULE THE ENTIRETY OF CREATION. TO BE UNABLE TO RULE YOURSELF IS TO HAVE LITTLE TO NO HOPE OF RULING ANYTHING OR ANYONE ELSE. RID YOURSELF OF THE CHILDISH NEED TO CONTROL ANYONE OR ANYTHING ELSE. CHANGE CAN ONLY BE AFFECTED IN THIS LIFE BY TRANSFORMING YOURSELF.

2

MASTER, HE WHO DEFINES, RULES. "BE THE MASTER OF YOUR OWN IMAGE RATHER THAN ALLOWING OTHERS TO DEFINE IT FOR YOU."[21] IT IS ONLY ONCE YOU REQUIRE NO APPROVAL FROM OUTSIDE OF YOURSELF THAT IT SHALL BECOME POSSIBLE FOR YOU TO BE THE RULER OF YOURSELF. THE MOST POWERFUL MEN ARE THOSE THAT DEFINE THEMSELVES AND PRESCRIBE THEIR OWN

---

[21] Robert Green, *The Laws of Human Nature*, 2018

LIMITS, REFUSING TO BE MOVED BEYOND THESE BY ANY EXTERIOR OR INTERIOR INFLUENCE. ONLY FOOLS REQUIRE OTHERS TO CALL THEM GREAT. TO BE TRULY GREAT, IT IS ONLY NECESSARY THAT YOU DO GREAT THINGS GREATLY.

3

MASTER, IN ALL OF THOSE WHOM LIFE HAS CREATED, THE VERY SAME POWER THAT CREATED THEM REMAINS AVAILABLE WITHIN THEM FOR THEIR OWN USE. YOU WERE CREATED BY LIFE SO THAT IT COULD BECOME AWARE OF ITSELF IN A WAY THAT IT HAS NEVER KNOWN ITSELF BEFORE. A MAN SHALL ALWAYS HAVE WITHIN HIS POWER THE ABILITY TO SEE HIMSELF, AND FASHION HIMSELF AS WHATEVER HE WILLS. ONCE YOU HAVE DECIDED SOMETHING ABOUT YOURSELF, MY SON, EVERYTHING IN THE OUTSIDE WORLD MUST CONFORM TO THAT DECISION. RENOUNCE THE BELIEF THAT THE OUTER WORLD HAS POWER OVER YOU. NEVER DEPEND ON ANYTHING OTHER THAN YOURSELF FOR YOUR OWN EVOLUTION. PEOPLE SHALL HAVE JUST AS MUCH AUTHORITY AS YOU ALLOW THEM TO HAVE OVER YOU. THE MORE YOU ALLOW THEM TO DICTATE YOUR VIEW OF LIFE AND THE WAY YOU CHOOSE TO LIVE, THE MORE POWER THEY SHALL HAVE OVER YOU AND YOUR KINGDOM. ALTHOUGH OTHERS MAY AT TIMES INDEED HINDER YOU FROM ACTING, THEY CAN NEVER CONTROL OR IMPEDE YOUR WILL UNLESS YOU ALLOW THEM TO DO SO.

4

MASTER, IT IS ONLY ONCE YOU ALIGN YOURSELF WITH THE TRUTH THAT YOU SHALL HAVE ACCESS TO POWER. THERE ARE ONLY TWO FORCES AT WORK IN THE UNIVERSE, MY SON,

POWER, AND THE AWARENESS OF THAT POWER, WHICH IS THE TRUTH. THE FIRST STEP IN OBTAINING POWER IS COMING TO THE REALIZATION OF THE TRUTH THAT YOU ARE POWER. BECAUSE YOU ARE POWER, YOU MUST ALWAYS HOLD YOURSELF IN AWE. THE GREATEST JOY, HAPPINESS, AND POWER SHALL COME TO YOU ONLY WHEN YOU BEGIN TO SEE AND RESPECT THINGS FOR WHAT THEY TRULY ARE. ALL POWER COMES FORTH FROM WITHIN YOURSELF. THUS, ALL POWER IS ULTIMATELY WITHIN YOUR CONTROL. POWER LIES IN NAUGHT BUT THE MASTERY OF IT. IN ORDER TO WHEEL THE GREATEST POWER, YOU MUST FIRST MASTER POWER ITSELF. YOU ARE THE FORCE THAT POWERS THE KINGDOM. YOUR KINGDOM IS BUT AN EXPRESSION OF THE POWER THAT YOU HAVE AND THAT YOU ARE. THOSE WHO CAN THINK THE FARTHEST AHEAD AND PATIENTLY BRING THEIR PLANS TO FRUITION APPEAR TO WIELD THE MIGHTY POWER OF THE OMNIPOTENT.

5

MASTER, ANGER MAKES YOU APPEAR UNWORTHY OF A CROWN. ANGER IS THE PROOF OF YOUR VERY OWN WEAKNESS. FEELING POWERLESS LEADS DIRECTLY TO RESENTMENT AND ANGER. ANGER ENTAILS BEING WOUNDED AND SUCCUMBING TO THOSE WOUNDS. A KING MUST LEARN TO EXPLOIT THE CHAOS OF THE WORLD RATHER THAN SUBMIT TO IT. TO REACT INSTEAD OF STRATEGIZING IS A SIGN OF WEAKNESS. EMOTIONAL PEOPLE ARE VULNERABLE PEOPLE OVER WHOM ONE CAN EASILY EXERT POWER. NEVER RELY UPON POWER THAT COMES FROM SOMEONE OR SOMETHING OTHER THAN YOURSELF. THE ONLY REAL POWER THAT EXISTS CONSISTS IN THE ABILITY TO CONTROL YOUR OWN MIND AND EMOTIONS. IN ORDER TO CONTROL THE DYNAMIC OF ANY GIVEN SITUATION, YOU MUST

LEARN TO CONTROL BOTH YOURSELF AND YOUR PASSIONS. NEVER TAKE A STANCE THAT LEAVES YOU NO OPTIONS. GETTING ANGRY AND LASHING OUT IS THE WORST THING THAT CAN HAPPEN TO A **KING**. ANGER IS A TRAITOR THAT LIMITS YOUR OPTIONS, AND THUS YOUR **POWER**. TO SPEAK TO A PERSON ANGRILY, OR TO SHOW YOUR HATRED BY WHAT YOU SAY OR HOW YOU LOOK, IS A MOST VULGAR PROCEEDING. FAR FROM INSPIRING LOYALTY OR RESPECT IN THOSE THAT HEAR THEM, PASSIONATE OUTBURSTS EXPOSE YOUR WEAKNESS, AND CREATES DOUBT AS REGARDS TO YOUR POWER. THE MOOD INTO WHICH A PERSON IS ABLE TO BRING YOU, LIES IN DIRECT CORRELATION TO THAT PERSON'S DOMINION OVER YOU. THE FREER YOUR MIND IS FROM PASSIONS, THE CLOSER YOU ARE TO FREEDOM AND **POWER**. MANY EQUATE STRONG PASSIONS WITH STRONG CHARACTER, BUT HE WHO IS MASTERED BY HIS PASSIONS IS A WEAK MIND. THE REAL **STRENGTH** OF A MAN IS MEASURED BY THE **POWER** OF THE FEELINGS THAT HE CONTROLS, NOT THOSE THAT CONTROL HIM. IT IS MORE POWERFUL TO PRAY FOR THE **POWER** NOT TO CHASE A THING THAN IT IS TO PRAY TO HAVE IT. SOMETIMES LETTING THINGS GO IS AN ACT OF FAR GREATER **POWER** THAN HOLDING ON TO THEM.

6

MASTER, THE DANCE OF **KINGS** IS THE DANCE WHOSE STEPS ALL THOSE THAT DESIRE TO ATTAIN **POWER** MUST LEARN. NOTHING IS STABLE OR CERTAIN IN THIS DANCE, AND NO MAXIM IS FIXED. ALL IN THE DANCE OF **KINGS** IS CONSTANTLY IN FLUX, AND IN IT, EVEN THE CLOSEST OF FRIENDS CAN BE TRANSFORMED INTO THE WORST OF ENEMIES. NEVER DEPEND UPON STABILITY OR LASTING ORDER IN THIS DANCE. ALWAYS

REMAIN AS FLUID AND GRACEFUL AS WATER, AND AS FORMLESS AS THE WIND. THERE SHALL BE TIMES IN THE DANCE OF **KINGS** WHEN YOU FIND YOURSELF IN A WEAK POSITION WITH NO SUBSTANTIAL **POWER**. IF YOU ARE WEAK AND STRIVE FOR LITTLE, LITTLE IS WHAT YOU SHALL UNDOUBTEDLY REMAIN. HOWEVER, IF YOU DEMONSTRATE **STRENGTH**, CONFIDENCE, RESOLVE, AND DETERMINATION, YOU SHALL ERADICATE YOUR OWN WEAKNESS AND EARN THE RESPECT OF ALL THOSE WHO BEAR WITNESS TO YOUR RESOLUTION. IF YOU REMAIN INDEPENDENT IN THE DANCE OF **KINGS**, YOU SHALL BECOME THE AXIS AROUND WHICH ALL OF YOUR FELLOW DANCERS SHALL PIVOT. THOSE THAT SURROUND YOU SHALL SOLICIT YOUR REGARD AND RESPECT WHICH SHALL GRANT YOU TREMENDOUS **POWER**. BECOME THE CRITICAL LINK IN THE CHAIN OF INFORMATION THAT FLOWS THROUGH YOUR REALM. PRODUCE SOMETHING OTHER PEOPLE DEPEND UPON. BE THE MEDIATOR EVERYONE NEEDS TO RESOLVE A DISPUTE. REMAIN UNTANGLED FROM ALL INDEBTEDNESS TO OTHERS. THE MOMENT YOU BECOME INDEBTED TO ANOTHER; YOUR **POWER** SHALL BE GREATLY REDUCED. NEVER DESPAIR AT HAVING TO DON THE MASK OF THE INCONSPICUOUS. IN THE DANCE OF **KINGS** IT IS YOUR UNREADABILITY THAT GIVES YOU THE MOST **POWER**. ANNIHILATE YOUR FEARS OF DEATH AND YOUR CONCERN FOR OTHER PEOPLE'S OPINIONS OF YOU. FOR THESE THINGS SHALL LIMIT YOUR POSSIBILITIES FOR ACTION. IN THE DANCE OF **KINGS**, HE WHO POSSESSES THE MOST POSSIBILITIES FOR ACTION SHALL ALWAYS POSSESS THE MOST **POWER**. IT IS ONLY THE FOOLISH WHO REST ON THEIR ACHIEVEMENTS AND BASK IN THEIR PAST GLORIES. FOR IN THE DANCE OF **KINGS**, THERE IS NEVER TIME TO REST.

7

M ASTER, IN ORDER TO BECOME POWERFUL, YOU MUST PERSONIFY **POWER**. A LL OF YOUR **POWER** LIES IN THE AWARENESS OF YOUR **POWER**. T HE SECRET TO **POWER** IS THE CONSCIOUSNESS OF IT. **POWER** PERCEIVED IS **POWER** ACHIEVED. **POWER** LIES IN BELIEVING, NOT IN WHAT YOU BELIEVE. U LTIMATE **POWER** LIES IN THE ABILITY TO DETERMINE THE BELIEFS OF OTHERS. H E WHO CONTROLS ANOTHER'S BELIEFS HAS NO NEED TO CONTROL THAT WHICH THEY DO.

POWER ITSELF FLOWS THROUGH **KNOWLEDGE**. I T SHALL NEVER BE WISE TO ESCHEW **KNOWLEDGE** OF ANY KIND. T HE **KNOWLEDGE** OF WHOM YOU ARE DEALING WITH, YOUR ABILITY TO MEASURE THEM, AND YOUR ABILITY TO DISCERN WHO IS BEST ABLE TO FURTHER YOUR INTEREST IN ANY GIVEN SITUATION ARE THE THREE MOST CRUCIAL SKILLS IN AMASSING AND PRESERVING **POWER**. W ITHOUT THESE SKILLS, YOU SHALL MAKE THE WRONG PEOPLE YOUR ENEMIES, AND CHOOSE THE WRONG PEOPLE WITH WHOM TO BUILD YOUR KINGDOM. M AKE ALL SEE YOU AS THE ANSWER TO THEIR PRAYERS. C HANNEL THE HUNGER OF YOUR PEOPLE TO BELIEVE IN SOMETHING INTO BELIEF IN YOU. P EOPLE WANT NOTHING MORE THAN TO BELIEVE IN GREATNESS, MY SON. T HEREFORE, YOU MUST ALWAYS BE GREAT. G REAT **POWER** LIES IN BEING ABLE TO OPEN A POSSIBILITY FOR MEN TO SEE THAT WHICH THEY DESIRE TO BELIEVE IN.

8

M ASTER, THE MAJORITY OF THE PEOPLE THAT YOU MEET SHALL PREFER ENDLESS DISCUSSION TO ACTION. N EVER ALLOW THIS TO

BE YOUR DISPOSITION. PEOPLE ADMIRE THE BOLD AND SHALL ALWAYS PREFER TO FOLLOW THEM OVER THE TIMID. THE SELF-CONFIDENCE OF THE BOLD **KING** AFFECTS HIS PEOPLE WITH COURAGE AND GIVES THEM THE AUDACITY TO HOPE. THE MAN WHO TAKES THE TIME TO CALCULATE TOO METICULOUSLY EVERY DIFFICULTY OR OBSTACLE, WHICH MAY OR MAY NOT LIE IN HIS PATH, FORFEITS **POWER** TO HESITATION AND INDECISION. HE THAT IS DARING AND INTREPID SEIZES AND ENSLAVES **POWER**, AND FORCES IT TO AID HIM IN HIS AMBITIONS. BE FEARLESS AND ALWAYS SEIZE THE INITIATIVE. THE RESPECT AND AWE THAT YOU GARNER BY SEIZING THE INITIATIVE SHALL ALWAYS TRANSLATE INTO GREAT **POWER**. FOR BY DOING SO, YOU CREATE YOUR OWN CIRCUMSTANCES RATHER THAN FEEBLY AWAITING WHAT TIME MAY OR MAY NOT BRING TO YOU.

9

MASTER, **POWER** IS NEVER FREELY GIVEN. IT MUST ALWAYS BE EARNED OR PAID FOR BY THE PAIN OF SACRIFICE. THE GREATER THE SACRIFICE THE GREATER THE **POWER** THAT IS BESTOWED UPON HE WHO IS DOING THE SACRIFICING. ALL HARDSHIPS EXIST IN ORDER TO MAKE DEMANDS UPON YOU TO REACH INTO THE VAST DEPTHS OF YOUR SPIRIT AND AWAKEN THE **POWER** NECESSARY TO OVERCOME THEM. JUST AS THERE CAN BE NO EXERTION OF FORCE WITHOUT OPPOSITION, THERE COULD BE NO MANIFESTATION OF YOUR **POWER** WITHOUT HARDSHIP.

10

MASTER, AMBITION CREEPS, AS WELL AS SOARS. LEARN TO LOOK BEYOND YOUR PRESENT SITUATION, CALCULATE AHEAD, FOCUS ON

YOUR ULTIMATE GOALS, AND ACT ACCORDINGLY. THOSE THAT POSSESS A VISION SHALL INEVITABLY GAIN **POWER**. THOSE WHO HAVE NO VISION SHALL ONLY BE THE PAWNS OF THOSE THAT POSSESS **POWER**. TRAIN YOURSELF TO THINK, NOT IN TERMS OF INDIVIDUAL BATTLES AND TACTICS, BUT IN TERMS OF OVERALL CAMPAIGNS AND STRATEGIES. IF YOU LEARN TO CONTROL THE TEMPTATION TO REACT TO EVENTS AS THEY HAPPEN, ALL OF YOUR ACTS SHALL BECOME THE STEPS THAT SHALL LEAD YOU TO THE ACTUALIZATION OF YOUR VISION. THE ABILITY TO PLAN PRUDENTLY WITH FORESIGHT AND IGNORE THE ILLUSIONS OF IMAGINED DANGERS AND ENTICING IMMEDIATE PLEASURES, SHALL ALWAYS TRANSLATE INTO **POWER**. THE FARTHER YOUR VISION EXTENDS AND THE MORE STEPS YOU PLAN AHEAD, THE MORE POWERFUL YOU SHALL BECOME. THE SECRET TO GAINING YOUR DESIRES IS TO NOT CHASE THEM AWAY. LIVE YOUR LIFE AS IF ALL OF YOUR DREAMS HAVE AND ARE ON THEIR WAY TO BEING FULFILLED. WHAT IS ALREADY YOURS CAN NEVER BE WITHHELD, AND TO WANT NOTHING IS TO HAVE EVERYTHING.

11

MASTER, A MISERLY MAN SHALL NEVER GAIN TRUE POWER. FOR HE SHALL NEVER HAVE AN ABUNDANCE OF FOLLOWERS WITH WHOM HE MAY WORK HIS WILL. THE PURPOSE OF WEALTH IS NOT MERELY FOR THE VAIN ATTAINMENT OF INANIMATE OBJECTS, BUT FOR THE USEFUL ATTAINMENT OF INFLUENCE. GENEROSITY IS A TOOL THAT YOU CAN LEARN TO USE STRATEGICALLY WITH A DEFINITIVE PURPOSE. THE PROPER GIFT SHALL ALWAYS PLACE HE WHO RECEIVES IT UNDER A SUBTLE DEBT TO HE WHO GAVE IT. THE MOST EFFECTIVE GIFTS FOR THIS PURPOSE ARE THOSE THAT SURPRISE THE RECIPIENT BY SEEMINGLY COMING OUT OF

NOWHERE AND INSPIRING AWE IN THEM FOR THE SIMPLE FACT THAT THEY HAVE NEVER RECEIVED A GIFT LIKE IT BEFORE.

12

MASTER, A SOLID REPUTATION BUILT UPON THE FOUNDATION OF GRACEFUL **STRENGTH** SHALL INCREASE YOUR PRESENCE, EXAGGERATE YOUR POSITIVE CHARACTERISTICS, AND CREATE A POWERFUL AURA AROUND YOU THAT SHALL INSTILL RESPECT AND ESTEEM FOR YOU INTO ALL THOSE THAT ENTER INTO YOUR CIRCUMFERENCE. OFTENTIMES, YOUR REPUTATION IS MORE DEPENDENT UPON WHAT YOU CONCEAL THAN WHAT YOU REVEAL. THE FOUNDATION OF YOUR **POWER**, AND THE MOST IMPORTANT SKILL IN WIELDING IT, SHALL ALWAYS BE YOUR ABILITY TO CONTROL YOUR EMOTIONS. EMOTIONAL REACTIONS BLIND YOU TO **THE TRUTH** CONCERNING SITUATIONS, AND PREVENT YOU FROM ACCURATELY PREPARING FOR, OR PRUDENTLY RESPONDING TO THEM. MUCH OF **POWER** LIES NOT IN WHAT YOU DO, BUT IN WHAT YOU DO NOT DO. INDEPENDENCE IS WORTH ANY PRICE WHICH YOU MAY HAVE TO PAY FOR IT. ELEVATE YOURSELF ABOVE THE PETTY SQUABBLES OF THOSE AROUND YOU AND RESIST THEIR DESPERATE ATTEMPTS TO DRAG YOU INTO FRIVOLOUS DISPUTES. THOSE WHO ARE QUICK TO RUSH TO THE AID OF OTHERS IN TRIVIAL SITUATIONS SUCH AS THESE SHALL GAIN LITTLE RESPECT FOR THEIR EFFORTS, WHILE THOSE WHO POSSESS AND EXHIBIT THE CONTROL NECESSARY TO AVOID BEING SUCKED INTO THE EMOTIONAL VORTEX OF THESE SITUATIONS SHALL ALWAYS BE BESIEGED BY ENTREATIES FOR SUPPORT. FOR THEIR DISPLAY OF CONTROL IS A DISPLAY OF GREAT **POWER**, AND AS A RESULT, ALL SHALL PLACE **POWER** IN THEIR HANDS.

13

Master, the main prerequisite of possessing POWER is the KNOWLEDGE of how to safely control that POWER. A KING must be a master of POWER. He must never allow POWER to master him. POWER is the ultimate currency. For POWER is one's ability to impose their will upon the world. With it, one shall be able to purchase whatsoever they may desire. POWER shall bestow upon you the ability to move all mountains and still any storm. Your POWER shall only be unassailable when people act as you wish them to act, and willingly give you that which you request without you having to resort to force. Ultimate POWER is the ability to have others move of their own volition, in whatever direction that you desire. The POWER of a kingdom is located in its foundation, in that which supports and impels it. It is of the utmost importance that you always believe in yourself, my son. For the KING is the foundation of every kingdom. POWER only resides where you believe that it resides. The ability to move in any direction at a moment's notice, which is independence and the essence of freedom, is the most vital skill that any KING can possess. Independence is POWER, and there is nothing that is as valuable, Master. Never allow a desire for money, material goods, or any sensual pleasure to entice you from your pursuit of POWER. If you make POWER your goal, all that you desire shall come to you as surely as fire shall always produce heat.

14

MASTER, YOUR REPUTATION IS THE CORNERSTONE TO YOUR POWER. IT IS ONLY FROM A POSITION OF UNQUESTIONED STRENGTH THAT TRUE PROGRESS SHALL BE ABLE TO BE FACILITATED. THEREFORE, YOU MUST SEE TO IT THAT YOUR REPUTATION ALWAYS REMAINS UNASSAILABLE. ONCE YOUR REPUTATION IS DIMINISHED IN ANY FASHION, YOU SHALL BECOME VULNERABLE TO ATTACKS FROM ALL SIDES, AND ALL THAT YOU HOPED TO BUILD SHALL COME CRUMBLING AROUND YOU. INSTEAD OF REACTING EMOTIONALLY TO EVENTS AS THEY OCCUR, TRAIN YOURSELF TO STEP BACK AND CONTEMPLATE THE LARGER EVENTS TAKING SHAPE BEYOND YOUR IMMEDIATE VISION. THOSE WHO WEAR THEMSELVES DOWN WITH THEIR PASSIONS AND SHACKLE THEMSELVES TO THEIR INFLEXIBILITY AND STUBBORNNESS HINDER THEMSELVES FROM BEING ABLE TO ADAPT TO CHANGE. IN THE DANCE OF **KINGS**, THEY ARE SWIFTLY SURPASSED BY THOSE DANCERS THAT ARE UNENCUMBERED BY SUCH HINDRANCES. WHILE THE OBSTINATE AND UNYIELDING MAY SEEM STRONG, THEIR RIGIDITY SHALL EVENTUALLY BE THE CAUSE OF THEIR PERDITION.

15

MASTER, AT ALL COST, MAINTAIN YOUR INNER SENSE OF INDEPENDENCE AND FREEDOM. IN THE DANCE OF **KINGS**, INDEPENDENCE IS **POWER**. TO LOSE YOUR INDEPENDENCE IS TO LOSE OTHERS' DEPENDENCE UPON YOU. NONE SHALL EVER BE ABLE TO RELY UPON A DEPENDENT PERSON. FOR THAT PERSON, BY BEING DEPENDENT, SHOWS THAT THEY ARE UNABLE TO DEPEND UPON THEMSELVES. ONCE YOUR INDEPENDENCE CEASES, ALL OF

THE COURTESY, RESPECT, AND DEFERENCE THAT ACCOMPANIED IT SHALL CEASE ALSO. FREE YOURSELF AS MUCH AS POSSIBLE FROM ALL COMMITMENTS, OBLIGATIONS, AND INDEBTEDNESS. FOR THESE THINGS ARE MORE OFTEN THAN NOT THE DEVICES OF THOSE THAT SEEK TO ENSNARE YOU INTO THEIR **POWER**. **POWER** DEPENDS UPON AWARENESS AND INTERACTION.

A **KING** MUST ALWAYS PLACE HIMSELF AT THE CENTER OF THE KINGDOM SO THAT HE MAY BE COGNIZANT OF ALL ACTIVITIES TAKING PLACE WITHIN IT. MAKE IT A POINT OF **HONOR** TO MAKE OTHERS COME TO YOU INSTEAD OF BEING ONE WHO CONSTANTLY BEGS OTHERS FOR SUPPORT. IF OTHERS SEE YOU AS A SOURCE OF SUCCOR, YOU SHALL ALWAYS HAVE CONTROL OF THE SITUATION WHEN THEY COME TO YOU. IN THE DANCE OF **KINGS**, HE WHO HAS CONTROL HOLDS THE **POWER** AND DEMANDS RESPECT. ALL MEN HAVE A PRICE, MY SON, WHETHER THAT PRICE BE MONEY, VALIDATION, **LOVE**, RESPECT, OR SOME TYPE OF SENSUAL PLEASURE. ALL MEN SHALL REVEAL THEIR PRICE TO YOU IF YOU WOULD BUT MASTER ONE OF THE MOST IMPORTANT SKILLS IN THE DANCE OF **KINGS**, WHICH IS THE ABILITY TO LISTEN. TO GAIN THE **KNOWLEDGE** OF A MAN'S MAINSPRING OF MOTIVE IS TO POSSESS THE KEY TO HIS WILL. SKILL, IN THE DANCE OF **KINGS**, CONSISTS IN LEARNING THE PRICE OF ALL THOSE THAT SURROUND YOU, AND BEING ABLE TO PRODUCE THE CURRENCY TO PAY IT. IF THERE IS SOMETHING AROUND YOU THAT YOU DESIRE BUT KNOW THAT YOU CANNOT HAVE, AT LEAST FOR THE TIME BEING, SHOW YOUR GREATNESS AND SUPERIORITY BY IGNORING IT, AND THEREBY DEEM IT AS WORTHLESS. INDIFFERENCE IS THE **POWER** OF A **KING**. FOR WHERE THE ATTENTION AND CONSIDERATION OF A **KING** LIES, THERE IS LIFE AND GROWTH. BUT THAT WHICH THE

KING TURNS HIS BACK ON SHALL PERISH FROM INSIGNIFICANCE.

16

MASTER, A KING'S KINGDOM IS HIS MESSAGE TO THE WORLD. IN ORDER FOR YOUR KINGDOM TO BECOME TRULY POWERFUL, YOU YOURSELF MUST EMPOWER THOSE IN IT. YOUR BEST GUARANTEE OF AUTHORITY RESIDES IN THE GOODWILL OF YOUR PEOPLE. THE STRENGTH OF A KING LIVES IN THE HEARTS AND MINDS OF THOSE WHO SUPPORT HIM. YOUR ENTIRE PURPOSE OF ATTAINING FREEDOM IS SO THAT YOU MAY CREATE IT FOR OTHERS. THE LIFE OF A KING IS ONLY VALUABLE AS LONG AS HE USES THE POWER OF HIS POSITION TO ORDER THE COURSE OF NATURE FOR THE UPLIFTING OF HIS KINGDOM. THE STORY OF YOUR RULE MUST BE BASED UPON POWER HELD ON THE BEHALF OF THOSE THAT INHABIT YOUR KINGDOM. KINGS ARE GIVEN POWER, RESOURCES, AND INFLUENCE FOR THE BENEFIT OF OTHERS. A KING IS GIVEN A KINGDOM FOR THE SAKE OF HIS PEOPLE, NOT HIMSELF. NEVER THINK THIS SHALL IMPEDE, OR HINDER, YOUR INDEPENDENCE IN ANY WAY. OTHERS' NEED OF YOU SHALL FREE YOU FROM THEM. THE MORE YOU ARE RELIED UPON, THE MORE FREEDOM, AND THUS POWER YOU SHALL HAVE. THE MORE ONE IS IMPRESSED BY POWER, THE EASIER THEY SHALL BE TO COMMAND. HE WHO KNOWS WELL HOW TO COMMAND SHALL ALWAYS BE OBEYED.

17

MASTER, THE ULTIMATE GOAL IN THE DANCE OF KINGS IS TO ERADICATE OTHERS' RESISTANCE TO YOUR INFLUENCE. CONTROL IS AN ELUSIVE PHENOMENON. THE HARDER YOU PULL AT PEOPLE,

THE LESS CONTROL YOU SHALL HAVE OVER THEM. YOUR CONDUCT SHALL ALWAYS HAVE POLITICAL CONSEQUENCES. THOSE AROUND YOU SHALL ANALYZE YOUR EVERY ACTION IN TERMS OF WHETHER IT AIDS OR HARMS THEM. SELF-INTEREST, THE MIGHTIEST MOTIVE OF ALL, IS THE LEVER THAT MOVES ALL PEOPLE. TAKING THIS FACT INTO ACCOUNT, YOU MUST FORM YOUR STRATEGIES WITH THE PURPOSE OF GAINING SUPPORT FROM OTHER PEOPLE, SO THAT YOU MAY STRENGTHEN YOUR **POWER** BASE. A **KING** MUST ALWAYS ATTUNE HIMSELF TO THE HEARTS AND MINDS OF THOSE BELOW HIM SO THAT HIS **POWER** BASE MAY BE SOLID. FOR WITHOUT THIS BASE, THE **POWER** OF A **KING** WOULD BE SO UNSTABLE THAT THE SLIGHTEST GUST OF THE WINDS OF ADVERSITY WOULD CAUSE HIM TO TOPPLE FROM THE THRONE, WITH THOSE BELOW HIM CHEERFULLY ASSISTING IN HIS DOWNFALL. WILLING COOPERATION SHALL PRODUCE A KINGDOM THAT POSSESSES ENDURING **POWER**, WHILE FORCED COOPERATION SHALL ALWAYS RESULT IN DEMISE. THE ABILITY TO WIN THE HEARTS OF YOUR PEOPLE LIES IN YOUR ABILITY TO BE ALL THINGS TO ALL MEN. IT IS OF THE UTMOST NECESSITY THAT YOU GAIN AND MAINTAIN THE ABILITY TO GLIDE FROM ONE SOCIAL CIRCLE TO THE NEXT AND BE ABLE TO MIX WITH ALL KINDS OF DIFFERENT TYPES OF PEOPLE.

IN THE DANCE OF **KINGS**, HE WHO MAKES NOT HIMSELF FAMILIAR WITH THE WORLD WHICH SURROUNDS HIM AND IS UNABLE TO DISCERN THE NATURES OF THE DIFFERENT BEASTS OF THE LAND IS DOOMED. FOR HE SHALL BE EASY PREY. IT IS CRUCIAL THAT YOU LEARN TO TELL THE WOLVES FROM THE LAMBS, AND THE LIONS FROM THE HYENAS. BEWARE OF ALL THOSE, WHO WITH HEARTS FULL OF HATE, FLATTER, AND WHO, WHILE DEVISING WAYS TO CRUSH THEIR ENEMIES, BOW BEFORE THEM.

THE GREATEST THING THAT A **KING** COULD EVER HOPE FOR IS THE **UNDERSTANDING** OF THE HIDDEN MOTIVES OF THOSE WHO SURROUND HIM. IT IS IMPERATIVE THAT YOU REALIZE THAT EVEN AS PEOPLE TRY TO CONCEAL THEIR DESIGNS CONSCIOUSLY, THEY UNCONSCIOUSLY DESIRE TO REVEAL THEMSELVES. THEY SHALL EMIT SIGNALS THAT REVEAL THEIR AMBITIONS AND DEEPEST DESIRES CONSTANTLY. IF YOU DO NOT NOTICE THEM, IT IS BECAUSE YOU ARE NOT PAYING CLOSE ENOUGH ATTENTION. ALWAYS BE PARTICULARLY ATTENTIVE TO A PERSON'S EYES. FOR IT IS A MOST DIFFICULT THING TO DISGUISE THE EYES' TESTIMONY CONCERNING ONE'S STATE OF MIND. WHEN MEASURING THOSE AROUND YOU, DO NOT BE LIKE THOSE FOOLS WHO RELY SOLELY UPON THEIR INSTINCTS. THERE IS NO SUBSTITUTE FOR CONCRETE **KNOWLEDGE**. STUDY THOSE THAT YOU WISH TO KNOW FOR AS LONG AS IT TAKES TO KNOW THEM. SOMETIMES THE BEST WAY TO BE WELL RECEIVED BY ALL IS TO CLOTHE YOURSELF IN THE HIDE OF THE DUMBEST OF BEASTS. LIBERALITY, ESPECIALLY FOR AN OUTSIDER, IS ALWAYS AN EFFECTIVE TOOL FOR CONSTRUCTING A SOLID **POWER** BASE.

TO DEFLECT THE ENVY THAT SHALL INEVITABLY COME IN THE DANCE OF **KINGS**, IT SHALL BE WISE AT TIMES TO MAKE A DISPLAY OF DEFERRING TO OTHERS AS IF THEY WERE SUPERIOR TO YOU. LEARN TO DON THE MASK OF THE UNAMBITIOUS. IT IS VERY DIFFICULT FOR PEOPLE TO ENVY THE PRESTIGE THAT THEY THEMSELVES HAVE GIVEN TO A PERSON WHO DOES NOT SEEM TO DESIRE IT. THE MASSES SHALL ALWAYS GIVE RESPECT AND **HONOR** TO THE UNCONVENTIONAL AND EXTRAORDINARY. JUST AS THE PLANETS REVOLVE AROUND THE SUN, IN EVERY GROUP, ALL SHALL REVOLVE AROUND A SINGULAR, POWERFUL PERSONALITY. NEVER MIND THOSE WHO CRITICIZE AND

CONDEMN YOU. POPULARITY IS SUPERFICIAL AND VAIN. AN INCOMPARABLY, POWERFUL PERSONALITY SHALL ALWAYS CARRY MORE WEIGHT THAN LIKEABILITY. IT TAKES BUT ONE INTREPID MIND AND INDOMITABLE SPIRIT TO TURN A FLOCK OF SHEEP INTO A PACK OF WOLVES.

18

MASTER, ISOLATION SHALL OFTEN EXPOSE YOU TO MUCH GREATER DANGERS THAN IT PROTECTS YOU FROM. TO BARRICADE YOURSELF IN A FORTRESS OF ISOLATION IS HIGHLY DANGEROUS. TO BE IN ISOLATION IS TO BE IGNORANT OF EVERYTHING THAT IS OCCURRING IN YOUR KINGDOM, INCLUDING PLOTS AGAINST YOU. IN A KINGDOM THREATENED BY DIVISION, **POWER** SHALL FALL IN YOUR LAP IF YOU ARE ABLE TO KEEP YOUR FORCES UNITED AND COHESIVE, AND YOUR MIND CLEAR AND FOCUSED UPON YOUR VISION. THE SOURCE OF THE **STRENGTH** OF YOUR KINGDOM SHALL ALWAYS BE ITS UNITY. THE FORMATION OF FACTIONS SHALL ALWAYS BE A KING'S GREATEST THREAT. FOR IN TIME, THESE FACTIONS SHALL COME TO PLACE THEIR OWN INTEREST AHEAD OF THOSE OF THE KINGDOM. WHEN DEALING WITH GRUMBLERS, WHO IN ORDER TO PROMOTE THEIR OWN INTEREST THRIVE ON DISCONTENT AND ENCOURAGE DISSENSION IN FACTIONALISM, KEEP YOUR PEOPLE CONTENT SO THAT THE POISON THAT THOSE GRUMBLERS DISPERSE CAN FIND NO PURCHASE IN THE HEARTS OF YOUR PEOPLE. ESTABLISH YOURSELF AS THE CENTER OF **POWER** IN YOUR KINGDOM, AND LET IT BE KNOWN THAT THERE IS MORE TO BE GAINED BY FOLLOWING YOU THAN TRYING TO FORM ANOTHER **POWER** BASE WITHIN THE KINGDOM. IF YOU DO THESE THINGS, ALL OF THE MALCONTENT GRUMBLERS SHALL DIE OFF ON THEIR OWN, BITTER AND ISOLATED.

As you dance, the dance of **KINGS**, my son, it is very likely that you shall create enemies. Never take their hatred personally. Vanity is the most prized possession of the majority of men. If you find yourself being hated for no apparent reason, it is more than likely that you have threatened the hater's sense of importance. Whenever possible, always work to make other people feel secure about themselves. Always murder the impulse to offend even if the other person appears deserving of offense. The satisfaction gained from insulting another is trifling and insignificant compared to the threat and danger of revenge. Be wary of the craft of those who deceive. Watch those who accuse you of being unfair, try to make you feel guilty, and talk about justice. For often, they are merely trying to gain an emotional advantage over you. Especially watch those who make an overwhelming display of morality. For their piety may be a cover for their nefarious desires.

19

Master, that which cannot be immediately understood inherently exudes **POWER**. That which is hidden is impossible to grasp. In the dance of **KINGS**, it is imperative that you surround yourself always with an air of secrecy and shroud your ambitions in the cloak of clandestine silence. Taciturnity shall always be more powerful than loquacity. Those who are the most powerful are often the ones who say the least. Because your enemies depend upon being able to read you in order to get some sense of your intentions, you must learn to

USE RETICENCE AS A SCREEN TO CONCEAL ALL OF YOUR DETERMINATIONS. TO PREVENT YOUR ENEMIES FROM SEEING THE HIDDEN PURPOSE BEHIND YOUR ACTIONS IS TO GIVE YOURSELF A TREMENDOUS ADVANTAGE OVER THEM. WHEN YOUR ENEMY'S ABILITY TO REASON ABOUT YOU BREAKS DOWN, AND THEY CANNOT FIGURE OUT WHAT YOU'RE ABOUT, A DEBILITATING AND DESTRUCTIVE DISORDER SHALL INFECT THEIR SYSTEM. THEY SHALL REACT TO YOUR ACTS IN WAYS THAT SHALL INEVITABLY WORK AGAINST THEM. IF YOU HAVE AN ENEMY THAT YOU DESIRE TO DESTROY, YOU MUST REPRESS YOUR COMPULSION TO REVEAL YOUR HOSTILITY WITH YOUR TONGUE. THIS SHALL ONLY REVEAL YOUR POSITION AND ALLOW YOUR ENEMIES TO LEARN YOUR AMBITIONS. WHATEVER SATISFACTION YOUR VANITY GAINS BY YOU EXPRESSING YOUR FEELINGS OPENLY SHALL NOT BE WORTH THE **POWER** TO CAUSE REAL DAMAGE THAT YOUR LOQUACIOUSNESS SHALL COST YOU.

MY SON, NEVER GIVE EXCESS ENERGY NOR UNDUE ATTENTION TO THE PETTY. CONSIGN THOSE WHO CANNOT DO YOU HARM IN THE LONG RUN TO OBLIVION AND BURY THEM ALONG WITH THEIR UNWORTHINESS IN THE GRAVE OF THEIR OWN INSIGNIFICANCE. TO GIVE SOMETHING YOUR ATTENTION IS TO GIVE IT YOUR **POWER**. WHEN A PETTY FOE HAS YOUR ATTENTION, YOU AND THEIR PETTINESS SHALL BECOME PARTNERS IN THE DANCE OF **KINGS**, WITH YOU REACTING TO THEIR PETTY MOVES. THE MORE ATTENTION YOU GIVE TO PETTINESS, THE MORE POWERFUL PETTINESS SHALL BECOME AND THE MORE UNWORTHY OF **POWER** YOU SHALL APPEAR. IT IS BY ACKNOWLEDGING PETTINESS THAT YOU GIVE IT VALIDITY AND OPEN YOURSELF TO ITS INFLUENCE. THAT PETTINESS THAT YOU DO NOT REACT TO SHALL NEVER BE ABLE TO DRAG YOU DOWN IN

A FUTILE ENGAGEMENT. NEVER SHOW DEFENSIVENESS IN THE FACE OF AN ENEMY. FOR TO SHOW DEFENSIVENESS IS TO ALLOW YOUR ENEMIES TO KNOW EXACTLY WHERE YOUR VULNERABILITIES LIE. YOUR ENEMIES SEEING THIS WEAKNESS, SHALL THEN UNDERSTAND HOW TO INJURE YOU. THE COMMON MAN, BECAUSE HE HAS NOT THE **POWER** AND RESTRAINT TO HOLD HIMSELF BACK, RESPONDS TO THE AGGRESSION OF HIS FOES BY BECOMING ENMESHED IN IT. THE WORST CONDITION IN WHICH AN AGGRESSIVE ENEMY CAN BE PLACED IS THAT OF HAVING NOTHING TO ATTACK. GIVE AN AGGRESSIVE ENEMY NOTHING TO STRIKE AT, AND THEIR OWN AGGRESSION SHALL BECOME THEIR DOWNFALL. CONFUSED AND DEBILITATED BY THE LACK OF OPPOSING ENERGY, YOUR ENEMIES SHALL BECOME UNBALANCED AND LOSE ALL **POWER** OF INTELLIGENT, STRATEGIC THOUGHT. IT IS IMPOSSIBLE TO ARGUE WITH SOMEONE WHO REFUSES TO RESPOND WITH AGGRESSION. THERE IS NOTHING MORE INFURIATING THAN ENGAGING WITH SOMEONE AND GETTING NO RESPONSE. UNDER ALL ATTACKS, USE SILENCE AS A SHIELD, AND MAKE YOUR FACE A FORMLESS BLANK MASK SO THAT YOU MAY CONFOUND AND FRUSTRATE ALL THOSE IGNOBLE SCOUNDRELS WHO CAN FIND NO WAYS TO DEFEAT YOU.

20

MASTER, **POWER** LIES NOT ONLY IN WHAT YOU HAVE, BUT ALSO IN WHAT YOUR ENEMIES BELIEVE THAT YOU MIGHT HAVE. AN ENEMY WHO CANNOT SEE WHAT YOU HAVE, OR WHERE YOU ARE HEADED, SHALL ALWAYS BE AT A SEVERE DISADVANTAGE. IN THE DANCE OF **KINGS**, IT IS ESSENTIAL THAT YOU LEARN THE ART OF INDIRECTION. NEVER REVEAL YOUR TRUE INTENTIONS. IN THE DANCE OF **KINGS**, HONEST STRAIGHTFORWARDNESS IS

A PERILOUS ENDEAVOR. IN THE FOREST, THE STRAIGHT TREES ARE OFTEN THE FIRST TO BE CHOPPED DOWN. LEARN TO DISARM YOUR ENEMY'S SUSPICIONS AND MAKE THEM MORE MANEUVERABLE BY MAKING THEM FEEL THAT THEY ARE STRONGER, MORE COMPETENT, AND MORE INTELLIGENT THAN YOU ARE. USE YOUR CHARM, HUMOR, GRACIOUSNESS, AND FLATTERY TO DIVERT THEIR ATTENTION AWAY FROM YOU, AND GIVE YOURSELF SPACE TO ENACT YOUR DESIGNS. WITH THEIR ATTENTION DIVERTED, THEIR DEFENSES SHALL BE LOWERED, AND YOU SHALL BE ABLE TO INFLUENCE THEM FAR MORE EFFECTIVELY.

WHILE TIMOROUSNESS HAS NO PLACE IN THE DANCE OF **KINGS**, IT IS OF THE UTMOST IMPORTANCE THAT YOU LEARN TO FEIGN IT AT TIMES. THERE SHALL BE TIMES WHEN YOU SHALL HAVE TO MASQUERADE AS THE LAMB SO THAT YOU MAY BE ABLE TO KILL THE WOLF. WHEN PLOTTING AGAINST YOUR ENEMIES, APPEAR FRIENDLY AND CALM SO THAT YOU MAY PRESENT TO THE WORLD A FACE THAT PROMISES THE OPPOSITE OF THAT WHICH YOU ARE TRULY PLANNING. LEARN TO CONTROL YOUR APPEARANCE AT ALL TIMES, SO THAT YOU MAY ALWAYS BE ABLE TO KEEP YOUR ENEMIES IN THE DARK.

IN THE DANCE OF **KINGS**, YOU MUST NEVER TAKE ANY ATTACK PERSONALLY, NOR MUST YOU EVER ALLOW ANY TO SEE THAT THEY HAVE BEEN ABLE TO HURT YOU IN ANY WAY. THE MAN THAT IS MADE TO FEEL INFERIOR OR DEFENSIVE, HOWEVER SUBTLY, SHALL INEVITABLY BEGIN TO ACT INFERIOR OR DEFENSIVE TO HIS OWN DETRIMENT. YOUR ENEMIES HARBOR THE SEEDS OF THEIR OWN PERDITION. IN ORDER TO DISCOVER THESE SEEDS, YOU MUST STEALTHILY SCRUTINIZE YOUR ENEMIES FROM BEHIND A KIND AND SYMPATHETIC EXTERIOR. ALLOW YOUR APPARENT GULLIBILITY TO INVITE THEM TO DROP THEIR GUARD AND OPEN UP THEIR MINDS

TO YOU.

21

MASTER, EVEN THE MOST POWERFUL OF MEN BLEED. ALL ARE AFFLICTED BY HUMAN WEAKNESS. A MAN'S GREATEST PASSION IS THE THING THAT IS MOST CAPABLE OF BECOMING HIS GREATEST VULNERABILITY. WHEN YOU FIND OUT WHAT A MAN LOVES, YOU HAVE GAINED THE TOOLS WITH WHICH HE MAY BE DESTROYED. THE GREEDIER SOMEONE IS, THE EASIER IT SHALL BE TO MANIPULATE THEM. WHEN A PERSON'S VANITY IS AT RISK, YOU SHALL BE ABLE TO MAKE THEM DO WHATEVER YOU LIKE. THE HOPE THAT WEALTH, FAME, OR SENSUAL GRATIFICATION MAY FALL INTO THEIR LAP IS THE BAIT THAT SHALL OFTEN LURE MEN INTO ACCEPTING THE MOST PREPOSTEROUS OF CONDITIONS. IN THE DANCE OF **KINGS**, ALTHOUGH IT SHALL BE NECESSARY AT TIMES FOR YOU TO INJURE THOSE THAT OPPOSE YOU, YOU MUST NEVER APPEAR IN PUBLIC WITH BLOOD ON YOUR HANDS OR DIRT ON YOUR FACE. IF A FIGHT WITH YOUR ENEMY IS INEVITABLE, ALWAYS BE SURE THAT THEY ARE THE ONES TO START IT. ALLOW THEM TO MAKE THE FIRST MOVE WHILE YOU AWAIT THE MISTAKES THAT SHALL DESTROY THEM. IF YOU CAN ARRANGE IT SO THAT YOUR ENEMIES APPEAR TO BRING THEIR MISFORTUNE UPON THEMSELVES, YOU SHALL NEVER HAVE TO FEAR THEIR REVENGE.

22

MASTER, IN THE DANCE OF **KINGS**, YOU MUST PERFORM ALL OF YOUR MANEUVERS WITH THE INTENTION OF MAKING YOUR ENEMIES EMOTIONAL AND BEFUDDLED. YOUR ENEMY'S **STRENGTH** SHALL ALWAYS BE INSEPARABLE FROM THEIR

ABILITY TO THINK STRAIGHT. TO AROUSE A PERSON'S EMOTIONS IS TO REDUCE THEIR CONTROL OVER THEIR WILL AND MAKE THEM MORE VULNERABLE TO PERSUASION. THIS SHALL ALWAYS BE MORE EFFECTIVE THAN FORCE. DISCONCERTED, FRUSTRATED ENEMIES ARE LIKE OVERRIPE FRUIT ON A LIMB. THE SLIGHTEST TOUCH SHALL DROP THEM. **POWER** SHALL NEVER WILLINGLY DISPLAY ITS WEAKNESS. THOSE WHO FEEL WEAK AND POWERLESS OFTEN DISPLAY VIOLENT OUTBURST OF EMOTION, SO THAT THEY MAY DISGUISE THEIR VULNERABILITIES, KEEP ALL THOSE AROUND THEM IN SUSPENSE, AND CREATE A MIRAGE OF **POWER** BY SEEMING MENACING AND FEROCIOUS. THOSE WHO ARE EMOTIONAL AND CONTROLLING ARE MERELY THOSE WHO USE THEIR EMOTIONS AND OBSESSIVE NEED TO CONTROL OTHERS, AS A MASK FOR THEIR WEAKNESSES AND INSECURITIES. THE RASH AND ARROGANT ARE PARTICULARLY EASY TO INFLUENCE AND MANEUVER. FOR THE RASH AND ARROGANT CHARGE AHEAD WITHOUT GIVING ANY THOUGHT AS TO WHERE IT IS THAT THEY ARE GOING.

IN THE DANCE OF **KINGS**, THE WISE **KING** SHALL ALWAYS STRATEGIZE AND STRIVE TO MANEUVER HIS FOES INTO POSITIONS OF WEAKNESS BEFORE ATTEMPTING TO DO BATTLE WITH THEM. ALL HAVE A SOURCE OF **POWER** UPON WHICH THEY DEPEND, MASTER. BECAUSE THIS SOURCE OF **POWER** HOLDS THEM UP, IT IS ALSO THEIR GREATEST VULNERABILITY. IT SHALL CAUSE THEM TO FALL IF IT IS TAKEN AWAY OR STRUCK. KNOWING INTIMATELY THE VULNERABILITIES OF YOUR ENEMIES SHALL ALWAYS MAKE YOUR BATTLES QUICKER AND LESS BLOODY, WHICH IS ALWAYS PRUDENT. EMBRACE YOUR ENEMIES CLOSELY. BARREL DEEP INTO THEIR HEART AND LEARN ALL OF THEIR CAPABILITIES. BOW TO THEM. BE SUBMISSIVE. FROM BEHIND A GENTLE, SUBSERVIENT FRONT, CONVINCE THEM TO TRUST YOU SO THAT

THEY MAY REVEAL TO YOU THEIR SITUATION. PRETEND TO ACCEPT THEIR IDEAS. SPEAK DEFERENTIALLY. LISTEN RESPECTFULLY. ACCORD WITH THEM IN EVERYTHING AND RESPOND TO THEIR AFFAIRS AS IF THEY WERE YOUR GREATEST FRIEND. FROM THERE IT SHOULD BE AN EASY MATTER TO GATHER VALUABLE INTELLIGENCE, SUCH AS WEAKNESSES TO ATTACK. BY BEING CHARMING AND ADAPTABLE TO THEIR MOODS, YOU SHALL BE ABLE TO SUBTLY INSINUATE YOURSELF INTO THE SOULS OF YOUR ENEMIES, AND INSIDIOUSLY BREAK THEM DOWN FROM THE INSIDE, JUST AS THE **KING** COBRA'S VENOM KILLS ITS PREY. NO STRUCTURE CAN STAND FOR LONG WHEN IT ROTS FROM WITHIN. ENTER DEEPLY INTO THE MINDS OF YOUR FOES AND LEARN TO THINK AS THEY THINK. ONCE YOU LEARN THE FRAILTIES OF YOUR ENEMIES, YOU SHALL HAVE THE MATERIAL WITH WHICH YOU MAY DESTROY THEM. NO ONE CAN DEFEND THEMSELVES AGAINST WHAT THEY CANNOT SEE. WHEN THE ULTIMATE DAY OF RECKONING FINALLY ARRIVES, MAKE IT SEEM AS IF HEAVEN ITSELF HAS DISMANTLED YOUR ADVERSARIES. IT IS FAR MORE DIFFICULT TO STOP A RIVER THAN IT IS TO REDIRECT IT TO A USEFUL PURPOSE.

23

MASTER, THE SECRETS OF RULERS AND **KINGS** SHALL ONLY BE GRASPED BY THOSE WHO POSSESS THE **UNDERSTANDING** TO USE THE **KNOWLEDGE** PROPERLY. YOUR FULL **POWER** SHALL ONLY MANIFEST ITSELF ONCE YOUR WILL, YOUR **KNOWLEDGE**, AND YOUR ACTIONS ARE ALL UNITED IN A FULL CIRCLE OF **UNDERSTANDING**. THE ACT OF **UNDERSTANDING** IS THE GENERATION OF THE MOST POWERFUL FORCE IN THE UNIVERSE. IT IS ONLY WHEN YOU HAVE

THE **LOVE** AND JOY THAT COMES FROM **UNDERSTANDING** THAT **POWER** AND **THE TRUTH** SHALL BE ABLE TO FLOW THROUGH YOUR BEING. AN **UNDERSTANDING KING** THAT SITS UPON A THRONE BUILT WITH RIGHTEOUSNESS POSSESSES THE **POWER** TO DISPERSE ALL EVIL IN HIS PRESENCE WITH BUT A LOOK FROM HIS EYES. THE ONLY GOOD REASON TO EXERCISE **POWER** IS IN THE SERVICE OF **UNDERSTANDING**. **POWER** IS DANGEROUS AND MAY TURN UPON ITS POSSESSOR AT ANY MOMENT. IF YOU POSSESS NOT **UNDERSTANDING,** YOUR **POWER** SHALL BE NAUGHT BUT AN ABERRATION AND MENACE. WITHOUT **UNDERSTANDING, POWER** SHALL PLACE YOU CLOSER TO THE ANIMALS THAN TO THE **DIVINE**. ALLOW ALL PLEASANTNESS TO COME FROM YOU, AND ALL UNPLEASANTNESS TO COME FROM OTHERS. THIS SHALL WIN YOU FAVOR AND SHIELD YOU FROM ANY ILL WILL. IF YOU ARE CRUEL AND MALEVOLENT, YOU SHALL NEVER BE ABLE TO ESCAPE HATRED. HOWEVER, TO BE GRACEFULLY MAGNANIMOUS IS TO WIN HEARTS AND SECURE A LASTING POSITION OF **POWER**. FOR GRACEFUL MAGNANIMITY SHALL SOFTEN PEOPLE'S WILL TO RESIST YOUR INFLUENCE.

24

MASTER, NOTHING IS ABLE TO CORRUPT A MAN AS MUCH AS THE PURSUIT OF **POWER**, AND IT IS THE FEAR OF LOSING **POWER** THAT CORRUPTS THOSE THAT HAVE IT. THOSE WHO POSSESS AN UNCHECKED DESIRE FOR **POWER** ARE LIKE CANCEROUS CELLS THAT DESTROY THE VERY SAME ORGANISM OF WHICH THEY ARE A PART. WHEN ONE ACQUIRES **POWER,** ALL OF THE DEFECTS IN THEIR SOUL SHALL BE REVEALED. JUST AS A PINPRICK IN A BALLOON CANNOT BE DETECTED AS LONG AS THE BALLOON IS

DEFLATED, BUT AT ONCE REVEALS ITSELF WHEN THE BALLOON IS FILLED WITH AIR, SO DISSOLUTE AND PERVERTED INDIVIDUALS RARELY EXPOSE THEIR DEFICIENCIES EXCEPT WHEN THEY ARE FILLED WITH AUTHORITY. FOR IT IS THEN THAT THE PRESSURES OF **POWER** SHALL CAUSE ALL OF THE TYRANNICAL URGES THAT THEY HAVE BURIED DEEP WITHIN THEMSELVES TO SPILL FORTH ON EVERY SIDE. THE FATAL FLAW OF **POWER** IS ARROGANCE. YOU MUST NEVER ENTERTAIN THE DEVIOUS LIES THAT PRIDE WHISPERS TO YOUR HEART. IT SHALL INTIMATE THAT YOU HAVE NO NEED TO LEARN OR ADAPT. IT SHALL DECLARE THAT YOU SHOULD ALLY YOURSELF WITH ANGER AND DESTROY ALL THOSE WHO WOULD DARE CHALLENGE YOU. IT SHALL BE THE SOURCE OF YOUR DEMISE, MY SON. FOR WHERE PRIDE IS ALLOWED TO PREVAIL, WAR AND RUIN MUST NECESSARILY FOLLOW.

BOOK EIGHT

1

MASTER, JUST AS THE CELESTIAL HEAVENS REFLECT TO THE WORLD A CERTAIN EFFIGY OF DIVINE BEAUTY AS IF IT WERE AN IMAGE IN A MIRROR, SO TOO ON EARTH IS A FAR TRUER REFLECTION OF THE ELEGANCE OF THE DIVINE FURNISHED BY THOSE GREAT KINGS WHO LOVE AND REVERENCE UNDERSTANDING, AND EXHIBIT TO THEIR PEOPLE THE RESPLENDENT LIGHT OF WISDOM ACCOMPANIED BY A LIKENESS OF THE DIVINE'S GENIUS. WITH GREAT KINGS SUCH AS THESE, THE DIVINE SHARES ITS RIGHTEOUSNESS, NOBILITY, AND AN INFINITUDE OF OTHER DEFINABLE BLESSINGS, WHICH SERVE AS A MORE DEFINITE PROOF OF DIVINITY TO THE EYES OF THE MASSES THAN EVEN THE VAST MAJESTY OF THE HEAVENS. IT IS THE DESTINY OF A KING TO BE A BEAUTIFUL FRUIT FOR ALL OF HUMANITY TO ENJOY. A KING IS A PORTAL THROUGH WHICH ENERGY FLOWS FROM THE UNMANIFEST SOURCE OF ALL LIFE FOR THE BENEFIT OF ALL MANIFESTATION. A GREAT KING IS SO CONSTITUTED THAT HE SEEMS NOT TO HAVE BEEN BORN, BUT PERSONALLY FORMED BY NATURE'S HANDS BECAUSE SHE WISHED TO SHOW OFF HER PROWESS BY BRINGING TOGETHER ENOUGH GREATNESS FOR A MULTITUDE IN A SINGLE MAN. A GREAT KING IS SO BLESSED THAT OTHERS' LIVES BECOME BETTER SIMPLY BY KNOWING HIM. HE HAS SUCH AN AIR OF MAGNANIMOUS GENTILITY THAT IS ACCOMPANIED BY SUCH A GRACIOUS HUMILITY THAT THE WORLD ITSELF SHALL ALWAYS SEEM TO BE TOO LIMITED FOR HIM. A KING SHALL BECOME TRULY WORTHY ONLY WHEN HE DEVELOPS A NOBLE, FORBEARING, KIND, AND GENEROUS SPIRIT. FOR IT IS THEN THAT HIS FAVOR SHALL

SHINE LIGHT, HIS SOUL SHALL FLASH **KNOWLEDGE** AND
POWER FROM HIS EYES, MAGNETISM SHALL RADIATE FROM HIS
BODY, AND HIS GOODNESS, TALENT, AND COURAGE SHALL MAKE
IT SEEM AS IF THERE IS NOTHING SO GREAT THAT IT MIGHT NOT
BE EXPECTED OF HIM.

2

MASTER, STRIVE TO ATTAIN FOR YOURSELF THE TITLE OF
SAGACIOUS GENTLEMAN, BY BEING GRACEFUL WITH YOUR
PRESENCE, BY ALWAYS MAINTAINING A GENTLE AND AGREEABLE
MANNER IN YOUR DAY-TO-DAY RELATIONSHIPS, AND BY BEING
INCESSANTLY COURTEOUS TO THE HIGHEST DEGREE. IN MATTERS
OF JUSTICE, ALWAYS BE FAIR, IMPARTIAL, AND ACCORDANT TO
THE TRUTH. THE **DIVINE**, WHOSE RESOURCES ARE
ENDLESS, IS THE TREASURER OF GENEROUS RULERS. WATCH FOR
ALL OPPORTUNITIES TO DO GOOD TO EVERYBODY AND OBLIGE ALL
WITH YOUR CONTINUAL BENEFICENCE. LEARN AS QUICKLY AS YOU
CAN THE VALUE OF ACCEPTANCE, AND NEVER CONDEMN OTHERS
FOR A MERE OPINION. A MIND THAT IS FREE TO THINK IN ANY
FASHION THAT IT DESIRES SHOULD BE RESPECTED, NOT
DESECRATED. TAKE KINDLY THE ADMONITIONS OF TIME, AND
GRACEFULLY SURRENDER THE THINGS OF YOUR YOUTH WHEN THE
TIME COMES FOR YOU TO LET THEM GO. BE ALWAYS VALIANT
AND MANNERLY, AND IN ALL OF YOUR ACTIONS, BEHAVE WITH
THE UTMOST DISCRETION AND PRUDENCE. RULE IN SUCH A WAY
THAT YOUR PEOPLE THEMSELVES BELIEVE THAT THEY WISH TO DO
THAT WHICH YOU COMMAND. ALWAYS SEEK THE COMPANY OF
THE JOYFUL. FOR MISERY IS BAD LUCK, AND THERE IS NO
CONDITION THAT IS MORE INFECTIOUS.

3

MASTER, EXCELLENCE OF CONVERSATION, WHICH GIVES TESTIMONY TO THE EMINENCE OF YOUR WISDOM, SHALL CAUSE YOU TO BE SEEN AS HONORABLE IN THE EYES OF MEN. WHEN YOU SPEAK, SPEAK WITH GENTLENESS AND HUMILITY, SO THAT YOU MAY BE OF SUCH A REPUTATION THAT WHENEVER PEOPLE SEE YOU, THEY BELIEVE THAT YOU SHALL HAVE SOMETHING AGREEABLE TO SAY. WHEN PROVERBS PERMANENTLY RESIDE WITHIN YOUR HEART AND UPON YOUR TONGUE, YOUR SPEECH SHALL BE AS DELICIOUS AS HONEY, YOUR INNER BEAUTY SHALL EXCELLETH ALL, AND EVERYTHING ABOUT YOU SHALL BE SURPRISING. COLOR ALWAYS YOUR CONVERSATIONS WITH THE DYE OF WIT AND GRACE. EMPLOY AGREEABLE PLEASANTRIES AND WITTICISMS IN SUCH A GRAND FASHION THAT YOUR WORDS, FAR FROM EVER BEING TEDIOUS AND BORING SHALL ALWAYS BE A SOURCE OF PLEASURE FOR OTHERS. WHEN DISCUSSING AFFAIRS OF THE KINGDOM, BE ELOQUENT, CIRCUMSPECT, AND PRUDENT ENOUGH TO KNOW HOW TO ADAPT YOURSELF TO THE CUSTOMS OF WHOEVER YOU MAY BE AMONGST, WHILE AT THE SAME TIME DISPLAYING SUCH GRACEFUL AND NONCHALANT SPONTANEITY THAT ALL ARE IMMEDIATELY SET AT EASE BY YOUR CANDOR.

4

MASTER, IN THE HEART OF EVERY KING, LIES IMPLANTED A CERTAIN MAGNIFICENT GREATNESS THAT IS COMPOSED OF REGAL SPLENDOR, READINESS OF SPIRIT, AND AN UNCONQUERABLE VALOR. LOVED AND RESPECTED BY ALL, EVEN IF A GREAT KING HAD NO DEEDS TO THEIR CREDIT, CHIEFLY FOR THEIR CHARACTER, THEY WOULD EARN RENOWN AND HONOR IN

THE WORLD. A TRUE **KING** FEARS NEITHER THE DARKNESS, NOR THE LIGHT. FOR A TRUE **KING'S** COURAGE IS OF SUCH ENERGY THAT IT REJOICES WHENEVER IT FINDS AN OPPORTUNITY TO DISPLAY ITSELF. BE ALWAYS MERCIFUL, DISCERNING, AND GALLANT. WITH THE EYE OF AN EAGLE AND THE JAWS OF A LION, CREEP LIKE A MOUSE, WHILE ALL THE WHILE MAINTAINING THE **UNDERSTANDING** THAT AT TIMES IT IS MORE COURAGEOUS NOT TO BECOME INVOLVED IN A WAR THAN IT IS TO WIN A BATTLE.

5

MASTER, A TRUE **KING** IS A FORCE OF NATURE THAT INHERENTLY BRINGS ORDER, INTELLIGENCE, AND COHERENCE. THE MERE PRESENCE OF A TRUE **KING** SHALL BRING HARMONY TO ANY SITUATION. A **KING** IS ANIMATED BY A SPIRIT OF PROFOUND SOLEMNITY FROM WHICH ALL OTHER TERRORS GLANCE OFF HARMLESSLY. A **KING** DWELLS IN THE ETERNAL CALM THAT LIES BENEATH THE WAVES OF THE OCEAN OF TRUTH, BEYOND THE REACH OF THE TEMPEST OF LIFE. TO THE EYES THAT WATCH THEM, THEY NEVER SEEM TO BE IN A HURRY, OR STRAINED BY THE BURDEN OF UPHOLDING THE KINGDOM. IGNORING THAT WHICH OFFENDS THEM, GREAT **KINGS** ARE LIKE THE MIGHTY LION THAT TOYS WITH THE INSIGNIFICANCE THAT CROSSES HIS PATH, REALIZING THAT ANY OTHER REACTION WOULD BE UNACCEPTABLE COMING FROM THE **KING** OF THE JUNGLE. BECAUSE THEY CREATE THEIR OWN, ONE SHALL NEVER HEAR A GREAT **KING** COMPLAIN ABOUT A LACK OF OPPORTUNITY. ABLE TO GO AT WILL TO A PLACE OF PURE CONCENTRATION IN TIMES OF INTENSE, PHYSICAL, AND EMOTIONAL TUMULTUOUSNESS, A GREAT **KING** MAINTAINS IN ADVERSITY A MIND SO UNMOVED,

AND IN SUCH ACCORDANCE WITH THE PRESENT MOMENT, THAT HE TESTIFIES TO THE ENTIRE UNIVERSE WITHOUT UTTERING A WORD, THAT CIRCUMSTANCE HAS NO DOMINION OVER HIM. CONSTANTLY, THE SAME THROUGH ALL VICISSITUDES OF FORTUNE, GREAT **KINGS** POSSESS THAT EXTRA QUALITY WHICH GIVES THEM THE ABILITY TO HOLD POISE, GRACE, AND RATIONAL THOUGHT, NO MATTER HOW DISASTROUS THE CONSEQUENCES OF FAILURE MAY BE. IT IS THIS EXTRA QUALITY WHICH ALLOWS THEM TO CARRY THEMSELVES WITH THE QUIET BUT FIRM RESOLVE THAT GIVES THEM THAT PARTICULAR AIR OF CONFIDENCE WHICH INSPIRES BELIEF IN EVERY HEART WHICH BEARS WITNESS.

6

MASTER, IT IS NOT HE THAT HOLDS THE SCEPTER, HE WHO HAS BEEN APPOINTED BY VOTE, NOR HE WHO HAS GAINED THE THRONE BY VIOLENCE OR GUILE THAT IS **KING**, BUT RATHER, ONLY HE WHO HAS A **KING'S UNDERSTANDING.** ALWAYS HUMANE, FILLED WITH COMPASSION AND CONSIDERATION, A TRUE **KING'S** ENEMIES SHALL ALWAYS OVERESTIMATE HIS FAULTS, AND HIS FRIENDS SHALL ALWAYS UNDERESTIMATE HIS VIRTUES. AS THE HEAVENS ARE HIGH AND THE EARTH IS DEEP, SO THE HEART OF A TRUE **KING** IS UNSEARCHABLE. THEY SHALL ALWAYS PURSUE **LOVE**, AND THEIR GREATEST PLEASURE IS TO ATTAIN SPIRITUAL GIFTS. TRULY GREAT **KINGS** ARE POSSESSORS OF A COMPASSION SO BOUNTIFUL THAT IT GIVES THEM THE CAPACITY TO HELP ANY LIVING CREATURE AT ANY GIVEN TIME. THEY ARE SO GIVING, FORGIVING, AND LOYAL BY NATURE THAT IT SHALL ALWAYS LIE BENEATH THEM TO EXHIBIT ANY FORM OF PETTINESS. WHEN A TRUE **KING** COMES INTO AUTHORITY, HE COMES WITH THE **UNDERSTANDING**

THAT THIS PRIVILEGE IS NOT SO THAT HE CAN NOW ARRANGE FOR HIS OWN COMFORTS, BUT THE COMFORT OF OTHERS. IT IS FOR THIS VERY REASON THAT THE LIFE OF A GOOD **KING** IS FREE, SAFE, AND AS DEAR TO HIS PEOPLE AS THEIR OWN LIVES ARE TO THEM. IT IS ONLY THE MOST SAVAGE OF BEASTS THAT RULE SIMPLY BECAUSE THEY ARE THE STRONGEST. A **KING** MUST BE A MAN OF MIGHTY CHARACTER AND CONVICTION, WHO LEADS BY EXAMPLE AND TRULY CARES FOR THE SUFFERING OF HIS PEOPLE. A GOOD **KING** WANTS HIS PEOPLE TO SHARE IN THE PROSPERITY OF THE REALM. ALTHOUGH HE MAY NOT BE ABLE TO FEEL THE PAIN OF HIS FOLLOWERS, HE SHALL FEAR THAT PAIN, NONETHELESS. FOR IT SHALL STING HIM AS DEEPLY AS HE THAT IS INJURED BY IT. TO BE A WISE **KING** IS TO BE AT PEACE WITH YOUR OWN CONSCIENCE, FAIR WITH YOUR FELLOW MAN, AND HONEST WITH YOURSELF. IF YOU WOULD BE ALL OF THESE THINGS, YOU SHALL NEVER FEAR THOSE OF EITHER HIGHER OR LOWER STATUS THAN YOURSELF.

BOOK NINE

1

MASTER, AT THE ROOT OF ALL OF YOUR DIFFICULTIES LIES YOURSELF AND YOUR **UNDERSTANDING** OF LIFE. IF YOU EVER FIND YOURSELF IN A HOLE, THE FIRST THING THAT YOU MUST DO IS STOP DIGGING. WHEN THINGS GO WRONG, IT IS IMPERATIVE THAT YOU LOOK DEEPLY WITHIN YOURSELF, NOT FOR THE PURPOSE OF SELF-CONDEMNATION, BUT TO GAIN **UNDERSTANDING**. WHILE YOU SHALL NEVER BE ABLE TO CONTROL EXACTLY WHAT HAPPENS IN LIFE, BECAUSE YOU ARE ABLE TO CONTROL YOUR OWN THOUGHTS, CONDUCT, AND AWARENESS, YOU SHALL ALWAYS HAVE THE ABILITY TO CONTROL HOW YOU RELATE TO WHATEVER IS HAPPENING. ALL PERTURBATIONS LIE NOT OUTSIDE OF YOU, BUT INSIDE OF YOU. YOUR OBSTACLES ARE NOT OTHER PEOPLE OR SITUATIONS, BUT RATHER YOUR OWN PERCEPTIONS. DIFFICULTIES ARE NOT EXTERNAL BUT ROOTED IN YOUR JUDGMENTS OF THAT WHICH YOU PERCEIVE TO BE AS EXTERNAL. ALL THINGS THAT YOU CONSIDER TO BE TROUBLES ARE ONLY TROUBLES FROM YOUR POINT OF VIEW. SPEND MORE TIME DEVELOPING YOUR OWN AWARENESS THAN STRUGGLING AGAINST OUTSIDE FORCES. IF YOU CEASE TO CREATE DISTURBANCES AND IMPEDIMENTS FOR YOURSELF, THEN IT SHALL BE IMPOSSIBLE FOR YOU TO BE DISTURBED OR IMPEDED. YOU SHALL NEVER HAVE ANYTHING TO FEAR FROM EXTERNAL THREATS. FOR THERE IS NO EXTERNAL WORLD. THERE IS ONLY YOU AND YOUR **SELF** UNFOLDING IN TWO WORLDS, THE INNER AND THE OUTER WORLD SIMULTANEOUSLY. THERE IS NOTHING THAT CAN HARM YOU

EXCEPT YOURSELF. YOU ARE NEVER A REAL SUFFERER, BUT BY YOUR OWN FAULT. ALL OF THE HARM THAT YOU SUSTAIN, YOU CARRY ABOUT WITH YOU. NEITHER MISERY, NOR HAPPINESS SHALL EVER COME FROM OUTSIDE OF YOU. IF YOU GAIN NOT THE ABILITY TO SUFFER, ENDURE, AND PROFIT FROM THE GRIEF THAT YOU EXPERIENCE ALONE, YOU SHALL NEVER BE ABLE TO BE **KING**. THE NEED TO GAIN THE APPROVAL AND ACCEPTANCE OF OTHERS, OR BLAMING OTHERS FOR YOUR OWN PROBLEMS, IS A TRAGIC FORM OF SELF-CONDEMNATION AND SHALL SEVERELY LIMIT YOUR **POWER**. THE ONE PERSON WHOM YOU SHALL ALWAYS BE ABLE TO RELY UPON, WITHOUT FAIL AND WITHOUT DISAPPOINTMENT, DURING THE DARK TIMES OF YOUR LIFE SHALL INVARIABLY BE YOURSELF. ALL THOSE FROM WHOM YOU CRAVE ATTENTION, APPROVAL, AND ACCEPTANCE TODAY SHALL BE THE SAME ONES WHOSE OPINIONS YOU SHALL HOLD IN CONTEMPT TOMORROW. AS **KING**, ALL DEPEND UPON YOU, MY SON. THEREFORE, YOU MUST ALWAYS SEE TO IT THAT YOU ARE ABLE TO DEPEND UPON YOURSELF AS WELL. SELF-RELIANCE IS THE SWORD WHICH SHALL SLAY ALL ADVERSITIES AND DILEMMAS.

2

MASTER, ONLY ONCE YOU HAVE LEARNED THE SPIRITUAL LESSON THAT A PARTICULAR CIRCUMSTANCE CONTAINS FOR YOU, SHALL THAT CIRCUMSTANCE PASS AWAY AND OTHER CIRCUMSTANCES TAKE ITS PLACE. WHEN YOU LEARN TO ACCEPT ALL ASPECTS OF LIFE, IT SHALL BECOME CLEAR TO YOU THAT YOU ARE ABLE TO LEARN FROM ANY SITUATION. HARDSHIPS SHALL TEACH A **KING** LESSONS WHICH HE COULD ONLY LEARN BY GOING THROUGH HARDSHIP. BEHIND EVERY CATASTROPHE, THERE ARE GREAT LESSONS TO BE LEARNED. INSTEAD OF WASTING VALUABLE

TIME WHINING AND COMPLAINING ABOUT YOUR DIFFICULTIES AND AFFLICTIONS, ALWAYS VIGILANTLY WATCH FOR THE HIDDEN LESSONS AND EDIFICATION WHICH LIE HIDDEN IN EVERY CALAMITY. OBSTACLES ARE MERELY OPPORTUNITIES FOR THE EXERCISE OF INTELLIGENCE. IF THE SEAS OF DISASTER ARISE, ALTHOUGH THEY MAY INDEED WASH AWAY YOUR POSSESSIONS, THEY SHALL NEVER HAVE THE **POWER** TO WASH AWAY YOUR ABILITY TO REASON. HE WHO IS NOT OPEN TO CRITICISM SHUTS HIMSELF OFF FROM IMPROVEMENT.

WHAT PEOPLE EXPERIENCE AS HINDRANCES IN LIFE ARE MERELY REFLECTIONS OF THEIR DECISION TO SHUT OUT **UNDERSTANDING**. IN EVERY TRIAL, THAT YOU FACE IN LIFE YOU HAVE ONLY ONE OF TWO CHOICES. EITHER YOU CAN MAKE YOUR HEART HARD AND PERISH, OR YOU CAN OPEN YOUR HEART AND LEARN. AS LONG AS YOU RETAIN THE ABILITY TO LEARN FROM YOUR ERRORS, YOU CAN NEVER FAIL. IT IS ONLY THE FOOLS' MISTAKES THAT ARE DISASTROUS. WHILE AN INTELLIGENT PERSON LEARNS FROM THEIR BLUNDERS AND BECOMES GREATER BECAUSE OF THEM, FOOLS REPEAT THEIR MISTAKES AND SUFFER TRAGEDY OVER AND OVER.

3

MASTER, CONTENTMENT BESTOWS UPON YOU THE **POWER** TO ACCEPT WHATSOEVER YOUR DESTINY MAY SEND YOUR WAY AND ASSIMILATE IT INTO THE GREATNESS WHICH YOU ALREADY POSSESS. BE NOT LIKE THE FEEBLE FLAME OF A SMALL CANDLE WHICH SHALL GO OUT AT THE SLIGHTEST GUST OF WIND, OR EVEN IF A PILE OF DRY AND FLAMMABLE TIMBER IS SUDDENLY THRUST UPON IT. INSTEAD, MAKE YOUR WILL AND MIND LIKE A BLAZING INFERNAL

CONFLAGRATION WHICH NOT ONLY GROWS STRONGER BECAUSE OF THE WIND, BUT BECAUSE OF ALL THAT IS PILED UPON IT. FREEDOM LIES NOT IN THE ELIMINATION OR SUPPRESSION OF ADVERSE SITUATIONS, BUT IN MASTERY OVER YOUR OWN INNER ATTITUDE TOWARDS THEM. TO PERCEIVE YOUR PREDICAMENT CLEARLY, WITHOUT THE DISTORTION OF NEGATIVE JUDGMENT, IS THE FIRST STEP IN BECOMING FREE FROM IT. YOUR PROBLEMS LIE NOT IN WHAT YOU EXPERIENCE, BUT IN YOUR OPINIONS CONCERNING YOUR EXPERIENCES. THERE IS NO EVIL OR VEXATION OF ANY KIND THAT IS ABLE TO GAIN ENTRANCE INTO YOUR HEART EXCEPT THAT YOU ALLOW. YOUR MERE OPINION IS ABLE TO RENDER ANY SITUATION OR CIRCUMSTANCE TOLERABLE, EVEN PROFITABLE, IF YOU REGARD THE CIRCUMSTANCES AS AN OPPORTUNITY FOR EDUCATION OR A MATTER OF YOUR DUTIES AS **KING**. YOU SHALL ALWAYS HAVE THE **POWER** TO ENDURE ANYTHING. NEVER THINK, "HOW WRETCHED AND UNFORTUNATE **I AM** THAT THIS HAS HAPPENED, AND I HAVE TO GO THROUGH THIS." BUT INSTEAD SAY, "HOW BLESSED AND FORTUNATE **I AM** THAT EVEN THOUGH THIS TERRIBLE THING HAS HAPPENED, AND I HAVE TO GO THROUGH IT, I AM ABLE TO VALIANTLY PERSEVERE. BECAUSE **I AM** STILL ALIVE, I HAVE THE OPPORTUNITY TO GROW STRONGER BECAUSE OF MY PLIGHT."

IF YOU REFUSE TO VIEW WHATEVER HAPPENS AS DETRIMENTAL AND GIVE UP YOUR DISSENTING OPINIONS CONCERNING THAT WHICH APPEARS TO CAUSE YOU PAIN, YOU SHALL BECOME IMPERVIOUS TO ALL MISFORTUNE AND NO HARM SHALL EVER BE ABLE TO REACH YOU. NEVER JUDGE ANY EXPERIENCE AS GOOD OR EVIL WHICH CAN HAPPEN TO BOTH THE GOOD AND EVIL MAN ALIKE. YOUR LIFE CAN NEVER BE MADE WORSE BY WHAT CANNOT MAKE YOU MORALLY WORSE. JUST AS THE LIGHTNING DISTURBS NOT THE

SKY THROUGH WHICH IT RIPS, SO TOO MUST THE MIND OF A **KING** BE UNFETTERED BY ADVERSITIES. THOSE WHO ALLOW THEMSELVES TO BE AFFECTED BY CIRCUMSTANCES SHALL ALWAYS HAVE SOMETHING TO WHINE AND COMPLAIN ABOUT. NO ONE SHALL EVER RESPECT THE **KING** WHO WHINES AND COMPLAINS. THE PRESENT MOMENT IS ALREADY THE CASE, AND THUS UNAVOIDABLE. INNER RESISTANCE TO THAT WHICH IS, IS A FUTILE AND FOOLISH ENDEAVOR. AVERSION AND REPUDIATION OF THE PRESENT MOMENT ARE TERRIBLE HABITS WHICH SHALL PREVENT YOU FROM FULLY ACCESSING YOUR **POWER**. TO BE IN A STATE OF INNER NONRESISTANCE TO WHAT HAPPENS, TO NOT JUDGE IT, OR MENTALLY LABEL IT AS GOOD OR BAD, BUT TO ALLOW IT TO BE AS IT IS, IS TO BE IN ALIGNMENT WITH **THE TRUTH**, AND TO HAVE YOUR THOUGHTS AND ACTIONS EMPOWERED BY LIFE ITSELF.

AS **KING**, MY SON, YOU HAVE A RESPONSIBILITY TO WORK INTELLIGENTLY WITH THAT WHICH YOU HAVE BEEN GIVEN BY FATE, AND TO NOT WASTE TIME FANTASIZING ABOUT WHAT YOU BELIEVE A PERFECT WORLD SHOULD BE LIKE. INSTEAD OF COVETING AND YEARNING FOR THAT WHICH YOU DO NOT HAVE, FIX YOUR ATTENTION, AND CONCENTRATE UPON ALL OF THE FINE AND GOOD THINGS THAT LIFE HAS GIVEN YOU TO FASHION YOUR KINGDOM WITH, AND IMAGINE HOW TERRIBLE THINGS WOULD BE IF YOU HAD NOT THESE THINGS IN YOUR POSSESSION. NEVER ALLOW AN EXTERNAL CAUSE TO COMPEL YOU TO GENERATE THAT WHICH IS HARMFUL TO YOURSELF. IT IS NOT THE ACTIONS OF OTHERS THAT TORMENT YOU, BUT RATHER YOUR JUDGMENTS CONCERNING THOSE ACTIONS. IN ORDER TO RID YOURSELF OF THE AGONY OF RESENTMENT, YOU NEED ONLY TO RELEASE THOSE JUDGMENTS THAT INFORM YOU THAT THE ACTIONS OF ANOTHER

ARE EVIL. ALTHOUGH PAIN MAY INDEED BE A PART OF LIFE, MISERY IS ALWAYS A CHOICE. MISERY, A CONTAGIOUS DISEASE AMONGST THE WEAK, COMES FROM ONE'S REFUSAL TO ACCEPT A SITUATION AS IT TRULY IS. THE MAJORITY OF PEOPLE HAVE NOT A CLUE AS TO WHAT THEY WANT. THEY ONLY KNOW THAT THEY DO NOT WANT WHAT IS. THE PRIMARY CAUSE OF MISERY IS NEVER THE SITUATION, BUT YOUR THOUGHTS ABOUT IT. FREEDOM FROM MISERY IS ATTAINABLE ONLY WHEN YOU FACE WHAT IS, DIRECTLY, RATHER THAN CONCOCTING NEGATIVE NARRATIVES ABOUT IT. IT IS ESSENTIAL THAT YOU LEARN TO SEPARATE **THE TRUTH** FROM THE STORY THAT YOUR MIND HAS MADE UP ABOUT IT. IT IS ONLY BY FACING **THE TRUTH** DIRECTLY, WITHOUT THE LIES OF NEGATIVITY, THAT YOU SHALL BE ABLE TO GAIN THE **POWER** THAT **THE TRUTH** OFFERS. THE THOUGHT, "I SHOULD NOT HAVE TO BE GOING THROUGH THIS," LIES AT THE ROOT OF ALL MISERY. IF YOU WERE TO ASK YOURSELF WHAT IS SO INSUFFERABLE, ODIOUS, OR UNMANAGEABLE ABOUT EACH TROUBLE IN YOUR LIFE THAT COMES TO YOU, A TRUTHFUL RESPONSE WOULD SOBER YOU OF ALL WRETCHEDNESS. ONCE YOU AWAKEN, YOU SHALL SEE THAT ALL THAT TROUBLED YOU WERE DREAMS, AND THE PRODUCTS OF A DISTURBED IMAGINATION.

4

MASTER, NO MATTER WHAT THE CIRCUMSTANCES MAY BE, IT SHALL ALWAYS BE WRONG TO DESPAIR. THE MEASURE OF A **KING'S** GLORY SHALL BE IN EXACT PROPORTION TO THE SCOPE OF THE ADVERSITY THAT HE EXPERIENCES AND OVERCOMES. HOPE IS A VERY COMPLEX THING FOR THE MAJORITY OF PEOPLE. IT IS DIFFICULT FOR MOST TO HOPE WITHOUT

CONTEMPORANEOUSLY BEING REMINDED OF ALL THOSE THINGS WHICH COULD BRING THEIR HOPE TO AN END. DESPAIR SHALL MOST ASSUREDLY COME TO ALL THOSE WHO LOSE SIGHT OF HOPE. IF YOU ALLOW THE COMPLEXITY OF A QUAGMIRE TO DISCOURAGE AND DEMORALIZE YOU, CAUSE YOU TO FALTER, OR LASH OUT EMOTIONALLY WITHOUT POISE, YOU SHALL LOSE MENTAL CONTROL, AND ADD MOMENTUM TO WHATEVER NEGATIVE FORCE MAY BE OPPOSING YOU. EVERY PROBLEM HAS CONTAINED WITHIN IT ITS OWN SOLUTION. THE ONLY QUESTION LIES IN YOUR ABILITY TO SEE IT. THERE IS NO BONDAGE SO TERRIBLE AS THAT OF HIM WHO HAS BEEN GIVEN OVER TO THE CONTROL OF THAT WORST TO TYRANTS, WHICH IS DESPAIR. REALITY IS PERCEPTION, MASTER. THE PERSON WHO DESPAIRS DOES SO BECAUSE THEY ARE TRAPPED BY NEGATIVE PERCEPTIONS OF THEIR OWN CREATION. DESPAIR SHALL PERSIST ONLY TO THE EXTENT THAT ONE ALLOWS THEMSELVES TO BE BEGUILED BY NEGATIVITY.

IN DIFFICULT MOMENTS, YOU MUST ABOVE ALL FIGHT YOUR INCLINATION TO DESPAIR. IN THE MIDST OF DIFFICULTIES, THE GREATEST DANGER COMES FROM LOSING HEART AND DOUBTING YOURSELF. DOUBT IS NOT WHAT IS NEEDED IN ADVERSE TIMES. WHAT IS NEEDED IS AN INTENSIFICATION OF YOUR DETERMINATION, AND A DOUBLING OF YOUR RESOLVE. ANY SITUATION CAN BE TURNED AROUND. IF YOU HAVE THE MENTAL **STRENGTH** AND FORTITUDE TO STEM THE WAVE OF DESPAIR WHICH THREATENS IN TIMES OF TRIBULATION, HOLD YOUR POISE, AND AWAIT THE PROPER MOMENT TO ACT, TIME ITSELF SHALL SHOW YOU THE PROPER STRATEGY WITH WHICH TO COUNTERACT ANY ADVERSE SITUATION, AND TURN YOUR POSITION OF DISADVANTAGE INTO A POSITION OF **POWER**. JUST AS A STEEL BEAM CAN BE PLACED INTO THE SUPPORT STRUCTURE OF THE

BUILDING SO FIRMLY THAT NOTHING, NOT EVEN AN EARTHQUAKE SHALL BE ABLE TO SHAKE IT LOOSE, SO TOO CAN YOU LODGE COURAGE AND HOPE SO FIRMLY WITHIN THE EDIFICE OF YOUR HEART THAT YOU REMAIN STEADFAST, POISED, AND GRACEFUL, NO MATTER WHAT CALAMITOUS EVENT MAY ARRIVE.

5

MASTER, LIFE IS FULL OF ANTIPATHY. ENMITY AND CONFLICT WITH OTHERS ARE INEVITABLE. NEVER IMAGINE THAT YOU SHALL ALWAYS BE ABLE TO AVOID CLASHES OF WILL WITH OTHERS. ACCEPT THAT THESE THINGS ARE A CERTAINTY OF EXISTENCE AND REALIZE THAT THE WAY IN WHICH YOU DEAL WITH YOUR ENEMIES SHALL DECIDE THE AMOUNT OF **POWER** THAT YOU'RE ABLE TO ATTAIN IN THE DANCE OF **KINGS**. RARE INDEED, MY SON, IS THE MAN THAT IS SO LUCKY THAT HE CAN LIE ON HIS DYING BED WITHOUT IT BEING SURROUNDED BY THOSE CELEBRATING HIS DEMISE. WISH NOT TO BE RID OF AN ENEMY. WISH INSTEAD TO BE ABLE TO RID YOURSELF OF THE DESIRE TO BE RID OF YOUR ENEMIES. WISE **KINGS** PROFIT MORE FROM THEIR ENEMIES THAN MOST PROFIT FROM THEIR FRIENDS. A WISE **KING** UNDERSTANDS THAT IN LIFE, HIS ENEMY SHALL FORCE UPON HIM A SENSE OF PRAGMATIC HUMILITY WHEN NOTHING ELSE IS CAPABLE OF DOING SO. ALWAYS THANK THE HEAVENS FOR YOUR ENEMIES. FOR THEY ARE LIKE MINES FILLED WITH GLORIOUS RICHES. THERE SHALL NEVER BE A BETTER TEACHER FOR YOU THAN AN ENEMY. BECAUSE IT SHALL ALWAYS BE MORE IN YOUR INTEREST THAN IT IS THEIRS TO LOCATE YOUR WEAKNESSES, IT IS ESSENTIAL THAT YOU OPEN YOUR HEART TO THE RECEPTION OF THE PRICELESS LESSONS THAT YOUR ENEMIES HAVE TO OFFER. NONE OTHER THAN YOUR ENEMY SHALL EVER TELL YOU WHAT YOUR

ENEMY IS GOING TO DO. NONE OTHER THAN AN ENEMY SHALL EVER TEACH YOU HOW TO CONQUER EVIL. ONLY AN ENEMY SHALL SHOW YOU WHERE YOU ARE VULNERABLE AND WEAK. AN ENEMY AT YOUR GATE SHALL FORCE YOU TO SHARPEN YOUR MIND AND BECOME FOCUSED LEST YOU BE DESTROYED.

WITHOUT HIS ENEMIES AROUND HIM, A **KING** WOULD RAPIDLY GROW LAZY AND CARELESS. NO **KING** HAS EVER BECOME GREAT WITHOUT HAVING A GREAT ENEMY. THERE COULD BE NO HERO IN ANY STORY WERE IT NOT FOR THE VILLAINS THAT CHALLENGED HIM ALONG HIS PATH TO HEROISM. WITHOUT A WORTHY ADVERSARY, YOU SHALL NEVER GROW STRONGER. WELCOME THE OPPOSITION OF OTHERS AS AN OPPORTUNITY TO PRACTICE PATIENCE, POISE, AND GRACIOUSNESS. THERE SHALL ALWAYS BE THOSE WHO HAVE NO OTHER PURPOSE IN THE DANCE OF **KINGS** BESIDES THAT OF STANDING ON THE SIDE OF THE DANCE FLOOR, ATTEMPTING TO TRIP DANCERS UP. AS **KING**, IT IS VITAL THAT YOU LEARN TO SUCCEED AND EXCEL DESPITE THE MYRIAD OBSTRUCTIONS THAT THOSE OF LESSER CHARACTER THRUST IN YOUR WAY. EVEN BETRAYAL, AS HORRENDOUS AS IT IS, IS OFTEN A WOUNDING THAT SHALL PROVIDE YOU AN OPPORTUNITY TO EMBRACE A NEW VIEW OF LIFE. WHENEVER YOU ENCOUNTER DIFFICULTIES AND OBSTACLES, WHETHER THEY MAY COME IN THE FORM OF TROUBLING CIRCUMSTANCES, OR IRKSOME PEOPLE, IT IS WISEST TO ACCEPT AND EMBRACE THE CIRCUMSTANCE, AND TURN THE OPPOSING ENERGY INTO A COOPERATIVE ONE. CHANGE THE ENEMY INTO AN ALLY. AN ENEMY WHO BECOMES A FRIEND IS DEFEATED AS SURELY AS ONE WHO HAS BEEN KILLED.

6

MASTER, REACHING OUT IN FRIENDSHIP IS NEVER WRONG. IF SOMEONE TRANSGRESSES, THAT IS THEIR OWN BUSINESS. ALL OF THEIR PROPENSITIES AND PROCLIVITIES ARE UP TO THEM ALONE, AND THEY ALONE SHALL EAT THE FRUITS OF THEIR ACTIONS. THE BEST RETALIATION FOR A **KING** AGAINST A PERSON WHO WRONGS HIM, IS SIMPLY TO NOT DO AS THEY DO. THE NOBLEST WAY OF TAKING REVENGE ON OTHERS IS BY REFUSING TO BECOME LIKE THEM. NEVER FEEL TOWARDS THE INHUMANE AND HEINOUS WHAT THEY FEEL TOWARDS EVERYONE ELSE. THOUGHTS OF PRAISING, BLESSING, AND GRATITUDE HAVE THE **POWER** TO DISSOLVE ALL MALIGNITY. LEARN TO PRAISE, BLESS, AND BE GRATEFUL FOR EVEN YOUR ENEMIES. FORGIVENESS IS MERELY THE ACCEPTANCE OF THE FACT THAT LIFE IS COMPRISED OF EVERYTHING WITHIN IT, AND EVERY POSSIBLE QUALITY OF LIFE IS GIVEN AN OUTLET FOR EXPRESSION. WHEN YOU GROW STRONG ENOUGH TO BE ABLE TO ACKNOWLEDGE THAT ALL OF YOUR SUFFERINGS, HEARTBREAKS, AND TRIBULATIONS PROVIDE YOU WITH THE OPPORTUNITY TO GAIN THE **UNDERSTANDING** THAT IS CRUCIAL TO YOUR GROWTH AND DEVELOPMENT, YOU SHALL NATURALLY FORGIVE, PRAISE, BLESS, AND BE GRATEFUL FOR ALL THOSE WHO COME INTO YOUR LIFE IN ORDER TO GIVE THESE PAINFUL, YET BENEFICIAL LESSONS.

NATURE HAS PROVIDED EVERY **KING** WITH MAGNANIMITY AS AN ANTIDOTE FOR THE POISON SPEWED BY THE ARROGANT AND DESPICABLE. AS A **KING**, YOU HAVE COME INTO BEING FOR THE SAKE OF THOSE WITHIN YOUR KINGDOM. THUS, YOU MUST EITHER TEACH THEM WITH GENTLE KINDNESS, OR ELSE LEARN TO BEAR THEIR IGNORANCE. YOU SHALL ALWAYS HAVE WITHIN YOUR

POWER THE ABILITY TO NOT ONLY NOT BE UPSET WITH THE SULLEN, INSENSITIVE, AND UNGRATEFUL, BUT EVEN TO SHOW THEM SYMPATHY, MERCY, AND BENEFICENCE. TO ALLOW MISANTHROPES TO DISTRACT YOU FROM YOUR GOALS BY BECOMING ANGRY WITH THEM FOR FOLLOWING THEIR NATURAL INCLINATIONS WOULD BE BOTH FOOLISH AND WEAK. UNLESS YOU GIVE IT TO THEM, THOSE WHO STAND IN YOUR WAY, AND ATTEMPT TO IMPEDE YOU FROM ACHIEVING YOUR AMBITIONS, HAVE NOT THE **POWER** TO TURN YOU AWAY FROM PRUDENT ACTIONS WHICH WOULD LEAD YOU TO THE FULFILLMENT OF YOUR GOALS, NOR DO THEY HAVE THE **POWER** TO DRIVE AWAY THE BENEVOLENT DISPOSITION THAT YOU HAVE TOWARDS THEM.

NEVER DISTRESS WHEN OTHERS ACCUSE, BLAME, OR SAY HURTFUL WORDS CONCERNING YOU OR YOUR CHARACTER. FOR IF YOU WERE TO LOOK DEEP WITHIN THE HEARTS OF THOSE TALEBEARERS AND BUSYBODIES, YOU WOULD QUICKLY SEE EXACTLY WHAT TYPE OF INDIVIDUALS THEY ACTUALLY ARE, AND HOW UNNECESSARY IT IS TO STRAIN AFTER THEIR GOOD OPINION. IF SOMEONE INFORMS YOU THAT ANOTHER HAS SPOKEN ILL OF YOU, REALIZE THAT THIS IS ALL THAT HAS HAPPENED, AND THAT YOU NOR YOUR CHARACTER HAVE BEEN INJURED IN THE LEAST BY THEIR VERBAL ASSAULT. IN FACT, YOU SHOULD RELISH THEIR ATTENTION, BE APPRECIATIVE TO THEM FOR THE OPPORTUNITY TO PROVE YOURSELF THAT THEY HAVE PROVIDED AND BE THANKFUL THAT YOU ARE IMPORTANT ENOUGH TO BE A TARGET WORTHY OF ATTACK.

7

MASTER, ON YOUR PATH TO THE THRONE, IT IS A MUST THAT YOU LEARN TO MAKE YOUR ENEMIES THE GRAVEL BENEATH YOUR FEET AND THE STEPPINGSTONES TO YOUR GREATNESS. IF EVER YOU SEE YOUR ENEMY IN QUICKSAND UP TO THEIR WAIST, IMMEDIATELY EXTEND THEM YOUR HAND AND QUICKLY PULL THEM FREE FROM THEIR PERIL. HOWEVER, IF YOU SEE THAT THEY ARE UP TO THEIR CHIN, SLOWLY PLACE YOUR FOOT UPON THE TOP OF THEIR HEAD AND PUSH THEM ALL THE WAY UNDER. HEROES ARE ONLY AS STRONG AS THE VILLAINS THAT OPPOSE THEM. IN THE LIFE OF A **KING**, HE USES HIS ENEMIES SO THAT HE MAY HAVE A MEANS OF GAUGING HIS **POWER**. IT IS ONLY BY OVERCOMING THE PEOPLE AND SITUATIONS THAT HAVE VEXED YOU THAT YOU SHALL REALIZE THE DEPTH OF YOUR **STRENGTH**. THE MIGHTIER YOUR ENEMIES, THE GREATER YOUR **HONOR** IF YOU ARE ABLE TO CONQUER THEM. BECAUSE IT IS BETTER TO LOSE TO A WORTHY RIVAL THAN TO OBLITERATE SOME FEEBLE FOE, THE GREATER SHALL BE YOUR REWARD EVEN IN DEFEAT. NEVER DEPEND UPON AN ENEMY NOT COMING. INSTEAD, ALWAYS DEPEND UPON BEING READY FOR THEM WHENEVER THEY DO COME. IN ALL SITUATIONS, YOU MUST CONSTANTLY TRAIN YOURSELF INTO THE FORMATION OF BETTER HABITS. FOR THE DAY SHALL ALWAYS COME WHEN GREATER ENEMIES SHALL RISE AGAINST YOU. NO MATTER HOW STRONG YOUR ENEMIES MAY SEEM, ALWAYS REMEMBER THAT ALL HUMANS HAVE VULNERABILITIES THAT CAN BE PREYED UPON. NEVER SEEK TO DEFEAT YOUR ENEMY, BUT RATHER HIS CONFIDENCE AND ASSURANCE IN HIMSELF. THE MAN WHO ALLOWS DOUBT TO TROUBLE HIM SHALL BE ABLE TO FOCUS UPON LITTLE ELSE. THE BEST WAY TO RID YOURSELF OF YOUR ENEMIES IS TO BANISH THEM

FROM YOUR KINGDOM ALTOGETHER. TO BANISH AN ENEMY IS TO RENDER THEM HARMLESS. FOR BY BANISHING THEM, YOU ROB THEM OF ALL OPPORTUNITIES TO DECEIVE OR HARM YOU.

8

MASTER, THOSE WHO ARE NOT WITH YOU DURING YOUR ADVERSITIES SHALL MOST ASSUREDLY BE AGAINST YOU IN YOUR PROSPERITY, EVEN IF THEY DARE NOT DECLARE IT OPENLY. IT IS THE WISE MAN THAT IS ABLE TO NAME HIS ENEMY. YOU MUST NEVER BECOME UPSET OR DISTRESSED WHEN SOMEONE DECLARES THEMSELVES TO BE YOUR OPEN ENEMY. NOT ONLY SHALL YOU ALWAYS BE SAFER KNOWING YOUR ENEMIES THAN NOT KNOWING THEM, BUT ONE WHO IS A GENUINE THREAT WOULD NEVER DARE REVEAL THAT THEY ARE YOUR ENEMY OPENLY. YOUR ENEMIES WISH YOU EVIL AND THERE IS NOTHING THEY WOULD LIKE MORE THAN SEEING YOUR DOWNFALL. HOWEVER, IF YOU ALLOW THEM TO BE, YOUR ENEMIES CAN BE THE LIGHT THAT SHALL GUIDE YOU TO VICTORY. KNOW YOUR ENEMIES, BUT ALWAYS BE AWARE OF YOUR FRIENDS AS WELL. FOR TO SEE AN ENEMY IN EVERYONE HAS BEEN THE DOWNFALL OF MANY TYRANTS.

9

MASTER, UNDERNEATH THE SURFACE APPEARANCE AND DIFFERENCES FOUND IN LIFE, ALL IS CONNECTED WITH EVERYTHING ELSE, AND TO THE SOURCE FROM WHICH ALL CAME. MISERY, AVERSION, AND HATE ALL ARISE FROM THE IGNORANT DELUSION THAT ONE IS A SEPARATE FRAGMENT THAT IS DISCONNECTED FROM THE **POWER** THAT LIES BEHIND ALL OF CREATION. RID YOURSELF OF THE CHILDISH NOTION THAT

ANYTHING IN THE LAND OF MATERIALITY BELONGS TO YOU OR OWES YOU A THING. A NOBLE MIND, THE MIND OF A **KING**, ACCEPTS ITS DESTINY, AND THAT WHICH LIFE PRESENTS IT WITH, WITHOUT RESERVATION, HESITATION, RESENTMENT, OR COMPLAINT. BECAUSE NO OTHER ENTITY WHETHER EXTERNAL, INTERNAL, OR EXISTING INDEPENDENTLY UPON ITS OWN, GOVERNS OR HOLD SWAY OVER LIFE, EVERY PART OF LIFE CONFORMS TO THE NATURE OF LIFE, AND SERVES ITS PURPOSE. LIFE CONTAINS NOTHING WHICH IS NOT BENEFICIAL TO ITSELF. BECAUSE EVERYTHING ORIGINATES IN, AND SPRINGS FORTH FROM THE ONE SOURCE OF LIFE, WHICH HAS NO INTEREST IN HARMING ITSELF OR ANY OF ITS PARTS, NO PART OF LIFE SHOULD EVER COMPLAIN ABOUT THAT WHICH IS ORGANIZED FOR THE GOOD OF ALL LIFE. LIFE WOULD NOT PROVIDE FOR BOTH PAIN AND PLEASURE WERE IT NOT INDIFFERENT TO BOTH.

HE WHO FAILS TO FOLLOW THE IMPECCABLE EXAMPLE OF LIFE BY ALSO BEING INDIFFERENT TO BOTH AND CHOOSES INSTEAD TO BEWAIL AND LAMENT AGAINST THE NATURE OF THINGS, OFFENDS AND REVOLTS AGAINST THE NATURE OF LIFE ITSELF, WHICH IS MADE UP OF NOTHING IF NOT THE NATURE OF ALL ITS MANIFOLD PARTS. ALL THINGS EITHER HAPPEN BY CHANCE OR BY THE DECREE OF DESTINY. IF THEY HAPPEN BY CHANCE, IT IS POINTLESS AND SILLY TO WHINE OR COMPLAIN. IF THEY HAPPEN BY AN OFFICIAL DECREE OF DESTINY, YOU HAVE NO AUTHORITY, NOR **POWER** TO TAKE DESTINY TO COURT. WHATEVER HAPPENS, THERE IS A REASON, MY SON. CONTRARY TO THE BELIEF OF THE WEAK, WHATSOEVER MAY HAPPEN, HAPPENS JUSTLY. BECAUSE THERE IS NOTHING THAT CAN HAPPEN THAT IS OUTSIDE OF THE ONE REALITY OF LIFE, NOTHING HAPPENS THAT IS NOT MEANT TO HAPPEN. EVERYTHING WHICH BEFALLS YOU, NO

MATTER HOW YOU MAY FEEL ABOUT IT, IS PART OF DESTINY'S DESIGN, AND THEREFORE HAS OCCURRED FOR A SPECIFIC PURPOSE. CONVERSELY, IF SOMETHING HAS NOT HAPPENED, THEN INDEED IT SHOULD NOT BE SO. FOR IF IT WERE IN HARMONY WITH THE WILL OF DESTINY, LIFE WOULD HAVE DONE IT. JUST AS NOTHING CAN HAPPEN TO A LION, A TREE, OR A STONE THAT IS NOT PROPER AND APPROPRIATE TO THE DESTINY OF A LION, A TREE, OR A STONE, THERE IS NOTHING THAT CAN HAPPEN TO A **KING** THAT IS NOT PROPER AND APPROPRIATE TO A **KING** AND HIS PARTICULAR DESTINY. WHATSOEVER MAY TRANSPIRE IN YOUR LIFE HAS BEEN ARRANGED BY FATE, BECAUSE IT IS IN SOME WAY CONDUCIVE TO THE PARTICULAR TASK THAT YOU HAVE BEEN DELEGATED BY LIFE. WHATEVER MAY HAPPEN TO YOU, MY SON, **LOVE** AND REJOICE IN EVERYTHING THAT YOUR DESTINY HAS ASSIGNED YOU. DELIGHT FROM THE DEPTHS OF YOUR BEING IN, AND CONTENT YOURSELF NOT WITH YOUR LOT IN LIFE, BUT IN THE FACT THAT YOU ARE PRESENT IN THE ETERNAL FLOW OF LIFE. EVERY EVENT IN LIFE IS EITHER GOOD FOR YOU OR DIRECTS YOUR ATTENTION TO THAT WHICH YOU NEED TO LOOK AT IN ORDER TO CREATE GOOD FOR YOURSELF AND SHOULD BE ACCEPTED AS READILY AS AN EXCELLENT DOCTOR'S COMMANDS, EVEN IF YOU FIND THESE EVENTS TO BE CRUEL OR DISAGREEABLE. FOR JUST AS TREATMENTS ARE PRESCRIBED BY A PHYSICIAN IN ORDER TO CURE A PATIENT OF THE WEAKNESS OF ILLNESS AND MAKE THEM STRONG AND HEALTHY, SO TOO ARE CIRCUMSTANCES PRESCRIBED BY LIFE IN ORDER TO CURE YOU OF THE ILLNESS OF WEAKNESS AND PREPARE YOU FOR THE FULFILLMENT OF YOUR DESTINY. THERE IS NOTHING THAT SHALL HAPPEN TO YOU THAT IS NOT A PART OF DESTINY'S PLAN. NOTHING SHALL EVER HAPPEN TO YOU THAT LIFE DOES NOT APPROVE OF. LIFE SHALL ALWAYS GIVE TO YOU WHATEVER EXPERIENCE IS MOST HELPFUL FOR YOUR EVOLUTION.

IT IS BECAUSE YOU ARE HAVING A PARTICULAR EXPERIENCE AT A PARTICULAR MOMENT THAT YOU SHALL KNOW THAT EXPERIENCE IS THE EXPERIENCE YOU MOST NEED. WHATEVER HAPPENED TO YOU, MASTER, WAS DESTINED TO HAPPEN SINCE BEFORE TIME BEGAN. IT WAS PRESERVED JUST FOR YOU, LIKE A THREAD WOVEN INTO THE TAPESTRY OF YOUR DESTINY. THEREFORE, EMBRACE IT, MY SON. FOR IT IS YOUR GIFT FROM FATE.

10

MASTER, IT IS ONLY IN ADVERSITY THAT THE TRUE KING SHALL BE DISCOVERED. LIFE SO ADMIRES GREATNESS THAT IT CHOOSES TO REVEAL IT THROUGH ADVERSITY AND THE HARSH BLOWS OF MISFORTUNE. THERE ARE NONE THAT KNOW THE FINAL END OF THOSE THINGS WHICH DESTINY SENDS. ONE CAN NEVER FORETELL WHEN A TEMPORARY OBSTACLE SHALL LEAD YOU TO A FUTURE GOOD. MISFORTUNE BORNE NOBLY IS GOOD FORTUNE. FOR GOOD FORTUNE LIES IN THE ABILITY TO NOBLY HANDLE WHAT MOST WOULD CALL MISFORTUNE. THE ONLY WAY THAT A MAN'S FORTUNE MAY BE CONSIDERED ILL, IS IF HE DOESN'T USE IT TO BENEFIT HIMSELF. IT IS ESSENTIAL THAT YOU LEARN TO USE TRAGEDY AND DISASTER AS A MEANS TO DEVELOP WILLPOWER, RESOLVE, AND DETERMINATION. CALMLY ACCEPT WHATEVER HAPPENS, AND NEVER DESPAIR WHEN YOU UNDERGO WHAT COMMON MEN REFER TO AS MISFORTUNE. LIFE CONTAINS NOTHING THAT IS NOT GOOD FOR IT, AND NOTHING CAN BE BAD FOR A PART OF LIFE THAT IS GOOD FOR LIFE AS A WHOLE. THE HARDSHIPS OF LIFE ARE NOT CONTRARY TO NATURE OR TO THE PROVIDENTIAL ORDERING OF THE COSMOS. FOR THEY ARE ORDAINED BY DESTINY, WHICH ALONE DETERMINES WHAT IS NEEDED FOR THE WELL-BEING OF THE UNIVERSE OF WHICH YOU

ARE A PART. BECAUSE DISGRACE AND **HONOR**, PAIN AND PLEASURE, POVERTY AND PROSPERITY, AND LIFE AND DEATH, CAN HAPPEN TO BOTH THE EVIL MAN AND THE GOOD MAN ALIKE, WITHOUT MAKING AN EVIL MAN MORE OR LESS EVIL, OR A GOOD MAN MORE OR LESS GOOD, NONE OF THESE THINGS CAN BE IN THEMSELVES EITHER EVIL OR GOOD. NEVER ALLOW ANY NEGATIVE OPINION OF YOUR PRESENT CIRCUMSTANCES, WHETHER IT BE YOUR OWN OPINION OR ANOTHER'S, TO DICTATE AND RULE YOUR FUTURE. IN ORDER TO ACHIEVE, IT IS NECESSARY THAT YOU LEARN, WHEN MISFORTUNE STRIKES, TO WAIT OUT ALL IMPEDIMENTS, HINDRANCES, AND ADVERSITIES TENACIOUSLY, PERSISTENTLY, AND PATIENTLY UNTIL THE NATURAL RHYTHMIC CYCLE OF LIFE CAUSES A CHANGE IN CIRCUMSTANCES THAT SHALL ALLOW YOU TO ADVANCE POSITIVELY TOWARDS YOUR AMBITIONS ONCE MORE. SO-CALLED MISFORTUNE, IF YOU ALLOW IT TO, SHALL TEACH YOU PRICELESS LESSONS ABOUT PERSEVERANCE, POISE, AND COURAGE. WHEN YOU GET INTO A DARK AND DESPERATE PLACE WHERE IT SEEMS THAT ALL HAVE FORSAKEN YOU, ALL FORCES ARE AGAINST YOU, AND YOU CAN HOLD ONTO HOPE NO LONGER, IT IS EXACTLY THEN THAT YOU MUST MURDER THE URGE TO DESPAIR AND ABANDON **FAITH** IN YOURSELF. FOR THIS IS PRECISELY THE MOMENT WHEN LIFE SHALL TURN IN YOUR FAVOR. LIFE SHALL ALWAYS FAVOR THE MAN WHO HAS THE DETERMINATION TO SEE THAT IT SHALL. REALITY IS WHATEVER IS, MY SON. OPPOSITION TO THAT WHICH ALREADY IS, IS THE GREATEST INDICATOR OF IGNORANCE. ALWAYS BEAR IN MIND THAT WHICH LIFE PROVIDES YOU WITH IS BEST FOR YOU, AND BEST TOO IS IT AT THE TIME THAT IT IS GIVEN. NEVER BE LIKE THOSE THAT CHASE AND LUST AFTER COMFORT AND PLEASURES AS IF THEY WERE THE GREATEST GOOD AND EVADE AND HATE HARDSHIPS AND DIFFICULTIES AS IF THEY WERE THE GREATEST

EVIL. THE PERSON WHO FEARS AND AVOIDS HARDSHIPS AND DIFFICULTIES IS AT ODDS WITH THE NATURAL ORDER OF LIFE, AND THUS SHALL NEVER ACHIEVE GREATNESS. HE WHO COVETS AND DESPERATELY CRAVES COMFORT AND PLEASURE SHALL NEVER HESITATE TO ACT UNJUSTLY.

11

MASTER, IN THIS LIFE, THAT WHICH IS GOOD FOR YOU IS THAT WHICH YOUR DESTINY GRANTS YOU AND CHANGE. CHANGE IS WHAT SUSTAINS AND REPLENISHES ALL THAT WHICH IS FOUND IN LIFE. LIFE IS NAUGHT BUT AN ENDLESS INCESSANT PROCESSION OF NAMES AND FORMS. ANYTHING THAT COMES GOES. EVERYTHING THAT YOU ARE NOW SEEING IS IN FACT CHANGING EVEN AS YOU WATCH IT AND SHALL NOT CONTINUE TO EXIST AS IT IS. ALL PARTS OF THE ENTIRETY OF LIFE SHALL IN A MOMENT CHANGE THEIR FORM AND SOON AFTER THAT, PERISH AND CEASE TO BE. LIFE EXULTS IN CHANGE. FOR IT IS ONLY BY CHANGE THAT NEW THINGS ARE ABLE TO COME INTO BEING.

DEATH AND CHANGE ARE TWO WORDS THAT MEAN THE VERY SAME THING. THE ESSENCE OF DEATH IS MERELY ONE FORM CHANGING SO THAT THEY MAY GIVE SPACE TO ANOTHER FORM. DEATH IS SIMPLY THE MEANS FOR LIFE TO REGENERATE. WHAT IS DEATH FOR ONE FORM IS BIRTH TO ANOTHER, AND DEATH IN ONE WORLD IS BIRTH IN ANOTHER. SOON, YOU SHALL BE BOTH NOWHERE AND NOBODY. NOBODY THAT NOW WALKS THE EARTH SHALL BE ALIVE, AND NONE OF THE THINGS THAT SURROUND YOU SHALL EXIST. IT IS ONLY BY **UNDERSTANDING** DEATH THAT YOU SHALL BE ABLE TO DEVELOP A PASSION FOR LIFE. BECAUSE IT IS THE NATURE OF ALL IN CREATION TO CHANGE

FORM AND DIE; OBVIOUSLY, DEATH IS AN ACT OF LIFE. THEREFORE, LIKE EVERYTHING ELSE IN LIFE, IT SHOULD BE DONE TO THE BEST OF YOUR ABILITY. ALL THINGS WHICH COME FROM THE EARTH ARE ONLY DUST. DEATH IS NOTHING MORE THAN THE NATURAL DISPERSAL AND DISTRIBUTION OF THIS DUST. THIS DISPERSAL AND DISTRIBUTION, BECAUSE IT CONFORMS TO THE LAWS OF NATURE, CANNOT BE BAD. NOTHING NATURAL IS BAD. JUST AS PEOPLE AWAIT THE BLESSED TIME WHEN THE CHILD IN A PREGNANT WOMAN'S BODY SHALL COME FORTH FROM THE WOMB IN THE NATURAL PROCESS OF CHILDBIRTH, SO TOO MUST YOU LEARN TO AWAIT WITH FORBEARANCE THE HOLY TIME WHEN YOUR SPIRIT SHALL EMERGE FROM ITS SHELL IN THE NATURAL PROCESS CALLED DEATH. YOU CAN NEVER LOSE THAT WHICH YOU ARE, WHICH IS YOURSELF. THEREFORE, YOU CAN NEVER DIE. YOU ARE LIFE. YOU DO NOT POSSESS A LIFE.

DEATH SHALL BE SEEN AS LIFE'S AGENT OF RENEWAL, LIKE A SNAKE SHEDDING ITS SKIN, ONLY IF YOU IDENTIFY WITH LIFE ITSELF, RATHER THAN WITH ITS PASSING PROCESSION OF PHENOMENA. TO THOSE IDENTIFIED AND INFATUATED WITH THE FORMS OF LIFE, ANY DEATH IS A REASON TO MOURN. JUST AS ONE WEARS CLOTHES UPON ONE'S BODY, THE BODY ITSELF IS APPAREL FOR THE SPIRIT. DEATH IS LIKE CHANGING AN OLD GARMENT AND PUTTING ON A NEW ONE. TOMORROW, YOU SHALL RETURN YOUR BODY TO THE SAME SOURCE FROM WHICH YOU ACQUIRED IT YESTERDAY, JUST AS YOU SHALL MOMENTARILY RELEASE YOUR BREATH BACK INTO THE SAME AIR FROM WHICH YOU JUST DREW IT. THE EARTH SHALL SOON COVER ALL WHO NOW LIVE, AND ITSELF CHANGE AGAIN AND AGAIN ON INTO TIMELESSNESS. BEFORE LONG, YOUR BODY SHALL CLOSE ITS EYES TO REST IN THAT ETERNAL SLUMBER, AND SOON AFTER THAT

SOMEONE SHALL BE GRIEVING FOR ALL THOSE WHO DUG YOUR GRAVE.

WHENEVER ANGER, FRUSTRATION, OR IMPATIENCE OVERTAKES YOU, REMIND YOURSELF OF HOW EVANESCENT AND EPHEMERAL ALL CIRCUMSTANCES ARE, AND HOW SOON YOU AND ALL YOUR VEXATIONS SHALL BE LAID OUT IN A GRAVE. SOON, YOU SHALL HAVE FORGOTTEN ALL, AND ALL SHALL HAVE FORGOTTEN YOU. SHORT ARE THE LIVES OF ALL WHO REMEMBER, AS WELL AS ALL WHO SHALL BE REMEMBERED. POINTLESS IS WORRY AND ANXIETY. FOR ALL THINGS OBEY THE DECREE OF FATE. BEFORE LONG, YOU SHALL BE BOTH NOBODY AND NOWHERE. IT IS ONLY IN THE FACE OF ONE'S MORTALITY THAT THE ENTIRE CONCEPT OF OWNERSHIP SHALL STAND REVEALED AS THE ULTIMATE INANITY. ONCE YOU DIE, EVEN THE BODY AND MIND THAT YOU ONCE CALLED YOURSELF SHALL NO LONGER BE YOURS AND SHALL NEVER AGAIN BE. IF YOU JUDGE GOOD AS ALL THAT HAPPENS IN ITS DUE TIME AND SEASON, AND CARE MORE THAT YOUR ACTS ARE RIGHTEOUS THAN THAT THEY ARE REWARDED, DEATH SHALL NEVER HAVE THE ABILITY TO HOLD YOU IN TERROR. NOTHING CAN BE HARMED BY COMING TO A CONCLUSION WHEN THE TIME FOR IT TO CEASE HAS ARRIVED.

12

MASTER, MANY ARE THE TRIALS AND TRIBULATIONS OF THE GREAT. THE GREATER THE SPIRIT OF A MAN, THE GREATER THE MAGNITUDE OF THE PROBLEMS HE SHALL FACE. ALL IS A PART OF A GREAT INDIVISIBLE AND INTENTIONAL DESIGN. YOU MUST ALWAYS BE GRACEFULLY REVERENT, CALM, AND TRUST IN THAT INTELLIGENCE WHICH GOVERNS ALL THINGS. EVERY STORM RUNS

OUT OF RAIN EVENTUALLY. THE SUN IS ALWAYS SHINING, WHETHER THE CLOUDS ARE THERE BLOCKING IT OR NOT. THE ONLY THING THAT CHANGES IN ADVERSITY IS THE MINDS OF MEN. TIME CARRIES ON UNPERTURBED IN TIMES OF ASCENDANCY, AS WELL AS IN TIMES OF CALAMITY. DARKNESS MUST EVENTUALLY PASS FOR THE DAY MUST COME. WHEN THE MORNING STAR BREAKS THE HORIZON, IT SHALL SHINE THAT MUCH BRIGHTER FOR THE MEMORY OF THE DARKNESS. NO OCCURRENCE OR CIRCUMSTANCE IS WORTHY OF YOUR SPIRIT BEING MADE HATEFUL, SPITEFUL, SELFISH, OR COWARDLY. THERE SHALL NEVER BE ANY REASONABLE JUSTIFICATION FOR A **KING** BECOMING LIKE THIS. YOU MUST HAVE A WILLINGNESS TO FACE THE DARKNESS BEFORE YOU SHALL EVER BE ABLE TO LET IN THE LIGHT. BEFORE YOU CAN DO ANYTHING TO CHANGE AN UNBEARABLE SITUATION, YOU MUST ACCEPT IT. NEVER ALLOW ANY DIFFICULTY TO HORRIFY YOU. FOR IF YOU ALLOW THEM TO, DIFFICULTIES SHALL REVEAL **STRENGTH** AND **POWER** TO YOU THAT YOU NEVER KNEW YOU POSSESSED. NO SHAME IS THERE IN FALLING. SHAME LIES ONLY IN THE REFUSAL TO STAND AGAIN. PAINFUL FAILURE IS THE LANGUAGE THAT LIFE USES TO TEACH HUMILITY, **WISDOM**, AND **UNDERSTANDING**. IT IS A LAW OF LIFE THAT EVERY **KING** WHO ACHIEVES GREATNESS MUST FIRST UNDERGO TESTING PERIODS OF ADVERSITY AND TRIALS OF FIRE. OFTENTIMES, MANY OF THEM SHALL BE TESTED FOR POISE, COURAGE, **FAITH**, AND THE MAGICAL **POWER** TO TURN HARDSHIP INTO OPPORTUNITY. BECAUSE NO MAN CAN FORETELL THE ULTIMATE CONSEQUENCES OF A DEFEAT, A **KING** MUST ALWAYS WELCOME DEFEAT AS A WAY TO INSPIRE HIMSELF TO BECOME TOUGHER AND STRONGER. NO MATTER WHAT MAY HAPPEN TO YOU, YOU EITHER HAVE THE **STRENGTH** AND **POWER** TO TENACIOUSLY PERSEVERE OR

YOU DON'T. IF YOU HAVE THE **POWER** TO PERSEVERE, YOU MUST NEVER WHINE, BUT INSTEAD THANK THE HEAVENS FOR YOUR **STRENGTH** AND PERSEVERANCE. IF YOU DO NOT POSSESS THE **POWER** TO PERSEVERE, YOU STILL SHOULDN'T WORRY OR COMPLAIN, FOR ONCE THE PUNY **STRENGTH** THAT YOU DO POSSESS EXPIRES, ALL OF YOUR DIFFICULTIES SHALL BE OVER.

EVERY **KING** MAKES MISTAKES. THIS IS HUMAN AND UNAVOIDABLE. THE TRICK THAT YOU MUST MASTER IS TO NEVER ALLOW YOUR MISTAKES TO DESTROY YOU. THE WISE **KING** NOTES THE INDICATIONS OF TRAGEDY AND AVOIDS THEM. THERE LIES NO GOOD IN WAITING UNTIL DANGER SURPRISES YOU TO PREPARE YOURSELF FOR IT. THE BLOW THAT KNOCKS ONE OFF THEIR FEET IS NOT SO MUCH THE HARD ONE AS THE ONE THAT COMES UNEXPECTED. ALWAYS BE ON GUARD AGAINST WHAT IS NOT YET IN SIGHT, AND ALERT FOR THAT WHICH IS AS YET UNHEARD. THIS IS WHAT SHALL GIVE YOU THE ABILITY TO DWELL IN THE MIDST OF HARDSHIP AS IF THEY DID NOT EXIST.

13

MASTER, JUST AS A DOCTOR, IN ORDER TO CURE AN ILL MAN OF ILLNESS MAY PRESCRIBE CERTAIN MEDICINES WHICH MAY TASTE TERRIBLE, IN ORDER TO CURE A **KING** OF WEAKNESS, LIFE PRESCRIBES ABANDONMENT, AFFLICTION, AND OTHER HARDSHIPS. ALL TROUBLES AND TRIBULATIONS ARE BLESSINGS IN DISGUISE. YOU MUST ALWAYS BE GRATEFUL FOR THESE EXPERIENCES RATHER THAN CRITICAL OF THEM. **POWER** WITHOUT RESISTANCE IS MEANINGLESS AND WEAK. IF SUCCESS IN LIFE CAME EASY, IT WOULD BE OF NO BENEFIT. THE VICTORIES WE CHERISH THE

MOST ARE FROM OUR MOST DIFFICULT BATTLES. YOUR PAIN AND SUFFERING, AS LONG AS IT ARISES OUT OF YOUR KINGLY TOILS, DUTIES, AND ENDEAVORS, ARE NOT CONTRARY TO THE WILL OF DESTINY. IF SOMETHING IS NOT CONTRARY TO THE WILL OF DESTINY, IT CANNOT POSSIBLY BE AN EVIL TO YOU. FOR THE BALL THAT HAS BEEN TOSSED UP INTO THE AIR, IT IS NO EVIL FOR GRAVITY TO CAUSE IT TO FALL BACK TO EARTH, NOR DID IT DO THE BALL ANY GOOD TO HAVE BEEN THROWN UP IN THE FIRST PLACE. IF IT IS EXCELLENT TO SAY OR DO SOME GREAT THING, THEN IT IS EVEN BETTER TO BE CRITICIZED FOR HAVING SAID OR DONE IT. ALL THAT IS CRITICIZED MUST AT A MINIMUM BE WORTHY OF SOMEONE'S NOTICE. EVERY GLORIOUS REIGN HAS HAD DARK PATCHES DURING WHICH THE CROWN HAS BEEN SULLIED BY THE MUD. TESTING PERIODS OF AFFLICTION ARE A GREAT PRIVILEGE TO A **KING** WHEN THEY COME TO HIM. THEY GRANT HIM THE OPPORTUNITY TO TAKE INVENTORY OF HIS POISE AND COURAGE SO THAT HE MAY SEE IF HE IS INDEED PREPARED TO TAKE THE THRONE. THE BEST PART ABOUT PAIN IS THE FACT THAT YOU CAN ALWAYS LEARN SOMETHING BECAUSE OF IT. OPPOSITION IS THE FUEL OF CREATIVITY. A KING'S CHARACTER IS FORGED IN THE FURNACE OF HUMILIATION. ADVERSITY MERELY SERVES TO PURIFY A **KING** AND PROVE HIS WORTH.

WHEN TRIBULATIONS COME, REMAIN CALM, SINCERE, AND DETERMINED. ACCEPT PATIENTLY THAT WHICH THE PRESENT MOMENT GIVES YOU. IT IS ONLY IN SUFFERING THAT YOU SHALL FIND THE TRUE MEASURE OF YOUR **STRENGTH**. SELDOM IS THE TIME WHEN BIRTH IS NOT A PAINFUL PROCESS. IT IS OFTEN OUT OF THE ASHES OF A RUINED PAST THAT NEW LIFE IS BEGUN. BEHIND EVERY DARK HAPPENING, BEHIND EVERY PREDICAMENT, THERE IS HIDDEN GOOD. EVERY CURSE IS A BLESSING IN

DISGUISE. THERE IS SOMETHING POSITIVE IN EVERY SETBACK. AS YOU DEVELOP THE **UNDERSTANDING** OF A **KING** AND BEGIN TO BE ABLE TO DISCERN EVER MORE CLEARLY THE LAWS OF LIFE, YOU SHALL CEASE TO FUSS, WHINE, WORRY, OR FUME OVER WHAT MOST WOULD CONSIDER HARDSHIP, AND BE ABLE TO MAINTAIN POISE, STEADFASTNESS, AND SERENITY AMIDST THE TEMPESTS OF CALAMITY. CIRCUMSTANCES DO NOTHING BUT REVEAL YOU TO YOURSELF. ANY EXPERIENCE CAN BE VALUABLE IF YOU WOULD BE WILLING TO RELEASE YOUR EXPECTATIONS, RESISTANCES, JUDGMENTS, AND CONCEPTUALIZATIONS CONCERNING IT. ANY EVENT IN YOUR LIFE CAN BE SEEN EITHER AS A MISTAKE OR MIRACLE DEPENDING UPON THE LENS WITH WHICH YOU CHOOSE TO VIEW LIFE. OBSTACLES ARE NAUGHT BUT THE BUILDING BLOCKS OF OPPORTUNITY, CLEVERLY DISGUISED. FAILURE IS NOTHING MORE THAN AN INSPIRATION FOR A GREATER AND MORE TENACIOUS EFFORT. THE **STRENGTH** OF A **KING'S** TRUE COURAGE SHOWS BEST DURING HIS SEASON OF ADVERSITY. ADVERSITIES ARE THE TESTS WHICH SHALL GIVE A **KING** THE CHANCE TO REALIZE THE SOURCE, AND NATURE OF HIS INNER **POWER**. THE THINGS THAT YOU GAIN SHALL ALWAYS BE PAID FOR BY THAT WHICH YOU LOSE. ALTHOUGH YOU MAY NOT GET ALL THAT YOU PAY FOR IN THIS LIFE, YOU SHALL CERTAINLY PAY FOR ALL THAT YOU GET. ALL MEN BECOME KIN IN SPIRIT AND DEED WHEN THEY ARE OVERTAKEN BY A COMMON CATASTROPHE. THOSE WHO IN TIMES OF PRECARIOUSNESS ARE INTENT UPON SUPPLYING THEIR OWN WANTS MUST NEVER BE TRUSTED BY YOU IN AN EMERGENCY. **POWER**, FAME, AND MATERIAL WEALTH, ESPECIALLY IF THEY COME TO HIM QUICKLY AND EASILY, CAN LEAD TO THE UNDOING OF A **KING** AS SURELY AS DISASTER. A **KING** IS TESTED FOR NOBLE CHARACTER, NOT ONLY DURING HIS SEASON OF GREAT TRAGEDY AND MISFORTUNE,

BUT ALSO DURING HIS SEASON OF GREAT VICTORY AND MATERIAL SUCCESS. MANY MORE **KINGS** SURVIVE THE TEST OF HARDSHIP AND DIFFICULTY THAN SURVIVE THE TEST OF PROSPERITY. NEVER TAKE FOR GRANTED THAT YOUR PAST SUCCESSES SHALL CONTINUE INTO THE FUTURE. NEVER ALLOW THEM TO LEAD YOU TO BELIEVE THAT YOU CAN DISREGARD OR DISPARAGE ANOTHER WITH IMPUNITY, WHO HAS NOT YET ATTAINED SUCCESS. TO GAIN THE CONFIDENCE OF A MAN WHEN HE IS POOR IS TO SHARE IN HIS HAPPINESS IF HE BECOMES SUCCESSFUL. STAND BY A MAN WHEN HE IS IN TROUBLE, IF YOU WISH TO STAY WITH HIM WHEN BETTER TIMES COME HIS WAY.

14

MASTER, MAN IS THE ONLY CREATURE ON EARTH THAT MUST BE ENCOURAGED TO STAY ALIVE. THE MAN WHO CHOOSES TO FOCUS ON PROBLEMS SHALL ALWAYS SEE PROBLEMS. WHEREAS HE WHO IS FOCUSED UPON SOLUTIONS, MAKES ALL PROBLEMS DISAPPEAR. NEVER CONCERN YOURSELF WITH RAIN. INSTEAD, LEARN TO WALK BETWEEN THE RAINDROPS. WHEN FACED WITH A DILEMMA, AND YOUR LIFE IS THREATENED BY SEEMINGLY INSURMOUNTABLE CATASTROPHE, YOU HAVE ONLY TWO OPTIONS. PERISH OR EVOLVE. HE WHO IS UNABLE TO ADAPT HIMSELF TO ALL CHANGING CIRCUMSTANCES AND ADVERSITIES WITHOUT LOSING HIS POISE AND GRACEFUL SENSE OF COMPOSURE IS UNFIT FOR THE THRONE. IN ANY CRISIS, YOU MUST REMAIN CALM, SO THAT YOU MAY HAVE THE **POWER** TO SIZE UP THE SITUATION ACCURATELY, AND EXPLOIT WHATEVER OPPORTUNITIES REVEAL THEMSELVES. AT SOME POINT, YOU MUST STOP RUNNING, TURN AROUND, AND BOLDLY FACE WHATEVER IS TRYING TO KILL YOU. THE HARD THING IS FINDING THE COURAGE TO MAKE THE

DECISION TO DO IT. AS LONG AS YOU CONTINUE TO BE REBORN, IT IS ALRIGHT TO DIE SOMETIMES, MY SON. ONE MOMENT OF PAIN IS TRIVIAL COMPARED TO A LIFETIME OF GLORY. LIFE NEVER ENDS, THUS THERE IS NO SUCH THING AS DEFEAT OR FAILURE UNLESS AND UNTIL YOU ACCEPT THEM AS SUCH. ALTHOUGH **STRENGTH** IS ALWAYS TESTED, **STRENGTH** ALWAYS PERSEVERES. FOR THIS IS WHAT MAKES IT **STRENGTH**. VALOR AND **FAITH** ARE YOUR BEST HOPE AND PROTECTION WHEN YOU ARE THREATENED WITH DOOM. WHEN A MAN FIGHTS, EVEN HIS ENEMIES RESPECT HIM. ESPECIALLY IF HE FIGHTS WITH INTELLIGENCE. NOTHING EVER HAPPENS TO A MAN THAT HE HAS NOT BEEN EQUIPPED BY NATURE TO HANDLE. IF YOU ACCEPT DIFFICULTY AS OPPORTUNITY, THEN YOU SHALL END UP WITH NO DIFFICULTIES AT ALL. IT IS ONLY WITH CONSTANCY, STEADINESS, AND PERSISTENCE THAT YOU SHALL ATTAIN **POWER**. JUST AS GOLD IS PURIFIED IN THE FIRE, SO ARE WORTHY MEN PURIFIED IN THE CRUCIBLE OF HUMILIATION. THE STRONG SHALL SHINE, NO MATTER HOW DARK IT MAY GET. NO MATTER HOW STRONG THE WIND, THE STARS SHALL REMAIN FIXED IN THEIR POSITION. IT IS A MOST SHAMEFUL AND DISGRACEFUL THING FOR YOUR SPIRIT TO QUIT WHEN YOUR BODY IS ABLE TO CONTINUE ON.

EVERY RATIONAL BEING HAS THE **POWER** TO TRANSMUTE ANY HINDRANCE WHICH THEY ENCOUNTER INTO MATERIAL THAT THEY CAN USE TO PROPEL THEM TO THE FULFILLMENT OF THEIR AMBITIONS. THE TREE THAT REFUSES TO BEND SHALL CRACK IN THE WIND. THOSE WHO GET THE BEST OUT OF LIFE ARE THOSE WHO MAKE THE BEST OUT OF WHATEVER LIFE BRINGS THEM. THINGS TURN OUT BEST FOR THOSE WHO ALWAYS MAKE THE BEST OUT OF THE WAY THAT THINGS TURN OUT. IN THE SCHOOL OF

AFFLICTION, PATIENCE IS THE FIRST SUBJECT THAT ONE MUST MASTER. ONLY THOSE WHO ENDURE TO THE END OF A THING SHALL BE SAVED. LIBERATION FROM TROUBLE SHALL BE OF NO AVAIL TO YOU IF YOUR EMANCIPATION COMES NOT BY YOUR OWN **POWER**. ONLY THOSE DELIVERANCES THAT DEPEND UPON YOU AND YOUR PROWESS ARE TRUSTWORTHY AND ENDURING. IN MOMENTS OF TUMULT AND TURMOIL, FORCE YOURSELF TO BE DETERMINED AND RESOLUTE. ACTING WITH RESOLUTION AND DETERMINATION IN TIMES OF TRAGEDY AND DISTRESS SHALL GARNER YOU RESPECT, AWE, AND IRRESISTIBLE MOMENTUM IN ALL OF YOUR ENTERPRISES.

15

MASTER, EVEN IF THE GROUND ITSELF GIVES WAY ON THE PATH BENEATH YOUR FEET, IT IS YOUR DUTY AS **KING** TO REMAIN STEADFAST, AND FIND A WAY TO CONTINUALLY MOVE FORWARD. AFTER THE STRUGGLE, YOU SHALL HAVE NO DOUBT DEFEATED THE DEMON. FREEDOM COMES AUTOMATICALLY ONCE ALL STRUGGLE CEASES. **KINGS** ARE JUDGED BASED UPON THE WAY THEY HANDLE CHAOS AND CONFUSION. THEREFORE, YOU MUST LEARN TO EMBRACE THEM AND MAKE THEM USABLE FOR YOUR OWN PURPOSE. ACHIEVEMENT TAKES PLACE ONLY IN THE FACE OF OPPOSITION. WHEN YOUR IMPEDIMENTS BECOME ALLIES AND PATRONS, LIKE GIFTS OR CONTRIBUTIONS, YOU NO LONGER HAVE ANY IMPEDIMENTS. DETERMINATION IS EVERYTHING, AND RESOLUTION IS INDISSOLUBLY BOUND UP WITH POISE. AS **KING**, YOU MUST REMAIN POISED AND GRACEFUL EVEN IN THE FACE OF CHALLENGES BEFORE WHICH YOU ARE POWERLESS. WHEN ILL FORTUNE BEFALLS YOU, IT WOULD BE JUST AS MUCH A WEAKNESS TO BECOME ACRIMONIOUS OR CRUEL, AS IT WOULD TO

FLINCH FROM ACTION AND ABANDON THE COURSE BECAUSE OF COWARDICE. THE **KING** WHO IS ALWAYS POISED, RESOLVED, AND DETERMINED TO KEEP HIS WITS ABOUT HIM SHALL NEVER NEED TO BECOME FEARFUL OR ALARMED WHEN ADVERSITY OR DANGER PRESENTS ITSELF. IF YOU OPPOSE AND RESIST WHAT HAPPENS, YOU SHALL PLACE YOURSELF AT THE MERCY OF WHAT HAPPENS, AND CIRCUMSTANCES SHALL ALWAYS DETERMINE YOUR HAPPINESS AND UNHAPPINESS. HOWEVER, TO EMBRACE WHAT HAPPENS AND BECOME COMPLETELY AT ONE WITH IT, IS TO ROB CIRCUMSTANCES OF ALL **POWER** OVER YOU. IF SOME CIRCUMSTANCE STANDS IN YOUR WAY AND HINDERS YOU FROM DOING SOMETHING THAT YOU WISH TO DO, IF INSTEAD OF REACTING AGAINST THE SITUATION THAT IS TROUBLING AND ALLOWING IT TO DISTRESS YOU, YOU WELCOME THE OBSTACLE, FLOW WITH IT, CALMLY ADAPT YOUR ACTIONS TO IT, AND DO SOMETHING THAT IS IN HARMONY WITH YOUR AMBITIONS, AND THE SORT OF KINGDOM THAT YOU ARE SEEKING TO BUILD, THE SOLUTION TO YOUR TROUBLE, SHALL NATURALLY ARISE OUT OF THE SITUATION ITSELF. BECAUSE THEY WERE UNABLE TO DO THESE VERY THINGS, MANY PEOPLE WHO WERE ON THE VERGE OF SUCCESS HAVE LOST THEIR PATIENCE AND FAILED IN THEIR UNDERTAKINGS. JUST AS PLEASURE HAS NO **POWER** TO WEAKEN YOU, PAIN HAS NO **POWER** TO HARM YOU. THAT WHICH DOES NOT MAKE YOU WORSE CANNOT POSSIBLY MAKE YOUR LIFE WORSE.

AS **KING**, YOU MUST BE THE JUTTING ROCK IN THE EDDYING SEA AGAINST WHICH, ALTHOUGH WAVES VIOLENTLY AND INCESSANTLY CRASH, ALL DISTURBANCES EVENTUALLY SETTLE AROUND AS A FROTHING FOAM. MOST DISGRACEFUL IS IT WHEN THE WILL OF A **KING** FALTERS EVEN BEFORE HIS BODY DOES.

HE WHO QUITS WHEN DIFFICULTY OVERTAKES HIM DECLARES TO ALL THAT HE MISTOOK PRETENTIOUS VANITY FOR TRUE GREATNESS. PERSEVERANCE SHALL ALWAYS BE MORE EFFECTIVE THAN PITIABLE LAMENTATIONS. FOR WHILE PITY DOES NOT FREQUENTLY GET YOU AID, ADMIRATION AT YOUR REFUSAL TO GIVE IN OFTEN SHALL. MANY HINDRANCES AND DIFFICULTIES THAT CANNOT BE SURMOUNTED IF YOU TRY TO OVERCOME THEM ALL AT ONCE, SHALL YIELD MOST ASSUREDLY IF YOU WOULD MASTER THEM LITTLE BY LITTLE. IN ADVERSITY, MANY SECRETS ARE DISCOVERED BY DETERMINED EFFORT, WHICH DISCOURAGEMENT AND DEJECTION WOULD HAVE HIDDEN FOREVER. TIME, AS IT PASSES, SHALL EVENTUALLY PRESENT OPPORTUNITIES TO YOU THAT YOU MAY NOT HAVE BEEN CAPABLE OF PREDICTING. FAILURE LIES NOT IN YOUR FALLING DOWN, BUT IN YOUR REFUSAL TO GET BACK UP. IT IS GREATNESS ALONE THAT SUBDUES ALL DIFFICULTIES. IT IS THE GREATNESS THAT FLOWS FROM THE POISE THAT A **KING** SUMMONS IN ADVERSITY THAT SHALL MANIFEST ITSELF IN THE FORM OF **POWER** AND **WISDOM**. ALWAYS REMEMBER, MY SON, WHEREVER THERE IS LIFE, GREATNESS THERE TOO IS POSSIBLE.

16

MASTER, EVERY FLIGHT COMMENCES WITH A FALL. THERE SHALL COME A TIME IN EVERY GREAT **KING'S** LIFE WHERE IF HE HAD NOT BEEN RUINED WHEN HE HAD, HE WOULD HAVE INDEED BEEN RUINED. GREAT **KINGS** LEARN THROUGH CALAMITY. THE FURNACE IS TO PURIFY, NOT TO CONSUME. YOU MUST LEARN TO USE DEFEAT AND FAILURE AS THE FUEL THAT FEEDS THE FIRE OF YOUR WILL. THE SHARPEST BLADES ARE THOSE THAT HAVE BEEN FORGED IN THE HOTTEST FIRES. A TRUE **KING** DOES NOT

SHATTER WHEN HE FALLS, RATHER HE BOUNCES TO ELEVATIONS NEVER BEFORE DREAMED OF. EVERY SOUL IS REBORN WHEN IT REFUSES TO ACCEPT DEFEAT AS FAILURE. NEVER SHOW SIGNS OF BITTERNESS OR DEFENSIVENESS IN THE FACE OF DEFEAT. INSTEAD, ALWAYS KEEP YOUR COMPOSURE, STAND TALL, BE GRACEFUL, AND USE DEFEAT AS A MEANS TO DEMONSTRATE THE EXCELLENCE OF YOUR CHARACTER TO THE UNIVERSE. ACCEPTING SUFFERING FOR A GREATER PURPOSE IS THE VERY DEFINITION OF DEDICATION AND THE FOUNDATION OF NOBILITY. THE ONLY WAY THAT A **KING** SHALL EVER REACH GREATNESS IS IF HE POSSESSES THE **STRENGTH** OF WILL NECESSARY TO UNDERGO DIFFICULTIES, AND ENDURE HARDSHIPS AND INCONVENIENCES WITHOUT ANIMOSITY, INDIGNATION, OR RESENTMENT. IT IS PRESSURE THAT TURNS COAL INTO DIAMONDS. THE DARKER THE SKY, THE BRIGHTER THE STARS SHINE.

A **KING** SHALL BECOME GREAT ONLY WHEN HE VANQUISHES THE HINDRANCES AND ADVERSITIES BY WHICH HE IS CONFRONTED. THUS, DESTINY, WHENEVER IT DECIDES TO INCREASE THE GREATNESS OF A **KING**, CAUSES ENEMIES TO ARISE AND CONSTRUCTS IMPEDIMENTS AGAINST HIM SO THAT HE MAY HAVE THE OPPORTUNITY TO OVERCOME THEM AND USE THEM AS THE FOOTHOLDS AND THE HANDHOLDS THAT SHALL ENABLE HIM TO CLIMB TO THE GLORIOUS HEIGHTS OF NEW MAGNIFICENCE. CRISES ARE MERELY OPPORTUNITIES FOR DEVELOPMENT IN THE PROCESS OF YOUR EVOLUTION. A **KING'S** NOBILITY IS SHOWN IN HIS RESPONSE TO ADVERSITY. OBSTACLES ARE PERFECT OPPORTUNITIES TO TEST YOUR DETERMINATION AND COURAGE. RATHER THAN DESPAIR WHEN DIFFICULTIES ARISE, YOU SHOULD REJOICE AND WELCOME HARDSHIP AS A CHANCE TO EXHIBIT YOUR MAGNANIMITY AND POISE. WHEN THE WORST THING THAT CAN

BEFALL YOU ACTUALLY OCCURS AND YOU BEAR IT, YOU SHALL EMERGE STRONGER THAN YOU EVER IMAGINED POSSIBLE. THERE HAS NEVER BEEN A STRONG **KING** WITH AN EASY PAST. THE WEAK TREES ARE LEVELED BY THE HURRICANE. ALTHOUGH ADVERSITY IS LIKE A POWERFUL TEMPEST THAT SEEKS TO HINDER YOU FROM GOING PLACES THAT YOU MIGHT OTHERWISE GO, IT ALSO SERVES THE PURPOSE OF TEARING ALL FAKE AND FRIVOLOUS THINGS AWAY FROM YOU, SO THAT AFTER THE STORM PASSES, YOU MAY BE LEFT WITH ONLY **THE TRUTH**. BLESSED ARE THOSE WHO HAVE ENTERED INTO THE PLACE OF DARKNESS AND OUT OF THE SHADOW OF DEATH COMES FORTH WITH NEW LIGHT. STAND POISED AND READY TO NOT ONLY ADJUST TO EACH AND EVERY CHANGE OF CIRCUMSTANCE THAT TIME DELIVERS, BUT ALSO TO SEIZE AND EXPLOIT EACH NEW OPPORTUNITY THAT EVERY CHANGE BRINGS. JUST AS THE POISON THAT PEACOCKS EAT PRODUCE THE BEAUTIFUL COLORS IN THEIR PLUMAGE, SO TOO MUST YOU USE THE NEGATIVE CIRCUMSTANCES OF YOUR LIFE TO ILLUMINATE YOUR NOBLE BRILLIANCE. JUST AS THE BEAUTIFUL LOTUS FLOWER GROWS OUT OF THE MOST DISGUSTING MUCK, SO TOO CAN THE MOST BEAUTIFUL ATTRIBUTES ARISE FROM THE MOST PAINFUL OF CIRCUMSTANCES. LIKE THE WOUNDED OYSTER, MEND THE DAMAGE THAT YOU SUSTAIN FROM ADVERSITIES WITH PRECIOUS AND PRICELESS PEARLS. EVEN IF YOU FIND YOURSELF GIVEN UP FOR DEAD, AND ABANDONED BY THOSE WHOM YOU **LOVE** MOST, YOU MUST NOT ALLOW YOURSELF TO LOSE HEART. FOR IF YOU MANAGE TO RETURN FROM THE BRINK OF DESOLATION, THOSE WHO GAVE UP ON YOU SHALL HAVE NO CHOICE BUT TO BOW BEFORE YOUR HONORABLE GREATNESS.

17

MASTER, IT IS IMPOSSIBLE TO TRULY UNDERSTAND WINNING IF YOU HAVE NEVER FELT WHAT LOSING FEELS LIKE. JOY ARRIVES ON THE HEELS OF SORROW. FAILURES ARE MERELY A **KING'S** STEPPINGSTONES TO SUCCESS. ADVERSITY IS AN ALLY IN A **KING'S** LIFELONG STRIVE FOR AMELIORATION. SUFFERING IS THE FIRE IN WHICH WEAKNESS BURNS ITSELF UP. AS GOLD IS REPEATEDLY HEATED AND COOLED IN ORDER THAT ITS PURITY MAY BE RAISED, SO TOO IS EVERY **KING** PURIFIED BY THE FIRES OF SUFFERING. ACHIEVEMENT IS BUT THE RESULT OF THE STRUGGLE AGAINST OPPOSITION. OBSTACLES ARE MERELY AN OPPORTUNITY TO CREATE SOMETHING NEW. **STRENGTH**, THE YOUNGER BROTHER OF STRUGGLE, SHALL ALWAYS FOLLOW ITS ELDER BROTHER WHEREVER IT GOES. TRUE **POWER** SHALL ONLY APPEAR WHEN A **KING** FACES HIS MOST ARDUOUS TEST. UNLESS THERE IS A SINCERE DEMAND FOR IT, **WISDOM** CANNOT BE GENERATED. THIS DEMAND CAN ONLY BE PROVIDED BY THE TRAGEDIES AND CALAMITIES THAT LIFE IMPARTS. ADVERSITY IS BUT A TOOL WHICH DESTINY GIVES TO A **KING** SO THAT WITH IT, HE MAY LEARN HOW TO ATTAIN SUCCESS AND GLORY. IF YOU CAN GAIN THE **POWER** TO SEE AND ACCEPT ADVERSITY AS AN INSPIRATION FOR GREATER EFFORT AND DETERMINATION AND PERSEVERE THROUGH EMOTIONALLY DEVASTATING CATASTROPHES AND FAILURES WITHOUT HAVING YOUR INNER SPIRIT SMOTHERED BY THESE EXPERIENCES, THESE VERY SAME EXPERIENCES SHALL INTRODUCE YOU TO THE HIDDEN FORCE WHICH RULES THE ENTIRETY OF LIFE. YOUR **FAITH** SHALL BECOME SO POWERFUL THAT IT SHALL DESTROY ALL OBSTACLES IN YOUR PATH, AND YOU SHALL GAIN THE **POWER** TO BECOME A MASTER OF WHATEVER YOU WISH TO MASTER. SOMETIMES THE MOST HORRIBLE

MISFORTUNE BRINGS ABOUT THE GREATEST UNFORESEEN RECOMPENSE. EMBRACE ADVERSITY SO THAT YOU MAY BE ABLE TO USE YOUR TRIBULATIONS TO ENHANCE YOUR REPUTATION AS A PILLAR OF **POWER** AND **STRENGTH** THAT CAN ALWAYS BE RELIED UPON IN TIMES OF DOUBT AND UNCERTAINTY. A **KING** LEARNS OBEDIENCE AND HUMILITY FROM THAT WHICH HE SUFFERS.

BOOK TEN

1

Master, terror is a swindler that shall steal your kingdom by robbing you of your initiative. While you must never fear death, you should always fear not reaching for life. Fear is a barrier to experience and serves no purpose besides that of restricting your vigor. To understand this thoroughly is to discover the dynamism of yourself, and to gain tremendous POWER and STRENGTH as a result of your discovery. In order to create greatness in your kingdom, it is essential that you replace all of the fear that you possess with UNDERSTANDING and FAITH in yourself. Men are most terrified by the unknown, and impossible is merely a name that the fearful give to the unseen.

As KING, you must never fear the unknowableness and unpredictability of change. Because change, the opening to new horizons, is that which allows growth and development, transitoriness shall never be a threat to you, nor should it ever be viewed as such. To believe in your own limitation is to live in fear. The desire for safety and security stands in stark opposition to every great and noble venture. The common man shall always go to far greater lengths to avoid what he fears than to obtain what he desires. He who from fear hesitates, shall never accomplish anything great. Fear automatically lowers your value and inscribes upon your soul, a self-fulfilling prophecy of incertitude and

TRAGEDY. WHILE FEARFUL HESITATION SHALL PLACE BARRICADES IN YOUR PATH, COURAGEOUS BOLDNESS SHALL OBLITERATE THEM. GREATNESS FEARS NO CONSEQUENCES. FEARS THEMSELVES ARE A FAR GREATER DANGER THAN AUDACITY. THE FEAR OF THE CONSEQUENCES OF A DARING MANEUVER IS NEVER IN ACCORD WITH **THE TRUTH**. FAILURE IS AN ILLUSION THAT IS CREATED BY ONE'S SENSE OF FEAR. THE FEAR OF FAILURE IS THE MOST COMMON CAUSE OF FAILURE. FOR TO FEAR FAILURE IS TO PLACE BOTH FEAR AND FAILURE IN YOUR HEART.

2

MASTER, DOUBT IS A **KING'S** WORST ENEMY. DOUBT IS A POISON THAT SHALL KILL YOUR **POWER**. THERE IS GREAT FEAR FOUND IN DOUBT. DOUBT AND FEAR ARE THE ARCHENEMIES OF SUCCESS. THE CHILDREN OF DOUBT AND FEAR ARE ALIBIS, EXCUSES, AND JUSTIFICATIONS FOR FAILURE. HE WHO DOUBTS MAKES NO PROGRESS. THOUGHTS OF DOUBT SHALL NEVER ACHIEVE ANYTHING BESIDES FAILURE. DOUBT AND FEAR ARE TREACHEROUS ENEMIES THAT SHALL CAUSE YOU TO LOSE THE WAR BY CONVINCING YOU NOT TO FIGHT. LIFE SHALL SUPPORT ALL OF YOUR UNDERTAKINGS ONCE THEY ARE BEGUN. HOWEVER, IF YOU DOUBT YOUR COURSE OF ACTION, THIS INCREDULITY SHALL CANCEL LIFE'S SUPPORT COMPLETELY. WHEN DOUBT IS BANISHED FROM THE KINGDOM, ABUNDANCE FLOURISHES, AND ANYTHING IS POSSIBLE. LIKE VINES GROWING BETWEEN MORTARED STONES, GIVEN ENOUGH TIME, DOUBT AND FEAR SHALL CAUSE EVEN THE STOUTEST OF HEARTS TO CRUMBLE. DOUBT OCCURS WHENEVER ONE LOOKS OUTSIDE OF THEMSELVES WHEN THEY ARE FACED WITH A CHOICE. WHEN MANY WAYS SEEM POSSIBLE, HE WHO TURNS AWAY FROM HIS INNER GUIDANCE IS HANDED OVER TO

FEAR. BECAUSE DOUBT IS DISAGREEABLE AND THREATENING, MOST PEOPLE NEVER ACTUALLY ANALYZE EVEN THEIR MOST CHERISHED BELIEFS TO FIND OUT IF IN FACT THEY ARE INDEED TRUE. HAVE NO FEAR OF THE FEARS THAT ACCOMPANY TRIBULATIONS. INSTEAD OF REPRESSING THEM, CONFRONT THEM, AND FACE THEM DOWN WITH YOUR MOST FORMIDABLE ALLY COURAGE BY YOUR SIDE. BY DELIBERATELY PUTTING YOURSELF IN PREDICAMENTS WHERE YOU HAVE TO FACE YOUR FEARS, YOU SHALL FAMILIARIZE YOURSELF WITH THEM, AND GAIN THE **POWER** AND CONFIDENCE THAT COME FROM OVERCOMING THEM. ALTHOUGH YOU MAY FEEL FEAR, IT IS IMPERATIVE AS A **KING** THAT YOU NEVER SUCCUMB TO IT AND BECOME AFRAID. FOR TO ENTER ANY ACTION AFRAID IS TO FAIL. NEVER MAKE CRITICAL DECISIONS WHEN YOU HAVE DOUBT PRESENT IN YOUR MIND. IF YOU ARE UNSURE OF A COURSE OF ACTION, YOU MUST NEVER ATTEMPT IT UNTIL YOU GAIN CERTAINTY. WHENEVER THERE IS DOUBT AS TO THE **WISDOM** OF AN ACTION WHICH YOU DESIRE TO COMMIT, THERE IS GREAT DANGER PRESENT ALSO. YOUR DOUBTS AND FEARS INDUCE TIMIDITY. TIMIDITY HAS BEEN THE RUIN OF MANY GLORIOUS ENTERPRISES. IF YOU BECOME INFECTED WITH TIMIDITY, YOUR TIMIDITY SHALL BE THE GERM THAT INFECTS YOUR KINGDOM WITH FEAR AND CAUSES THE DISEASE OF DOUBT TO SPRING UP LIKE A PLAGUE. IT IS ONLY BY BEING UNAFRAID OF CONSEQUENCES THAT YOU SHALL BE ABLE TO GAIN ANY CONTROL OVER YOUR SITUATION. FANATICISM AND DEFENSIVENESS ARE TWO OF DOUBT'S MOST CLEVER DISGUISES. FANATICISM IS NOTHING MORE THAN OVERCOMPENSATED DOUBT, AND HE WHO BECOMES DEFENSIVE IS A PUPPET WHOSE STRINGS ARE BEING PULLED BY DOUBT.

3

MASTER, FEAR IS NAUGHT BUT ANTICIPATED PAIN. WORRY IS FEAR IN A CLEVER MASK. ONCE YOU GAIN AN **UNDERSTANDING** OF THE TRANSIENCE OF ALL PHENOMENA AND THE INEVITABILITY OF CHANGE, IT SHALL BE EASY FOR YOU TO ENJOY THE PLEASURES OF LIFE WITHOUT FEAR OF LOSS, OR ANXIETY ABOUT THE FUTURE. FEAR AND ANXIETY ARE ONLY WINDS THAT YOU MUST ALLOW TO BLOW PAST YOU. WHEN YOU REMOVE ANXIETY AND FEAR FROM ANY SITUATION, ALL THAT REMAINS IS **LOVE** AND **FAITH**. ANXIETY AND FEAR ARE IRREFUTABLE INDICATIONS OF SPIRITUAL IMMATURITY AND INSECURITY. THE MAN WHO GROWS ANXIOUS AND FEARFUL TESTIFIES TO THE UNIVERSE THAT HE HAS NO **FAITH** IN HIMSELF. IF YOU WOULD SEEK **KNOWLEDGE** AND GAIN **UNDERSTANDING** OF YOUR FEARS, THEY SHALL ALL BE OVERTHROWN AND REPLACED BY **FAITH**.

NO GOOD HAS EVER COME FROM DESPAIR, NOR FROM DWELLING UPON THE NEGATIVE SIDE OF ANY SITUATION. ALWAYS TRUST IN HOPE. HOPE IS THE LIGHT THAT SIGNALS THE END OF A DARK NIGHT OF DISCOURAGEMENT. IT IS THE ONE THING THAT SHALL NEVER FORSAKE YOU NO MATTER HOW DARK TIMES MAY GET. FAILURE IN ITSELF IS NOTHING. BUT TO LIVE DEFEATED, TO LOSE HOPE, AND SIMPLY GIVE UP, IS TO FAIL EVERY DAY THAT YOU LIVE. ALL FEARS ARE BASED UPON THE FEAR OF DEATH. ONCE YOU REALIZE THAT YOUR TRUE SELF IS IMMORTAL, AND YOU BEGIN TO SEE YOURSELF AS A PART OF ETERNITY, ALL OF YOUR FEARS SHALL AUTOMATICALLY DISAPPEAR, AND YOU SHALL BE ABLE TO FACE ANYTHING, AND LOOK ANYONE IN THE EYE WHILE DOING SO. IF UNCERTAINTY IS UNACCEPTABLE TO YOU, YOUR UNACCEPTANCE

SHALL TURN INTO FEAR. FEAR SHALL BECOME THE DOMINANT FACTOR IN YOUR DECISION MAKING AND PREVENTS YOU FROM TAKING THE POSITIVE ACTION NECESSARY TO INITIATE POSITIVE CHANGE. IF YOU LEARN TO ACCEPT UNCERTAINTY, AND BECOME COMFORTABLE WITH IT, YOUR ACCEPTANCE SHALL TURN INTO ALERTNESS AND CREATIVITY. INFINITE POSSIBILITIES SHALL OPEN UP IN YOUR LIFE, AND NO CIRCUMSTANCE SHALL EVER BE ABLE TO FETTER YOUR AMBITIONS.

4

MASTER, TERROR, AND DESPAIR ARE CAPABLE OF CONFUSING EVEN THE STRONGEST OF MEN. THEY ARE ANY MAN'S MOST POWERFUL FOES. TERROR AND DESPAIR MAKE MEN ACT AGAINST THEIR OWN BEST INTEREST. THEY HAVE THE ABILITY TO CHANGE ANY MAN INTO SOMETHING THAT HE DOES NOT WISH TO BE, WHICH IS A COWARD. THE MOST COMMON CAUSE OF THE MISTAKES OF MEN IN THEIR ENTERPRISES LIES IN BEING TOO FEARFUL OF PRESENT DANGERS, AND NOT AWARE ENOUGH OF THOSE DANGERS WHICH ARE REMOTE AND, AS YET UNSEEN. IT IS BY FEARFULLY FLEEING THE HUNTER THAT THE TERRIFIED RABBIT IS ENSNARED IN HIS TRAP. TERROR AND DESPAIR ARE TRAITORS THAT SHALL ALWAYS IMPART FALSE COUNSEL. THEY SHALL CAUSE YOU TO MISCONSTRUE EVEN THE VERY BEST OF INTENTIONS AND MAKE EVEN A TRUSTED FRIEND APPEAR TO BE AN ENEMY. OFTENTIMES, PEOPLE WHO DEPLOY CYNICISM ARE MERELY ATTEMPTING TO DISGUISE THEIR OWN FEELINGS OF INSECURITY AND FEAR. EVEN THE WISE SHALL BLIND THEMSELVES WHEN THEY ARE AFRAID TO SEE **THE TRUTH**.

5

MASTER, IT IS IMPOSSIBLE TO INSPIRE AN ARMY WITH COURAGE WHEN YOU YOURSELF ARE OPPRESSED BY THE HORROR OF DESPAIR. A TRUE **KING** IS FREE FROM THE MANACLES OF FEAR. THROUGH HIS COMPASSION, HE IS SKILLED IN LIBERATING OTHERS FROM THEIR STATES OF FEAR. WHEN YOU REACH BEYOND YOURSELF TO OFFER GENUINE AID TO ANOTHER, YOU ARE LED PAST YOUR OWN FEARS AND LIMITATIONS. THE MOST EFFECTIVE WAY OF CONVINCING YOUR PEOPLE THAT THEY NEED NOT BE AFRAID IS TO SHOW THEM THAT YOU ARE NOT. FEAR, ALONG WITH GREED, AND THE LUST FOR **POWER** ARE THE MAIN PSYCHOLOGICAL MOTIVATING FORCES BEHIND ALL CONFLICT AND VIOLENCE. VICTORY, IF IT IS GAINED BY YOUR ENEMY, SHALL BE GAINED NOT BY THE NUMBER OF YOUR PEOPLE THAT THEY KILL, BUT BY THE NUMBER OF YOUR PEOPLE THAT THEY FRIGHTEN. THOSE THAT ALLOW THEIR FEARS TO ROB THEM OF THEIR COURAGE SHALL SURRENDER THEIR WITS AND SKILL, AS WELL. FEAR, DOUBT, AND DEJECTION HAVE THE ABILITY TO SPREAD THROUGH YOUR KINGDOM LIKE WILDFIRE. WHEN YOU SEE THEM STIRRING, YOU MUST EXTINGUISH THESE FLAMES OF NEGATIVITY BEFORE THEY BLAZE INTO A CONFLAGRATION OF PANIC AND MUTINY. IN NORMAL CIRCUMSTANCES, INDIVIDUALS WHO BECOME FRIGHTENED CAN REGAIN THEIR POISE OVER TIME, ESPECIALLY IF THEY ARE AROUND OTHERS WHO ARE CALM. HOWEVER, IN A PANIC-FILLED GROUP, THIS IS NOT POSSIBLE. THOSE WHO ARE INFECTED WITH PANIC AND MUTINOUS IMPULSES EXPERIENCE A TYPE OF PSYCHOSIS IN WHICH THEY LOSE CONTACT WITH **THE TRUTH**. IN ORDER TO STOP FEAR FROM REACHING THIS POINT IN YOUR KINGDOM, YOU AS **KING**, MUST BECOME AWARE OF THE STIRRINGS OF FEAR AS SOON AS THEY

BEGIN. APPEAL TO THE **HONOR** AND **DIGNITY** OF THOSE CONTAMINATED AND INSPIRE THEM WITH THE LIGHT OF YOUR VALOR.

THE FRIGHTENED MAN SHALL ALWAYS BE DEFEATED. TO FEAR SOMETHING IS TO GIVE THAT THING **POWER** OVER YOU. MOST FEAR CHANGE, EVEN IF THAT CHANGE IS FOR THE BETTER. EVERYTHING IN LIFE FEARS THAT WHICH IS STRANGE. THE UNSEEN ENEMY SHALL ALWAYS BE FRIGHTENING. HOWEVER, WHEN YOU CEASE TO FEAR WORLDLY **POWER**, A FAR GREATER **POWER**, WHICH IS YOUR OWN, SHALL ARRIVE TO SUPPORT YOU. ONE OF THE GREATEST DEFECTS FOUND IN THE COMMON MAN IS THAT HE TENDS TO UNDERVALUE THOSE THINGS OF WHICH HE IS AFRAID. FEAR, ESPECIALLY WHEN IT IS REPRESSED, OFTEN DISGUISES ITSELF AS AGGRESSIVE CONTEMPT, AND EXCESSIVE ATTEMPTS TO DEFAME, DISCOUNT, OR DISPARAGE THAT WHICH FRIGHTENS. IT IS ONLY WHEN A MAN IS IN THE PRESENCE OF SOMETHING THAT SCARES HIM THAT HE FEELS THE NEED TO DISRESPECT AND DERIDE IT AND LET OFF A PLETHORA OF REFERENCES TO HIS **POWER**, CLEVERNESS, OR PROWESS. THOSE THAT FEEL SAFER TRYING TO PREDICT WHAT YOU CANNOT BE, RATHER THAN SEEING AND CELEBRATING THE POTENTIAL GREATNESS WHICH YOU POSSESS, SHALL ALWAYS SEEK TO FORCE THEIR OPINION OF YOU UPON YOU, AND PLACE LABELS UPON YOU IN AN ATTEMPT TO LIMIT YOUR **POWER**. NEVER ALLOW THEIR PETTINESS TO BOTHER YOU OR MAKE YOU DEFENSIVE. THERE IS NO WORSE FATE THAN BEING HABITUALLY DEFENSIVE. FOR THAT MEANS THAT YOU ARE ALWAYS AFRAID OF THE TRIFLING JUDGMENTS OF THE INSIGNIFICANT. WEAKNESS SHOWN SHALL ALWAYS BE FAR WORSE THAN WEAKNESS FELT. ALLOW YOUR LAUGHTER TO BE DEATH TO YOUR OWN FEARS, AND BIRTH TO

YOUR ENEMY'S. ALTHOUGH IT IS NATURAL FOR ONE TO DESIRE TO IMITATE THE DEPORTMENT OF A BELOVED PERSON, THERE IS ALSO A TENDENCY TO ECHO THE BEHAVIORS OF THOSE WHOM ONE FEARS, SO THAT THEIR **POWER** MAY BE ATTAINED. YOU MUST NEVER ALLOW YOURSELF TO BECOME INTOXICATED WITH THE **POWER** THAT INFLICTING FEAR UPON OTHERS BRINGS YOU. ALTHOUGH IT MAY BE USEFUL IN TIMES OF DEFENSE, YOU MUST NEVER USE FEAR AS AN OFFENSIVE WEAPON OF CHOICE. IN THE LONG RUN, FRIGHTENING PEOPLE HABITUALLY SHALL CEASE TO WORK, AND YOU SHALL CREATE INTRACTABLE BITTER ENEMIES IN THE PROCESS. SHAME IS NAUGHT BUT THE INTERNALIZED FEAR OF THE OPINIONS OF OTHERS. NO MAN DREADS THAT HIS NAME BE SPOKEN OPENLY, BUT FOR SOME REASON OF POTENTIAL SHAME. AS A **KING**, YOU MUST WITHDRAW TOTALLY FROM PURPOSELY SHAMING OTHERS. GOSSIPING ABOUT PEOPLE, TEARING THEM DOWN, OR TRYING TO LOOK SUPERIOR TO THEM ARE ALL TRICKS THAT ONE EMPLOYS IN ORDER TO CAMOUFLAGE THEIR OWN FEARS OF VULNERABILITY.

6

MASTER, ALL ANXIETIES ARE DUE TO EXPECTATIONS. NERVOUSNESS IS MERELY ENERGY MIXED WITH FEARFUL THOUGHTS. FEAR HAS NO PLACE IN THE DECISIONS OF THE MIND OF A **KING**. UNDER NO CIRCUMSTANCE MUST YOU EVER ALLOW THE SUPPOSITIONS AND ASSUMPTIONS OF YOUR IMAGINATION TO LEAD YOU TO COWARDICE. THERE IS NEVER ANY REASON TO BE AFRAID, NO MATTER WHAT THE PARTICULAR CIRCUMSTANCE, WHETHER THAT CIRCUMSTANCE BE IN THE PRESENT MOMENT, IN THE FUTURE, OR IN DEATH ITSELF. IF SOMETHING OCCURS IN THE PRESENT THAT YOU DEEM WORTHY

OF FEAR, RECALL TO YOUR MIND THAT ON ANY SUBJECT YOU ARE ALWAYS CAPABLE OF FORMING A CORRECT JUDGMENT, AND SOUND OPINION. IF YOU ANTICIPATE SOME FEARFUL THING HAPPENING IN THE FUTURE, REMEMBER THAT YOU SHALL FACE THE FUTURE WITH THE VERY SAME WILL, AND MIND WHICH GUIDES, SUPPORTS, AND SUSTAINS YOU IN THE PRESENT MOMENT. IF DEATH FRIGHTENS YOU, REMIND YOURSELF THAT TO FEAR DEATH IS TO FEAR FREEDOM. IF ONE DOES NOT FEAR DEATH, ONE CANNOT POSSIBLY BE THREATENED OR CONTROLLED BY IT. FEAR SHALL IMPEDE THE FLOW OF YOUR **POWER** AND SERVES ONLY TO NARROW YOUR AWARENESS. IT IS THE ASSASSIN OF OPTIMISM. THE BUTCHER OF ENTHUSIASM. THE MURDERER OF **FAITH**. THE BLINDER OF VISION. THE EXECUTIONER OF POSITIVE AND CREATIVE EFFORT. THE ANNIHILATOR OF SERENITY. WHILE FEAR IS DEBILITATING, IF YOU ALLOW IT TO GROW INTO TERROR, IT SHALL PARALYZE YOU. ONCE TERROR HAS SEIZED YOUR MIND, IT IS LIKE A VICE THAT SHALL CRUSH YOUR WILL. TERROR CAN HAVE TERRIBLE CONSEQUENCES. TERROR SHUTS DOWN YOUR RATIONAL THOUGHT PROCESS AND RENDERS YOU USELESS. THE TURMOIL OF EMOTIONS THAT ARISE FROM TERROR CAUSE TIME AND EVENTS TO MOVE AT A SEEMINGLY UNCONTROLLABLE RATE. HOWEVER, IF YOU LEARN TO KEEP YOUR PRESENCE OF MIND AND RESPOND TO ALL EVENTS WITH GRACE, TIME ITSELF SHALL SEEM TO MOVE MUCH MORE SLOWLY, AND YOUR POISE SHALL OPEN UP POSSIBILITIES THAT TERROR WOULD HAVE OTHERWISE CLOSED OFF.

ALL NEGATIVE EMOTIONS HAVE THEIR FOUNDATIONS IN FEAR, AND ALL NEGATIVE EMOTIONS, SUCH AS HATRED, ANXIETY, ENVY, DISMAY, AND THE LIKE DISRUPT THE ENERGY FLOW OF THE BODY AND CAUSE ILL HEALTH. FEAR RULES BY CREATING DISTORTIONS IN PEOPLE'S **KNOWLEDGE**. THE BEST WAY TO CRIPPLE A

PERSON'S WILL AND DESTROY THEIR CAPACITY TO THINK STRAIGHT IS TO CONSCIOUSLY CREATE UNCERTAINTY, CONFUSION, AND APPREHENSION. FEAR THRIVES ON THE UNKNOWN. THERE IS NONE SO BRAVE THAT THEY ARE NOT DISTURBED BY SOMETHING UNEXPECTED. FAMILIARITY SHALL SOOTHE THE FEARS OF YOUR PEOPLE. MOST ARE ONLY THREATENED, AND THUS FRIGHTENED, WHEN THEIR **KNOWLEDGE** CANNOT EXPLAIN WHAT IS HAPPENING IN THEIR LIFE. ALWAYS BE CONTENT WITH THE UNKNOWABLE OBSCURITY OF UNCERTAINTY. TO BE CONTENT IN ALL SITUATIONS IS TO RID YOURSELF FOREVER OF THOSE IMPLACABLE DEMONS, FEAR, AND DESPAIR. ALL EVIL QUALITIES STEM FROM FEAR. IF YOU CONTROL YOUR FEAR, ALL OF YOUR EVIL QUALITIES SHALL VANISH.

ONE OF THE MOST CLEVER TRICKS THAT FEAR USES TO CONTROL PEOPLE IS TO CONVINCE THEM THAT IT DOES NOT EXIST. YOU MUST FIRST BECOME AWARE OF YOUR WEAKNESSES BEFORE THEY CAN BE TURNED OFF. IN ORDER TO DISCOVER YOUR COURAGE, IT IS A MUST THAT YOU FIRST COME TO KNOW YOUR FEARS. IT IS ONLY BY IDENTIFYING YOUR FEARS THAT YOU SHALL BE ABLE TO TAKE AWAY THEIR COVERT **POWER** TO DETERMINE YOUR THOUGHTS AND DECIDE YOUR ACTIONS. IF YOU FIND YOURSELF POSSESSED BY THE DEMON OF FEAR, WASTE NOT TIME TRYING TO DESTROY THIS DEMON. RATHER FOCUS UPON AND CULTIVATE THE ANGEL OF COURAGE, AND THE DEMON SHALL FLEE OF ITS OWN ACCORD. THE MAN THAT IS REPLETE WITH FEAR HAS NO ROOM LEFT FOR PURPOSE AND VISION. IT IS ONLY WHEN YOU CONQUER THE FEAR AND DOUBT THAT RESIDE WITHIN YOUR MIND, AND FREE YOUR MIND FROM THE AUTOMATIC RESPONSES THAT FEAR AND DOUBT INDUCE, THAT YOU SHALL CONQUER FAILURE AND REALIZE YOUR BOUNDLESS POTENTIAL. ONCE YOU

SUBJUGATE THESE VIRULENT TRAITORS OF THE MIND, ALL OF YOUR THOUGHTS AND ACTIONS SHALL BE ALLIED WITH THEIR TRUE COMPATRIOT, **POWER**, AND ALL OF YOUR CRISES AND DILEMMAS SHALL BE BRAVELY MET AND OVERCOME. ALL FEAR IS BASED UPON LIES OF THE IMAGINATION. IT IS ONLY THE LABELING OF A FEELING THAT GENERATES FEAR AND NOT THE OBJECT OF WHICH YOU ARE AFRAID. FEAR DOES NOT EXIST UNTIL A CERTAIN FEELING THAT YOU HAVE IS LABELED AND OBJECTIFIED AS SUCH, HAS RULES ABOUT HOW YOU SHOULD REACT TO IT, AND IS GIVEN A SPECIFIC CHARACTER AND DEFINITION. WHEN YOU RELINQUISH YOUR THOUGHTS, CONCEPTS, AND EXPECTATIONS CONCERNING THEM, AND SIMPLY OBSERVE YOUR FEARS, YOU SHALL CLEARLY SEE THAT BECAUSE THEY ARE SIMPLY MENTAL PATTERNS THAT YOU HAVE CREATED, AND FORM NO ESSENTIAL PART OF YOUR NATURE, THERE IS NOTHING TO BE AFRAID OF. FEAR IS MERELY A STATE OF MIND. BECAUSE YOU HAVE ALWAYS THE **POWER** TO CHOOSE YOUR STATE OF MIND, YOU NEED TO TOLERATE YOUR FEARS ONLY SO LONG AS YOU WISH. IT IS ALWAYS WITHIN YOUR **POWER** TO LET YOUR FEARS GO. YOU MUST NEVER DWELL UPON THEM OR ATTEMPT TO REASON WITH THEM. FOR THESE ARE MERELY FEAR'S CLEVER DEVICES TO HOLD ON TO YOU. NEVER MAKE THE MISTAKE OF THINKING THAT BEING AFRAID MAKES YOU WEAK, FOR IT DOESN'T. IT SIMPLY MEANS THAT YOU HAVE NOT YET LEARNED HOW TO LET YOUR FEARS GO.

BOOK ELEVEN

1

MASTER, ALL THINGS ARE INTERTWINED AND CONNECTED, AND AS A RESULT OF THIS INTERCONNECTION, A NATURAL INCLINATION KNOWN AS LOVE, WHICH UNITES ALL THINGS IN AWARENESS, IS ALWAYS PRESENT, ALTHOUGH IT IS FELT IN VARYING DEGREES. THE GREATEST GIFT THAT YOU CAN EITHER GIVE OR RECEIVE IS LOVE. IT IS ONLY ONCE YOU REALIZE THAT YOU ARE THE SOURCE OF ALL LOVE THAT YOU SHALL BE ABLE TO FIND IT. THE MOST POWERFUL FORCE IN THE ENTIRE UNIVERSE LIES WITHIN YOUR VERY OWN HEART. LOVE IS THE RECOGNITION OF ONENESS IN THIS WORLD OF DIFFERENCES AND OPPOSITES. IT IS THE RECOGNITION OF ONENESS IN THIS WORLD OF DUALITY. TO LOVE ANOTHER IS TO RECOGNIZE YOURSELF IN ANOTHER. THE REALIZATION OF THE ONENESS OF YOURSELF AND ANOTHER IS TRUE COMPASSION. HOW YOU REACT TO PEOPLE AND CIRCUMSTANCES, PARTICULARLY WHENEVER ADVERSITIES AND DIFFICULTIES ARISE, IS THE BEST INDICATOR OF HOW MUCH YOU TRULY LOVE YOURSELF. LOVE IS THE MOTIVATING FORCE OF THE UNIVERSE, MY SON, AND THE GREATEST OF ALL MOTIVES IS LOVE. DILIGENCE IS GREATLY AIDED BY FEELINGS OF AFFECTION, AND THE ANXIETY TO PLEASE THAT AFFECTION STIMULATES.

IN ORDER TO BE A GREAT KING, IT IS IMPERATIVE THAT YOU LEARN TO MASTER AND DIRECT THE POWER GENERATED BY THE EMOTION OF LOVE. IT SHALL ALWAYS BE BETTER TO RULE WITH THE HEART THAN WITH THE SWORD. A KING THAT IS WISE, NOBLE, AND GOOD, SHALL ALWAYS RULE WITH LOVE. IN ORDER

TO TRULY **LOVE**, YOU MUST MINISTER TO, SACRIFICE FOR, GIVE ATTENTION TO, EMPATHIZE WITH, APPRECIATE, AFFIRM, ENCOURAGE, AND INSPIRE ALL THOSE PEOPLE WHOM YOU **LOVE**. THE GREATER THE CONVICTION WITH WHICH YOU **LOVE**, THE MORE **LOVE** YOU SHALL DRAW UPON YOURSELF. HE THAT LOVES, TRANSMUTES THE NOBILITY AND MAGNIFICENCE OF THAT WHICH HE LOVES INTO HIS VERY OWN GREATNESS. EVEN A MAN WITH BLIND EYES IS ABLE TO SEE MORE THAN HE WHO POSSESSES A BLIND HEART. TO GIVE YOUR HEART TO SOMETHING IS TO GIVE YOUR ALL TO SOMETHING. BE AS FIERCE AND LOYAL IN YOUR **LOVE** AS YOU WOULD BE IN WAR. ONE SHALL ALWAYS BE ABLE TO LEARN A GREAT DEAL ABOUT THE TRUE NATURE OF A PERSON BY SEEING WHAT THEY **LOVE**, OBSERVING THE WAY THAT THEY **LOVE**, AND LEARNING WHY THEY **LOVE**. THERE CAN BE NO TRUE **LOVE** WHERE THERE IS NO SACRIFICE. IT IS IMPOSSIBLE TO TRULY SERVE WITHOUT **LOVE**.

WITHOUT FAIL, THOSE **KINGS** THAT HAVE BECOME TRULY GREAT HAVE OFFERED LOVING SERVICE TO THEIR PEOPLE INCESSANTLY. ALL TRULY GREAT **KINGS** UNDERSTAND THAT TO GIVE OF YOURSELF WITH **LOVE** IS TO LOSE NOTHING AND GAIN EVERYTHING. TO **LOVE** SIMPLY FOR THE JOY OF IT, IS TO NEVER HAVE THAT JOY FALL AWAY. HOWEVER, TO **LOVE** ONLY FOR THE SAKE OF WANTING SOMETHING IN RETURN FROM THOSE WHOM YOU **LOVE**, IS TO SURELY BE DISAPPOINTED IN TIME.

2

MASTER, THE MOST FORTUNATE PEOPLE IN THIS WORLD ARE THOSE THAT HAVE BEEN LOVED SINCE THEIR BIRTH. THERE IS NO FORTUNE WORTH THE PRICE OF TRUE **LOVE**. IT IS A MUCH

GREATER FAULT TO BE FOUND LACKING IN **LOVE** THAN ANYTHING ELSE. TIME IS **LOVE'S** GROWTH SEEN IN DEGREES. **LOVE** IS THAT WHICH BONDS YOU TO THE HARMONIC RHYTHM OF THE UNIVERSE. **LOVE** MAKES ALL THINGS GREAT. FOR **LOVE** IS THE FORCE THAT LURES THE PATTERNS OF MAGNIFICENCE OUT OF THE VOID. THE TREE OF **LOVE** ALWAYS DESIRES TO GROW. YOU ONLY HAVE TO PLANT THE SEEDS. **LOVE** HUMBLES ALL ATTACKERS AND IS IMPREGNABLE IN DEFENSE. **LOVE** ALONE BINDS EVIL. BECAUSE **LOVE** IS CAPABLE OF STEALING FREE WILL, USING NO WEAPON BUT ITSELF, THE EMOTION OF **LOVE** PROVIDES A GREAT EXCUSE FOR EVERY KIND OF FAULT. HOWEVER, MY SON, **LOVE,** ALTHOUGH GREAT, IS NEVER A PLAUSIBLE EXCUSE FOR TREACHERY. **LOVE** IS NOTHING WITHOUT TRUST. YOU SHALL ALWAYS GAIN THE MOST **KNOWLEDGE** ABOUT YOURSELF FROM THOSE YOU INTENSELY **LOVE,** AS WELL AS THOSE YOU INTENSELY DISLIKE. FOR THOSE YOU INTENSELY **LOVE,** REFLECT YOUR HIGHEST ASPIRATIONS, WHILE THOSE YOU INTENSELY DISLIKE REFLECT YOUR DEEPEST FEARS OF WHAT LIES WITHIN YOURSELF. VIOLENCE CAUSES **LOVE** TO BREAK DOWN AND TURNS IT INTO FEAR AND HATRED. A SECOND SPENT IN HATRED IS AN ETERNITY WITHDRAWN FROM **LOVE.** AS VIOLENCE BEGETS VIOLENCE, **LOVE** BEGETS **LOVE.** A FIRE SHALL NEVER STOP A FIRE. ACCEPTING INSULT WITHOUT RETALIATION IS THE HIGHEST PRACTICE. TO POUR **LOVE** ON HATE IS TO POUR WATER ON FIRE. IT SHALL ALWAYS BE WITHIN YOUR **POWER** TO **LOVE** EVEN THOSE WHO HAVE WRONGED YOU. ALWAYS KEEP IN MIND THAT THE MORE YOU **LOVE,** THE MORE LOVABLE YOU BECOME. THOSE THAT WRONG YOU, DO SO UNINTENTIONALLY, OUT OF THEIR OWN IGNORANCE. THOSE WHO DO EVIL CAN NEVER TRULY HARM YOU, AS LONG AS YOU DO NOT SULLY YOUR CONSCIENCE OR DISGRACE YOUR INNER BEING

3

MASTER, THERE IS MUCH MORE GENIUS REQUIRED TO MAKE LOVE THAN IS REQUIRED TO COMMAND ARMIES. THE MORE HEARTS ARE WORTH THE CAPTURE, THE MORE DIFFICULT THEY ARE TO BE WON. A SONGBIRD SHALL ALWAYS SING MUCH MORE GRACEFULLY IF YOU CAN PERSUADE IT TO FLY INTO THE CAGE ON ITS OWN. AS LOVE ARISES FROM AFFECTION, SO AFFECTION IS PROMPTED BY THE BEAUTY OF ATTRACTIVE MANNERS, WISDOM, GRACIOUS SPEECH, CHARMING GESTURES, AND A FEELING THAT ONE IS LOVED ONESELF. ALTHOUGH IT MAY INDEED BE POSSIBLE TO BUY A PERSON'S HAND, IT SHALL NEVER BE POSSIBLE TO PURCHASE THEIR HEART. LOVE CAN ONLY BE ATTRACTED BY LOVE. IT IS ONLY POSSIBLE TO ATTRACT AND HOLD ONTO AS MUCH LOVE AS YOU FEEL FOR YOURSELF. IN ORDER TO BE LOVED AND RESPECTED, YOU MUST FIRST LOVE AND RESPECT YOURSELF.

ALL OF THE WORLD LOVES A LOVER, MASTER. IF YOU WISH TO FIND LOVE IN ANOTHER, YOU MUST FIRST SEE YOURSELF AS LOVABLE. THE MAN WHO SEARCHES OUTSIDE OF HIMSELF FOR LOVE, IS AS FOOLISH AS HE WHO ATTEMPTS TO SEE HIS OWN EYES WITHOUT A MIRROR. IT IS EXTREMELY DIFFICULT FOR ONE TO REFUSE ANYTHING TO ONE BY WHOM THEY FEEL THEY ARE DEARLY LOVED. ONLY HE WHO IS VALUED, ESTEEMED, AND LOVED SHALL BE MISSED IN HIS ABSENCE. EVEN THE MOST DEADLY, DANGEROUS, OBNOXIOUS, AND HATEFUL PERSON HAS A SOFT SPOT SOMEWHERE THAT IS VULNERABLE AND CAPABLE OF BEING ABSORBED BY LOVE. YOU SHALL NEVER CONVINCE

ANOTHER TO **LOVE** YOU BY BEING HATEFUL. IT IS IMPOSSIBLE TO HAVE A BOND WITH SOMEONE THAT YOU REFUSE TO PAY ATTENTION TO. FOR YOU SHALL NEVER UNDERSTAND THAT WHICH YOU DO NOT PAY ATTENTION TO. ATTENTION AND **UNDERSTANDING** DRIVE RELATIONSHIPS FORWARD. **LOVE** SPRINGS FROM **UNDERSTANDING** AND ATTENTION, RATHER THAN MYSTERY. FOR ONE GROWS TO **LOVE** ONLY THOSE THINGS WHICH THEY ARE AWARE OF AND UNDERSTAND. THERE IS NOTHING MORE DREADFUL AND SADDER THAN THE PAINFUL PANGS OF A HOPELESS **LOVE**. FOR EVERYONE ALIVE LOVES TO HAVE THEIR AFFECTIONS RETURNED.

4

MASTER, A **QUEEN**, THE SYMBOL OF LOYALTY IN A KINGDOM, IS THE SOLACE FOR ALL OF THE BITTERNESS IN A **KING'S** LIFE, AND IS THE MUCH-NEEDED COMPENSATION FOR ALL OF HIS RISKS, STRUGGLES, AND SACRIFICES THAT HAVE ALL ENDED IN DISAPPOINTMENT. NO **KING**, NO MATTER HOW PLEASANT, GRACEFUL, OR COURAGEOUS SHALL EVER PERFORM GALLANT ACTS OF CHIVALRY UNLESS THEY ARE INSPIRED BY THE BEAUTY OF A WOMAN. FAR FROM DISTRACTING HIM, A BEAUTIFUL WOMAN SHALL AWAKEN THE MIND OF A **KING** AND MAKE HIM FEARLESS AND BOLD BEYOND MEASURE. WITHOUT WOMEN, MEN WOULD LACK CHARM, AND BE MORE UNCOUTH AND BARBAROUS THAN EVEN A WILD BEAST. ALL THAT A **KING** CAN UNDERSTAND, A **QUEEN** CAN ALSO. WHEREVER A **KING'S** INTELLECT CAN PENETRATE, SO ALONG WITH IT CAN A **QUEEN'S**. THE BEAUTY OF WOMEN IS A SOOTHING BALM THAT CAN ASSUAGE THE ANXIETIES, MISERIES, AND WRETCHED ILL HUMORS THAT AT TIMES OCCUPY THE HEARTS OF MEN. ALWAYS GIVE ALL THE HELP IN

YOUR **POWER** TO LADIES, DAMSELS IN DISTRESS, AND NEVER ON PAIN OF DEATH AND ETERNAL DISGRACE MUST YOU DO ANY EVIL THING TO A WOMAN. WHETHER HE IS TELLING **THE TRUTH** OR NOT, THE MALIGNANT MAN WHO MAKES A VILE BOAST OF HAVING ENJOYED SOME LADY'S FAVORS, DESERVES THE MOST DASTARDLY PUNISHMENT IMAGINABLE. ALTHOUGH IT MAY INDEED BE TRUE THAT SOME WOMEN ARE AFFLICTED BY THE FAULT OF HAVING IRRATIONAL OPINIONS, IN ALL CIRCUMSTANCES AND UNDER ALL CONSIDERATIONS, YOU MUST SHOW RESPECT AND REVERENCE FOR WOMEN, ESPECIALLY IF THERE IS ANY QUESTION OF IMPUGNING THEIR **HONOR**. THE **KING** WHO COULD NOT PUT UP WITH HARSH WORDS FROM A WOMAN WOULD BE OF LITTLE WORTH. WHEN A WOMAN CRITICIZES OR DISPARAGES YOU, IT IS WITH THE INSTINCTIVE AIM OF COMPELLING YOU TO TAKE A SUPERIOR POSITION IN ORDER TO MAKE YOU INTO A SYMBOL OF AWE AND VENERATION, SO THAT SHE MAY THRUST THE ROLE OF HERO UPON YOU. INDEED, MY SON, WOMAN SHALL BE BOTH YOUR CROWNING GLORY AND YOUR GREATEST DANGER. FOR SHE SHALL DEMAND FROM YOU YOUR GREATEST AND RECEIVE IT. BUT ONLY IF YOU HAVE IT IN YOU TO BRING FORTH.

5

MASTER, ROYAL WOMEN WERE MADE FOR ROYAL MEN. MANY OF THE VIRTUES OF ABILITY THAT ARE REQUISITE FOR A **KING** ARE EVEN MORE SO FOR HIS **QUEEN**. IT IS ESSENTIAL THAT BOTH **KING** AND **QUEEN** BE POSSESSORS OF THE ABILITY TO SHUN PRETENTIOUSNESS, THE ABILITY TO BE BOTH ELEGANT AND GRACIOUS, THE ABILITY TO BE WELL-MANNERED, AND THE ABILITY TO BE ADROIT AND PRUDENT, WHILE AT THE SAME TIME POSSESSORS OF THE ABILITY NOT TO BE PROUD, ENVIOUS,

ACRIMONIOUS, VAIN, CONTENTIOUS, OR INEPT. JUST AS IT IS GOOD FOR A **KING** TO DISPLAY A CERTAIN STURDY AND VIGOROUS MANHOOD, SO IT IS FITTING FOR A **QUEEN** TO DISPLAY A CERTAIN SOFT, DELICATE, YET FIRM AND GENTLE TENDERNESS, WITH SUCH AN AIR OF FEMININE SWEETNESS IN HER EVERY MOVEMENT, THAT SHE ALWAYS APPEARS AS AN AMELIORATING REFLECTION OF HER **KING**.

EVERY WOMAN, MY SON, IS EXTREMELY ANXIOUS TO BE BEAUTIFUL OR AT LEAST TO APPEAR SO. WHEN, IN HER OPINION, NATURE HAS FAILED HER IN THIS, SHE SHALL ENDEAVOR TO REMEDY THE FAILURE BY ANY ARTIFICIAL MEANS THAT SHE DEEMS NECESSARY, WHETHER THOSE MEANS BE VIRTUOUS OR NOT. MUCH IS LACKING TO THE WOMAN WHO LACKS THE BEAUTY OF GOODNESS IN HER HEART AND SOUL. MOST WOMEN WHO HAVE THE EXTREME MISFORTUNE TO BE TOO CLOSELY RESTRICTED, OR ABUSED BY THEIR HUSBANDS AND FATHERS, ARE LESS CHASTE THAN THOSE WHO ENJOY A CERTAIN MEASURE OF LIBERTY. IN **LOVE**, MAKE SURE THAT THE WOMAN YOU CHOOSE TO ADMIRE IS ONE THAT REGARDS DISHONOR AS A FATE WORSE THAN DEATH. FOR EVEN SENSIBLE MEN DO THE MOST FOOLISH THINGS WHEN THEY ARE HEAD OVER HEELS IN **LOVE** WITH A DISHONORABLE WOMAN. **LOVE** WITH A WOMAN WHO IS DISHONORABLE AND LAWLESS SHALL INEVITABLY TURN INTO FEAR AND GROW DARK AND WILD. YOU SHOULD APPRECIATE A SMILE, LAUGH, WORD, OR ACT OF GENTLE KINDNESS, HOWEVER SMALL, FROM AN HONORABLE WOMAN, FAR MORE THAN ALL OF THE BLANDISHMENTS, ADULATIONS, AND CARESSES OF DISHONORABLE WOMEN WHO, IF THEY ARE NOT RIBALD AND LASCIVIOUS, WITH THEIR LACK OF SHAME, THEIR LOQUACITY, THEIR BRASHNESS, AND THEIR VULGAR BEHAVIOR CERTAINLY APPEAR TO BE SO. THE WOMAN WHOM YOU

LOVE MUST NOT ONLY BE ABOVE REPROACH, BUT ALSO BEYOND EVEN SUSPICION. NO MAN HAS IT IN HIS **POWER** TO OVERRULE THE DECEITFULNESS OF A WOMAN. YOU MUST NEVER ALLOW YOUR THOUGHTS, EMOTIONS, ACTIONS, OR FATE BE DECIDED BY WHAT A WOMAN DECIDES TO PUT INSIDE OF HER VAGINA.

6

MASTER, ONCE THE FLAME OF LOVE FOR A BEAUTIFUL WOMAN IS BURNING IN YOUR HEART, COWARDICE CAN NEVER POSSESS IT. IF YOU DESIRE TO BE LOVED BY A WOMAN, YOU YOURSELF MUST LOVE, AND BE LOVABLE. THE TENDER AND GENTLE SOULS OF LADIES ARE VERY SUSCEPTIBLE TO HARMONY AND SWEETNESS. ALTHOUGH THEIR INITIAL FEELINGS MAY BE FEAR, THE HEARTS OF WOMEN ARE FILLED WITH ADMIRATION FOR HE WHO IS CALM, AMICABLE, AND HANDSOME. WOMEN SHALL ALWAYS SCRUTINIZE THEIR FIRST IMPRESSIONS FAR MORE THAN ANY OTHER. AT THE BEGINNING, THEIR EYES AND MIND, AVID FOR NOVELTY, TAKE NOTE OF EACH LITTLE THING AND ARE IMPRESSED BY IT, WHEREAS BY AND BY, THEY ARE NOT ONLY SATED, BUT BORED BY WHAT THEY SEE. THE BEST WAY TO WIN ESTEEM FROM LADIES IS TO SERVE AND PLEASE THEM. BECAUSE A TRUE LADY ALWAYS CONSIDERS IT AN INSULT WHEN A MAN SHOWS A LACK OF RESPECT BY SEEKING TO GAIN HER ESTEEM BEFORE HE HAS SERVED HER, A MAN WHO IS TRULY IN LOVE MUST DEVOTE ALL OF HIS THOUGHTS TO SERVING AND PLEASING THE WOMAN THAT HE LOVES. WOMEN WHO ARE BEGGED, ALMOST ALWAYS, REFUSE TO GIVE IN TO THE ONE WHO BEGS THEM. THERE IS NO ENDEAVOR IN ALL THE WORLD MORE WORTHWHILE THAN MAKING A BEAUTIFUL WOMAN SMILE. IF YOU GIVE A WOMAN FRUSTRATION,

YOU SHALL RECEIVE NAUGHT BUT HELL IN RETURN. TWO THINGS A WOMAN SHALL NEVER BE ABLE TO RESIST ARE ATTENTION AND THE PULL OF A SECRET DESIRE THAT HAS COME TO LIFE BEFORE HER VERY EYES.

IN ALL THINGS, WHAT WOMEN MOST DESIRE IS TO HAVE THEIR WILL. IF YOU DESIRE A WOMAN, IT IS OFTEN BEST TO COURT HER SISTER FIRST. MOST WOMEN ARE EXCEEDINGLY CURIOUS, AND THUS EXTREMELY EAGER TO LEARN SECRETS. WITH A WOMAN, A SHARED JOURNEY WITH A BIT OF HARDSHIP SHALL DO MORE TO CREATE A DEEP AND LASTING BOND THAN SHALL EXPENSIVE GIFTS AND VAIN LUXURIES. WHEN GREAT RIVERS DIVIDE INTO NUMEROUS CHANNELS, THEY DIMINISH INTO SMALL STREAMS.

WHEN A MAN GIVES HIS **LOVE** TO MORE THAN ONE WOMAN, IT LOSES MUCH OF ITS FORCE. AS IN EVERYTHING ELSE, IF YOU ARE IN **LOVE** WITH A WOMAN, YOU MUST BE SINCERE AND GENUINE. FOR IF THE DISHONORABLE AND TREACHEROUS BETRAYAL OF EVEN A LUKEWARM ACQUAINTANCE CAN BE PROPERLY HELD TO BE A VILE AND DISGUSTING TRANSGRESSION, CONSIDER HOW MUCH WORSE A CRIME IS THE VILLAINOUS BETRAYAL OF THE WOMAN WHO LOVES YOU. DEVOTE ALL OF YOUR TOILS AND TROUBLES TO THE PRINCIPAL AIM OF THE CONQUEST OF A WOMAN'S BEAUTIFUL SOUL, RATHER THAN VICTORY OVER HER DECAYING FLESH. FOR TO CONQUER THE FORTRESS OF A BEAUTIFUL WOMAN'S MIND, MELT THAT COLD ICE, AND BREAK THOSE HARD DIAMONDS THAT GUARD THE HEART WHICH LIES WITHIN HER GENTLE BREAST, IS TO BE REWARDED WITH THE SPLENDID RADIANCE OF ALL OF HER BEAUTIFUL DEVOTION AND DEDICATION.

A **KING** MUST DEMONSTRATE HIS **LOVE** SO CLEARLY THAT THE WOMAN HE LOVES CANNOT CONCEAL THAT SHE KNOWS SHE

IS LOVED. HE MUST ALWAYS DO THIS WITH THE UTMOST DISCRETION AND MODESTY, AS TO AVOID ANY SUGGESTION OF DISRESPECT. IT IS ALWAYS MILDLY EMBARRASSING FOR A WOMAN TO SEE THAT SHE IS ADORED INTENSELY. FOR MEN CAN DISPLAY THEIR AFFECTIONS AND ENDEARMENTS WITH FAR LESS RISK THAN WOMEN. ABOVE ALL, IT IS ESSENTIAL TO PLEASE THE WOMAN THAT YOU **LOVE**, AND TO AVOID OFFENDING HER WHENEVER POSSIBLE. BEFORE MAKING ANY DECLARATION OF INFATUATION TO A WOMAN, YOU MUST MAKE SURE THAT YOU DO NOT OFFEND HER BY DOING SO. FOR TO OFFEND HER IS TO NOT DECLARE YOUR **LOVE** AT ALL. ALTHOUGH IT IS TRUE THAT IN MATTERS OF **LOVE**, A WOMAN SHOULD ALWAYS HEAR WHAT SHE DESIRES TO BE TOLD. OFTENTIMES, A WOMAN IS BETTER PERSUADED BY WHAT SHE GUESSES THAN BY WHAT SHE HEARS. WHEN YOU WISH TO DECLARE YOUR **LOVE** TO A WOMAN, YOU SHOULD DO SO BY SUBTLE ACTION, SUCH AS SIGHS, GESTURES OF RESPECT, CERTAIN SHYNESSES, OR THE USE OF THE EYES, WHICH COMMUNICATE HIDDEN FEELINGS AND CARRY FAITHFULLY THE MESSAGES WRITTEN IN YOUR HEART MORE EFFECTIVELY THAN ANYTHING ELSE, RATHER THAN VOLUMES OF WORDS AND INCESSANT WAGGING OF THE TONGUE. BY COMMUNICATING IN SUCH A DISCREET MANNER, YOU SHALL VERY OFTEN AROUSE AFFECTION IN THE HEART OF THE WOMAN THAT YOU ADORE. IF YOU DO DECIDE TO DECLARE YOUR AFFECTIONS BY WAY OF SPEAKING OR WRITING, YOU SHOULD DO SO WITH SUCH MODESTY AND CARE THAT YOUR WORDS SEEM WHOLLY AMBIGUOUS AND AFFECT YOUR BELOVED IN SUCH A WAY THAT SHE CAN LEGITIMATELY PRETEND, IF SHE WISHES TO AVOID EMBARRASSMENT, NOT TO UNDERSTAND WHAT IS MEANT BY YOUR WORDS. IT IS IN THIS WAY THAT YOU SHALL BE ABLE, IF YOU RUN INTO DIFFICULTY, TO WITHDRAW EASILY AND PRETEND TO HAVE SPOKEN OR WRITTEN WITH SOME OTHER AIM IN VIEW.

Never follow any other method of trying to deprive your rival of a lady's favor besides that of loving her, serving her, being discreet, humble, and worthier than your rival. Remember always that the man who shows that he is afraid that his lady may leave him for someone else, betrays the fact that he knows that he is inferior in merit and worth to his rival.

BOOK TWELVE

1

Master, in the formation of your kingdom, it shall be essential for you to build a POWER base. Human beings are POWER. A devoted and dedicated army of adherents shall be able to do things for you that money cannot buy, and thus always shall be more valuable than material riches. Only the ignorant feel superior or inferior to anyone else. The wise understand that race, social class, and caste are merely frivolous foolishness, which serve only to obscure and veil the light of the unconditioned potential that lies hidden within each and every individual. If your kingdom is to endure, my son, communication, the glue that holds all kingdoms together, must dwell there. Any kingdom divided, rots from the inside, and shall soon be laid waste. There are three types of people in this world. There are those that shall leave you alone. There are those that shall help you. And there are those that shall try to hurt you. Your greatest dangers in life shall not come from those who openly oppose you and proclaim themselves your enemies, but from counterfeit allies who pretend to support you, while deviously scheming to sabotage you and steal your kingdom. One of the most important attributes that you must cultivate within yourself is the ability to be patient with negative people, without allowing yourself to resent them for their negativity. Negative people are only negative because they feel that this is best. It shall always be a most cruel thing to

RESENT AND BLAME A PERSON FOR PURSUING WHAT APPEARS PROPER AND BENEFICIAL TO THEM. EVEN IF THEY ARE MISTAKEN IN THEIR NEGATIVE VIEW, IT IS NOT NECESSARY THAT YOU BECOME IRRITATED IN ORDER TO ENLIGHTEN THEM. NEITHER IS IT REQUISITE THAT YOU HATE OR RESENT SOMEONE IN ORDER TO WISH TO AVOID AND STAY CLEAR OF THEM.

THE PEOPLE IN YOUR LIFE REFLECT ASPECTS OF YOURSELF. THE FIRST STEP IN ESTABLISHING YOUR THRONE IN RIGHTEOUSNESS IS TO REMOVE THE WICKED FROM BEFORE YOU. ALWAYS SURROUND YOURSELF WITH THOSE WHOM EXCELLENCE IS THE PRIME CHARACTERISTIC OF ALL THEIR ACTIONS. EVEN IF YOU ESTABLISH YOURSELF IN THE BOSOM OF JUSTICE, IF YOU SURROUND YOURSELF WITH THOSE WHO WOULD TAKE BRIBES, YOU SHALL SOON BE OVERTHROWN. IF YOU PAY ATTENTION TO FOOLISHNESS, LIES, DECEPTIONS, OR MENDACITY, YOU YOURSELF SHALL BECOME WICKED. THAT WHICH YOU SURROUND YOURSELF WITH, IS THAT WHICH YOU SHALL BECOME. IT SHALL NEVER BE TO YOUR ADVANTAGE TO BE ASSOCIATED, IN ANY MANNER, WITH THOSE WHO HAVE ACCEPTED IGNORANCE AS THEIR WAY OF LIFE. TIME IS MUCH TOO PRECIOUS OF A RESOURCE TO WASTE SPENDING IT IN A FELLOWSHIP OF PEOPLE WHO CONTRIBUTE NOTHING TO THE WELFARE OF YOUR KINGDOM. THOSE WHO DO NOT INCREASE YOU, SHALL INEVITABLY DECREASE YOU. ANYTIME YOU TOLERATE MEDIOCRITY IN OTHERS, IT INCREASES YOUR OWN. THE FIRST OPINION PEOPLE FORM OF YOU, AND OF YOUR **UNDERSTANDING** COMES BY OBSERVING THOSE THAT YOU HAVE AROUND YOU. IT SEEMS NATURAL FOR LIKE TO ATTRACT LIKE. TO FRATERNIZE WITH THE IGNORANT OR INIQUITOUS IS TO BE TAKEN FOR IGNORANT OR INIQUITOUS. TO ASSOCIATE WITH THE GOOD AND DISCREET IS TO BE TAKEN FOR

GOOD AND DISCREET. WHEN THOSE WHO SURROUND YOU ARE REMARKABLY EXCELLENT AND LOYAL, YOU SHALL ALWAYS BE CONSIDERED TO HAVE EXCELLENT **UNDERSTANDING**. FOR YOU HAVE UNDERSTOOD HOW TO RECOGNIZE THE REMARKABLE AND EARN THEIR LOYALTY. WHEN THOSE AROUND YOU ARE VILE, DISHONORABLE, AND DOUBLE CROSSERS, A GOOD OPINION CANNOT BE FORMED OF YOU BECAUSE OF THE BAD JUDGMENT YOU HAVE SHOWN IN CHOOSING THE PEOPLE YOU SURROUND YOURSELF WITH. TO RUN WITH WOLVES IS TO LEARN TO HOWL. TO ASSOCIATE WITH EAGLES IS TO LEARN TO SOAR TO GREAT HEIGHTS. WHEN LEADING, THOSE THAT YOU LEAD SHALL ALL HAVE THEIR OWN AGENDAS. THE MORE YOU CAN GET YOUR PEOPLE TO THINK OF THE KINGDOM, THE LESS THEY SHALL THINK OF THEMSELVES. TO MAKE THEM FEEL PART OF A GROUP THAT IS FIGHTING FOR SOMETHING WORTHY, TO INVOLVE THEM IN A CRUSADE THAT ALLOWS THEM TO SEE THEIR PERSONAL GLORY AS TIED TO THE GLORY OF THE KINGDOM AS A WHOLE, IS TO DISTRACT THEM FROM PETTINESS AND SATISFY THEIR NEED TO FEEL A PART OF NOBLE GREATNESS.

2

MASTER, TO BE STARVED FOR HUMAN TOUCH IS FAR WORSE THAN TO STARVE FOR BREAD. FAMILY AND TRUE FRIENDSHIPS ARE THE MOST BEAUTIFUL PART OF ANY **KING'S** LIFE. MERCY ONLY COMES FROM FAMILY AND TRUE FRIENDS. YOU CAN TRUST THEM IN A WAY THAT YOU CAN NEVER TRUST ANYONE ELSE. THERE IS NOTHING THAT CAN COMPARE TO FAMILY AND FRIENDS, ESPECIALLY IF THEY HAPPEN TO BE NOBLE AND COMPETENT. THERE ARE NO LOVES NOR HATES SO INTENSE AS THOSE FOUND WITHIN A FAMILY. NEVER FORGET HOW MUCH YOUR MOTHER

SUFFERED WHEN YOU WERE BORN. NEVER SEEK TO GAIN **HONOR** FOR YOURSELF AT YOUR FATHER'S EXPENSE. ONE'S **HONOR** COMES FROM THE RESPECT THAT THEY SHOW TO THEIR PARENTS. THE RELATIONSHIP WITH ONE'S PARENTS IS THE RELATIONSHIP THAT SETS THE TONE FOR ALL SUBSEQUENT RELATIONSHIPS. A CHILD IS CRIPPLED BY NOT BEING ALLOWED TO BECOME WHO AND WHAT THEY CAN BECOME. IF CHILDREN ARE WELL TENDED AND PROPERLY BROUGHT UP, THEY NEARLY ALWAYS RESEMBLE THOSE FROM WHOM THEY SPRANG, AND ARE OFTEN EVEN BETTER. HOWEVER, IF NO ONE GIVES THEM PROPER ATTENTION, THEY GROW WILD, AND NEVER REACH MATURITY. A PARENT'S DUTY IS TO RAISE THEIR CHILDREN WITH EXCELLENCE AND SEE TO IT THAT THEY RECEIVE THE **KNOWLEDGE** TO BE GOOD PEOPLE AND GOOD LEADERS WITH THE CAPACITY TO BE ABLE TO PASS ON THEIR BEAUTIFUL THOUGHTS TO OTHERS. BECAUSE THEY ARE UNABLE TO LET GO OF THE NEED TO BE NEEDED BY THEIR CHILD, SOME PARENTS HAVE A HARD TIME LETTING GO OF BEING A PARENT, EVEN WHEN THE CHILD GROWS INTO BEING AN ADULT. IF A CHILD'S PARENT IS NOT ASSISTING THEM IN THEIR GROWTH, AND IS SIMPLY ATTACHED TO THAT CHILD, PLACING OBSTACLES AND EMOTIONAL PAIN IN THEIR CHILD'S PATH, THAT CHILD HAS NO OBLIGATION TO THAT PARENT, EXCEPT THAT OF EXCELLING THEM IN GOODNESS. HOWEVER STARTLED AND DISAPPOINTED YOU MAY BE BY THE WEAKNESSES YOU OBSERVE IN THOSE YOU ADORE; YOU MUST LOOK AT THEIR CONDUCT OBJECTIVELY FROM ALL SIDES AND FOCUS ONLY UPON THOSE QUALITIES IN THEM WHICH LIFT YOUR SPIRIT AND EDIFY YOUR MIND.

CHILDREN HAVE THE DUTY TO BRING **HONOR** TO THEIR PARENTS. IT IS THROUGH THE CHILDREN THAT THE MOTHER

AND FATHER ARE PRAISED. IT SHALL ALWAYS BE A PAINFUL ENDEAVOR FOR A WISE CHILD TO ATTEMPT TO ADVISE THEIR PARENTS. FOR EVEN IF A CHILD HAS THE ABILITY TO TEACH, IT IS A MOST DIFFICULT THING FOR THE PRIDE OF THEIR PARENTS' HEARTS TO ALLOW THEM TO LEARN. IT IS MOST UNFORTUNATE THAT IT IS SO FATALLY EASY TO MAKE YOUNG CHILDREN BELIEVE THAT THEY ARE HORRIBLE. HE WHO IS NOT A FATHER TO HIS CHILDREN CAN NEVER BE A REAL **KING**. A SON'S **FAITH** BEGINS WITH HIS FATHER. A BOY BECOMES INVISIBLE WHEN HE IS NOBODY'S SON.

3

MASTER, WITHOUT FRIENDSHIP, MEN WOULD BE THE MOST MISERABLE OF ALL OF THE CREATURES THAT WALK UPON THE FACE OF THE EARTH. THE DREAMS OF FUTURE KINGDOMS OFTEN BEGIN SITTING AROUND TALKING TO DEAR FRIENDS. YOU DESTROY YOUR ENEMIES WHEN YOU VIEW THEM AS FRIENDS. NO MATTER WHAT DISASTERS OR CATASTROPHES MAY STRIKE, TRUE FRIENDS SHALL ALWAYS FIND EACH OTHER. YOU SHALL NEITHER ATTAIN NOR RETAIN SUCCESS WITHOUT THE FRIENDLY COOPERATION OF OTHERS. CONCORDANT COORDINATION OF EFFORT IN YOUR KINGDOM SHALL ALWAYS BE FAR MORE IMPORTANT THAN THE INDIVIDUAL SKILL WHICH LIES WITHIN IT. FRIENDSHIP AND HARMONIOUS COOPERATION ARE PRECIOUS AND PRICELESS ASSETS THAT CAN ONLY BE OBTAINED BY GIVING THEM IN RETURN. FRIENDSHIP, LIKE EXCELLENT WINE, SHALL ONLY BECOME STRONGER AS IT GROWS OLDER. A LOYAL, DEVOTED FRIEND IS LIKE A SAFE SHELTER. IF YOU FIND ONE, YOU SHALL BE SAVED FROM THE STORM. MAKE THE PURPOSE OF ANY FRIENDSHIP IN WHICH YOU ARE INVOLVED A SHARED EVOLUTION.

THE REAL PURPOSE OF FRIENDSHIP IS TO ENCOURAGE AND INSPIRE YOUR FRIENDS TO GREATNESS AND VIRTUE, AND TO DETER THEM FROM FOLLY. THERE CAN BE NO FRIENDSHIP WITHOUT CONFIDENCE, AND NO CONFIDENCE WITHOUT GREAT VIRTUE. WHENEVER TWO FRIENDS ARE SEEN, WHOEVER KNOWS ONE, IMMEDIATELY ASSUMES THE OTHER TO BE OF THE SAME CHARACTER. THOSE THAT SHARE A COMMON QUALITY ARE NATURALLY DRAWN TO ONE ANOTHER. JUST AS ANIMALS OF THE SAME SPECIES FLOCK TOGETHER, SO TOO DO PEOPLE PREFER TO KEEP COMPANY WITH THOSE LIKE THEMSELVES. THOSE THAT ARE NOT ALIKE SHALL NOT COME TOGETHER. EVERY CREATURE PREFERS TO ASSOCIATE WITH HIS OWN KIND. FOR THE GOOD OR BAD, YOU BECOME LIKE THOSE WITH WHOM YOU HAVE CLOSE ASSOCIATION. WHOEVER YOUR FRIENDS ARE, YOU SHALL BE ALSO. WHILE A MIRROR REFLECTS A MAN'S FACE, WHAT THAT MAN IS TRULY LIKE IS SHOWN BY THE FRIENDS THAT HE CHOOSES. IT IS ONLY THOSE WHO LOVE PURITY OF HEART, ADORE EXCELLENCE, AND HAVE GRACE ADORNING THEIR LIPS THAT YOU MUST COUNT AS FRIENDS. THERE IS NOTHING THAT CHEERS THE HEART AS MUCH AS THE IMAGES OF GREATNESS THAT ARE REFLECTED IN THE CHARACTER OF GOOD FRIENDS.

4

MASTER, ALTHOUGH IT MAY PROVE DIFFICULT, IT IS IMPERATIVE THAT YOU DEVELOP PATIENCE FOR THOSE WHOSE OPINIONS HAVE NO BASIS IN FACTS. ALTHOUGH YOU MAY NEVER BE ABLE TO CARRY A FRIEND'S BURDEN, YOUR **LOVE** SHALL ALWAYS ENABLE YOU TO CARRY A FRIEND. A TRUE FRIEND WOULD RATHER DIE THEMSELVES THAN ALLOW A FRIEND TO FACE DEATH ALONE. REALLY SEEKING TO UNDERSTAND ANOTHER PERSON IS THE MOST

IMPORTANT STEP IN FORMING RELATIONSHIPS. PEOPLE BECOME FRIENDS BY LISTENING TO EACH OTHER. ALL FRIENDSHIPS EXIST ENTIRELY IN **UNDERSTANDING**. THE DETERMINING FACTOR IN ANY FRIENDSHIP IS THE LEVEL OF **UNDERSTANDING** INVOLVED IN THAT FRIENDSHIP. GENUINE FRIENDSHIPS EXIST ONLY WHEN THERE IS AN OUTWARD FLOW OF OPEN AND ALERT ATTENTION TOWARDS THE OTHER PERSON, IN WHICH THERE IS DESIRE FOR NOTHING BESIDES **UNDERSTANDING**. THOSE WHO TRULY UNDERSTAND YOU SHALL SHARE WITH YOU NOT ONLY YOUR GREATNESS, BUT ALSO YOUR DESPERATION TO REALIZE THAT GREATNESS. NEVER MAKE CAPRICIOUS, OR EXTRAVAGANT DEMANDS UPON YOUR FRIENDS. HE WHO NEVER EXPECTS GRATITUDE FROM A FRIEND SHALL ALWAYS BE PLEASANTLY ASTONISHED WHEN THAT FRIEND DOES SHOW GRATITUDE. LEARN HOW TO ACCEPT THE APPARENT TRIBUTES, FAVOR, AND GIFTS OF FRIENDS WITHOUT ARROGANTLY FEIGNING INDIFFERENCE TO THEM OR FEELING YOURSELF UNDER OBLIGATION BECAUSE OF THEM. BECAUSE THEY HAVE SURELY DONE SO OUT OF IGNORANCE, AND A MISTAKEN VIEW, BE QUICK TO ACCEPT THE APOLOGY OF ANY TRUE FRIEND WHO HAS HURT OR OFFENDED YOU.

IN ORDER TO KEEP YOUR FRIENDS FAITHFUL AND BE LOVED AND HONORED BY THEM, YOU MUST STUDY THEM, **LOVE** THEM, **HONOR** THEM, ENRICH THEM, DO THEM KINDNESSES, AND SHARE WITH THEM BOTH YOUR GLORY, AND YOUR CONCERNS. BE A LOYAL AND STEADFAST FRIEND THAT IS COURTEOUS, COMPASSIONATE, GENEROUS, AFFABLE, AND CHARMING AS A COMPANION. BE VIGOROUS AND DILIGENT IN PROMOTING THE **HONOR** OF YOUR FRIENDS, WHETHER THEY ARE ABSENT OR PRESENT. TOLERATE THEIR NATURAL AND EXCUSABLE DEFECTS,

AND NEVER BREAK WITH THEM FOR TRIFLING REASONS. DEPART FROM THOSE WHO SHOW DISHONOR, ARE ARROGANT, REVEAL YOUR SECRETS, OR TURN ON YOU UNEXPECTEDLY. JUST AS THROWING A STICK AT A BIRD IS TO CAUSE IT TO FLY AWAY, TO INSULT A FRIEND IS TO BREAK UP A FRIENDSHIP. NOT ONLY WELCOME, BUT ENCOURAGE PLAIN-SPOKEN DISAGREEMENT WITH YOUR OPINIONS, AND ALWAYS DELIGHT IN BEING SHOWN A BETTER WAY. DO NOT BE LIKE THOSE WHO ARE CONTENTIOUS OVER EVERY TRIFLING THING AT ALL THE WRONG TIMES. THOSE WHO SEEK TO CENSOR WHAT THEY DO NOT DO THEMSELVES. THOSE WHO ALWAYS FIND CAUSE TO COMPLAIN OF THEIR FRIENDS, WHICH IS A MOST HORRID HABIT. THOSE WHO ALWAYS PUSH IN FRONT OF OTHERS, IN ORDER TO SECURE THE FIRST AND MOST HONORED PLACE FOR THEMSELVES. RESPECT ALL OF YOUR FRIENDS ACCORDING TO THEIR WORTH AND MERIT, AND ASSOCIATE MORE WITH THOSE WHO ARE HIGHLY REGARDED, NOBLE, AND RECOGNIZED AS WISE, THAN WITH THOSE WHO ARE UNCOUTH, INDOLENT, AND OF LITTLE WORTH, SO THAT YOU IN TURN MAY BE ADORED AND VENERATED BY THE GREAT AND BE NUMBERED AMONGST THEM.

5

MASTER, THE SADDEST THING ABOUT BETRAYAL IS THAT IT ALWAYS COMES FROM A FRIEND. FOR THE LAMB, THE FRIENDSHIP OF THE WOLF IS A DECEITFUL TRAP. AFFECTED SINCERITY IS A SNARE. A FRIEND CAN HARDLY BE A FRIEND IF HE IS ALSO YOUR BETRAYER. THOSE FRIENDS THAT REFUSE TO HELP YOU CLIMB DO SO BECAUSE THEY DESIRE YOU TO CRAWL. JUST AS TERMITES CAN SILENTLY DESTROY THE MOST SOLID AND STURDY WOOD, SO TOO CAN ENVY SILENTLY DESTROY THE MOST DEPENDABLE FRIENDSHIPS.

Anyone who turns traitor once, is sure to do so again as soon as fortune shines upon a new master. You must never trust one that would betray his own people. Harmony is easier achieved with two instruments than several. To have one close and intimate friend is better than to have many. However, although it may indeed be wise to **LOVE** and secure one person above all others according to merit, worth, and excellence, it is most unwise to trust so much in this tempting trap of familiarity as to have cause for repentance later on. It is foolish to trust anyone or anything completely besides yourself. There are so many clandestine secrets and recesses in the minds of men that it is nearly impossible to discover and discern all of the insincere charlatanism that may be hidden there.

In life, you must arm yourself with discretion and never completely lie down those arms, not even for friends. Never allow words from an enemy to terrify you, nor advice from a colleague to beguile you. Desire is a most contagious disease. If someone sees that you are desired by another, for no other reason besides this one, they shall find you desirable as well. Some shall attempt to use the cover of friendship as a means to disguise their aggressive ambitions. They shall offer assistance and alliance, so that they may do you harm, or advance their own interest at your expense. In times of prosperity, it is a most difficult thing to tell who your true friends are. However, in adverse times, they shall be impossible to miss.

As a magnet attracts metal, so too does the wealth that

A MAN POSSESS ATTRACT THE GREED THAT RESIDES WITHIN THE HEARTS OF MEN. THE POSSESSION OF MATERIAL WEALTH SHALL ATTRACT MANY WHO PROFESS FRIENDSHIP THAT THEY DO NOT GENUINELY FEEL. THE LOSS OF OPULENCE DISCLOSES THE TRUE IDENTITY OF ALL WHO PROCLAIM THEMSELVES AS FRIENDS. EVEN IF WHAT HE SAYS IS FOLLY, WHEN A RICH PERSON SPEAKS, EVERYONE SHALL BE SILENT, AND WHEN HE IS DONE, THEY SHALL ALWAYS PRAISE HIM TO THE SKIES FOR WHAT HE SAYS. WHEN ONE IS SUCCESSFUL, EVEN THOSE THAT HATE HIM, SHALL PRETEND TO BE HIS FRIENDS. THOSE FRIENDSHIPS THAT ARE OBTAINED BY ANY OTHER MEANS BESIDES MAGNANIMOUS NOBILITY OF MIND MAY INDEED BE GARNERED, BUT THEY SHALL NEVER BE SECURE, AND IN TIMES OF HARDSHIP, THEY CANNOT BE RELIED UPON. WHENEVER YOU OBSERVE ONE WHOM YOU WISH TO CONSIDER A FRIEND, THINKING MORE OF THEIR OWN WELFARE THAN YOURS, AND SEEKING INWARDLY THEIR OWN ADVANTAGE IN EVERYTHING, UNDERSTAND IMMEDIATELY THAT SUCH A PERSON SHALL NEVER MAKE A GOOD FRIEND, NOR SHALL YOU EVER BE ABLE TO TRULY TRUST THEM WITH WHAT IS MOST DEAR TO YOU.

BOOK THIRTEEN

1

MASTER, IT IS ONLY BY SEEING THINGS FOR WHAT THEY ARE, THAT YOU SHALL BE ABLE TO USE THEM FOR WHAT THEY ARE WORTH. JUST AS YOU ARE THE **KING** OF YOUR KINGDOM, **THE TRUTH** IS THE **KING** OF THE UNIVERSE. **THE TRUTH** IS THE SOURCE AND CAUSE OF ALL THINGS. **THE TRUTH** IS THE ONLY TEACHER IN THE UNIVERSITY OF LIFE AND THE ONLY SUBJECT THAT IT TEACHES IS ITSELF. DESPITE THE VULGAR OPINIONS OF THE MASSES, HARMONY AND GRACEFULNESS ARE THE INEFFACEABLE TRUTH OF THE UNIVERSE. **THE TRUTH** IS THE STANDARD AGAINST WHICH ALL ELSE IN YOUR KINGDOM MUST BE MEASURED. THE STANDARD OF TRUTH, BY WHICH YOU MUST JUDGE YOUR KINGDOM, IS PEACE. BEAUTY IS **THE TRUTH**, AND **THE TRUTH** IS BEAUTY. **THE TRUTH** IS PERFECTION, AND PERFECTION IS **THE TRUTH**. WHEN **THE TRUTH** RULES YOUR KINGDOM, **LOVE** SHALL REIGN SUPREME. WHERESOEVER **THE TRUTH** STANDS, **UNDERSTANDING** SHALL STAND ALONGSIDE OF IT. IT IS ONLY BY THOROUGHLY **UNDERSTANDING** AND LIVING IN HARMONY WITH **THE TRUTH** THAT ONE SHALL BE ABLE TO BE A SOURCE OF GRACE AND BEAUTY TO ALL. IN THE NAME OF **THE TRUTH**, A **KING** MUST BE WILLING TO SACRIFICE EVERYTHING. JUST AS FLOWERS CANNOT BE FORCED TO OPEN, BUT OPEN TO PERFECTION GRADUALLY AND GRACEFUL IN THE LIGHT OF THE SUN, SO TOO MUST YOU AS **KING** OPEN YOUR KINGDOM TO PERFECTION BY SHINING UPON ALL THE LIGHT OF **THE TRUTH**.

2

Master, the sword of truth shall forever give POWER to your hand. The entire universe is but a single, living entity possessed of one substance, THE TRUTH. THE TRUTH is the source of POWER, and the force that not only moves the universe, but holds it together as well. POWER was the first created. THE TRUTH has always existed. Desires, circumstances, and perception shall come and go. However, the foundation of your being, which is THE TRUTH, is forever unchanging. No matter what one becomes, one shall always "BE." THE TRUTH never tries to be anything. It simply is what it is. There is no need to dress up THE TRUTH, and THE TRUTH needs no defense. THE TRUTH always has the POWER to stand alone. THE TRUTH is beyond all belief. Therefore, THE TRUTH needs no one to believe in it. THE TRUTH simply is, and is magnificent, whether one believes it or not. THE TRUTH is like a great rock jutting from the turbulent sea. Solid and immovable, whether you like, or even choose to acknowledge it.

A soul that is shipwrecked should never curse the rock because it is solid and immovable. On the contrary, it should cling to that rock because it is solid and immovable. For that rock is the only refuge from the raging waters. Although the shadows of ignorance may appear to be dark, they are exposed to be as nothing before the light of THE TRUTH. Everyone prospers, and everything is fulfilled around the KING who is

ALWAYS ON THE SIDE OF **THE TRUTH**. ALTHOUGH MEN SHALL AT TIMES FORGET **THE TRUTH**, TO THE UNIVERSE NOTHING ELSE EXISTS. THERE IS NOTHING AS UNCOMPROMISING AS JUSTICE. ALTHOUGH THE MORAL CURVE OF THE UNIVERSE MAY INDEED BE LONG, IT SHALL ALWAYS BEND TOWARDS **THE TRUTH**. TIME AND **THE TRUTH** SHALL EVENTUALLY CORRECT ALL EVILS, AND RIGHT ALL WRONGS. ONLY RESPECT FOR **THE TRUTH** SHALL ALLOW ONE TO LIVE TRUTHFULLY. LEARNING TO ACCEPT **THE TRUTH** IS THE FIRST STEP TOWARD GAINING CONTROL OF YOUR FATE. ANYTHING IS POSSIBLE ONCE ONE IS ABLE TO PERCEIVE **THE TRUTH**.

NEVER ALLOW ANYONE ELSE TO WRITE THE STORY OF YOUR LIFE. TO TAKE RESPONSIBILITY OF YOUR DESTINY, IT IS ONLY NECESSARY FOR YOU TO TAKE RESPONSIBILITY FOR YOUR OWN PERSONAL TRUTH. THE EVENTS IN YOUR LIFE SHALL ALWAYS REFLECT YOUR PERSONAL TRUTH. FOR YOUR PERSONAL TRUTH IS THE SUM TOTAL OF ALL OF YOUR THOUGHTS, WORDS, AND ACTIONS.

3

MASTER, IN THE LAND OF THE BLIND, ONLY THE ONE-EYED MAN IS KING. KINGS ARE THOSE PRECIOUS FEW IN EXISTENCE WHO TRULY KNOW AND UNDERSTAND **THE TRUTH**. THERE IS ONLY ONE ABSOLUTE TRUTH, AND ALL OTHER TRUTHS ARE BUT EMANATIONS OF IT. ALL ARE BUT DIFFERENT MANIFESTATIONS OF THE SAME ENTITY, WHICH IS **THE TRUTH**. ALTHOUGH EVERYTHING IS MADE FROM THE ONE ESSENCE OF **THE TRUTH**, DIFFERENT NAMES HAVE BEEN GIVEN TO THE INFINITE FORMS THAT IT TAKES. IF YOU ARE ABLE TO SEE BEYOND THE REALM OF WORDS, BEYOND THE REALM OF NAME, AND BEYOND

THE REALM OF FORM, YOU SHALL BE ABLE TO SEE **THE TRUTH**. THE UNIVERSE, WHICH IS **THE TRUTH**, SHALL FOREVER REMAIN THE SAME, NO MATTER HOW MANY CHANGES APPEAR TO TAKE PLACE WITHIN IT. IF YOU WISH TO SEE **THE TRUTH**, YOU MUST REMOVE THE LABEL FROM THAT WHICH YOU PERCEIVE. ONE CAN NEVER KNOW **THE TRUTH** UNTIL IT IS REVEALED. WHILE THE GLORY AND GREATNESS OF THE UNIVERSE LIE MANIFEST IN ITS ABILITY TO CONCEAL **THE TRUTH**, THE GLORY AND GREATNESS OF A **KING** LIE MANIFEST IN HIS ABILITY TO DISCERN IT. JUST AS IT IS ONLY BY MUCH DIGGING AND EXPLORATION THAT GOLD, DIAMONDS, AND RUBIES ARE OBTAINED, SO TOO IS IT ONLY BY SEARCHING DEEP WITHIN THE MINE OF HIS SOUL THAT A **KING** SHALL BE ABLE TO DISCOVER **THE TRUTH**. WHEN YOU BEGIN TO SEE YOURSELF AS THE POINT AROUND WHICH EVERYTHING IS REVOLVING, YOU SHALL BEGIN TO PERCEIVE **THE TRUTH** OF THE UNIVERSE. ONCE YOU DISCOVER **THE TRUTH** OF THE UNIVERSE, THE WHOLE WORLD SHALL BECOME YOURS.

TO SEE THE GOOD IN OTHERS, YOU MUST FIRST SEE **THE TRUTH** WITHIN YOURSELF. **THE TRUTH**, ALTHOUGH PRESENT AND VISIBLE AT ALL TIMES, AND UNMISTAKABLE ONCE DISCERNED, IS ALWAYS CONCEALED IN PLAIN SIGHT, AND RARELY IF EVER ACKNOWLEDGED. IN ORDER TO PERCEIVE IT, ONE MUST FIRST LEARN TO FOCUS, SO THAT ONE MAY BE ABLE TO QUIET THE TURMOIL INSIDE OF ONE'S BEING. IT IS ONLY THIS TURMOIL THAT PREVENTS ONE FROM APPREHENDING **THE TRUTH**. WHEN PEOPLE'S EMOTIONS ARE ENGAGED, IT IS NEARLY IMPOSSIBLE FOR THEM TO SEE **THE TRUTH** AS IT TRULY IS. ANALYSIS AND SEEING **THE TRUTH** ARE BOTH DEPENDENT UPON SELF-CONTROL. BECAUSE **THE TRUTH** CAN BE

EXPERIENCED ONLY IN THE COMPLETE SILENCE OF THE MIND, IT IS IMPOSSIBLE TO COMMUNICATE WITH, OR REALIZE **THE TRUTH**, WITHOUT A CALM MIND AS ONE'S INSTRUMENT. THE ONLY REAL TRUTH TO BE FOUND IN THIS WORLD IS **THE TRUTH** THAT IS FOUND IN SILENCE. **THE TRUTH** NEEDS NO WORDS TO EXPRESS ITSELF. ONLY LIES DO. WHILE WORDS MAY INDEED POINT YOU TO **THE TRUTH**, THEY MUST NEVER BE CONFUSED WITH **THE TRUTH**. IT IS IMPOSSIBLE FOR ONE TO FULLY EXPRESS **THE TRUTH**. ONE CAN ONLY PERCEIVE IT. IN ORDER TO EXPRESS TRUTH, ONE MUST USE WORDS AND SYMBOLS THAT CAN ONLY REPRESENT OR SYMBOLIZE TRUTH. **THE TRUTH** SPEAKS LOUDER THAN WORDS. IT IS IMPOSSIBLE TO FILL YOUR SOUL WITH TRUTH, UNTIL YOU FIRST EMPTY IT OF ALL OF YOUR BELIEFS AND OPINIONS. ONCE YOU CEASE TO CHERISH YOUR OPINIONS, **THE TRUTH** SHALL NATURALLY ARISE. IT IS ONLY WHEN ONE DOES NOT FOCUS UPON AN ASSUMPTION, THAT THEY CAN SEE **THE TRUTH**.

DUALITY HAS TWO SIDES. THE OBJECT OF PERCEPTION, WHICH IS **THE TRUTH**, AND ONE'S INTERPRETATION OF **THE TRUTH**, WHICH IS MERELY A POINT OF VIEW. BOTH SIDES OF ANY ARGUMENT ARE EQUALLY TRUE. THE BELIEF THAT ONE IS IN SOLE POSSESSION OF **THE TRUTH**, IS A BELIEF THAT CAN CORRUPT ONE'S ACTIONS AND THOUGHTS TO THE POINT OF TYRANNICAL MADNESS. A PERSON'S BELIEF SYSTEM OR RELIGION DOESN'T NECESSARILY SHOW THEM WHAT IS TRUE, BUT ONLY WHAT THEY BELIEVE. **THE TRUTH** DOES NOT NEED A VERSE ATTACHED TO IT IN ORDER TO BE TRUE. ONLY INFORMATION IS GIVEN IN BOOKS. NOT THE TRUTH. AT ALL COSTS, YOU MUST ALWAYS REMAIN OPEN TO THE RECEPTION OF **THE TRUTH**. NEVER MISTAKE YOUR EDUCATION FOR **KNOWLEDGE** OF

THE TRUTH. Seeing the world through old expectations and beliefs only reinforces ignorance and covers up **THE TRUTH**.

4

Master, the man who refuses to listen shall never even hear, much less comprehend **THE TRUTH**. **THE TRUTH** shall never become known unless one first seeks it out for themselves. If something is true, it matters not that a billion to one believe it not. Truth can never be established by consensus. The greatest impediment to the development of the ability to know **THE TRUTH** is the delusion of determining what is valid through the fact that the masses hold a certain belief. When information concerning **THE TRUTH** is offered gratuitously, the ignorant shall resent this, and even the wisest **KING** shall not be able to communicate it effectually. When bringing **THE TRUTH** to those who are ignorant of it, you shall always be more effective if you are responding to a person who is making inquiries concerning it. Just as the closer one gets to a dog's bone, the more that dog shall bark. The closer one gets to a truth about a person that doesn't want that information found out, the more that person shall cry out. Like a man whose head is on fire, and running for water to put it out, nothing shall be able to stop a sincere seeker of **THE TRUTH**.

No habit produces nobility of the spirit, like the habit of examining methodically and honestly everything that you encounter in this life and determining its true place

IN THE ORDER OF THINGS. INFORMATION BASED ON GOSSIP AND OPINIONS ARE LIKE PEBBLES IN A POND. PLENTIFUL AND FREE. HOWEVER, FACTS AND TRUTH ARE LIKE RARE AND PRECIOUS JEWELS. FOR THEIR PRICE IS THE METICULOUS LABOR NECESSARY TO EXAMINE THEM FOR VERACITY. LOOK THOROUGHLY INTO ALL SITUATIONS AND SEE THEM FOR WHAT THEY REALLY ARE. DO WHAT IS RIGHT AND SPEAK ONLY **THE TRUTH** WITH EVERY FIBER OF YOUR BEING. ALLOW **THE TRUTH** TO PERMEATE YOUR THOUGHTS AND WELCOME IT AS THE SOURCE FROM WHICH YOUR VERY BEING FLOWS. HAVE GREATNESS IN YOUR ACTIONS, SPEECH THAT REFUSES TO UTTER DECEPTION, AND A DISPOSITION GLAD OF WHATEVER COMES.

NO MAN SHALL EVER FULLY UNDERSTAND A TRUTH UNTIL HE HAS STRUGGLED AGAINST IT. THE ONLY TRUTH THAT YOU MUST KNOW ABOVE ALL OTHERS, IS **THE TRUTH** OF YOURSELF. YOU MUST NOT ONLY ACQUIRE TRUTH, YOU MUST LIVE IT AS WELL. IT IS ONLY BY LIVING A TRUTH THAT ONE MAKES IT TRUE TO THEM. WITHOUT MANIFESTATION, **THE TRUTH** CANNOT BE USED, UNDERSTOOD, OR REALIZED. YOU DELIVER YOUR MESSAGE EACH AND EVERY TIME YOU SPEAK. IF YOU DO NOT DELIVER **THE TRUTH**, IT IS BECAUSE YOU HAVE NOT GAINED A TRUE **KNOWLEDGE** OF YOURSELF. LIFE BRINGS ALL SITUATIONS, AND EACH LIFE CONTAINS ITS OWN TRUTH. WHAT IS TRUE ONE TIME IS NOT ALWAYS TRUE THE NEXT. EVERY MOMENT CONTAINS ITS OWN REVELATION. ACCEPT A THING BEFORE YOU ATTEMPT TO CHANGE IT. FOR TO ACCEPT SOMETHING IS TO SEE ITS TRUTH.

5

Master, never allow any difficulty of hardship to cause you to abandon **THE TRUTH.** Just as gold and diamonds remain beautiful, whether they are praised or slandered, kindness, truth, and humility remain beautiful no matter what the opinions of others may say. Every fool confuses their opinions and viewpoints with fact. Many are those who have been misled by opinions. Wrong ideas can warp the judgment of even the most intelligent. Oftentimes, amongst the masses, **THE TRUTH** is drowned in a sea of opinions. Though an opinion may not be true and be totally false, that opinion can become so convincing that people begin to believe in it. Once a person begins to believe in any opinion, that opinion shall gain control over them, whether it is truth or not. Opinions and rumors are merely the hopeful fancies of folly. In serious matters concerning your kingdom, it is of the utmost necessity that you always demand evidence concerning the veracity of the information furnished you. **THE TRUTH** is a wind that blows away the poisonous gas clouds of false opinion. Because the world is ruled by force, opinion uses force to accomplish his goals. **THE TRUTH** is always the first casualty in a war of opinions. Each position in every conflict has its own truth, as felt by each side. Any truth that a man can utter is but a half truth.

6

MASTER, THE MAJORITY OF THE FACTS AND BELIEFS THAT MOST PEOPLE HOLD AS TRUTH ARE NOT TRUE AT ALL. ONLY THE TRULY WISE ARE ABLE TO CONSISTENTLY DISCERN THE DIFFERENCE BETWEEN LIES AND **THE TRUTH**, YET THE IGNORANT ARE SO ARROGANT IN THEIR BELIEFS THAT THEY ALWAYS CAN, THAT IT SHALL ALWAYS BE EXCEEDINGLY EASY TO FOOL THEM. BELIEVING IN LIES IS HOW ONE CREATES THEIR OWN PERSONAL HELL. KNOWING **THE TRUTH** IS HOW ONE IS ABLE TO CREATE THEIR OWN PERSONAL HEAVEN. EMOTIONAL PAIN SHALL BECOME YOUR PERPETUAL COMPANION WHEN A LIE IS THE FOUNDATION OF YOUR LIFE. ALMOST ANYONE CAN BE CONVINCED TO BELIEVE ALMOST ANYTHING. PEOPLE SHALL WILLINGLY BELIEVE A LIE WHEN THEY WISH IT TO BE TRUE, OR WHEN THEY ARE AFRAID THAT IT MAY BE TRUE. TO FEAR THAT SOMETHING IS TRUE IS TO ACCEPT THE POSSIBILITY THAT IT MAY BE TRUE. TO ACCEPT THE POSSIBILITY THAT SOMETHING MAY BE TRUE IS THE FIRST STEP IN MAKING IT YOUR PERSONAL TRUTH. REMAIN ETERNALLY WATCHFUL AND CONTINUALLY SEEK **THE TRUTH** IN EVERY SITUATION. EVEN THE FEELINGS OF THE BEAUTIFUL EMOTION OF AFFECTION MAY CLOUD YOUR VISION AND CAUSE YOU TO COLOR EVENTS TO COINCIDE WITH YOUR DESIRES. THAT WHICH APPEARS AS TRUTH AT ONE TIME AND DISAPPEARS LIKE A MIST AFTER A WHILE IS A LIE. **THE TRUTH** IS THAT WHICH PERSISTS AT ALL TIMES AND IN ALL CIRCUMSTANCES.

REAL IS THAT WHICH IS PERMANENT. THE UNREAL IS THAT WHICH CHANGES. **THE TRUTH** HAS NO NEED TO PROVE ITSELF. IT EXISTS WHETHER ONE BELIEVES IT OR NOT. LIES, ON THE OTHER HAND, EXIST ONLY IF SOMEONE CREATES THEM, AND

THEY SURVIVE ONLY IF ONE BELIEVES IN THEM. NOTHING CAN EVER BE TAKEN AWAY FROM **THE TRUTH**. ONE CAN ONLY COVER IT WITH LIES. A LIE WITH A HEART OF TRUTH IS A MOST POWERFUL AND DANGEROUS THING. SKEPTICISM SHALL REVEAL **THE TRUTH** AND DESTROY ALL LIES. THE DARKNESS OF LIES STANDETH NOT A CHANCE IN THE PRESENCE OF THE BRILLIANT EFFULGENCE OF **THE TRUTH**. THE MERE RECOGNITION OF THE LIE IS ALREADY THE ARISING OF **THE TRUTH**. A **KING** MUST ALWAYS SCRUTINIZE WHAT HE HEARS EXTENSIVELY. FOR WHILE SOME OF WHAT IS HEARD IS TRUE, MOST OF WHAT IS HEARD IS NOT. IT SHALL ALWAYS BE BETTER TO ASK A QUESTION AND GET **THE TRUTH**, RATHER THAN MAKE AN ASSUMPTION AND GET A LIE. REALIZATION OCCURS WHEN ONE IS ABLE TO SEE THE SIMPLICITY OF **THE TRUTH** HIDDEN BEHIND THE SOPHISTICATED COMPLICATION OF LIES. WHILE YOU MUST ALWAYS RESPECT SOUND LEARNING AND THOSE WHO SEEK **THE TRUTH**, YOU MUST ALSO ALWAYS REMAIN ON GOOD TERMS WITH ALL THE REST, BUT FROM A SAFE DISTANCE.

7

MASTER, FOOLISH IS THE FEAR THAT THIS LIFE SHALL SOMEDAY END. FOR THIS IS AN INEVITABILITY. WISE INDEED, HOWEVER, IS THE FEAR THAT A LIFE THAT IS IN HARMONY WITH **THE TRUTH** MAY NEVER BEGIN. HE WHO REFUSES TO ACCEPT **THE TRUTH** IS DESTINED TO BE ASSASSINATED BY LIES. THE GREATEST AND MOST FOOLISH FEAR IN THIS WORLD IS THE FEAR OF **THE TRUTH**. FEAR, PRIDE, AND IGNORANCE ARE MUCH MORE INTERESTED IN THEIR SELF-PRESERVATION THAN THEY ARE IN **THE TRUTH**. **THE TRUTH** HAS NEVER TRULY HARMED ANYONE. MANY PEOPLE ARE AFRAID OF **THE**

TRUTH BECAUSE THEY HAVE LEARNED TO BELIEVE IN SO MANY LIES. HARM COMES FROM CONTINUING IN SELF-DECEPTION, PERSISTING IN ERROR, AND CLINGING TO IGNORANCE. ANY ATTEMPT TO CONCEAL **THE TRUTH** SHALL ULTIMATELY PROVE FUTILE. **THE TRUTH**, LIKE OIL IN WATER, SHALL ALWAYS RISE TO THE SURFACE. NEVER DENY **THE TRUTH** SIMPLY BECAUSE IT IS ACCOMPANIED BY PAIN. ONE GETS TO CHOOSE NOT WHAT IS TRUE, ONLY WHAT THEY SHALL DO WITH IT. THERE ARE NO ARGUMENTS OR DISCUSSIONS THAT CAN REVEAL **THE TRUTH** TO THOSE WHO ARE NOT YET READY OR EVOLVED ENOUGH TO RECEIVE IT. THE MAJORITY OF THE PEOPLE YOU SHALL ENCOUNTER IN THIS LIFE SHALL NOT BE PREPARED TO HEAR **THE TRUTH**. OPPOSITION TO **THE TRUTH** IS INEVITABLE, ESPECIALLY IF IT TAKES THE FORM OF A NEW IDEA. ALWAYS USE **WISDOM** AND GREAT CAUTION BEFORE REVEALING THE WHOLE TRUTH OF A MATTER TO A PERSON. DIMINISH THE DEGREE OF RESISTANCE TO **THE TRUTH** BY NOT ONLY GIVING THOUGHT TO THE AIM, BUT ALSO TO THE METHOD OF APPROACH. AVOID DIRECT ATTACKS ON LONG-ESTABLISHED POSITIONS. INSTEAD, LEARN TO TURN THE DISCUSSION, SO THAT A MORE PENETRABLE SIDE IS EXPOSED TO THE THRUST OF THE SWORD OF TRUTH. A PERSON SHOULD NEVER BE CONDEMNED BECAUSE THEY BELIEVE A LIE, BUT RATHER BECAUSE THEY REFUSED TO BELIEVE **THE TRUTH** WHEN IT WAS PRESENTED BEFORE THEM. ONLY A FOOL IS FOOLISH ENOUGH TO ARGUE WITH A TRUTH THAT HAS BEEN DEMONSTRATED.

BOOK FOURTEEN

1

MASTER, PATIENCE PRODUCES IMMEDIATE RESULTS. THE MOST IMPORTANT OF THESE RESULTS IS SERENITY OF MIND, WITH WHICH ALL MAY BE ACCOMPLISHED. SERENITY IS THE KEY TO THE LOCKED VAULTS OF **WISDOM**, **POWER**, AND **UNDERSTANDING**. COURAGE IS MERELY THE REALIZATION OF YOUR INNER SERENITY DURING TIMES OF DISTRESS. TO MASTER THE ABILITY TO BE SERENE IN DIFFICULT SITUATIONS IS TO ALWAYS FIND THE COURAGE TO FACE THEM. ANY **KING** WITHOUT SERENITY SHALL DEFEAT HIMSELF EVENTUALLY. THE GENTLE AND CALM MAN, NOT THE MAN THAT IS ALWAYS ANGRY AND VEXED, HAS TRUE **STRENGTH**, POISE, COURAGE, AND GRACE. THE CLOSER A MAN IS TO BEING UNAFFECTED BY CIRCUMSTANCES, THE CLOSER HE SHALL BE TO REAL **POWER**. FRUSTRATION, EXCESSIVE SORROW, AND ANGER ARE ALL SURE SIGNS OF WEAKNESS. HE WHO GIVES IN TO ANY OF THESE THINGS SHOWS THAT HE HAS NOT ONLY BEEN INJURED, BUT THAT HE HAS SUCCUMBED TO HIS INJURIES AS WELL.

AS **KING**, IT IS A MUST THAT YOU TRAIN YOURSELF TO REMAIN CALM AND TRANQUIL IN SPITE OF THE STORMS OF LIFE. TO BE ABLE TO DO THIS IS TO BE THE LIGHTHOUSE THAT GUIDES OTHER SHIPS AT SEA TO SAFETY. WHENEVER FACING THOSE THINGS THAT ARE OUTSIDE OF YOUR CONTROL, IT IS A MUST THAT YOU FOCUS UPON THE SILENCE THAT DWELLS WITHIN YOUR HEART SO THAT YOU MAY BECOME A HIEROGLYPH OF GRACE AND POISE, AND EXUDE SUCH A SENSE OF SERENITY THAT THOSE AROUND YOU ARE LEFT FEELING MORE AT PEACE, LESS THREATENED, AND MORE AT

GENTLE EASE. LEARN TO EMANATE PEACE LIKE A FORCE FIELD AND ALL CONFLICT AND DISCORD SHALL BE SUBDUED IN YOUR PRESENCE. IT IS ONLY THROUGH **UNDERSTANDING** THAT YOU SHALL LEARN TO LIVE PEACEFULLY. IF YOU GAIN AN **UNDERSTANDING** OF **THE TRUTH**, YOU SHALL HAVE PEACE AND TRUE **LOVE** TO THE END OF YOUR DAYS. EVERYONE IS THE CAUSE OF THEIR OWN VEXATION. NOTHING CAN HINDER YOU, BESIDES YOURSELF. EVERYTHING DEPENDS UPON YOUR PERCEPTION OF IT. TRUE SERENITY IS A STATE OF PEACE THAT NOTHING CAN DISTURB, AND IT IS THE PRINCIPAL REQUIREMENT FOR THE MANIFESTATION OF REAL **POWER**. YOUR FEELING OF SERENITY IN SITUATIONS THAT OTHERS CONSIDER TUMULTUOUS IS NOT AN INDICATION THAT YOU ARE CALLOUS, CRUEL, OR INDIFFERENT, BUT RATHER IT IS SIMPLY A CHOICE THAT YOU AS **KING** MUST MAKE. BY BECOMING ONE WITH YOUR SERENITY, YOU BECOME AN INSTRUMENT OF **LOVE**. IT IS BY BECOMING AN INSTRUMENT OF **LOVE** THAT YOU SHALL BE ABLE TO ERADICATE ALL PROBLEMS. IT IS ONLY ONCE YOU DISCOVER WHO YOU TRULY ARE THAT YOU SHALL BECOME A TOOL OF HEAVEN, CAPABLE OF BRINGING PEACE AND HARMONY TO ALL. IN ORDER TO GROW POWERFUL, YOU MUST OBTAIN SERENITY. IN ORDER TO OBTAIN SERENITY, YOU MUST ACCEPT **THE TRUTH**. THROUGH SERENITY, YOU SHALL GAIN **STRENGTH**. THROUGH **STRENGTH**, YOU SHALL GAIN **POWER**. THROUGH **POWER**, YOU SHALL GAIN VICTORY. THROUGH VICTORY, YOU SHALL GAIN YOUR KINGDOM. BEFORE ANYTHING CAN BE CREATED, A FOUNDATION BASED UPON ORDER MUST BE PUT IN PLACE. UNITY CAN ONLY BE MAINTAINED BY ORDER. ORDER CAN ONLY BE CREATED BY A MIND THAT IS SERENE AND QUIESCENT.

2

MASTER, BETTER IS PEACE THAN ALWAYS WAR. PEACE, OR EQUILIBRIUM, IS A STATE IN WHICH POSITIVE AND NEGATIVE FORCES ARE BALANCED. HE WHO REFUSES TO BE GOVERNED BY PEACE IS DESTINED TO BE RULED BY TURMOIL. PEACE IS THE END OF IGNORANCE. STILLNESS IS THE STATE OF THE **DIVINE**. THE WORST CONFUSION IMAGINABLE IS THE CONFUSION BORNE OF PANIC. PANIC AND ITS FOLLOWING CONSEQUENCES ARE MUCH MORE HARMFUL THAN THAT WHICH MADE YOU PANIC IN THE FIRST PLACE. OUTER CHAOS IS MERELY A REFLECTION OF INNER TURMOIL. UNCONDITIONAL **LOVE**, YOUR NATURAL STATE, SHALL SHINE THROUGH ONLY WHEN YOUR SPIRIT IS NOT OBSCURED BY THE STORM CLOUDS OF IGNORANCE AND TURMOIL. UNCONDITIONAL **LOVE** THAT IS PERVASIVE THROUGHOUT ONE'S LIFE IS CALLED SERENITY. THE ONLY MAN WILLING TO DISTURB THE PEACE OF OTHERS IS ONE WHO IS NOT AT PEACE WITH HIMSELF. IF YOU ACT AS PEACEMAKER AMONGST YOUR PEOPLE, YOUR KINGDOM SHALL BE UNITED AND PEACEFUL IN FRIENDSHIP. THERE HAS NEVER BEEN A GREAT KINGDOM WHOSE DESIGN WAS BASED UPON CHAOS AND TURMOIL. NO TREE HAS BRANCHES THAT ARE FOOLISH ENOUGH TO FIGHT AMONGST THEMSELVES. JUST AS GREATNESS SHALL NEVER BE ACHIEVED BY A KINGDOM WITHOUT SOCIAL HARMONY AND PEACE, GREATNESS SHALL NEVER BE ATTAINED BY A **KING** IF HE HAS NOT INNER HARMONY AND PEACE.

TO BE AT ONE WITH THE SILENT STILLNESS WITHIN YOUR HEART IS TO INCREASE YOUR **POWER** BY ALLOWING YOURSELF TO HAVE PEACE AND HARMONY WITHIN YOURSELF. THE DESTINY OF A **KING** IS TO UNITE, NOT TO DIVIDE. THE PEACE OF KINGDOMS

IS TOTALLY DEPENDENT UPON THE INDIVIDUALS WITHIN THAT KINGDOM ACHIEVING HARMONIOUS UNITY WITHIN THEMSELVES. WHERE THERE IS TRUE **LOVE**, THERE SHALL BE ORDER AND UNITY. HOWEVER, WHERE DISORDER AND DISUNITY PREVAIL, THERE IS NO **LOVE**, ONLY FEAR, AND THUS HATRED. HATRED IS A POISON WHOSE ONLY ANTIDOTE IS UNCONDITIONAL **LOVE**. IT IS UNCONDITIONAL **LOVE** THAT PRESERVES AND MAINTAINS YOUR HEART WITH THE HEALING BALM OF SERENITY. ONLY HE THAT IS FREE FROM FEAR AND HATRED OF ANY KIND SHALL EXPERIENCE SERENITY. WITHOUT THE INFLUENCE OF SERENITY, NO PRODUCTIVE CHANGE SHALL EVER OCCUR. TO REMOVE THE TENSIONS IN YOUR KINGDOM IS TO PUT THE CREATIVE THINKERS ON CENTER STAGE, BY CREATING THE IDEAL ENVIRONMENT FOR MINDS OF GREAT VISION TO INFLUENCE THE FUTURE. NOTHING IN LIFE SHALL BE OF VALUE IF YOU ARE NOT AT PEACE WITH IT.

TRAIN YOURSELF TO LIVE WHOLEHEARTEDLY THE ONLY LIFE THAT YOU POSSESS, WHICH IS LIFE IN THE PRESENT MOMENT, SO THAT YOU MAY BE ABLE TO SPEND YOUR REMAINING DAYS FREE FROM ANXIETY, KINDLY DISPOSED TOWARDS ALL, AND AT PEACE WITH ANYTHING WHICH DESTINY MAY DECIDE TO BESTOW UPON YOU. IT IS ONLY SERENITY THAT SHALL GIVE YOU THE ENHANCED INTUITION AND **POWER** NEEDED TO SEE **THE TRUTH** IN SITUATIONS OF TURMOIL. BY MAINTAINING INNER SERENITY AND ALLOWING THE FIRE OF **THE TRUTH** TO BURN STEADILY WITHIN YOU DURING UNBLESSED TIMES, YOU SHALL DO FAR MORE GOOD, THAN IF YOU WERE TO BECOME DISCONTENTED, ARGUMENTATIVE, OR VEXED OVER DISAGREEABLE CONDITIONS. TO REACT NEGATIVELY DURING TIMES OF ILL, SHALL DO NAUGHT BUT FAN THE FLAMES OF FEAR AND HATE, UNTIL THEY BURN AND CONSUME ALL THAT THEY COME INTO CONTACT WITH. SACRIFICE

IS THE KEY TO PEACE. WITHOUT PEACE, THERE SHALL BE NO JOY. FOR THE TWO ARE ONE AND THE SAME.

3

MASTER, IT IS ONLY ONCE YOU HAVE PREPARED YOURSELF FOR WAR THAT YOU SHALL TRULY HAVE PEACE. PEACE IS WORTH PRESERVING MORE THAN ANYTHING ELSE. IN ORDER TO KNOW PEACE, YOU MUST BECOME IT. RESPECT IS THE FOUNDATION OF ALL PEACE. WITHOUT RESPECT, YOU SHALL NEVER HAVE PEACE IN YOUR KINGDOM. IF YOU ARE ABLE TO MAKE YOUR NATURE AN UNCONQUERABLE SERENITY, THERE SHALL BE NOTHING, OR NO ONE IN THE WORLD THAT COULD EVER BE AGAINST YOU. IF YOU WISH TO BE A GREAT **KING** IN ALL OF YOUR THOUGHTS, WORDS, AND ACTIONS, YOU MUST FASHION YOURSELF INTO AN IMAGE OF SERENITY THAT NOTHING CAN DISTURB. SERENITY IS MAINTAINED BY THE EQUILIBRIUM OF FORCES, AND SHALL CONTINUE AS LONG AS THIS EQUILIBRIUM EXISTS, AND NO LONGER. SERENITY SHALL COME ONLY TO THOSE WHO ARE ABLE TO CONTROL THEIR MIND WITH PROPER SELF-DISCIPLINE. YOUR INNER SERENITY IS MUCH TOO IMPORTANT TO BE HELD RANSOM TO FACTORS OUTSIDE OF YOUR CONTROL. YOUR INNER SILENCE IS THE SOURCE OF YOUR **POWER.**

AS **KING**, YOU MUST BE THE EMPTY SPACE AT THE CENTER OF THE WHEEL THAT ALLOWS THE WHEEL TO TURN. THE SPACE IN THE CUP THAT GIVES THE CUP ALL OF ITS **POWER**. THE EYE IN THE MIDDLE OF THE STORM THAT IS THE SOURCE OF THE **POWER**, AND YET UNTOUCHED BY IT. LEARNING TO ACCEPT ADVERSITY COURAGEOUSLY SHALL ALLOW YOU TO ALWAYS BE SERENE. ANY SITUATION THAT YOU MAY FIND YOURSELF IN CAN

BE USED FOR ENHANCEMENT, IF ONLY YOU WOULD MANIFEST THE PROPER ATTITUDE OF SERENITY. ALL EXPERIENCES COME TO YOU IN ORDER TO GIVE YOU AN OPPORTUNITY TO RECLAIM AND STRENGTHEN YOUR ORIGINAL SERENITY. IT IS ONLY THROUGH SERENITY THAT YOU SHALL ACQUIRE **WISDOM** AND **POWER**. FREEDOM FROM INNER TURMOIL, THE VERY DEFINITION OF SERENITY IS THE HIGHEST FREEDOM THAT THERE IS. IN ORDER TO TRULY BE A **KING**, MY SON, IT IS A MUST THAT YOU BE FREE. THEREFORE, IN ORDER TO BE A **KING**, IT IS A REQUISITE THAT YOU DEVELOP INNER CALM. IT SHALL DO YOU NO GOOD TO APPEAR OUTWARDLY CALM WHILE REMAINING A SEETHING VOLCANO AWAITING ERUPTION INWARDLY. FOR SOONER OR LATER, FEAR AND DESTRUCTION SHALL SPEW FORTH FROM YOUR SOUL. IT IS YOUR DUTY AS **KING** TO BE ALWAYS A MESSENGER OF ORDER AND SERENITY, NOT ONLY THROUGH YOUR WORDS, BUT THROUGH YOUR VERY BEING. THE SOLE REASON THAT YOU ARE **KING** IS BECAUSE YOU ARE THE ONLY ONE CAPABLE OF BRINGING FORTH TRANQUILITY AND HARMONY TO YOUR KINGDOM. IT SHALL BE IMPOSSIBLE FOR YOU TO EXTEND PEACE IF YOU DO NOT FIRST CULTIVATE IT WITHIN YOURSELF. IT IS IMPOSSIBLE TO GIVE WHAT YOU YOURSELF DO NOT POSSESS. ALTHOUGH A GREAT MANY PEOPLE SPEND THE MAJORITY OF THEIR LIVES IN THE STATE OF DISCONTENT, YOUR GOAL IN LIFE MUST BE TO LIVE IN TOTAL SERENITY. YOU SHALL ONLY FIND SERENITY BY BECOMING **THE TRUTH**. CHERISH THE LIFE THAT YOU HAVE BEEN GIVEN, MASTER, AND **LOVE** ALL THAT HAS BEEN WOVEN INTO YOUR DESTINY. ALL MEN'S DAYS ARE NUMBERED. THEREFORE, YOU MUST USE ALL THOSE THAT YOU HAVE REMAINING TO OPEN THE WINDOWS AND CURTAINS OF YOUR MIND TO THE EDIFYING LIGHT OF SERENITY.

IT IS OF THE UTMOST FOLLY TO GIVE WAY TO FEAR OR IRRITATION. FOR TO SUCCUMB TO FEAR OR IRRITATION IS TO WISH THAT THINGS PAST, PRESENT, OR FUTURE WERE DIFFERENT THAN THE SUPREME INTELLIGENCE, WHICH ORDERS THE ENTIRE UNIVERSE, ASSIGNED THEM TO BE. YOU SHALL HAVE MORE CONTROL OVER YOUR OWN SERENITY BY CONTINUALLY RETURNING TO IT. WHENEVER ANYTHING CAUSES YOU TO BECOME DISTURBED, RETURN QUICKLY TO THE BOSOM OF SERENITY, AND LOSE NOT YOUR HANDLE OVER YOUR **POWER** ANY LONGER THAN IS ABSOLUTELY NECESSARY. IT IS ONLY WHEN YOUR MIND DOESN'T MIND BEING VEXED AND ACCEPTS IT, THAT THE VEXATION SHALL DISAPPEAR. VEXATION ABOUT BEING VEXED IS MERELY ANOTHER LAYER OF VEXATION. SERENITY COMES NATURALLY WHEN THERE IS INNER ACCEPTANCE AND UNCONDITIONAL **LOVE** FOR WHATEVER YOU ARE EXPERIENCING IN THE PRESENT MOMENT. BEING SERENE AND BEING THE **KING** ARE ONE IN THE SAME. THE ONLY OPPORTUNITY FOR BEING AT PEACE IS NOW. FOR PEACE SHALL COME TO YOU ONLY WHEN YOU MAKE PEACE WITH THE PRESENT MOMENT. THE MOMENT YOU STOP WANTING ANYTHING OTHER THAN THE PRESENT MOMENT, YOU SHALL HAVE **POWER** AND PEACE. THE MAN WHO ALWAYS WANTS AND WISHES FOR SOMETHING ELSE SHALL BE FOREVER FILLED WITH TURMOIL, BLAME, AND EXCUSES FOR HIS FAILURE. YOUR PURSUIT OF SERENE HARMONY SHALL BE SUBVERTED BY YOUR PRIZING THINGS OF LITTLE VALUE AND FEARING THAT DEATH SHALL ROB YOU OF THESE THINGS. TO GAIN SERENITY, IT IS NOT NECESSARY THAT YOU GIVE UP ANYTHING IN THIS WORLD. ONLY YOUR ATTACHMENT TO THIS WORLD. WHILE YOU MAY RULE THE WORLD IF YOU WISH, YOU MUST NEVER ALLOW THE WORLD TO RULE YOU. BY NATURE, MEN ARE AT EASE AND SERENE. HOWEVER, DUE TO EFFORTS AIMED AT

SATISFYING SELFISH DESIRES OF THE LOWER NATURE, THEY
DISTURBED THEIR EASE AND SERENITY.

ENJOYMENT IN THIS WORLD CONSISTS OF USING THINGS WELL,
WHILE REMAINING UNAFFECTED BY THEM. IT IS THE SELFLESS
PEOPLE THAT ARE THE MOST POWERFUL. THOSE THAT ARE WISE
FEAR TO BE SELFISH. FOR THE WISE UNDERSTAND THAT
SELFISHNESS CAUSES ONE TO LOSE THEIR SERENITY. TO HAVE
EXPECTATIONS FOR A RETURN WHEN YOU GIVE IS TO ALWAYS
DISTURB YOUR OWN SERENITY LATER ON. THERE IS MUCH
SERENITY FOUND IN SILENCE. IT IS ONLY WHEN YOU LET GO OF
LABELING YOUR EXPERIENCES THAT YOU SHALL BE ABLE TO FIND
THE SERENITY OF DETACHMENT. INNER SERENITY SHALL COME
ONLY WHEN YOU LEARN TO ACCEPT AND FORGIVE, RATHER THAN
JUDGE AND CONDEMN. WHERE THERE IS AN INCAPACITY TO
ACCEPT, THERE SHALL ALWAYS BE NO ACCEPTANCE, AND HENCE NO
SERENITY.

WELL, THERE IT IS, MY SON. THE THOUGHTS OF YOUR FATHER WRITTEN EXPRESSLY FOR YOU SO THAT THEY MAY BE YOUR GUIDE TO THE THRONE. A MANUAL WRITTEN JUST FOR YOU, CONCERNING THE ART OF KINGSHIP. I PRAY THAT I HAVE AN OPPORTUNITY TO MEET YOU. FOR MY **KNOWLEDGE**, **WISDOM**, AND **UNDERSTANDING** INCREASE EXPONENTIALLY BY THE DAY. **I AM** ALREADY LIGHT YEARS AHEAD OF THE INFORMATION FOUND IN THESE LETTERS TO YOU. AND SINCE YOU HAVE NOT YET EVEN BEEN BORN, I SHALL BE EVEN FURTHER AHEAD BY THE TIME THAT I MEET YOU. UNTIL THAT WONDERFUL DAY, MY SON, KNOW THAT MY EVERY MOMENT SHALL BE DEDICATED TO BECOMING GREATER, SO THAT I MAY PROVE MYSELF A WORTHY FATHER FOR YOU. I **LOVE** YOU, MASTER, AND I ALWAYS SHALL.

WITH **LOVE**, YOUR FATHER,

THE DIVINE KING

ABOUT THE AUTHOR

Antionelle Owens, an inspirational speaker, entrepreneur, and spiritual advisor, was born in Orangeburg, South Carolina, but raised in the early part of his life in St. Matthews before moving to Columbia in his adolescence. He attended A.C. Flora High School, where he played basketball for the late Don Bell. Antionelle earned a scholarship and majored in Political Science at King University in Bristol, Tennessee.

After college, he spent a year coaching girls' basketball at Crayton Middle School in Columbia, SC. He then had the opportunity to play basketball professionally in Lausanne, Switzerland. After returning home from this experience, different circumstances began to push him towards discovering his true purpose by arranging it so that he would have to spend time with the downtrodden in prison.

This is what led Antionelle to author the kingship initiation series which he has entitled, *Chronicles of the KING*, of which the three books, *Prince Micah the Magnificent, A KING MUST UNDERSTAND: Thoughts of a Divine King: A Manual Concerning the Art of Kingship*, and *For He Comes Out of Prison to be King* are a part.